Foundations of Criminal Law

Interdisciplinary Readers in Law
ROBERTA ROMANO, *General Editor*

Foundations of Contract Law
RICHARD CRASWELL and **ALAN SCHWARTZ,** *Editors*

Foundations of Employment Discrimination Law
JOHN J. DONOHUE III, *Editor*

Foundations of the Economic Approach to Law
AVERY WIENER KATZ, *Editor*

Foundations of Criminal Law
LEO KATZ, MICHAEL S. MOORE, and
STEPHEN J. MORSE, *Editors*

Foundations of Tort Law
SAUL LEVMORE, *Editor*

Foundations of Environmental Law and Policy
RICHARD L. REVESZ, *Editor*

Foundations of Corporate Law
ROBERTA ROMANO, *Editor*

Foundations of Administrative Law
PETER SCHUCK, *Editor*

Foundations
of Criminal Law

Edited by
**LEO KATZ, MICHAEL S. MOORE,
AND STEPHEN J. MORSE**

New York   Oxford
Oxford University Press
1999

Oxford University Press

Oxford   New York
Athens   Auckland   Bangkok   Bogotá   Buenos Aires
Calcutta   Cape Town   Chennai Dar es Salaam   Delhi   Florence
Hong Kong   Istanbul   Karachi   Kuala Lumpur   Madrid
Melbourne   Mexico City   Mumbai   Nairobi   Paris   São Paulo
Singapore   Taipei   Tokyo   Toronto   Warsaw

and associated companies in
Berlin   Ibadan

Copyright © 1999 by Oxford University Press, Inc.

Published by Oxford University Press, Inc.
198 Madison Avenue, New York, NY 10016

Oxford is a registered trademark of Oxford University Press

Library of Congress Cataloging-in-Publication Data
Katz, Leo.
    Foundations of criminal law / Leo Katz, Michael S. Moore, and
Stephen J. Morse.
        p.   cm. — (Interdisciplinary readers in law)
    ISBN 0-19-509495-6; 0-19-509496-4 (pbk.)
    1. Criminal law—United States.   I. Moore, Michael S., 1943–   .
II. Morse, Stephen J.   III. Title.   IV. Series.
KF9218.K376   1998
364—dc21   97-52247

1 3 5 7 9 8 6 4 2

Printed in the United States of America
on acid-free paper

Contents

4 The General Part: Accomplice, Attempt, and Conspiracy Liability, 223

5 Justification and Excuse, 249

Foundations of Criminal Law

Introduction

Avoiding being the victim of wrongful harmdoing is for most people as essential to a good life as avoiding hunger or the deprivation of other basic needs. Indeed, the ability of people and societies to provide for basic needs is dependent on minimal levels of security. Although private prevention practices and private responses to the behaviors commonly deemed criminal are possible, the most basic forms of force and misappropriation of property are everywhere and in all types of polities considered proper objects of state regulation. In complex societies, some forms of harmdoing threaten personal autonomy and security so grievously that they can be regulated adequately only at a societal level; the effort requires more coordination and efficiencies of scale than most individuals can provide privately. Such regulation could occur without criminal law, however. As Samuel Butler described in his novel *Erewhon*, criminal behavior could be treated as a matter of social hygiene. In such a system, harmdoing humans, like bacteria, would not be blamed or punished, practices that connote moral evaluation; instead, they would be subject to whatever prophylaxis was necessary to render them harmless. Any pain occasioned by such treatment would be the regrettable side effect rather than the precise point of the response. Such a system sounds plausible and even desirable to many people.

Despite the plausible availability of alternative forms of regulation, a specifically *penal* code is an omnipresent feature of all modern societies that have a legal system. Penal codes define crimes, commission of which is generally thought morally blameworthy, and announce punishments, which are supposed to cause pain and are generally thought to be deserved by the criminal. Blame, punishment, and, typically, more rigorous procedural protections for the alleged harmdoer than are provided by civil law are the features that distinguish penal from nonpenal regulation. But how does a society decide which forms of harmdoing require penal forms of regulation? How does the law justify state blame and punishment generally and the doctrines of the criminal law specifically?

Substantive criminal law is traditionally divided into two categories: the general part and the special part.[1] The former refers to the basic doctrines of culpability that apply to all crimes, including, for example, doctrines about how crimes and defenses should be defined. The special part includes doctrines concerning specific crimes, such as murder, robbery, rape, and theft. The more basic general part therefore constrains how the state can define liability for specific crimes. Although both parts of the criminal law are essential to a complete penal code, this book considers only the foundational general part. Once the general part is understood, it is relatively easy to understand the issues concerning how to define particular behaviors that the state may wish to prohibit by criminal law, such as homicide or burning the property of another without permission.

The selections included in the chapters that follow come from scholarship and commentary in many fields, but, not surprisingly, they are drawn primarily from law, philosophy, and social science. The relevant literatures are vast and continue to grow. Crime is an ever-present feature of society in the United States (and elsewhere) that threatens and sometimes terrifies us. It immorally intereferes with pursuit of the good life, degrading, in different ways, both the perpetrators and their victims. Given the importance of crime to the maintenance of a well-ordered society, it is no wonder that it attracts the attention of public policy analysts and political commentators. Because criminal behavior also fascinates, research devoted to theorizing about and researching the causes and responses to crime thrives in scholarly disciplines like psychology, sociology, economics, demography, and psychiatry, as well as in criminology itself. Recent substantive criminal law scholarship has been heavily influenced by the learning of these disciplines.

Ultimately, however, crime is personal, involving an individual or individuals behaving in ways that harm their fellow citizens. The doctrines of the criminal law are thus addressed to the behavior of individual persons. Now, we tend to think that understanding human behavior is simply a scientific problem that the social and physical sciences will solve when they become sufficiently sophisticated. But the sciences can make progress toward explaining human behavior only if scientists understand what they are doing conceptually, a prerequisite aided immeasurably by philosophy, especially the philosophy of mind and action. Moreover, criminal law is largely dependent upon morality. When one person harms another grievously, moral evaluation of the harmdoer and the act inevitably occur, raising questions about whether con-

---

1. Neither part addresses criminal procedure—the rules for the conduct of a criminal case that guide both the prosecution and defense. Criminal procedure is an important, related field, but this book addresses only criminal law itself.

demnation is warranted. Science cannot answer such questions because they are not factual; they are issues of value, about which philosophy once again clarifies one's thinking, even if it does not provide answers. Consequently, many of the selections in this volume employ philosophical methods and concepts to clarify crucial issues of culpability.

The selections in chapter 1 explore a topic often largely ignored in substantive criminal law courses: the crime problem. In this first chapter we try to provide a broad overview of important theoretical and factual issues about crime in the United States. These materials cover behavior that virtually everyone would agree is harmful, evil, and unproblematically criminal. In a sense, these discussions may not seem foundational for the substantive criminal law, which is why they are often omitted from the standard criminal law course, but the criminal law is a primary social response to harmdoing that we hope will reduce crime as well as do justice. If the criminal law seems to adopt doctrines or policies divorced from the best theories and facts about criminal behavior, is it likely to be successful or to claim the allegience of thoughtful people? On the other hand, it is possible that crime is a much larger problem than can be dealt with by the criminal law. Perhaps the most we can expect is that the criminal law will respond in morally adequate ways to problems that are not of its making and that in so doing it will not make a bad situation worse. As you consider the materials on substantive criminal law in the chapters that follow the first, ponder whether these unavoidable substantive criminal law issues can be resolved in ways that will have much influence on the crime problem.

The chapters that follow the first consider in turn definitions of punishment and its justifications; questions of what behaviors ought to be the subject of criminal prohibition; general issues concerning how crimes should be defined, which individuals involved in criminal activity ought to be liable, and the extent to which behavior that only threatens harm should be criminal; limitations on the state's ability to punish apparently evil conduct; defenses; and sentencing. Each chapter and major subsection is preceded by an introduction that will guide your thinking generally about the selections that follow. Each major subsection is then followed by notes and questions that provide further information and help sharpen analytic understanding of the issues.

1

The Crime Problem:
Theory and Evidence

Crime seems always to be near or at the top of the nation's consciousness. It is often perceived to be our most pressing problem. Yet what concerns the average citizen is not the entire range of behaviors that modern codes criminalize, because most crimes do not directly threaten the security and safety of our persons and property. Although misbehavior in business, ill treatment of the environment, and a host of other misdeeds arguably harm society sufficiently to warrant criminal penalties and can produce outrage in particular cases, they do not create the same sense of moral outrage and fear aroused by the "traditional" crimes against persons and property. When Americans wonder what to do about crime, they are not thinking about shady practices on Wall Street or the illicit transfer of food stamps. Rather, they want to know what causes and how to prevent homicide, rape, serious assaults, arson, burglary, auto theft, robbery, and similar forms of harmdoing that virtually everyone agrees are morally wrong, frightening, and deserving of state sanction.

The criminal law is of course a central institution for responding to crime, but most courses in criminal law do not pay much attention to the "crime problem." Although brief reviews of the theories of punishment, including crime prevention mechanisms such as deterrence and incapacitation, are common, substantial attention to criminal behavior is rare. This chapter attempts to remedy this omission by providing some thought-provoking materials. Because the crime problem is huge, we cannot cover even a tiny fraction of what a good reader in criminology would offer, but this introduction explains our choice of selections, points you to other reading, and attempts to guide your thinking about the selections that follow.

There is a rich theoretical tradition in criminology that includes explanations derived from biology, psychology, and sociology. For example, some researchers and theorists have offered genetic explanations for some criminal behavior. Others have provided individualistic, rational choice, or personality trait models. Yet others are concerned with environmental variables, such as peer group pressure, the influence of deviance labels, or the outcomes of the material conditions of society. Virtually all continue to attract adherents, but none commands the field. The causes of crime are still essentially contested territory.

Because the theoretical terrain is so rich, complicated, embattled, and dependent on basic research from allied disciplines, we have chosen not to include basic theory among the readings. Instead, the readings first address phenomenological and statistical facts about crime that any decent causal theory and proposed remedy should address. The bulk of the selections concern policy proposals concerning what to do about crime and implicitly draw on causal, explanatory theories as well as on the facts. The proposals focus primarily on "traditional" crimes, because they most concern us and because they have been the dominant subject of criminological attention. Readers should consider, however, whether proposed responses to the traditional crimes can be usefully generalized to other types of conduct that are now routinely deemed criminal. Is a general explanation for and a proposal for how to reduce crimes of violence—assuming that such are possible—likely also to apply to the dumping of toxic waste material or the operation of an unlicensed liquor still?

Writings about the crime problem that go beyond bare descriptions of facts are influenced by explicit or implicit theories of human nature and political visions. Indeed, many would argue that even which facts we collect and how we describe them, such as the commonly collected and described differences between the crime rates of the two sexes, are implicitly theory driven. For example, one would care about sex as a variable only if one thought that it was likely to have causal significance or that it was important to some political or moral agenda.

Although many bemoan the uselessness of political and moral labels such as "liberal" and "conservative," scholars and others do tend to interpret data and to make proposals that appear to fit preconceived theoretical positions. Often, it seems, the arguments are not really about data but are instead about what kind of beings humans are and about how they should live together. Readers should therefore be alert to the theory of human nature and the politics that at least in part motivate the authors of the selected essays. We have tried to include in the selections that follow a reasonably representative sample of the political spectrum that includes the predominant views, but space constraints make comprehensiveness impossible.

Recognition that preexisting theories and politics inevitably influence scholarship about crime does not mean that all writing about the crime problem is nothing more than the expression of personal preferences. Some social science and public policy writing meets high standards of objectivity and some does not. Attention to the rigor of a writer's methodology and argument is crucial, especially when considering a topic like crime, which tends to engage and even emotionally inflame us. Ask yourself how much we really know about the causes and prevention of crime. Which assertions are soundly verified or convincingly argued and which are "armchair inductions" or weakly reasoned?

Cross-cultural and historical materials enrich our understanding of the influence of culture on criminal behavior, but space constraints again prevent the inclusion of such material. As you read the selections in this section, however, try to consider the extent to which the explanations presented for crime may be limited to the context—primarily the United States today—that they seek to explain.

What is the relevance of the substantive criminal law to the crime problem? Although some traditional justifications for punishment—notably deterrence and incapacitation—aim at crime prevention, few scholars think that the doctrines of substantive criminal law have much to do with the causes or prevention of criminal behavior. Of course, no behavior is a legal crime unless the criminal law prohibits it, and if more behaviors are prohibited, there will be more crime. But these are banal tautologies. Remember, we are concerned with harms to the person and property that are condemned morally and legally virtually everywhere and at all times. The precise contours of the substantive criminal law addressing this harmdoing are unlikely to be weighty explanatory variables for such behaviors. As we have seen, to explain crime and its rates, commentators place far more emphasis on sociological, psychological, and economic variables and on the efficiency of law enforcement, prosecution, and punishment. Redefining the mens rea elements for specific crimes or reforming the test for legal insanity, for example, is far less likely to affect crime in the streets than is the state of the economy or the perceived likelihood of apprehension, conviction, and punishment. Substantive criminal law does not have much effect on the major variables that do seem to explain crime, including the nondoctrinal operation of the criminal justice system. This will explain why so few writers about the crime problem even mention the substantive criminal law.

Is this apparently consensual supposition about the irrelevance of substantive criminal law to the crime problem correct? There are at least two important exceptions. Consider first how the decision to expand the scope of behavior prohibited by the criminal law can affect the crime problem more generally. For example, our society's decision to criminalize the recreational use of many substances that affect behavior, including drugs such as the opiates and cocaine, has profound consequences. Although drug use might have undesirable effects even if it were decriminalized, the decision to criminalize it and seriously to attempt to enforce these laws commits the criminal justice system to an enormous expenditure of resources at every stage of the process, from detection to incarceration. Regulation by criminal justice is very expensive, and resources allocated to enforcing any criminal law could clearly be reallocated to enforce other laws. If the prisons are full, as they now are, cells devoted to minor drug dealers cannot be given to more serious criminals. Moreover, as some commentators controversially suggest, criminalization of private, voluntary, recreational drug use may in part produce other crime, such as the violence between rival illicit dealers or the corruption of public officials with "drug money." Thus, the decision to define certain conduct as criminal can indeed affect the crime problem. Consider this issue again when you read chapter 2, "Crime and Punishment."

The second exception concerns decisions about the appropriate punishments for various offenses. Deciding which types of crimes deserve imprisonment and for how long surely affects criminal justice resource allocation and, more controversially, the deterrent and incapacitative effects of the criminal justice system. The latter, as the selections disclose, are more controversial because commentators disagree about whether substantial increases in the penalties for various crimes and greater willingness to sentence convicted criminals to prison have much effect on the crime rate. Still, it is surely plausible to suppose that there is an effect on crime rates and that sentencing policies affect resource allocation. Nonetheless, the system may not be efficient and may have disproportionately negative impacts on certain groups. These issues are also considered in chapter 6, "Sentencing Theory and Practice."

As you ponder the following discussions of the crime problem, try to imagine other ways in which the substantive criminal law can have a substantial effect on crime rates.

1.1   WHY IS CRIME ATTRACTIVE?

Seductions and Repulsions of Crime

JACK KATZ

The readily available, detailed meaning of common criminality has been systematically ruled out as ineligible for serious discussion in the conventions of modern sociological and political thought. Something important happened when it became obscenely sensational or damnably insensitive to track the lived experience of criminality in favor of imputing factors to the background of crime that are invisible in its situational manifestation. Somehow in the psychological and sociological disciplines, the lived mysticism and magic in the foreground of criminal experience became unseeable, while the abstractions hypothesized by "empirical theory" as the determining background causes, especially those conveniently quantified by state agencies, became the stuff of "scientific" thought and "rigorous" method. . . .

The closer one looks at crime, at least at the varieties examined here, the more vividly relevant become the moral emotions. Follow vandals and amateur shoplifters as they duck into alleys and dressing rooms and you will be moved by their delight

From *The Seductions of Crime* (New York: Basic Books, 1988), pp. 311–24.

in deviance; observe them under arrest and you may be stunned by their shame. Watch their strutting street display and you will be struck by the awesome fascination that symbols of evil hold for the young men who are linked in the groups we often call gangs. If we specify the opening moves in muggings and stickups, we describe an array of "games" or tricks that turn victims into fools before their pockets are turned out. The careers of persistent robbers show us, not the increasingly precise calculations and hedged risks of "professionals," but men for whom gambling and other vices are a way of life, who are "wise" in the cynical sense of the term, and who take pride in a defiant reputation as "bad." And if we examine the lived sensuality behind events of cold-blooded "senseless" murder, we are compelled to acknowledge the power that may still be created in the modern world through the sensualities of defilement, spiritual chaos, and the apprehension of vengeance.

Running across these experiences of criminality is a process juxtaposed in one manner or another against humiliation. In committing a righteous slaughter, the impassioned assailant takes humiliation and turns it into rage; through laying claim to a moral status of transcendent significance, he tries to burn humiliation up. The badass, with searing purposiveness, tries to scare humiliation off; as one ex-punk explained to me, after years of adolescent anxiety about the ugliness of his complexion and the stupidity of his every word, he found a wonderful calm in making "them" anxious about *his* perceptions and understandings. Young vandals and shoplifters innovate games with the risks of humiliation, running along the edge of shame for its exciting reverberations. Fashioned as street elites, young men square off against the increasingly humiliating social restrictions of childhood by mythologizing differences with other groups of young men who might be their mirror image. Against the historical background of a collective insistence on the moral nonexistence of their people, "bad niggers" exploit ethnically unique possibilities for celebrating assertive conduct as "bad."

What does the moral fascination in the foreground of criminal experience imply for background factors, particularly poverty and social class? Is crime only the most visible peak of a mountain of shame suffered at the bottom of the social order? Is the vulnerability to humiliation skewed in its distribution through the social structure? To address these questions, we should examine the incidence and motivational qualities of what is usually called "white-collar" crime. Perhaps we would find a greater level of involvement in criminality, even more closely linked to shameful motivations. But the study of white-collar crime has been largely a muckraking operation from the outside; despite isolated exceptions, we have no general empirical understanding of the incidence or internal feel of white-collar crime. This absence of data makes all the more remarkable the influence, within both academic and lay political thought on crime, of the assumption of materialist causation. . . .

Whether their policy implications point toward increasing penalties to decrease crime or toward increasing legitimate opportunities or "opportunity costs" to decrease crime, modern causal theories have obliterated a natural fascination to follow in detail the lived contours of crime. Perhaps the indecisive battle among competing determinist theories of crime is itself an important aspect of their persistent popularity. . . . Methodological innovations, policy experiments, and the latest wave of governmental statistics continually stimulate the ongoing dialogue, with no side ever gaining a decisive advantage but all sharing in an ideological structure that blocks un-settling encounters with the human experience of crime.

What would follow if we stuck with the research tactic of defining the form of de-viance to be explained from the inside and searching for explanations by examining how people construct the experience at issue and then, only as a secondary matter, turned to trace connections from the phenomenal foreground to the generational and social ecological background? We would have to acknowledge that just because blacks have been denied fair opportunity for so long, and so often, the criminality of ghetto blacks can no longer be explained by a lack of opportunity. Just because the critique of American racial injustice has been right for so long, as criminological ex-planation it now is wrong. . . . For how many generations can a community maintain a moral independence of means and ends, innovating deviance only to reach con-ventional goals? How does a people restrict its economic participation only to the stunted spiritual engagement permitted over centuries of racism? By what anthropo-logical theory can one hold his real self somehow outside the cynical hustles he de-vises day by day, his soul, untouched by a constant pursuit of illicit action, waiting with confident innocence in some purgatory to emerge when a fair opportunity ma-terializes? The realities of ghetto crime are literally too "bad" to be confined to the role of "innovative means" for conventional ends. This is not to deny that the history of racial injustice makes a morally convincing case for increasing opportunities for the ghetto poor. It is to say that materialist theories refuse to confront the spiritual challenge represented by contemporary crime.

The profundity of the embrace of deviance in the black ghetto and the tensions that will emerge among us if we discuss the lived details of these phenomena form one set of the contemporary horrors our positivist theories help us avoid facing. Another blindness they sustain is to the lack of any intellectual or political leadership to confront the massive bloodletting of mate against mate and brother against brother that continues to be a daily reality in the inner city. Each time the sentimentality of materialism is trotted out to cover the void of empirically grounded ideas, it seems more transparent and less inspiring; each time the exhortation to positivism carries a more desperate sentiment that it *has* to be right. And, finally, there is the incalculable chaos that would break out if the institutions of social science were to apply the meth-ods of investigation used here to deviance all across the social order.

Theories of background causes lead naturally to a reliance on the state's defini-tion of deviance, especially as assembled in official crime statistics, and they make case studies virtually irrelevant. But the state will never supply data describing white-collar crime that are comparable to the data describing street or common crime. Politically, morally, and logically, it can't.

The problem is due not to political bias in the narrow sense, but to the dialectical character of white-collar crime as a form of deviance that necessarily exists in a moral metaphysical suspense. To assess the incidence and consequences of common crimes like robbery, one can survey victims and count arrests in a research operation that may be conducted independently of the conviction of the offenders. But individual victims generally cannot authoritatively assert the existence of tax cheating, consumer fraud, insider trading, price fixing, and political corruption; when prosecutions of such crimes fail, not only can the defendants protest their personal innocence, but they can deny that *any* crime occurred. We are on especially shaky grounds for asserting with methodological confidence that white-collar crimes exist before the state fully certifies the allegation through a conviction.

On the one hand, then, white-collar crime can exist as a researchable social problem only if the state officially warrants the problem; on the other hand, white-collar crimes will *not* exist if the state gets too serious about them. The existence of prohibitions against white-collar crimes distinctively depends on the prohibitions not being enforced. The strength of public and political support for robbery and murder prosecutions is not weakened with increased enforcement. But if the official system for prosecuting tax cheating, pollution violations, and even immigration fraud becomes too vigorous, pressure will build to reduce the prohibitory reach of the underlying laws. At the extreme, any group that becomes subject to massive state treatment as criminally deviant is either not an elite or is a class engaged in civil war. . . .

1.2 FACTS

Facts a Theory of Crime Ought to Fit

JOHN BRAITHWAITE

Below [is] a list of what I [believe] to be . . . the strongest and most consistently supported associations in empirical criminology, bearing in mind that we are concerned with a general theory and not with propositions relevant only to specific types of crime. Any credible theory would at least have to be consistent with these findings, and preferably would offer an explanation for most of them.

1. *Crime is committed disproportionately by males.*
In most, if not all, societies men constitute over 90 percent of adult prison populations. Arrest and court data also consistently show in all countries a massive overrepresentation of men in criminal statistics, while self-report measures tend to show much more modest gender differences in offending rates. Smith and Visher's (1980) review of forty-four studies suggests that the more serious the type of offense, the greater the gender differences in rates of offending.

Following up on modest gender differences in self-report studies, some have suggested that women benefit from a "chivalry" factor in enforcement and criminal sentencing, but this has been hotly disputed in the literature. Any evidence of "chivalry" in the criminal justice system is certainly insufficient to explain a finding of twenty times as many male as female homicide offenders in a nation's prisons.

Some contend that the gap between male and female offending rates is shrinking, while others conclude that any such increases have been modest or restricted to prop-

From *Crime, Shame, and Reintegration* (Cambridge: Cambridge University Press, 1989), pp. 44–53.

erty offenses of the type traditionally engaged in by females. What is beyond doubt is that massive gender differences remain.

The other source of data consistently confirming this is victim surveys, where victims are asked to recall, where possible, the gender of their offender(s). . . . Even observational data on as "traditionally female" an offense as shoplifting has shown men proportionally twice as likely to shoplift as women.

As . . . many others have pointed out, traditional criminological theory has tended to concentrate on male delinquency and has failed utterly in explaining why massive gender differences in offending persist in all societies at all points of time for which data exist.

2. Crime is perpetrated disproportionately by 15–25 year olds.
Data on persons found guilty or cautioned in England and Wales for indictable offenses show that offenses per 100,000 population increase sharply from age 10 to peak at ages 15–18 and then decline sharply to reach low levels by the late 20s, which gradually become even lower for the remainder of the life cycle. A similar pattern with minor variations can be seen in all societies. Hirschi and Gottfredson conclude that this age structure of offending has been essentially invariate across cultures and historical periods and for different types of crime. Greenberg has challenged the sweeping nature of this claim by suggesting that youth in some historical and societal contexts are more marginalized and more prone to crime than others.

There is a more fundamental problem with the seemingly uncontroversial conclusion that crime is perpetrated disproportionately by 15–25 year olds. This is that for the major category of crime barely captured in criminal statistics—white collar crime—the opposite is probably true. People under 25 are the age group least likely to engage in white collar crime because to do so requires incumbency in high-status occupational roles which most under-25s have yet to attain . . .

Thus, a more appropriately qualified expression of this generalization from the literature would be that *for those offenses which persons of all ages have opportunities to commit, crime is committed disproportionately by 15–25 year olds;* or a more precise formulation might be, *for those offenses which do not require incumbency in high-status occupational roles, crime is committed disproportionately by 15–25 year olds.*

3. Crime is committed disproportionately by unmarried people.
The same qualification about white collar crime applies here. Nevertheless, putting aside white collar crime, there can be no doubt about the strong and consistent bivariate association between being unmarried and higher offending.

Unfortunately, however, the literature has devoted little attention to the question of the extent to which married people have lower crime rates because they are older on average than unmarried persons. The Cambridge study found only a very modest tendency for those who had married by age 21 or 22 to engage in fewer subsequent offenses by age 24. Sutherland and Cressey report residual marital status effects after some controls for age. In the face of these limited data, the question of whether the marriage effect is no more than a consequence of the age effect must remain open.

4. *Crime is committed disproportionately by people living in large cities.*
Crimes are reported to the police at a higher rate in larger cities than in smaller cities, at a higher rate in smaller cities than in rural areas, and within larger cities at a higher rate in the core cities than in the suburbs. Victim surveys also support the association between large city life and high crime rates, as do self-reported delinquency surveys. In the United States there is a positive correlation between city size and the proportion of the population which is black; however, an association between urbanism and crime does remain after controlling for percentage black. There are no systematic data on the ecological distribution of white collar crime, but almost all instances described in the literature occur in cities, mostly large cities where financial and industrial activity is concentrated.

5. *Crime is committed disproportionately by people who have experienced high residential mobility and who live in areas characterized by high residential mobility.*
Geographical mobility was a key variable in the social disorganization school; Shaw and McKay and their University of Chicago followers felt that mobile individuals who were liable to move at any time did not feel concerned about enforcing informal social control in the neighborhood and were in turn less susceptible to informal controls exercised by others. From the 1930s an impressive body of evidence accumulated associating residential mobility and crime.

6. *Young people who are strongly attached to their school are less likely to engage in crime.*
. . .This is the first of a number of propositions which only have application to juvenile offenders, in this case because adults rarely attend school.

7. *Young people who have high educational and occupational aspirations are less likely to engage in crime. . . .*

8. *Young people who do poorly at school are more likely to engage in crime. . . .*

9. *Young people who are strongly attached to their parents are less likely to engage in crime. . . .*

10. *Young people who have friendships with criminals are more likely to engage in crime themselves. . . .*

11. *People who believe strongly in the importance of complying with the law are less likely to violate the law.*
This association . . . has been consistently supported in the literature. There has been limited attention in the literature to the possibility that law-breaking behavior causes a diminution in respect for the law, rather than the reverse. With self-report studies there has also been a neglect of the likelihood that social desirability bias might cause the error in reports of respect for the law and reports of law breaking to be negatively correlated.

12. *For both women and men, being at the bottom of the class structure, whether measured by socioeconomic status, socioeconomic status of the area in which the person lives, being unemployed, being a member of an oppressed racial minority (e.g., blacks in the U.S.), increase rates of offending for all types of crime apart from those for which opportunities are systematically less available to the poor (i.e., white collar crime).*

This used to be uncontroversial, but became controversial in the 1960s and 1970s with a large number of self-report studies of delinquency which produced slight and statistically nonsignificant class differences or differences between blacks and whites in the United States. . . . My contention is that self-report measures have biases which exaggerate the proportion of delinquency perpetrated by middle class juveniles, and that massive class and race differences for officially recorded offenses of high reportability such as homicide and car theft cannot be explained away. It is also difficult to explain away the finding that surveys of victims of crimes in the U.S. reveal that of the offenders whose racial identity could be discerned by their victims, about half were black; for the most serious offenses two-thirds were black. . . . Nevertheless, this is perhaps the most controversial entry on our list.

13. *Crime rates have been increasing since World War II in most countries, developed and developing. The only case of a country which has been clearly shown to have had a falling crime rate in this period is Japan.*

Interpol statistics and other sources suggest that, apart from the classic case of Japan, crime rates from countries for which reasonably reliable data are available have tended to increase in the period since World War II. Apart from Japan, Switzerland is the only country that might be construed as having an overall fall in the crime rate since World War II. As Wilson and Herrnstein conclude, the general increase can be partly explained by the changing age structure of the population; but, controlling for age, "between 1960 and 1973, the arrest rate for homicide of persons in the age group fifteen to twenty-four increased by 69 per cent [in the U.S.]."

The trend has not in all cases been continuously upward and consistently reflected for all types of offenses. For example, between 1980 and 1984 the rate of reported index offenses in the United States dropped 15 per cent, but even so in 1984 it was still higher than it was in the mid-seventies and much higher than before the crime explosion of the 1960s. In some countries, crime trends during the twentieth century might be conceived as conforming to a U-curve, with decreases early in the century, a mid-century trough, and then the postwar increase. . . . The data from most countries are simply not available to make generalizations on longer term trends. The only generalization we can make with confidence about historical crime trends is one of a general post-war increase.

Most of the entries on this checklist would be uncontroversial to those familiar with the criminological literature. Most debate would center on what else should be added to a list of what we most confidently know.

1.3 EXPLANATIONS AND PROPOSALS

Causes of Violence

JOHN MONAHAN

I warn you in advance that what I cannot do—what no one can honestly do—is offer a neat, simple story that explains why there is so much violent crime in America. Only people on the extremes of the political spectrum have that luxury and that conceit. The root cause of violence, says the right, is bad genes or bad morals. Not so, says the left; the root cause of violent crime is bad housing, bad schools, or dead-end jobs.

I am here to tell you that while doing something about the causes of violence surely requires a political ideology, the only way we have a prayer of finding out what those causes are in the first place is if we check our ideologies at the door and try to keep our minds open as wide, and for as long, as we can bear it. I urge you to give it a try. If you do, what I think you will find is that violence does not have one root cause.

Let's talk about the biological causes first. They are the easiest to talk about because there is not much to say. Many biological or health factors have been nominated as candidates for causes of violence—hormones like testosterone, transmitters in the brain like serotonin, and blood abnormalities like hypoglycemia are only a few that have been mentioned. Biological factors do not have to be hereditary. They can be caused by environmental events, such as exposure to lead paint, head injury, or poor nutrition.

Fortunately for us, the National Academy of Sciences just reviewed hundreds of studies on the relationship between biology and violence, and it came to one clear bottom-line conclusion: "No patterns precise enough to be considered reliably biological markers for violent behavior have yet been identified." The National Academy found many promising leads that should be vigorously pursued by researchers, but so far nothing it could point to as a proven or even close-to-proven biological risk factor for future violence.

Next come the sociological causes. We know the most about social factors and violence because social factors such as demography are relatively easy to measure and because people have been measuring them for a long time. What do we know? We know a great deal about a relatively small number of things.

- We know that to live in America is to live in the land of the brave as well as in the home of the free. We are all familiar with depressing statistics about our trade deficit with Japan. But more depressing is our crime surplus. Compared with Japan, a nation of roughly comparable industrialization, with cities much more crowded than ours, our homicide rate is more than five times higher, our rape rate is 22 times higher, and our armed robbery rate is an astounding 114 times higher.

From *Drugs and Violence in America,* United States Sentencing Commission, ed. (Washington, D.C.: U.S. Government Printing Office, 1993), pp. 77–83.

- We know that, within America, violence is subject to great regional variation. The murder rate, for example, is almost twice as high in the South as it is in the Northeast, but the robbery rate is almost twice as high in the Northeast as it is in the South.
- We know that communities within all regions of America differ drastically among themselves in how violent they are. In general, the smaller the community, the lower the rate of violence. Within the same city, some neighborhoods have rates of violent crime 300 times higher than other neighborhoods.
- We know that people who commit violence on the street are disproportionately poor and unemployed; jail inmates had on average an annual income prior to their arrest at about the federal government's official "poverty level," and about half were unemployed at the time they committed a violent crime.
- We know that the overwhelming majority—close to 90 percent—of the people arrested for crimes of violence are men and that, despite enormous changes in gender roles in recent decades, this 90 percent figure has not budged for as long as we have kept criminal records. Indeed, there is no place in the world where men make up less than 80 percent of the people arrested for violence, now or at any time in history.
- We know that violence is primarily the work of the young. People in their late teens and 20s are much more likely to be arrested for violence than younger or older people.
- We know that the arrest rate—and the victimization rate—for violent crime for African-Americans is now about six times higher than for whites.
- Finally, we know that official violent crime rates, as high as they are, drastically underestimate the actual rate of violence in America, particularly violence within the family.

After this, what we know about the sociological correlates of violence falls off rapidly. Note that I said "correlates," and not "causes." Two problems keep us from knowing which of these things really matter in causing violence and which are irrelevant. One problem is that each of these factors relates not only to violence but to other sociological factors as well. Call this the "ball of wax" problem. Poverty and race, for example, are related not just to violence, but to each other. If you take poverty into account, the effect of race on violence decreases drastically, and in some studies disappears entirely. The second problem is that it is sometimes hard to tell which came first, the sociological factor or the violence. Call this the "cause and effect" problem. It is true, of course, that violence does not cause people to be male or to be young. But whether unemployment leads people to commit violent acts or whether for at least some people their violent acts lead employers not to want to hire them is not so clear. (It is also possible that, at least for some people, a third factor—like an "impulsive" temperament—causes them both to be violent and to be unlikely to keep a steady job.)

Finally come the psychological causes. If research on violence were like stock on Wall Street, then where I would put my money right now is on psychology. By this I most emphatically do not mean mental disorder. The best epidemiological evidence indicates that major mental disorder accounts for at most three percent of the violence in American society. What I mean instead are the developmental processes that we all go through, most of us more or less successfully but some of us with great difficulty. I mean particularly the family—the filter through which most of the sociological factors, such as a parent's being unemployed, and many of the biological factors, like poor nutrition, seem to have their effect on a child growing up.

There is a risk, of course, whenever someone talks about families and children, that he or she is invoking images that may never have existed except on 1950s television and, even if they did once exist, surely no longer reflect the great variety of relationships in contemporary America. But whether we prefer Ozzie and Harriet Nelson or Murphy Brown, there is one important thing we should not forget, and that is that all types of families share something in common. Whether they are married or cohabiting, biological or adoptive or foster, single or dual, gay or straight, and whatever their ethnicity, virtually all parents try to raise their children to be neither the victims nor the perpetrators of violence. Fortunately, most of each of these types of families succeed. Unfortunately, some of each of these types of families fail.

What do we know about families and children and violence?

- We know that while many aggressive children go on to be law-abiding adults, aggression at age eight significantly predicts violent convictions well into the 30s in every culture in which it has been studied.
- We know that while most children who have been physically abused by their parents go on to be perfectly normal adults, physical abuse doubles the risk that a boy will have convictions for violent crime as an adult.
- We know that failure of a child in school is one of the most enduring correlates of later violence. Four out of five violent offenders in prison never finished high school.
- We know that stability matters; the more changes of placement a foster child experiences while he or she is growing up, the more likely he or she will later be arrested for a violent crime.
- We know that a lack of parental supervision has been consistently related to delinquency, including violent delinquency. One study, for example, found that ten percent of nondelinquents were poorly supervised by their parents, one-third of one- and two-time delinquents were poorly supervised, and more than three-quarters of repeat offenders were poorly supervised. Another study found that for children growing up in very disadvantaged and violent neighborhoods, who look like they have everything going against them, the one factor that seems to protect against the child growing up to be violent is having a parent—overwhelmingly, a mother—who supervises her child very strictly and who nips misbehavior in the bud rather than waiting for the principal to call or the police officer to knock on the door.
- Finally, we know much about the relationship between illegal drugs and violence—information that others on this panel are presenting. But it is important to remember that the connection between one legal drug—alcohol—and violence is beyond dispute. About one-third of all violent offenders are alcoholic, and the earlier an adolescent starts to drink, the more likely he or she will be violent as an adult.

These findings are not immune from either "ball-of-wax" or "cause-and-effect" problems. Failure in school, for example, is associated not only with violence but with poor parental supervision as well. And it is not obvious whether frequent changes of placement for a foster child lead to violence, or whether a child's violence at home leads foster parents to give him or her back to the agency. But surely the accumulated findings give us reason to believe that families have an enormous influence, for better or worse, on how children develop.

None of this in any way negates the influence of social conditions in giving rise to violence. Poor people without adequate child care, for example, may have a much more difficult time monitoring their children's behavior than affluent people with live-in help. Nor do they necessarily negate the possible influence of biological factors. Nutrition, to give another example, is something that parents literally put on the table for the child to eat. But it is through the family that these things have their effects and through the family that those effects might best be redirected.

So we know some important things about violence, and particularly about the home environment and violence. But we do not know nearly enough about how to prevent violence in the first place or how to stop it from happening again once it begins.

Malign Neglect

MICHAEL TONRY

Throughout this century, black Americans, especially men but increasingly also women, have been more likely than whites to commit violent and property crimes. They have also been more likely to be in jail or prison, on probation or parole. People of goodwill, from W. E. B. Du Bois at the turn of the century through Gunnar Myrdal in the 1940s, to most contemporary scholars of crime, agree that disproportionate black criminality is the product of social and economic disadvantage, much of it traceable to racial bias and discrimination, more overt in earlier times than today.

For at least seventy years, scholars have differed on how much more involved in crime blacks are than whites. Bias in police arrest and crime-recording practices, insufficient sympathy for black victims, exaggerated sympathy for white victims, and official practices adverse to blacks are often said to distort official statistics. The disagreements, however, have principally concerned the extent, not the existence, of higher levels of black crime.

Racial disparities in prisons, jails, and other corrections programs trigger larger and harsher disagreement. Some argue that the disparities result from racial bias operating at every criminal justice stage from arrest to parole release. However, although no one denies that there is bias in the system, many scholars and most officials believe that racial disproportions result largely from different racial patterns of criminality and that bias is a relatively small, though immensely important, part of the problem.

So summarized, it might appear that these are chronic problems about which broadly shared understandings have emerged. That appearance would be deceptive.

From *Malign Neglect* (New York: Oxford University Press, 1995), 3–4, 6–7, 17–31, 39–47.

Crimes and punishments of blacks are acute social problems; their ramifications dig deeply into the fabric of American life; and there is no agreement on their solution.

Crime by blacks is not getting worse. The proportions of serious violent crimes committed by blacks have been level for more than a decade. Since the mid-1970s, approximately 45 percent of those arrested for murder, rape, robbery, and aggravated assault have been black (the trend is slightly downward). Disproportionate punishments of blacks, however, have been getting worse, especially since Ronald Reagan became president. Since 1980, the number of blacks in prison has tripled. Between 1979 and 1992 the percentage of blacks among those admitted to state and federal prisons grew from 39 to 54 percent. Incarceration rates for blacks in 1991 (1,895 per 100,000) were nearly seven times higher than those for whites (293 per 100,000). Widely publicized studies in 1990 showed that 23 percent of black males aged 20 to 29 in the United States were under criminal justice system control (as were 23 percent in New York and 33 percent in California). Studies by the National Center on Institutions and Alternatives showed that in 1991 in Washington D.C., and Baltimore, 42 and 56 percent, respectively, of black males aged 18 to 35 were under justice system control.

Those numbers are, or ought to be, shocking to every American. . . .

Particularly since 1980, the effects of crime control policies have been a major contributor to declining levels of lawful employment by young black males. The extraordinary levels of black male involvement with the justice system—far, far higher than twenty years ago—are a serious impediment to the achievement of welfare policy goals. Many disadvantaged black males start out with bleak life chances, and disadvantaged young men ensnared in the criminal justice system have even bleaker prospects. No solution to problems of the urban underclass or, more broadly, of black poverty can succeed if young men are not part of it. The crime problem is no longer simply a criminal justice system concern. Unless America can devise ways to make its crime control policies less destructive of poor black males and poor black communities, there can be no solution to the problems of the black underclass.

The traditional left/right disagreement over whether crime control efforts should concentrate on root causes or on the preventative effects of punishment, exemplified by then Attorney General Richard Thornburgh's acerbic remark at a 1991 "Crime Summit," "We are not here to search for the roots of crime or to discuss sociological theory," is obsolete. The issue is no longer whether social disorganization and economic disadvantage predispose the people affected by them to crime; it is whether crime control policies and justice system practices can be made less socially destructive.

. . . For at least twenty-five years, researchers have shown and honest politicians have known that manipulations of penalties have relatively little or no effect on crime rates. In 1993, for example, a National Academy of Sciences report commissioned and paid for by the Reagan administration's Department of Justice, noting that the average prison time per violent crime had *tripled* between 1975 and 1989, asked, "What effect has increasing the prison population had on levels of violent crime?" The answer, "Apparently, very little."

No one doubts that society is safer having some penalties for crime rather than none at all, but that choice is not in issue. On the real-world question of whether in-

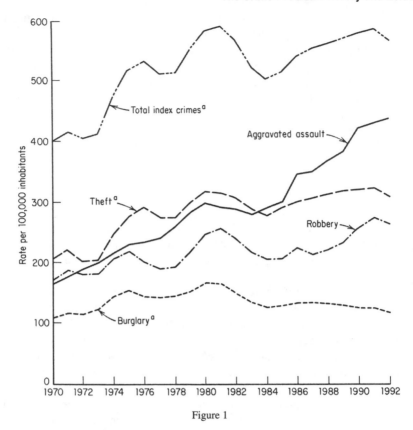

Figure 1

creases in penalties significantly reduce the incidence of serious crimes to which they attach, the answer is maybe, a little, at best, but usually not. Minor misconduct is a different matter. Parking patterns do change, for example, when ticketing becomes more common, towing is more often used, or "boots" immobilize illegally parked vehicles. . . .

The evidence concerning the limited influence of penalties on ordinary crimes against people and property comes from research in many countries on the deterrent and incapacitative effects of penalties, from evaluations of mandatory penalty laws in the United States, and from governmental surveys in the United States, Canada, Australia, and England of knowledge concerning the effects of penalties. . . . Recent national administrations, however, on the basis of deceptive and distorted presentations of data, have claimed the contrary. The baldest claims came from . . . William Barr, attorney general during the Bush administration's final months. . . .

. . . [A] look at data on crime trends provides a necessary backdrop. . . . Figure 1 shows police data from the FBI's *Uniform Crime Reports* on aggravated assaults, robberies, burglaries, thefts, and total index crimes from 1970 to 1992. Rates for burglary, theft, and total index crimes have been divided by 10 in order to show trends for all these offenses in a single figure. The broad pattern is of an increase in rates for most crimes until the early 1980s, followed by declines until the mid-1980s and in-

Table 1.　Crime and Incarceration Rates, State and Federal Prisons, 1960–90 (per 100,000 population)

	1960	1970	% Change 1960–70	1980	% Change 1970–80	1990	% Change 1980–90
"All crimes"	1,887	3,985	+111	5,950	+49	5,820	−2
Violent crimes	161	364	+126	597	+64	732	+23
Incarceration	117	96	−18	138	+44	292	+112

Sources: William P. Barr, "The Case for More Incarceration" Washington D.C.: U.S. Department of Justice, Office of Policy Development, 1992), Table 2; Bureau of Justice Statistics, *Prisoners in America,* various years.

creases thereafter. Among important offenses not shown in Figure 1, the homicide rate in 1980 was 10.2 per 100,000 population, falling to 7.9 in 1984 and 1985 and returning to 9.3 in 1992. The rape rate in 1980 was 36.8 per 100,000 and in 1992 was 42.8. Because public attitudes have rightly become less tolerant of assaults and sex offenses, in recent decades most analysts believe that significant parts of the apparent increases for rape and aggravated assault result from the greater likelihood that incidents will be reported to the police and that the police will record them as crimes. That this is so for assaults can be seen by comparing the steadily growing rates for assault with the mild decline for homicide. A homicide is a lethally successful assault. Given the greater availability of ever more lethal firearms, the proportion of assaults proving fatal (that is, the ratio of homicides to assaults) should be increasing. To the contrary, it has steadily fallen. This suggests that much of the apparent rise in assault rates reflects higher reporting and recording rather than a higher incidence of assault.

Barr's "Case for More Incarceration" came from deceptive presentation of some of the data shown in Table 1. Barr explained that Table 1 shows a declining incarceration rate in state and federal prisons in the 1960s, when crime rates increased, and sharply increased incarceration rates in the 1970s and 1980s, when violent crime rates also rose but at lower percentage rates; the rates for "all crimes" fell slightly during the 1980s. From this comparison, Barr claimed that reduced use of incarceration led to the substantial increase in rates for "all crimes" between 1960 and 1970 and that the 112 percent increase in incarceration between 1980 and 1990 led to a 2 percent decline in crime rates.

The problems with Barr's analysis can be seen in Table 2, which repeats Table 1 but in highlighted form fills in missing data so that differences are shown at five- rather than ten-year intervals. It becomes apparent that the years Barr compared were chosen deceptively. For example, had he compared the crime rates in 1985 with those in 1990, a five-year period when the percentage and absolute increases in prison populations were the largest in the nation's history, he would have found it difficult to claim a cause-and-effect relation between incarceration and crime rates. Crime rates overall rose 12 percent, and violent crime rates climbed more than 32 percent. There is little to celebrate in a one-third increase in violent crime.

Barr also deceptively selected the crime rates to be compared: "From 1960 to 1970, the crime index rate [for all crimes] more than doubled, increasing by 111 per-

Table 2. Crime and Incarceration Rates, State and Federal Prisons, 1960–90 (per 100,000 population)

	1960	1965	% Change 1960–65	1970	% Change 1965–70	1975	% Change 1970–75	1980	% Change 1975–80	1985	% Change 1980–85	1990	% Change 1985–90
"All crimes"	1,887	2,449	+30	3,985	+63	5,282	+33	5,950	+13	5,206	–13	5,820	+12
Violent crimes	161	200	+24	364	+82	482	+32	597	+24	556	–7	732	+32
Incarceration	117	108	–8	96	–11	111	+16	138	+24	200	+45	292	+46

Sources: William P. Barr, "The Case for More Incarceration." Washington D.C.: U.S. Department of Justice, Office of Policy Development, 1992), Table 2; FBI. *Uniform Crime Reports*, various years; Bureau of Justice Statistics, *Prisoners in America*, various years.

Note: **Bold** data not provided in "The Case for More Incarceration."

cent; from 1970 to 1980, it rose by 49 percent; but from 1980 to 1990, it actually *declined* by 2 percent" (emphasis in original). By focusing on 1980 and 1990 rates for "all crimes," Barr could claim that a decade's more-than-doubling of incarceration rates had produced a slight decrease in crime rates (from 5,950 per 100,000 population to 5,820). Had he focused on changes in violent crime rates during the same years, he would have had to acknowledge (and explain away) a 23 percent increase. . . .

Who Is in Prison?

A second defense of law-and-order imprisonment policies is the claim that any sympathy with prisoners is misplaced because the vast majority of those sent to prison are dangerous people who have committed very serious crimes. . . . Thus Steven Dillingham at the Attorney General's 1991 Crime Summit: "National statistics reveal that 95 percent of state prisoners have been convicted of violent crimes, or are recidivists." This suggests that prisons are used parsimoniously and are reserved for violent and other serious offenders. That impression is false, for two reasons.

First, the combination of violent offenders and "recidivists" in one category suggests that both are equally threatening. They are not. Numerous minor nonviolent offenders have been convicted before of theft, shoplifting, passing bad checks, selling small amounts of marijuana or other drugs, or other trifling crimes. This makes them recidivists, but neither very important nor very scary ones, and certainly not ones who need to be held in expensive prisons.

So what proportion of the 95 percent are violent offenders, most of whom presumably deserve to be in prison, and what proportion are recidivists who may or may not deserve to be in prison? We know the answer for 1991, the latest year for which sufficiently detailed national data have been published. In that year, 46.6 percent of those in state prisons on a census date had been convicted of violent crimes (another 25 percent had been convicted of property crimes, 21 percent of drug crimes, and 7 percent of "public-order" crimes). And of those in prison in 1991, 38 percent had not been incarcerated before. In other words, well over half of state prisoners had been convicted of crimes not involving violence, and two-fifths had never before been sentenced to jail or prison. The claim that only 5 percent of prisoners are nonviolent first offenders begins to take on a different, less threatening, hue.

Second and more important, the 95 percent claim confuses prison populations with prison admissions. Because people convicted of violent crimes deservedly receive longer sentences than do people convicted of most property crimes, they remain in prison longer. On any day, the proportion of violent prisoners among those in prison is larger than the proportion of violent offenders among those admitted to prison. The proportion of those admitted to prison for violent crimes has been declining steadily (down from 42 percent in 1977 to 35 percent in 1985 to 27 percent in 1990). . . .

In thinking rationally about imprisonment policies, what we should want to know is who goes to prison, not what percentage of those in prison are "nonviolent first offenders." We know the answer for 1990. Twenty-seven percent were violent offenders; 32 percent each were property and drug offenders; 8 percent were "public-order" offenders, and 1 percent were "other." There is lots of room for debate about the wisdom of contemporary patterns of prison use.

The Cost-Effectiveness of Imprisonment

The final disingenuous explanation for why more imprisonment is appropriate is that incarcerating offenders saves money and that building more prisons will save more money. As former Attorney General Barr put it in the 1992 "Case for More Incarceration," "inadequate prison space *costs* money" (emphasis in original). This implausible proposition is based on a series of discredited cost-benefit analyses of prison use. . . .

Reasonable people disagree over what penalties should attach to what crimes and over the general directions that crime control efforts should follow. There are, however, important costs to alternative choices, and one of the most important is the effects of policies of historically unprecedented harshness on members of minority groups. The claims of the Reagan and Bush administrations notwithstanding, these are and should be hard choices, not easy ones.

The Burden on Black Americans

American crime policies since 1980 have had disastrous consequences for black Americans. On any given day, blacks are six to seven times more likely than whites to be in jail or prison. Astonishingly high percentages of young black males are under the control of the criminal justice system. These patterns, all of which have worsened steadily since 1980, do not result from increases in the proportions of serious crimes committed by blacks.

Black Americans are far more likely than whites to be in prison or jail. Although blacks make up less than 13 percent of the U.S. population, they comprise nearly half of the populations of U.S. prisons and jails and, in recent years, more than half of those sent to jails and prisons. Most people's first reaction is to compare 13 percent of the general population with 50 percent of the prison population and to be surprised that black imprisonment rates are four times higher than they ought to be. Although the surprise is warranted, the calculation is misleading because it understates racial disparities.

What should be compared is the likelihood, relative to their numbers, that black and white Americans will be locked up. In 1991, the black rate was 6.47 times higher than the white rate. Among black Americans, 1,895 per 100,000 were in prison or jail on the counting dates. Among white Americans, 293 per 100,000 were in prison or jail. Between December 1991 and December 1993, the number of jail and prison inmates grew by more than 150,000. Both the incarceration rates by race and the black-white differentials have also grown.

Another, even more remarkable pattern of black-white disparities has been revealed by a series of studies attempting to determine the proportions of blacks under the control of the criminal justice system on a given day. Of all the people in prison or jail, on probation or parole, or released on bail or recognizance pending trial, what percentage are black? The first such analysis, in 1990 by Marc Mauer of The Sentencing Project, showed that nationally 23 percent of black males ages 20 to 29 were under justice system control. Table 3 shows the findings of five such recent studies.

Basic changes in the social and economic conditions that shape the lives of dis-

Table 3. Percentages of Young Black Males Under Justice System Control

Source	Area	Coverage	Year	Ages	Percent
Correctional Association of New York (1990)	New York State	JPPP	1990	20–29	23
Mauer (1990, The Sentencing Project)	United States	JPPP	1990	20–29	23
Center on Juvenile and Criminal Justice (1990)	California	JPPP	1988/89	20–29	33
Miller (1992a, National Center on Institutions and Alternatives)	Washington, D.C.	JPPP, PTAW	1991	18–35	42
Miller (1992b, National Center on Institutions and Alternatives)	Baltimore	JPPP, PTAW	1991	18–35	56

JPPP = Jail, prison, probation, parole.
PTAW = Pretrial release or sought on arrest warrent.

advantaged black Americans and cause their disproportionate involvement in crime are beyond the power of the criminal justice system. However, although we do not know much about using the criminal justice system to do good, we do know how to change its policies so that they do less harm. Such a harm-reduction strategy would have six elements.

First, be honest. Admit that no war against crime will ever be won, that criminal sanctions have at most a modest influence on short-term crime rates, and that locking up many more people is not likely to produce a demonstrably safer America. Crime is part of all human societies and is shaped by the ways in which societies organize themselves. If crime rates in America are to decline in the long term, the causes will lie in major changes in social policies toward job creation, income maintenance, medical care, housing, education, drugs, and firearms. . . .

Second, think about the foreseeable effects of crime control policies on members of minority groups. When policies are likely to burden members of minority groups disproportionately and, through them, their families and communities, reconsider the policies. One extreme example is the 100-to-1 distinction made between crack and powder cocaine in federal law and the federal sentencing guidelines. Presumptive sentences vary directly with the amount of illicit substance involved, and the guidelines direct judges to multiply quantities of crack by 100 in order to determine the amount on which the sentence will be based. The problem is that crack, though it is pharmacologically indistinguishable from powder, tends to be used and distributed by blacks, and powder by whites. One federal court of appeals reported that 95 percent of federal crack defendants are black and 40 percent of powder defendants are white. As could have been expected, blacks convicted of crack offenses receive much harsher sentences in federal courts than do whites convicted of powder offenses.

Another extreme example is the War on Drugs. All sources of relevant knowledge, ranging from experienced police narcotics squad members to ethnographers studying inner-city street life, supported predictions that the enemy troops would consist mostly of young minority males. Any experienced police official could have predicted that policies of wholesale arrests of dealers would sweep up mostly young minority user-dealers in the cities. This is not necessarily because more members of minorities use or sell drugs, but because arrests are easier to make in disorganized inner-city areas where many minority dealers operate than they are in middle- and working-class neighborhoods where white dealers operate. As could have been expected, the number of blacks in prison for drug crimes has risen sharply. In 1986, among white non-Hispanic state prisoners, 8 percent had been convicted of drug crimes, compared with 7 percent of black non-Hispanic prisoners. By 1991, the white percentage had increased by half to 12 percent, and the black percentage had increased by three and one-half times to 25 percent. . . .

Third, establish sentencing guidelines with strong presumptive upper limits on punishment severity. Experience with guidelines in the United States has been mixed. Some guidelines are broad and flexible and place few constraints on judges' discretion. Others are narrow and rigid and greatly constrain judges' options. Most have reduced sentencing disparities and racial differences in sentencing. Some are followed most of the time; others are often ignored. In every system on which data are available, we know that judges much more often impose sentences less severe than the guidelines direct than more severe, and that sentences more severe than the guidelines direct are everywhere uncommon.

The worst injuries that biased sentencing can produce are cases in which racial bias or judicial idiosyncrasy results in the imposition of aberrantly severe penalties. . . .

There are two solutions. First, cut the statutory maximums. . . . The second solution is to establish sentencing guidelines that, if past experience is repeated, will reduce sentencing disparities in general to some degree and will greatly lower the risk of aberrantly long, racially motivated sentences. Even if the guidelines are exceptionally harsh, like the current federal guidelines, they will lessen the risks of even longer extraordinary sentences.

Fourth, abolish all mandatory penalties. The evidence is overwhelming that mandatory penalties for serious crimes have few if any deterrent effects (which, if they exist, soon waste away), are frequently circumvented by judges and lawyers, and sometimes result in imposition of penalties that everyone involved believes are too severe. Moreover, they are often applied to drug and other crimes with which blacks are disproportionately likely to be charged and accordingly have a disproportionate impact on blacks.

Mandatory penalties are an especially pernicious part of contemporary punishment policies. Their principal purposes are political and short term—to allow officials at a time of heightened concern about crime to show that they are "tough on crime." Such laws, however, once passed, are seldom repealed and continue to affect the lives of offenders long after the concern that produced them has dissipated. . . .

Fifth, empower and encourage judges to mitigate sentences to take account of in-dividual circumstances. Minority offenders would especially benefit from broadened judicial discretion. The movement in the last twenty years toward systems of rigid sentencing standards based solely on offenders' crimes and criminal records, and premised on just-deserts theories, was a mistake. Ethically and humanly relevant dif-ferences among offenders extend well beyond their crimes, and most judges and many prosecutors want to take account of some of those differences. . . .

Sixth, greatly limit the use of imprisonment, and use part of the money saved to support enhanced community corrections and treatment programs. The rest can be applied to putting state and federal budgets back in balance. If the combined prison and jail population was lowered to 1980 levels, adjusted for population increase and a bit more, $10 billion to $20 billion a year could be saved on institutional corrections budgets, and additional billions could be saved (or reallocated) on police, prosecuto-rial, and court operations. Crime rates in 1993 were about the same as in 1980 when the prison and jail population was under 500,000, which makes 600,000 a reasonable target to set for 1999. Between 1980 and 1993, the resident population of the United States rose by less than 12 percent. Thus 600,000 inmates would allow for popula-tion growth and still permit some increase over 1980 levels. It would also generate a national incarceration rate of 225 per 100,000 population, which is somewhat higher than the 1980 rate and would still be two to five times higher than that of any other country with which the United States ordinarily wants to be compared. Many would still find these levels unacceptably high in light of recent evidence that American crime rates, except for gun crimes, are about the same as those of most Western na-tions.

Several questions arise. How could inmate populations be cut so sharply? If my first two proposals, be honest and worry about race effects, were taken seriously by policymakers, the answers would be easy. Stop imprisoning most user-dealers and most property offenders. Revise sentencing standards and guidelines to prescribe prison sentences for violent offenses at 1980 levels. Rescind all mandatory penalty laws retroactively. Create special parole boards with the power to consider the release of every prisoner who is over age fifty and has served at least five years and every prisoner who has served ten years or more. The only valid general criterion for deny-ing release would be that, on actuarial grounds, the offender presents an unacceptable risk of future violent criminality. Denying release might also be justified for espe-cially notorious offenders like political assassins and serial murderers.

How much money would be saved? At a modest estimate of $25,000 in annual operating costs per inmate, the gross savings from 900,000 fewer inmates would be $22.5 billion. The net would be less; experience with deinstitutionalization of men-tal health programs demonstrates that governments have difficulty terminating em-ployees and closing facilities that are no longer needed. However, many new jobs would open up in community corrections and in treatment programs for which cur-rent corrections workers would be qualified. There would also be one-time charges as out-moded facilities were closed forever, offset to some extent by gains from con-verting some prisons and jails to other uses. Whatever the details, in the end the an-nual net savings would permit a massive rise in funding for community corrections and treatment programs and still lower government spending by many billions.

What would be done with the diverted offenders? For some, nothing. Most former prisoners over age thirty-five present little threat of violence or other serious offending. The best thing to do is to let many of those released early get on with their lives. For current offenders, depending on the gravity of their crimes, confinement or community penalties are the answer. Those confined should receive sentences scaled down at least by half from current levels of time served to 1980 levels and never more than is commensurate with the relative severity of the offenses. Most, however— again depending on the gravity of their crimes—should be sentenced to community penalties like intensive supervision probation, community service, house arrest, daytime or nighttime confinement, and financial penalties coupled when appropriate with compulsory participation in treatment programs. When it is feasible, restitution or community service should routinely be ordered. Conditions of community penalties should be vigorously enforced, with prompt but graduated consequences attaching to violations.

From a public safety perspective, a combination of community penalties and greatly expanded treatment programs for offenders is more effective than the current program of excessive incarceration and insufficiently supported community punishments and treatment programs. Community penalties do no worse than prisons in regard to recidivism, and sometimes better.

What to Do About Crime

JAMES Q. WILSON

When the United States experienced the great increase in crime that began in the early 1960s and continued through the 1970s, most Americans were inclined to attribute it to conditions unique to this country. . . .

Now, 30 years later, any serious discussion of crime must begin with the fact that, except for homicide, most industrialized nations have crime rates that resemble those in the United States. . . .

America, it is true, continues to lead the industrialized world in murders. There can be little doubt that part of this lead is to be explained by the greater availability of handguns here. Arguments that once might have been settled with insults or punches are today more likely to be settled by shootings. But guns are not the whole story. Big American cities have had more homicides than comparable European ones for almost as long as anyone can find records. . . .

But except for homicide, things have been getting better in the United States for over a decade. Since 1980, robbery rates (as reported in victim surveys) have declined by 15 percent. And even with regard to homicide, there is relatively good news: in 1990, the rate at which adults killed one another was no higher than it was in 1980, and in many cities it was considerably lower.

From *Commentary,* Sept. 1994, pp. 25–34.

This is as it was supposed to be. Starting around 1980, two things happened that ought to have reduced most forms of crime. The first was the passing into middle age of the postwar baby boom. By 1990, there were 1.5 million fewer boys between the ages of fifteen and nineteen than there had been in 1980, a drop that meant that this youthful fraction of the population fell from 9.3 percent to 7.2 percent of the total.

In addition, the great increase in the size of the prison population, caused in part by the growing willingness of judges to send offenders to jail, meant that the dramatic reductions in the costs of crime to the criminal that occurred in the 1960s and 1970s were slowly (and very partially) being reversed. Until around 1985, this reversal involved almost exclusively real criminals and parole violators; it was not until after 1985 that more than a small part of the growth in prison populations was made up of drug offenders. . . . But suddenly, starting around 1985, even as adult homicide rates were remaining stable or dropping, *youthful* homicide rates shot up. . . . Between 1985 and 1992, the homicide rate for young white males went up by about 50 percent but for young black males it *tripled.*

. . .

The United States, then, does not have *a* crime problem, it has at least two. Our high (though now slightly declining) rates of property crime reflect a profound, worldwide cultural change: prosperity, freedom, and mobility have emancipated people almost everywhere from those ancient bonds of custom, family, and village that once held in check both some of our better and many of our worst impulses.

. . .

There are only two restraints on behavior—morality, enforced by individual conscience or social rebuke, and law, enforced by the police and the courts. If society is to maintain a behavioral equilibrium, any decline in the former must be matched by a rise in the latter (or vice versa). If familial and traditional restraints on wrongful behavior are eroded, it becomes necessary to increase the legal restraints. But the enlarged spirit of freedom and the heightened suspicion of the state have made it difficult or impossible to use the criminal-justice system to achieve what custom and morality once produced.

This is the modern dilemma, and it may be an insoluble one, at least for the West.

. . .

Then, of course, there is gun control. Guns are almost certainly contributors to the lethality of American violence, but there is no politically or legally feasible way to reduce the stock of guns now in private possession to the point where their availability to criminals would be much affected.

. . .

As for rehabilitating juvenile offenders, it has some merit, but there are rather few success stories. Individually, the best (and best-evaluated) programs have minimal, if any, effects; collectively, the best estimate of the crime-reduction value of these programs is quite modest, something on the order of 5 or 10 percent.

Much is said these days about preventing or deterring crime, but it is important to understand exactly what we are up against when we try. Prevention, if it can be made to work at all, must start very early in life, perhaps as early as the first two or three years, and given the odds it faces—childhood impulsivity, low verbal facility, incompetent parenting, disorderly neighborhoods—it must also be massive in scope. Deterrence, if it can be made to work better (for surely it already works to some degree), must be applied close to the moment of the wrongful act or else the present-orientedness of the youthful would-be offender will discount the threat so much that the promise of even a small gain will outweigh its large but deferred costs.

In this country, however, and in most Western nations, we have profound misgivings about doing anything that would give prevention or deterrence a chance to make a large difference.

. . .

Prompt deterrence has much to recommend it: the folk wisdom that swift and certain punishment is more effective than severe penalties is almost surely correct. But the greater the swiftness and certainty, the less attention paid to the procedural safeguards essential to establishing guilt. . . .

Yet the more draconian the sentence, the less (on the average) the chance of its being imposed; plea bargains see to that. And the most draconian sentences will, of necessity, tend to fall on adult offenders nearing the end of their criminal careers and not on the young ones who are in their criminally most productive years. (The peak ages of criminality are between sixteen and eighteen; the average age of prison inmates is ten years older.) I say "of necessity" because almost every judge will give first-, second-, or even third-time offenders a break, reserving the heaviest sentences for those men who have finally exhausted judicial patience or optimism. . . .

What, then, is to be done? Let us begin with policing, since law-enforcement officers are that part of the criminal-justice system which is closest to the situations where criminal activity is likely to occur.

It is now widely accepted that, however important it is for officers to drive around waiting for 911 calls summoning their help, doing that is not enough. As a supplement to such a reactive strategy—composed of random preventive patrol and the investigation of crimes that have already occurred—many leaders and students of law enforcement now urge the police to be "proactive": to identify, with the aid of citizen groups, problems that can be solved so as to prevent criminality, and not only to respond to it. This is often called community-based policing. . . .

The new strategy might better be called problem-oriented policing. It requires the police to engage in *directed,* not random, patrol. The goal of that direction should be to reduce, in a manner consistent with fundamental liberties, the opportunity for high-risk persons to do those things that increase the likelihood of their victimizing others.

For example, the police might stop and pat down persons whom they reasonably suspect may be carrying illegal guns. . . . Since three-fourths of all convicted offenders (and a large fraction of all felons) are in the community rather than in prison, there are on any given day over three million criminals on the streets under correctional supervision. Many are likely to become recidivists. Keeping them from carrying weapons will materially reduce the chances that they will rob or kill. The courts might also declare certain dangerous street gangs to be continuing criminal enterprises, membership in which constitutes grounds for police frisks. . . . The police can also offer immediate cash rewards to people who provide information about individuals illegally carrying weapons. . . .

Getting illegal firearms off the streets will require that the police be motivated to do all of these things. But if the legal, technological, and motivational issues can be resolved, our streets can be made safer even without sending many more people to prison.

The same directed-patrol strategy might help keep known offenders drug-free. . . .

Almost everyone agrees that more treatment programs should exist. But what many advocates overlook is that the key to success is steadfast participation, and many, probably most, offenders have no incentive to be steadfast. To cope with this, patrol officers could enforce random drug tests on probationers and parolees on their beats; failing to take a test when ordered, or failing the test when taken, should be grounds for immediate revocation of probation or parole, at least for a brief period of confinement.

The goal of this tactic is not simply to keep offenders drug-free (and thereby lessen their incentive to steal the money needed to buy drugs and reduce their likelihood of committing crimes because they are on a drug high); it is also to diminish the demand for drugs generally and thus the size of the drug market.

Lest the reader embrace this idea too quickly, let me add that as yet we have no good reason to think that it will reduce the crime rate by very much.

. . .

Both anti-gun and anti-drug police patrols will, if performed systematically, require big changes in police and court procedures and a significant increase in the resources devoted to both, at least in the short run. . . .

Another promising tactic is to enforce truancy and curfew laws. This arises from the fact that much crime is opportunistic: idle boys, usually in small groups, sometimes find irresistible the opportunity to steal or the challenge to fight. . . . While it is possible to deter the crimes they commit by a credible threat of prompt sanctions, it is easier to reduce the chances for risky group idleness in the first place.

. . .

All these tactics have in common putting the police, as the criminologist Lawrence Sherman of the University of Maryland phrases it, where the "hot spots" are. Most people need no police attention except for a response to their calls for help. A small fraction of people (and places) need constant attention. Thus, in Minneapolis, *all* of the robberies during one year occurred at just 2 percent of the city's addresses.

. . .

The sheer number of police on the streets of a city probably has only a weak, if any, relationship with the crime rate; what the police do is more important than how many there are, at least above some minimum level. Nevertheless, patrols directed at hot spots, loitering truants, late-night wanderers, probationers, parolees, and possible gun carriers, all in addition to routine investigative activities, will require more officers in many cities. Between 1977 and 1987, the number of police officers declined in a third of the 50 largest cities and fell relative to population in many more. Just how far behind police resources have lagged can be gauged from this fact: in 1950 there was one violent crime reported for every police officer; in 1980 there were three violent crimes reported for every officer.

I have said little so far about penal policy, in part because I wish to focus attention on those things that are likely to have the largest and most immediate impact on

the quality of urban life. But given the vast gulf between what the public believes and what many experts argue should be our penal policy, a few comments are essential.
. . .

The expert view, as it is expressed in countless op-ed essays, often goes like this: "We have been arresting more and more people and giving them longer and longer sentences, producing no decrease in crime but huge increases in prison populations. As a result, we have become the most punitive nation on earth."

Scarcely a phrase in those sentences is accurate. The probability of being arrested for a given crime is lower today than it was in 1974. The amount of time served in state prison has been declining more or less steadily since the 1940s. Taking all crimes together, time served fell from 25 months in 1945 to 13 months in 1984. Only for rape are prisoners serving as much time today as they did in the 40s.

The net effect of lower arrest rates and shorter effective sentences is that the cost to the adult perpetrator of the average burglary fell from 50 days in 1960 to 15 days in 1980. That is to say, the chances of being caught and convicted, multiplied by the median time served if imprisoned, was in 1980 less than a third of what it had been in 1960.

Beginning around 1980, the costs of crime to the criminal began to inch up again—the result, chiefly, of an increase in the proportion of convicted persons who were given prison terms. By 1986, the "price" of a given burglary had risen to 21 days. Also beginning around 1980, as I noted at the outset, the crime rate began to decline.

It would be foolhardy to explain this drop in crime by the rise in imprisonment rates; many other factors, such as the aging of the population and the self-protective measures of potential victims, were also at work. . . .

Yet it is worth noting that nations with different penal policies have experienced different crime rates. According to David Farrington of Cambridge University, property-crime rates rose in England and Sweden at a time when both the imprisonment rate and time served fell substantially, while property-crime rates declined in the United States at a time when the imprisonment rate (but not time served) was increasing.

Though one cannot measure the effect of prison on crime with any accuracy, it certainly has some effects. . . .

Nor, finally, does America use prison to a degree that vastly exceeds what is found in any other civilized nation. Compare the chance of going to prison in England and the United States if one is convicted of a given crime. . . . Your chances were higher in England if you were found guilty of a rape, higher in America if you were convicted of an assault or a burglary, and about the same if you were convicted of a homicide or a robbery.
. . .

Of late, drugs have changed American penal practice. In 1982, only about 8 percent of state-prison inmates were serving time on drug convictions. In 1987, that started to increase sharply; by 1994, over 60 percent of all federal and about 25 percent of all state prisoners were there on drug charges. In some states, such as New York, the percentage was even higher.

This change can be attributed largely to the advent of crack cocaine. Whereas snorted cocaine powder was expensive, crack was cheap; whereas the former was distributed through networks catering to elite tastes, the latter was mass-marketed on street corners. People were rightly fearful of what crack was doing to their children and demanded action; as a result, crack dealers started going to prison in record numbers.

Unfortunately, these penalties do not have the same incapacitative effect as sentences for robbery. A robber taken off the street is not replaced by a new robber who has suddenly found a market niche, but a drug dealer sent away is replaced by a new one because an opportunity has opened up.

We are left, then, with the problem of reducing the demand for drugs, and that in turn requires either prevention programs on a scale heretofore unimagined or treatment programs with a level of effectiveness heretofore unachieved. Any big gains in prevention and treatment will probably have to await further basic research into the biochemistry of addiction and the development of effective and attractive drug antagonists that reduce the appeal of cocaine and similar substances.[1]

In the meantime, it is necessary either to build much more prison space, find some other way of disciplining drug offenders, or both. There is very little to be gained, I think, from shortening the terms of existing non-drug inmates in order to free up more prison space. Except for a few elderly, nonviolent offenders serving very long terms, there are real risks associated with shortening the terms of the typical inmate.

Scholars disagree about the magnitude of those risks, but the best studies, such as the one of Wisconsin inmates done by John DiIulio of Princeton, suggest that the annual costs to society in crime committed by an offender on the street are probably twice the costs of putting him in a cell.

. . .

But I caution the reader to understand that there are no easy prison solutions to crime, even if we build the additional space. The state-prison population more than doubled between 1980 and 1990, yet the victimization rate for robbery fell by only 23 percent. Even if we assign all of that gain to the increased deterrent and incapacitative effect of prison, which is implausible, the improvement is not vast.

. . .

Recall my discussion of the decline in the costs of crime to the criminal, measured by the number of days in prison that result, on average, from the commission of a given crime. That cost is vastly lower today than in the 1950s. But much of the decline (and since 1974, nearly all of it) is the result of a drop in the probability of being arrested for a crime, not in the probability of being imprisoned once arrested.

. . . I have defended the use of prison both to deter crime and incapacitate criminals. I continue to defend it. But we must recognize two facts. First, even modest additional reductions in crime, comparable to the ones achieved in the early 1980s, will require vast increases in correctional costs and encounter bitter judicial resistance to mandatory sentencing laws. Second, America's most troubling crime problem—the increasingly violent behavior of disaffected and impulsive youth—may be especially hard to control by means of marginal and delayed increases in the probability of punishment.

1. I anticipate that at this point some readers will call for legalizing or decriminalizing drugs as the "solution" to the problem. Before telling me this, I hope they will read what I wrote on that subject in the February 1990 issue of *Commentary*. I have not changed my mind.

Possibly one can make larger gains by turning our attention to the unexplored area of juvenile justice. Juvenile (or family) courts deal with young people just starting their criminal careers and with chronic offenders when they are often at their peak years of offending. We know rather little about how these courts work or with what effect.

. . .

The key, unanswered question is whether prompt and more effective early intervention would stop high-rate delinquents from becoming high-rate criminals at a time when their offenses were not yet too serious. Perhaps early and swift, though not necessarily severe, sanctions could deter some budding hoodlums, but we have no evidence of that as yet.

For as long as I can remember, the debate over crime has been between those who wished to rely on the criminal-justice system and those who wished to attack the root causes of crime. I have always been in the former group because what its opponents depicted as "root causes"—unemployment, racism, poor housing, too little schooling, a lack of self-esteem—turned out, on close examination, not to be major causes of crime at all.

Of late, however, there has been a shift in the debate. Increasingly those who want to attack root causes have begun to point to real ones—temperament, early family experiences, and neighborhood effects. The sketch I gave earlier of the typical high-rate young offender suggests that these factors are indeed at the root of crime. The problem now is to decide whether any can be changed by plan and at an acceptable price in money and personal freedom.

If we are to do this, we must confront the fact that the critical years of a child's life are ages one to ten, with perhaps the most important being the earliest years. During those years, some children are put gravely at risk by some combination of heritable traits, prenatal insults (maternal drug and alcohol abuse or poor diet), weak parent-child attachment, poor supervision, and disorderly family environment.

If we knew with reasonable confidence which children were most seriously at risk, we might intervene with some precision to supply either medical therapy or parent training or (in extreme cases) to remove the child to a better home. But given our present knowledge, precision is impossible, and so we must proceed carefully, relying, except in the most extreme cases, on persuasion and incentives.

We do, however, know enough about the early causes of conduct disorder and later delinquency to know that the more risk factors exist (such as parental criminality and poor supervision), the greater the peril to the child. It follows that programs aimed at just one or a few factors are not likely to be successful; the children most at risk are those who require the most wide-ranging and fundamental changes in their life circumstances. The goal of these changes is, as Travis Hirschi of the University of Arizona has put it, to teach self-control.

. . .

In this country we tend to separate programs designed to help children from those that benefit their parents. The former are called "child development," the latter "welfare reform." This is a great mistake. Everything we know about long-term welfare recipients indicates that their children are at risk for the very problems that child-helping programs later try to correct.

The evidence from a variety of studies is quite clear: even if we hold income and ethnicity constant, children (and especially boys) raised by a single mother are more likely than those raised by two parents to have difficulty in school, get in trouble with the law, and experience emotional and physical problems. Producing illegitimate children is not an "alternative life-style" or simply an imprudent action; it is a curse. Making mothers work will not end the curse; under current proposals, it will not even save money.

. . .

What we really want is *fewer illegitimate children,* because such children, by being born out of wedlock are, except in unusual cases, being given early admission to the underclass. And failing that, we want the children born to single (and typically young and poor) mothers to have a chance at a decent life.

Letting teenage girls set up their own households at public expense neither discourages illegitimacy nor serves the child's best interests. If they do set up their own homes, then to reach those with the fewest parenting skills and the most difficult children will require the kind of expensive and intensive home visits and family-support programs characteristic of the four successful experiments mentioned earlier.

One alternative is to tell a girl who applies for welfare that she can only receive it on condition that she live either in the home of *two* competent parents (her own if she comes from an intact family) or in a group home where competent supervision and parent training will be provided by adults unrelated to her. Such homes would be privately managed but publicly funded by pooling welfare checks, food stamps, and housing allowances.

Group homes funded by pooled welfare benefits would make the task of parent training much easier and provide the kind of structured, consistent, and nurturant environment that children need.

. . .

My focus on changing behavior will annoy some readers. For them the problem is poverty and the worst feature of single-parent families is that they are inordinately poor. Even to refer to a behavioral or cultural problem is to "stigmatize" people.

Indeed it is. Wrong behavior—neglectful, immature, or incompetent parenting; the production of out-of-wedlock babies—*ought* to be stigmatized.

. . .

. . . If we fail to stigmatize those who give way to temptation, we withdraw the rewards from those who resist them. This becomes all the more important when entire communities, and not just isolated households, are dominated by a culture of fatherless boys preying on innocent persons and exploiting immature girls.

We need not merely stigmatize, however. We can try harder to move children out of those communities, either by drawing them into safe group homes or facilitating (through rent supplements and housing vouchers) the relocation of them and their parents to neighborhoods with intact social structures and an ethos of family values.

Much of our uniquely American crime problem (as opposed to the worldwide problem of general thievery) arises, not from the failings of individuals but from the concentration in disorderly neighborhoods of people at risk of failing.

. . .

I seriously doubt that this country has the will to address either of its two crime problems, save by acts of individual self-protection. We could in theory make justice swifter and more certain, but we will not accept the restrictions on liberty and the weakening of procedural safeguards that this would entail. We could vastly improve the way in which our streets are policed, but some of us will not pay for it and the rest of us will not tolerate it. We could alter the way in which at-risk children experience the first few years of life, but the opponents of this—welfare-rights activists, family preservationists, budget cutters, and assorted ideologues—are numerous and the bureaucratic problems enormous.

Unable or unwilling to do such things, we take refuge in substitutes: we debate the death penalty, we wring our hands over television, we lobby to keep prisons from being built in our neighborhoods, and we fall briefly in love with trendy nostrums that seem to cost little and promise much.

NOTES AND QUESTIONS

1. We appear to know a great deal about the scope of the crime problem, about the rates and location of crime and about the characteristics of offenders and victims. Moreover, there is increasingly good evidence about these matters available from other western countries. Unlike commentators of the relatively recent past, those of today, representing all political preferences, appear not to dispute these matters very much. As the readings disclose, however, there is substantial debate about theoretical and factual issues concerning the causes of the current crime problem and the proposed solutions.

2. The majority of criminological writing is presented in what Jack Katz terms the "positivist" mode. That is, it focuses on the empirical causes and correlates of crime, not on the individual criminal and his or her experience of how it feels and what it means to offend. As a result, criminal behavior is often presented as the purely mechanical outcome of largely impersonal forces of biology, psychology, society, and economics. The concept of the criminal as an agent is lost. This type of presentation lends itself to thinking of crime as the inevitable symptom of a disease or a product of socioeconomic forces. Paradoxically, such thinking makes it easier for "us," the law-abiding, to distance ourselves from "them," the criminals, because "we" do not understand their experience and think we don't share it. Katz's virtue is that he rescues the full-blooded criminal self from positivistic annihilation, demonstrating that crime has attractions that all people can understand and that can motivate even evildoing. Simultaneously, the attractions of crime help explain why large numbers of people disadvantaged by exposure to comparatively few alternative attractions find crime such a ready outlet. Still, Katz, reminds us, at the end of the positivist's bio-psycho-sociocultural-economic causal chain, there is a flesh-and-blood person making an understandable choice. Is Katz's picture persuasive, or does it tend to "blame the victim"?

3. Theory is supposed to guide our thinking and research about phenomena, and the crime literature suffers from no shortage of theoretical hypotheses, ranging from rational-choice models of individual conduct to broader, sociological formulations that focus on the environmental forces that shape behavior. Each reasonably influential theory appears to have enough internal consistency and enough external empirical support to suggest its plausibility. But each also suffers from conceptual and empirical deficiencies. For example, key variables are vaguely defined, and embarrassing, contradictory findings can always be found. Braithwaite claims that none of the dominant theories of crime can explain all the uncontroversial facts about crime

that his selection provides. Considering the enormous complexity of individual behavior and of society and the lack of agreement among experts, what is a lay reader, including an intelligent lawyer or legislator, to think? How does one not trained in the social sciences or other disciplines from which the work under consideration is derived assess the merits of that work per se and in comparison to other work?

Consider the differences between the causal analyses and the policy prescriptions of Wilson and Tonry. Both are highly influential scholars, widely steeped in the relevant literatures and exemplars of an analytic approach. They read the same sources but differ markedly in the conclusions they draw. On occasion there are dispositive arguments or findings that cause scholars to abandon a position, but this is relatively rare. Virtually always the data are unclear or quite capable of alternative readings, allowing the commentator interpretive latitude. Can the differences between Wilson and Tonry be explained simply by their obviously different politics and theoretical predilections? Who is more persuasive to you? Can you defend why you think so?

Suppose that you were a legislator faced with conflicting policy prescriptions. Assuming that you would try to do the right thing rather than simply satisfy the perhaps temporary preferences of your constituents, what would you do? Is a judge or jury member in a substantially different position when asked to assess conflicts between expert witnesses concerning matters not within the factfinder's ken? Can anyone—a legislator, judge, or member of a jury—do anything more than exercise one's best judgment concerning the facts and arguments presented, trying to take into account biases of which one is aware?

4. Theoretical understanding of the causes of problems seems useful because it appears to hold the key to solutions. For example, once the germ theory of infectious disease was understood, it was far easier to determine how to prevent the transmission of and to treat these diseases. Such thinking supports the search for the so-called "root causes," of which crime is allegedly a symptom. Even if this is the right way to think, as many claim, a number of observations warrant both caution and perhaps some optimism. First, human behavior, especially at the larger level of groups, is notoriously hard to understand because the phenomena are so complicated and because controlled experimentation on important questions is difficult or impossible for practical or ethical reasons. We can't cause neonatal brain damage to a random sample of infants and then compare their development to undamaged controls. It would be nice to know the independent effects of undesirable variables such as racism or poverty by introducing them in a subject group and comparing the subjects with controls, thus holding everything else constant. But we can't do this either. Now, some experimental work is possible, and nonexperimental methodologies can produce reliable results of high probable validity, but it is always hard because individual people and groups in realistic conditions simply cannot be manipulated to test hypotheses as easily as infrahuman species or much of nature can be.

Second, even if we understand the causes of a phenomenon, once again we may not be able to affect those causes for practical or ethical reasons. Suppose there exists reasonably convincing evidence that a genetic predisposition in part causes certain types of antisocial behavior. Suppose, too, that we can't yet identify or fix the alleged genetic culprit. At best we might be able to identify the infants at risk, but then what? Our causal knowledge has told us only in which group of people the problem will arise, but it as yet offers no clue to the remedy. That will have to come from knowledge about how to combat the effects of genetic defects nongenetically. Moreover, not every infant at risk will become antisocial in the absence of an effective intervention. Depending on the strength of the causal variable, we can only say probabilistically what the chance is that any particular individual in the risk group will ultimately manifest the problem. Should all of them be treated, however? And if so, at whose expense? Is there an ethical problem with stigmatizing an infant as being at risk? How certain would you have to be to justify this?

Consider another example. Despite the cautions of Wilson and others about the validity of the claim that poverty is a root cause of crime, most commentators believe that poverty is a powerful cause and call for various social programs to eliminate it. But do we really know how to do this and, if so, can we do it in ways that are consistent with other values that we cherish? Is comparison with other societies that appear to do better in this regard entirely fair? After all, their histories and values are quite different from ours, and the relative equality of resources in some other places is a quite recent phenomenon that may not be destined to last; the wealth and social equality of these societies may succumb to external forces beyond their control or it may create other unacceptable problems in the long-term.

Third, symptoms can often be controlled or cured without understanding their causes by methods unrelated to those causes, because we have better data and theories about the symptom than the cause. For example, early childhood programs that use psychological methods to help kids learn to control impulsiveness problems that may lead to crime might succeed in diminishing crime even though the potential problem has genetic roots. Indeed, many proposed anticrime programs fit precisely this model of thinking about how to address crime.

5. Despite a growing data base and increasing theoretical sophistication, the difficulties besetting understanding the roots of crime and how to address them often lead to a search for quite partial solutions. Until the doctor comes and tells us how to rid ourselves of poverty, racism, brain damage, and the like, we apparently must content ourselves with the less basic proposals that virtually all commentators propose. This is the more pragmatic approach that many students and agents of the criminal justice system have always preferred and that has been the dominant response. The difference now is that most scholars and intervention providers and consumers understand that all new programs should be accompanied by a rigorous evaluation component to see if they really work. That an expert who designed the program on the basis of the best theory and evidence guarantees that it will work is not sufficient assurance that it finally does.

How would you go about evaluating the outcomes of many of the proposals the selections include? Suppose for example, that minor drug dealers were no longer incarcerated, as Tonry proposes. What would happen to prison populations? If drug use increased in inner-city neighborhoods, on balance would the proposal be a success even though fewer disadvantaged and nonviolent offenders went to prison?

6. In criminal justice debates, arguments and proposals based on social science and policy analysis often confront moral counterclaims and value preferences that cannot be avoided by factual findings. Returning to the hypothetical case described in the previous note, suppose that we no longer incarcerated minor drug dealers and that, so far as we can tell, doing so creates no further negative results and even saves some money in the long run. What is the appropriate response if a critic nonetheless says that she is a just-deserts theorist and that even minor drug dealing is an offense sufficiently heinous to require that dealers serve significant jail terms? Or what if there is a proposal for selective incapacitation—giving longer sentences to convicts predicted to be specially dangerous than to other convicts convicted of the same crime but who are not predicted to be dangerous—and the evidence is that it is likely ultimately to be successful at reducing crime and may even save money. Again, what is the appropriate response to the just-deserts critic who says that enhancing the punishment of offenders for what they *may* do in the future is simply unjust, even if the program "works"? Finally, what if the "war on drugs" does prevent more rampant drug use, an outcome that seems to justify the war's associated costs. How does the drug warrior respond to the libertarian who says that what people consume privately for their own enjoyment or any other reason is not the government's business and that criminal prohibition of use is wrong?

In these cases, liberals and conservatives alike tend to become impatient with the critics, accusing them of being naïve and impractical. Arguments from pure principle frustrate policy analysts dedicated to solving serious social problems. But understandable impatience is not a reasoned response to the critics. How should the critics be answered?

7. A major dispute that deserves specific attention is whether criminal prohibition and imprisonment have deterrent effect. (Chapter 6 also addresses these questions.) One's armchair induction is that they certainly would, assuming that conviction and imprisonment are sufficiently unpleasant. One would even expect, contrary to the claims of many, that crimes of impulse would be generally suppressed by the general, implicit caution that fear of unpleasant consequences inculcates in almost everyone, albeit with lessened effect among impulsive people. In the face of these armchair inductions, earlier critics of the recent, vast increases in the rate of imprisonment and the size of the prison population pointed out that crime rates scarcely declined despite the increases and that there is little reason to believe that they would have climbed even higher if the tougher new sentencing policies had not been adopted. Thus the deterrent and incapacitative effects of the increasing use of imprisonment seemed minimal, at best. Although the data can be disputed, the criticism seemed quite plausible. In recent years, however, the rates of imprisonment have continued at high levels *and* the rates of serious crimes have dropped substantially in most major cities and in virtually all areas of the United States. Proponents of incarceration believe that the very recent decrease in crime is attributable in substantial measure to the deterrent and incapacitative effects of the increased use of imprisonment. Opponents think that other variables, such as the strength of the economy, better explain the decrease. Explanations abound for the drop in crime, but none is entirely convincing. What should a sensible legislator do? Should society continue the present policy of heavy use of imprisonment, with its attendant fiscal costs and possible racial bias? What kind of data or arguments would persuade you to retain or abandon present policy?

But how much do potential criminals have to fear from the criminal justice system? Liberals argue correctly that an extremely high percentage of convicted felons now serve prison terms and, consequently, the average term for an offender caught and prosecuted for a crime will be lengthy. Conservatives respond that proportionally few offenders are actually caught and prosecuted to conviction. Thus, if one calculates the average term for a crime by dividing the total time served for that crime in a given time period by the number of times that crime was actually committed, the average will be low. Even if the average expected sentence for each crime has risen, the rates of unprosecuted serious crime are sufficiently high to keep that average still quite low. Do criminals know this? They may not know many of the doctrinal intricacies of the substantive criminal law that may influence their cases if they are caught and prosecuted, but it beggars belief to claim that they are unaware of the risk of going to prison. Most potential offenders know that if they continue offending, they will surely be caught sometime and that if caught, their chance of going to prison is now higher than in the past. For the many people with little stake in our society, especially disadvantaged and minority young males, the odds of going to prison for any specific offense may still be sufficiently low to fail adequately to deter them. Or so the conservatives claim.

Suppose the conservative explanation is correct. What follows? If more criminals were caught and convicted, would lesser average sentences suffice to protect the public? What would be the marginal gain in deterrence from keeping average sentences lengthy nonetheless? Suppose the liberals are correct. Would the proper response be to reduce the prison population, as Tonry and others suggest, from 1.5 million to 600,000 by incarcerating only the most violent and notorious offenders for considerably shorter terms? Given the rates of serious crimes like robbery, rape, aggravated assault, and burglary, would there be a sufficient number of successful prosecutions and prison terms to maintain minimal deterrence and incapacitation? And what about the property offenders, who will not be imprisoned? Will lesser sanctions deter them, especially since law enforcement is likely to decrease detection resources if the criminal justice system signals by failing to imprison that these are not serious matters? What would you do?

8. Drug policy is a crucial criminal justice issue that the selections mention only briefly. This is a topic of enormous complexity that cannot adequately be addressed in a brief selection, but students should be aware of some of the crucial issues, including the theoretical and practical depth of the disputes about drug policy. Virtually every important issue—ranging from the relationship of drug use to other crimes to the success rate of law enforcement in diminishing either supply or demand—is intensely debated. Some facts are undeniable: an enormous percentage of felons arrested in major cities test positive for controlled substances; drug cases clog the courts of our major cities; a very high percentage of prisoners in federal and state prisons are serving terms for drug offenses, often of a relatively minor nature. Drug enforcement apparently consumes a disproportionate amount of criminal justice resources. Nevertheless, there is little agreement about what these facts mean or what to do about them.

Those who consider drugs an unmitigated evil applaud continuing law enforcement efforts and wish more resources expended. Others survey the landscape and think the war on drugs has been lost and cannot be won. Consequently, decriminalization or legalization has gained fervent support from scholars, such as Milton Friedman and Ethan Nadelmann; politicians, such as Kurt Schmoke, the mayor of Baltimore; and journals of opinion, such as *The Economist*. Advocates of decriminalization variously believe (1) that a drug war using criminal law enforcement as its weapon cannot conceivably halt the demand or supply of easily secreted substances that consumers want; (2) that the criminal law's war on drugs creates more problems, such as more crime and corruption, than it solves; and, (3) that the government has no legitimate right to prevent the private use of substances by consenting adults. Other critics of the drug war, who are not committed to decriminalization, nevertheless share some of the reservations of the decriminalizers but have other criticisms, such as the disproportionate amount of money spent on law enforcement rather than drug treatment and the disproportionate impact of criminalization on disadvantaged people. Advocates of maintaining a strong law enforcement response, most of whom also genuinely applaud treatment and noncriminal prevention efforts, claim that the free availability of substances that which would follow decriminalization would surely increase use and the ravages that uncontrolled drug consumption produces. Thus, they argue, the law enforcement approach is a regrettable but necessary stopgap.

Since the most recent "war" was proclaimed in reaction to the widespread appearance and use of the "crack" form of cocaine, law enforcement agencies in the Untied States and abroad have had many laudable successes, but the illegal supply of controlled substances of ever greater purity and ever cheaper prices has not abated. It is of course possible that society would be even worse off had we not continued to fight the drug wars. Indeed, James Q. Wilson's attack on decriminalization, referred to in the selection above, suggested that this would have been true and predicted that if we had decriminalized drugs, future generations would have wondered what kind of people would have allowed the horrors that Wilson is certain would occur. Once again we observe a conflict. Tonry accuses the government of taking steps certain to harm minority, predominantly African American, citizens, and wonders how people of goodwill could do this. Wilson wonders how people of goodwill could have done anything different.

What should a legislator of goodwill do when various proposals for dealing with the drug crisis are made? Virtually no one opposes the suggestion that more resources should be allocated to treating those who are treatable according to the best research. But the debate rages concerning whether the law enforcement approach to the drug war should continue, and if so, in what way.

9. The introduction to this chapter suggested that, with few exceptions, the substantive criminal law did not make much difference in the rates of crime we experience. Are you now persuaded that this suggestion was correct? Can you think of other ways the substantive criminal law could be reformed to help, or at least to do less harm?

2

Crime and Punishment

The readings in this chapter are organized around three large questions: first, what is punishment; second, why should punishment ever be inflicted; and third, what sorts of behaviors should be punished? The answers to these questions are usually called, respectively, a definition of punishment, a theory (or justification) of punishment, and a theory of criminal legislation.

Each of these three major questions is introduced in the beginnings of the subsections that follow. Preliminarily, however, we should be alive to the possibility that the questions are not as separable from each other as our organization might suggest. There seem to be implications from certain answers to one of these questions for the possible answers to the others. For example, if in answering the definitional question (of what punishment is) one adopts the functionalist answers of Posner or Moore, that will have a bearing on the second question of why we punish. To see this, suppose that what makes a legal sanction a punishment is the purpose for which it is imposed. Suppose further that that purpose is either crime prevention (Posner) or retribution (Moore). With such supposed answers to the first question, it should come as no surprise that one's answer to the second is close in terms of the goods of crime prevention or retribution. After all, if to say what something is is to say what it is good for (which is what a functionalist definition of punishment does), then by so defining it one has already partly justified why we have such a thing in terms of the goods that it serves.

As a second example, consider the relationship between the second question and the third. Suppose we answer the second question (of why we punish) with the answer, "to exact retribution." Such a retributive theory of punishment lies uneasily with a harm-prevention theory of what it is we should prohibit with criminal legislation. For if we prohibit actions in order to prevent harms to others, how can our theory of why we punish those who transgress such prohibitions be anything other than a harm-prevention sort of theory of punishment?

Despite these relationships between possible answers to these three basic questions, it is useful to separate the questions, as we do in the readings below. If nothing else, such separation allows one to enquire into the sorts of relations that may exist between varying answers to these distinct questions.

2.1   THE NATURE OF PUNISHMENT AND THE BOUNDARIES OF THE CRIMINAL LAW

The existence of areas or departments of law has received scant attention by legal theorists. Mostly the existence of tort law, contract law, property law, criminal law, etc., is simply taken for granted by lawyers and legal academics, even after legal history shows us how contingent are the developments of these areas of law. What makes a given law, rule, or process part of *criminal* law? Is it the content of the norm, its prohibiting force, its punitive purpose, the sanctions attached to noncompliance, or something else?

Each of the selections that follow approaches this question about the essence and the boundaries of criminal law through the key notion of punishment. The assumption is that if we can say what punishment is, we are a good ways down the road to answering the questions about criminal law's essence and boundaries.

"What is punishment?" is one of those "what is . . . " questions that seems to call for a description of something by way of an appropriate answer. If we ask, "what is an intention?" or "what is mental illness?" we expect an answer in the form of a description of a kind of thing. This pragmatic expectation is what makes answers like "never having to say you're sorry" (Eric Segal) or "the lonely voice of youth" (Johnny Cash) sound elliptical when given to questions like "What is love?" or "What is truth?"

Each of the selections below seeks to give a description in answer to the question, "what is punishment?" but what is being described may differ from author to author. Kent Greenawalt seeks to elucidate our *concept* of punishment. He does so in terms of "typical instances" (what some would call standard instances, clear cases, paradigmatic examples, or paradigms) or punishment, each of which possess the five features he explores. Greenawalt recognizes that in some secondary or perhaps metaphorical sense, institutions, practices, or actions could be punishments even though they lack one or more of these features. Still, for Greenawalt the indisputable instances of punishment are those that possess all five features.

Richard Posner approaches the nature of punishment differently. Although Posner seeks the "meaning" of the criminal law, he is not doing so by seeking to define either punishment or criminal law. Rather, he seeks a "positive theory" of criminal law doctrine. Such a positive theory will be a description of the criminal law we have, not an explanation of why we have it nor an evaluation of it as a good thing to have. Yet Posner's descriptive theory is given in terms of the hidden function served by the criminal law doctrines that we have. Such function, Posner urges, is (mediately) to prevent market bypassing by individuals and (ultimately) to promote economic efficiency.

Like Posner, Michael Moore eschews giving any analysis of our concepts of punishment or of criminal law as an area of law. Rather, Moore too seeks to describe the nature of the thing to which our concepts of criminal law and punishment apply. Also like Posner, Moore seeks an answer in terms of the function(s) served by criminal law and punishment. Moore's major differences with Posner here seem to be two: first, the good that criminal law serves is the achieving of retributive justice, not the achieving of economic efficiency; and second, although the theory that gives such an answer is properly called a descriptive theory, Moore argues that when the thing described is a "functional kind," any accurate description will also be a limited kind of evaluation.

Punishment

KENT GREENAWALT

Punishment is not an exclusive province of the law. Parents punish their children, and members of private associations punish their wayward fellows. Like most concepts, "punishment" has no rigid boundaries. One useful way to understand its central aspects and uncertain borderlines is to identify the features of typical instances of punishment, and to inquire how far their absence would lead one to say that something other than punishment is taking place.

Typical and Atypical Instances

In typical cases of punishment, persons who possess authority impose designedly unpleasant consequences upon, and express their condemnation of, other persons who are capable of choice and who have breached established standards of behavior.

From *Encyclopedia of Crime and Justice* (New York: Macmillan, 1983), reprinted in *Journal of Criminal Law and Criminology,* Vol. 74 (1983), pp. 343–45.

Responsible Agents

Punishment is a practice that is performed by, and directed at, agents who are responsible in some sense. God and humans can punish; hurricanes cannot. People, but not faulty television sets, are fit subjects of punishment. A higher level of capacity is required to impose punishment than is minimally necessary to make one subject to it. To be subject to it, one need have only sufficient mental control over one's actions to refrain from disfavored behavior, a degree of control that quite small children and some animals possess. To punish, one must be able consciously to inflict harmful consequences because of a wrong that has been committed.

Unpleasant Consequences

Punishment involves designedly harmful consequences that most people would wish to avoid. Medical treatment and other forms of therapy may also be painful, but their unpleasantness is an unfortunate contingent fact; pleasing or painless substitutes, if available, would be preferred. Unpleasantness is, on the other hand, part of the basic nature of punishment; if the response to those who break rules was to give them something they wanted, such as more money, one would not consider the response to be punishment, even if the aim were to reduce future violations.

Condemnation

The unpleasant consequences of punishment are usually preceded by a judgment of condemnation; the subject of punishment is explicitly blamed for committing a wrong. The close link between punishment and condemnation is attenuated in some instances. When a teacher punishes an entire class because one child has been naughty, he may not be condemning the other members of the class. The teacher's choice of collective punishment will reflect his belief either that the group as a whole is capable of constraining the actions of its members or that one student will hesitate to be the source of mischief for his classmates; but the teacher need not suppose that all the other members of the class are actually partly responsible for the particular naughty act. A similar analysis applies to vicarious punishment. Punishing one person for the sins of another may serve a purpose even if the victim of punishment is not condemned for the specific wrong.

For certain violations of law, condemnation may be wholly absent, except in the most formal sense. Some actions may be deemed antisocial and worth discouraging by unpleasant consequences even if no one really blames the persons who perform them. This is perhaps exemplified by the attitude American society now takes toward most parking violations. For a different reason, a reflective judgment of condemnation may be absent when very young children are punished. Parents may evince anger and impose simple penalties in the belief that this is the most effective way to teach acceptable behavior. They may thus treat their children as blameworthy, even though they doubt that the children are experienced enough actually to merit blame for performing the offending actions.

Condemnation is not in itself usually considered punishment. If members of a society regarded a formal condemnation as extremely shameful, one might think of that as a possible punishment in itself rather than merely a complement of more substantial consequences; this discussion will adopt the common assumption that punishment involves more than condemnation.

Authority

Punishment is imposed by people who have authority to do so—authority conferred by legal rule, associational standard, or social morality. A father can punish his own small children, but he cannot punish a neighbor's child unless the neighbor has given him power to do that. Only public officials can punish a thief for breaking the law. Authority may be conceived in a somewhat extended sense, whereby one can speak of a person's being punished by the community when his offensive behavior is met by the negative informal reactions of its members.

Standards

Punishment ordinarily follows some breach of established rules of behavior; the notion that people should have fair warning as to what behavior is punishable, and to what degree, is now an established principle of most legal systems. Yet, especially in informal family settings, people may be punished for doing things they should have realized were wrong, even though they were not warned in advance about that specific sort of behavior. Even then, one can usually point to some relevant, more general standard that the children have been taught, such as taking care of family property, not harming brothers and sisters, and not disturbing parents. Many legal systems also contain some standards of misbehavior that are quite open-ended. Much more extraordinary is punishment of persons for actions they had no reason to suppose were wrong at the time they committed them.

Misperceptions

The assumption thus far has been that those who impose punishment, and the community at large, perceive circumstances as they really are. However, people may be woefully mistaken about critical facts. An innocent person may be punished because he is thought guilty, or all epileptics may be punished in the belief that having that disease evidences extreme moral fault. Misperceptions may also occur because of conscious manipulations by those aware of the actual facts. If officials successfully persuade others that a woman they know to be innocent is guilty, her condemnation and imprisonment will, in the public perception, constitute genuine punishment. Whether the knowledgeable officials should regard this as instance of (unjust) punishment or something else is debatable. The crucial inquiry, in any event, is not whether what follows such deviations from the bases for imposing punishment can accurately be called punishment, but whether deviations of this sort can ever be morally justified. . . .

Legal Punishment and the Criminal Law

Parts of the civil law authorize punitive consequences, but in advanced legal systems, legal punishment is linked to the criminal law. That law consists of prohibitions of antisocial behavior backed by serious sanctions. Not every criminal conviction is necessarily followed by punishment—alternative dispositions are often possible—but a set of mandatory rules that did not provide for punishing of violators would not be part of the criminal law. The meaning and possible justification of legal punishment are, therefore, very closely related to the meaning and possible justifications of the criminal law.

NOTES AND QUESTIONS

1. Linguists often and usefully distinguish two kinds of definitions: *lexical* definitions, which try to capture the meaning of words as they are used by the relevant linguistic community; and *stipulative* definitions, which recommend that a certain meaning be given to words irrespective of whether those words have been hitherto used with that meaning in mind. Which sort of definition of "punishment" is Greenawalt seeking to give?

2. Why might it be useful to seek either kind of definition for "punishment"?

3. Does Greenawalt's definition define punishment for all cultures? Or is his an explication only of the Anglo-American concept of punishment, recognizing that other cultures could have different concepts of punishment?

4. Does Greenawalt intend his five features of typical instances of punishment —responsible agents giving and receiving it, it being unpleasant to receive, the expression of condemnation in the giving of it, it being given by one in authority over the one receiving it, it being in response to a breach of standards—to be individually necessary, jointly sufficient conditions for the correct use of the word "punishment"? If not, what other sense of definition could Greenawalt intend? Try to define "religion." Did you mention as one factor "belief in a supernatural, person-like Being"? If so, is the presence of such a factor *necessary* for something to be a religion? If not, could such a factor still be part of the definition or the meaning of "religion"?

5. What would (or should) Greenawalt say of the following idiomatic bit of English: "As a judge sentencing Jones for drunk driving, I gave him a light sentence because I thought he had already been punished enough—after all, his wife and children were killed in the accident, he was crippled, and he lost his job."

6. Is it conceptually possible to punish a thoroughgoing masochist? How about a thoroughgoing optimist, who believes that whatever happens is for the best?

An Economic Theory of the Criminal Law

RICHARD A. POSNER

Introduction

I think . . . that the substantive doctrines of the criminal law, as of the common law in general, can be given an economic meaning and can indeed be shown to promote efficiency. . . . I certainly do not want to be understood, however, as arguing that every rule of the criminal law is efficient, or that efficiency is or ought to be the only social value considered by legislatures and courts in creating and interpreting the rules of the criminal law.

My analysis can be summarized in the following propositions:

1. The major function of criminal law in a capitalist society is to prevent people from bypassing the system of voluntary, compensated exchange—the "market," explicit or implicit—in situations where, because transaction costs are low, the market is a more efficient method of allocating resources than forced exchange. Market bypassing in such situations is inefficient—in the sense in which economists equate efficiency with wealth maximization—no matter how much utility it may confer on the offender.

2. Much of this market bypassing cannot be deterred by tort law—that is, by privately enforced damage suits. The optimal damages that would be required for deterrence would so frequently exceed the offender's ability to pay that public enforcement and nonmonetary sanctions such as imprisonment are required.

3. Such sanctions are extremely costly for a variety of reasons, and this, together with the socially worthless character of most of the sanctioned conduct, has a number of implications for efficient criminal law doctrine, such as that unsuccessful attempts should be punished in order to economize on costlier punishments for completed crimes. The threat of punishing attempts, as we shall see, makes the completed crime more costly in an expected sense and therefore less likely to be committed. I contend that the main differences between substantive criminal law and substantive tort law can be derived from the differences in (1) the social costs of criminal and tort sanctions and (2) the social benefits of the underlying conduct regulated by these two bodies of law. I contend, in short, that most of the distinctive doctrines of the criminal law can be explained as if . . . the objective of that law were to promote economic efficiency.

From *Columbia Law Review,* Vol. 85 (1985), pp. 1194–99.

The Function of Criminal Law

An Economic Typology of Crimes

In this section I try to derive the basic criminal prohibitions from the concept of efficiency; I argue that what is forbidden is a class of inefficient acts. As this is a controversial endeavor, I think it important to note that the rest of the article does not depend on it—that it would be little affected if I took as given that society wants to prevent the acts that it calls murder, theft, rape, etc., and did not inquire why.

When transaction costs are low, the market is virtually by definition, the most efficient method of allocating resources. Attempts to bypass the market will therefore be discouraged by a legal system bent on promoting efficiency. If I covet my neighbor's car, it is more efficient to force me to negotiate with my neighbor—to pay him his price—than it is to allow me to take his car subject to being required by a court to pay the neighbor whatever the court decides the car is worth. If I happen to have no money but want a car, it would be inefficient to let me just take a car. Indeed, unlike the first case, this transfer cannot possibly improve the allocation of resources—that is, it cannot move resources from a less to a more valuable employment—because value is a function of willingness to pay. Since I am unwilling (because unable—but it does not matter why) to pay my neighbor's price for the car, it follows that the car would be less valuable in an economic sense in my hands than in his.[1] Moreover, if I am allowed to take the car, I will have an incentive to expend resources on taking it and my neighbor will have an incentive to expend resources on preventing it from being taken, and these expenditures considered as a whole, yield no social product.

In short, it is inefficient to allow pure coercive transfers of wealth—"pure" implying that the transfer is not an incident of a productive act: But this is an important qualification. The invention of a new product or process can also cause all sorts of wealth transfers that are involuntary from the standpoint of the losers, but invention increases, as well as transfers, wealth in a way that merely taking someone's wealth from him does not. Invention is not just a coercive or involuntary transfer, and it would be infeasible to force the inventor to identify and negotiate terms of compensation with all the losers.

The role of the criminal law in discouraging market bypassing is obscured by the fact that the market transaction that the criminal bypasses is usually not a transaction with his victim. If someone steals my car, normally it is not because he wants that car and would have bought it from me if the criminal law had deterred him from stealing it. He steals to get money to use in buying goods and services from other people. The market transaction that he bypasses is the exchange of his labor for money in a lawful occupation. But it is still market bypassing.

Although the market-bypassing approach provides a straightforward economic rationale for forbidding theft and other acquisitive crimes—such as burglary, robbery, fraud (false pretenses), embezzlement, extortion (by threat of violence), most kid-

---

[1]The car might, of course, confer more utility (pleasure, satisfaction) on me than on my neighbor, but there is a difference between utility in a broad utilitarian sense and value in a (perhaps narrow) economic sense, where value is measured by willingness to pay for what is not yours already, or willingness to accept payment for what is yours.

napping, some murder, some assault and battery, some rape—we must also consider "crimes of passion," which loom large in thinking about the criminal law and which may seem to have nothing to do with bypassing markets. Such crimes can be defined in economic terms as crimes motivated by interdependent negative utilities. An example is murdering someone because you hate him rather than because you want his money. These are not wealth transfers in any obvious sense and may seem to have nothing to do with bypassing the market. It might seem therefore, that before we could pronounce such conduct inefficient we would have to compare the offender's utility with the victim's disutility. We could not do this without exceeding the conventional limits of economics, which do not allow interpersonal comparisons of utilities, just as we could not describe a theft as efficient because the impecunious thief would derive greater pleasure from his act than the pain suffered by his wealthy victim.

Now as a matter of fact it is a pretty safe empirical guess that most such conduct does create net disutility. The whole idea is to inflict as much disutility on the victim as possible, and it is unlikely that every disutile experienced by the wretched victim confers an equal and opposite utile on the offender. Indeed, there would seem to be a fundamental asymmetry between the pleasure that one would obtain from killing another person who has sullied one's honor, and the victim's pain, broadly defined to include the disutility to him of losing his life. But I want to emphasize four other economic, rather than utilitarian, points:

1. Coercion arising from interdependent negative utilities cannot increase the wealth of society and therefore cannot be an efficient act. If A kills B because the resulting disutility to B confers utility on A, the wealth of the society is not increased even in the unlikely event that the total amount of human happiness is increased.

2. The dichotomy between acquisitive crimes and crimes of passion is overstated. Acquisitive crimes bypass explicit markets: crimes of passion often bypass implicit markets—for example, in friendship, love, respect. . . . Less obviously, crimes of passion often bypass explicit markets too. The essential characteristic of a market, and the source of the ethical appeal of market systems, is that in a market people have to be compensated for parting with the things that have value to them, unless transaction costs are prohibitive. Someone who gets his satisfactions in life from beating up other people, without compensating them, rather than from engaging in trade with them is thus bypassing explicit markets. This point is obscured by the fact, noted earlier in the context of acquisitive crimes, that the victims of the crimes and the people that the aggressor would be trading with if he were not committing crimes are different people.

To sum up, one who spends his time brawling rather than working is bypassing an explicit market;[2] if he spent his time raping rather than dating women he would be bypassing an implicit market. The essential point in both cases is that he would not be deriving his satisfactions in life from acts that confer benefits on other people.

3. Allowing coercion would create incentives for potential victims to spend heavily on self-protection and for potential aggressors to spend heavily on overcoming the victims' self-protective efforts. All this spending would yield little if any net social product.

---

[2]Professional boxing would be an example of a lawful market alternative to battery.

4. Some crimes of passion are costly and inefficient efforts at self-help. A slanders B, and B, instead of suing A, kills him. The suit would have given B almost the satisfaction that killing A did, and at far lower social cost.

. . . Suppose a rapist derives extra pleasure from the coercive character of his act. Then there would be (it might seem) no market substitute for rape, suggesting that rape is not a pure coercive transfer and should not, on economic grounds, anyway, be punished criminally. But the argument would be weak:

a. Because there are heavy penalties for rape, the rapes that take place—that have not been deterred—may indeed be weighted toward a form of rape for which there are no consensual substitutes; it does not follow that the rape that is deterred is generally of this character.

b. Put differently, the prohibition against rape is to the marriage and sex "market" as the prohibition against theft is to explicit markets in goods and services.

c. Given the economist's definition of "value," even if the rapist cannot find a consensual substitute (and one such substitute, prostitution, is itself illegal), it does not follow that he values the rape more than the victim disvalues it. There is a difference between a coerced transaction that has no consensual substitute and one necessary to overcome the costs of consensual transactions; only the second can create wealth, and therefore be efficient. Indeed, what the argument boils down to is that some rape is motivated in part or whole by the negative interdependence of the parties' utilities, and this, as I have argued in connection with crimes of passion, is no reason for considering the act efficient.

d. As with my earlier discussion of crimes of passion, it is important not to take too narrow a view of market alternatives. Supposing it to be true that some rapists would not get as much pleasure from consensual sex, it does not follow that there are no other avenues of satisfaction open to them. It may be that instead of furtively stalking women they can obtain satisfactions from productive activities, that is, activities in which other people are compensated and thus derive benefits. this is an additional reason to think that the total wealth of society would be increased if rape could be completely repressed at a reasonable cost.

All this may seem to be a hopelessly labored elucidation of the obvious, that rape is a bad thing; but I think it useful to point out that economic analysis need not break down in the face of such apparently noneconomic phenomena as rape.

NOTES AND QUESTIONS

1. Posner hopes that his economic analysis will be "helpful in explaining the basic structure of . . . the criminal law." In what sense does he intend his theory to *explain* the structure of the criminal law? Does it count against his theory doing any *explaining* (in this sense) that "judges and legislators do not often speak the language

of economics"? Is Posner giving up any truly explanatory ambitions for his theory when he states that "most of the distinctive doctrines of the criminal law can be explained as if the objective of that law were to promote economic efficiency"?

2. Do you think that Posner thinks economic efficiency is good? If so, does that evaluation influence his discovery of economic efficiency as the hidden objective of criminal law? Should it?

3. What does Posner mean by "economic efficiency?" Is it (1) stable trade points in markets where transaction costs are zero, (2) any Pareto-optimal distribution where no one can be made better off (as judged by him) without making someone else worse off (as judged by her), or (3) maximal wealth production? Can these three different notions be combined in some way for a unitary notion of efficiency?

4. How does forcing people to use voluntary exchanges in a market promote economic efficiency? Does it always or only usually serve efficiency to force people into markets?

5. In noncapitalist societies where there are very limited (explicit) markets, what function would Posner assign to the criminal law?

6. Posner makes much of the differences between his economic theory of the criminal law and the utilitarian theory. Consider the following questions:

a. Despite the differences, what are the similarities? Why does Posner call his a pure deterrence theory?

b. One difference between utilitarianism and Posner's theory arises when the distribution of wealth is such that willingness to pay in a market is not proportional to intensity of preference. You may want a Jaguar more than anyone else in the world, but if you have no wealth and no means to attain it, your intense preference will find no market expression. Posner points out that to the economist the reason why you cannot pay is irrelevant: "Value in a (perhaps narrow) economic sense . . . is measured by willingness to pay." When willingness to pay is *not* expressive of intensity of preference, in what sense is it a measure of value?

c. Elsewhere Posner has emphasized the difference between efficiency in the sense of wealth maximization, and the preference-satisfaction maximization distinctive of some forms of utilitarianism. If more wealth is not preferred, in what way could it be better? Indeed, is the notion of wealth always a function of some preference order (so that unpreferred wealth is a contradiction)? Or can wealth be need-relative, not preference-relative, and still be an intrinsic good?

d. Under what conditions would a utilitarian think that rape should be prohibited by the criminal law? How do these compare to Posner's economic analysis of the prohibition against rape?

e. What idea of "satisfaction" is Posner using when he claims that the slander victim who kills rather than sues his slanderer derives no more *satisfaction* from the killing than the lawsuit? Did not the slander victim choose the killing over the suing when both were open to him? A (cardinal) utilitarian may recognize that the slander victim's free choices do not maximize his satisfactions, but can a free market economist like Posner?

7. To what extent are there implicit markets for crimes of violence like rape and murder? Can there be explicit or implicit markets—i.e., places for voluntary exchange—if what is wanted is a coerced "exchange"? How does Posner respond to this worry?

The Nature of a Theory of the Criminal Law

MICHAEL S. MOORE

The Function of the Criminal Law

We cannot begin any taxonomizing of criminal law theories until we settle the question of what kind of kind the criminal law is and what sort of good . . . it can achieve. These are distinct questions, but, as we shall see, the answer to one highly influences the answer to the other.

Few people believe that criminal law is only a nominal kind—that its doctrines are grouped together as an area of law only because of the accidents of history, that there is no nature such doctrines share that sets them apart from other areas of law other than the convention of our system to call them, or the agencies that administer them, "criminal." More typical is the use of the allegedly distinctive sanctions of the criminal law as the criterion of its identity and individuation. This more typical view holds that what marks law as criminal law is the loss of life or liberty attendant upon criminal liability, a deprivation not attendant upon any other (i.e., civil) liability.

Such a view finds criminal law's essence in a feature of its structure—namely, in its remedy—and is what I earlier called something like a natural kind view of an area of law. Such a view need not be indifferent to criminal law's function(s). To be justified, such severe sanctions must serve some good, even if the good served is not the essence of criminal law. Typically, those viewing criminal law as identified by its distinctive sanctions hold a mixed view as to its functions. Such a view may hold that punitive sanctions are justified when they attain a sufficient level of incapacitation, deterrence, reform, and retribution (the traditional big four of punishment theory). Since locking people up, scaring them, and changing them are not intelligible as intrinsic goods, such a mixed theory is better described, first, in terms of a crime-prevention function (itself served by incapacitation, deterrence, and reform, and itself serving the utilitarian goal of making us all better off); second, in terms of the function of achieving retributive justice; and third, in terms of the function of achieving distributive justice by devoting extra social resources to those less advantaged members of the population (criminals) who need them. There are other mixed theories of criminal law's function, of course, that do not mix all three of these types of intrinsic goods (retributive justice, utility, distributive justice) but mix only two, such as a mixed utilitarian/retributive theory or a mixed rehabilitative/utilitarian theory. One can also "mix" the goals in different ways, lexically ordering the achievement of one goal over another as opposed to simultaneously maximizing both.

In any case, such mixed punishment theories go hand in hand with the remedy-based view of criminal law because such a theorist has already fixed the essence of

From "A Theory of Criminal Law Theories," *Tel Aviv University Studies in Law,* Vol. 10 (1990), pp. 134–40.

criminal law (by its remedy) and then asks, how should that remedy be used? A natural answer is, "to maximize all the goods there are," leading to some form of mixed theory of punishment.

What's wrong with this remedy-based view of the criminal law can be seen by inquiring into the intelligibility of asking, "What is a punishment?" if one does not already have in mind an answer to the question, "Why do we punish?" For if the structural feature that allegedly fixes criminal law's essence—punitive sanctions—is itself described only by the function served, then criminal law is a functional and not a natural kind.

Admittedly, we are not bereft of structural intuitions about what sanctions constitute punishments. Sanctions that are severely unpleasant to endure like death, confinement, the ducking stool, etc., seem easy examples. Yet would even these sanctions—let alone monetary fines—be punishment if they were not imposed for a punitive purpose? If a pound of flesh is the stipulated damages to be paid upon breach of some contract, the remedy, although very unpleasant to endure, is still for breach of contract, not a crime. Moreover, could not a gift of flowers be a punishment—as when we punish our friends' derelictions by being especially nice to them in order to heighten their feelings of guilt? If our purpose is punitive, the sanctions inflicted will be a punishment, no matter what their structural features might be. To explicate what a punishment is, then, one must first explicate what a punitive purpose is.

The supposed structural essence of criminal law in terms of its distinctive remedy of punishment turns out to involve us in criminal law's function. This is not raised to argue for a retributive function for the criminal law based on what Herbert Hart once aptly called the "definitional stop." No argument has yet been presented for any particular function of the criminal law. The only point so far is that one cannot get a handle on what sanctions constitute a punishment unless one has *some* function in mind as the goal of the criminal law. The result is that the criminal law is not to be identified with, nor can it be individuated by, any structural features of its allegedly distinctive remedies. Criminal law is *an* area of law only because it serves some distinctive good that we honor as its function.

We can satisfy ourselves that criminal law is a functional kind only if we can satisfy ourselves as to what its function is. To do this, we must first have some idea of how in general we find the function of anything, an area of law included.

There are two components in our judgments of a thing's function. One is a judgment about its capacity: What can it cause? Such capacity judgments are heavily influenced by what sorts of effects the item has brought about in the past, which is why we often look for a thing's function in the actual consequences of its activities. The second component judgment is one of goodness: of all the states of affairs within the capacity of some thing to bring about, are any of them intrinsically good? If none of the effects a thing can cause are good, then it has no function (although like a poison it may of course have an evil *use*); if a thing can bring about some intrinsically good state of affairs, then that consequence is what the thing is "good for," i.e., that is the thing's function.

Consider by way of example the current debate in psychology about the function of dreaming. Does dreaming serve the function of keeping us asleep (Freud's hypothesis), some other function, or no function at all? We answer this question by first inquiring what dreaming has the capacity to cause. Does it cause the relaxation of that vigilant sentinel of our good opinions of ourselves, the Freudian "censor," who while "asleep at his post" lets by usually repressed wishes that find fantasized satisfaction in the dream and thus discharge their otherwise sleep-disturbing energy? Current research into that causal question suggests that the answer is "no," that dreaming does not cause the prolongation of sleep through Freudian or any other mechanisms. But for illustration, suppose the evidence were the other way, so that it did appear that dreaming tends to protect sleep from otherwise disturbing stimuli. We need a second kind of judgment to decide that the function of dreaming is to guard sleep. We need to judge that sleep is good. Sleep does not appear to be an intrinsic good—unless one's life is so bleak that death looks pretty inviting too—so sleep must bring about something else that is good. And this embroils us in another large debate in psychology: what is sleep good for? There are lots of causal hypotheses here too (one of which is, incidentally, that we sleep in order to dream).

What researchers are looking for as they search for, and then sift among, the effects of dreaming and of sleeping is some contribution these processes make to something that is intrinsically good, namely, health, Unless they find some causal linkage between these processes and health, they will not have found such processes' functions.

If we apply this process to the criminal law, the same two kinds of judgments are involved. First we ask, what consequences does the criminal law have the capacity to bring about? Remembering that this is an exercise in particular jurisprudence, I ask this question about the criminal law that I most intimately know, that of the Anglo-American system. Can Anglo-American criminal law bring about emphatic denunciation of wrongdoing? Can it bring about social cohesion? Can it predict violent propensities and incapacitate those with such propensities from hurting others? Can it educate people out of wanting to hurt others? Can it achieve retributive justice? Can it reinforce existing wealth disparities? Can it dampen movements for social change, and thereby entrench those in power?

Suppose for the moment that criminal law has the capacity to cause all of these effects to some significant degree. Which might be its function? Some of these effects are not only not intrinsically good, they do not even contribute to something else that is intrinsically good. Maintaining wealth disparities and dampening social change are in this category, so these cannot be the criminal law's function. If these were the only effects of criminal law, then it would have no function. Others on this list are not intrinsic goods, but they may well have the capacity to contribute to something else that is intrinsically good which could then be criminal law's function. Denouncing wrongdoing, maintaining social cohesion, incapacitating or educating people are in this category. These are perhaps good depending on what else they cause. Typically, though not inevitably, the further good thing each of these things is thought to cause is the prevention of crime. Murder, rape, mayhem, etc. are bad, and their prevention is intrinsically good, so perhaps this is the function of criminal law. Yet the achieving of retributive justice is also good for its own sake—or so I have argued. So should we say that the criminal law has two functions of equal dignity, crime-prevention and retribution? Many people have said this, and it is not an implausible thing to say. Yet there are two considerations that suggest that the only function of our criminal law is the achievement of retributive justice. One is the tension that exists between crime-prevention and retributive goals. This tension is due to retributivism's inability to share the stage with any other punishment goal. To achieve retributive justice, the punishment must be inflicted because the offender did the offense. To the extent that someone is punished for reasons other than that he deserves to be punished, retributive justice is not achieved.

This is seen most easily in situations where the offense committed deserves a certain range of punishment, and then extra punishment is tacked on for crime-prevention reasons (such as to induce the criminal to talk and implicate others, or to strike a blow for general deterrence). That others cannot be convicted without an accused's testimony, or that his crime has become a popular one and his case a very public one, making his punishment a useful object lesson to others, are factors irrelevant to what the accused deserves. There is no retributive justice achieved in the imposition of such an increment of punishment.

Now suppose no identifiable increment of punishment is added for crime-prevention reasons. Rather, the accused is punished no more than he deserves. Yet part of the reason motivating those who punish him is that his punishment will serve as an example to others. Such a criminal may have no grounds for complaint, but we do; the criminal system is not achieving retributive justice. By seeking to achieve other goods through punishment, we necessarily lessen our ability to achieve the good of retribution.

The tension between retribution and any other goal of punishment such as crime-prevention prevents us from any comfortable "mix" of goods for punishment. We cannot happily seek both goals and kill two birds with the proverbial one stone, for by aiming at one of the birds we will necessarily miss the other.

The second consideration militating against a mixed theory of criminal law's function stems from the structure of Anglo-American criminal law. The criminal law we have has a great deal more capacity to cause the achievement of retributive justice than it does the prevention of crime. Partly this is due to factors extraneous to the doctrines of the criminal law, such as the limited efficacy of deterrence. More important is the shape of our criminal law doctrines themselves. If one were seeking to maximize deterrence, or incapacitation, we would not have the doctrines we do. Consider but one example, the differential punishment for intentional homicide. Typically under American state law, intentional killing may be first degree murder if it was premeditated, voluntary manslaughter if it was done in a rage brought on by the victim's provoking act, or second degree murder if it was neither provoked nor premeditated. On crime-prevention grounds of deterrence or incapacitation, these are hard distinctions to justify. The more impulsive the killing, the more punishment there should be on deterrence grounds, for such draconian measures may be the only way to get the impulsive killer to stop and think. Analogously, second degree murders are typically intra-family killers who are highly nonrescidivist, so on incapacitation grounds this class of criminals should be punished least. As we know, however, this is not how punishment is scaled by our homicide laws. Such laws make sense only if they are seen as attempting to grade culpability (by the degree of control exercised by the killer as he acted).

Examples of this sort abound in the criminal law. Such doctrines make utilitarianism look like so many "bad reasons for what we believe on instinct anyway" (F.H. Bradley's characterization). It is thus difficult to make the utilitarian goal of crime prevention into even *a* goal of Anglo-American criminal law, given how often that goal's apparent implications are flouted by the doctrines supposedly serving it.

I thus assume in what follows an exclusively retributive function for Anglo-American criminal law. Our criminal law exists in order to achieve retributive justice. I have of course only lightly sketched the argument for this conclusion.

The first question of a theory of the criminal law is the question of why we punish. My answer—to exact retribution—influences the possible shape of the rest of a criminal law theory. Alternative answers in terms of the utilitarian goal of crime-prevention or the distributive justice goal of rehabilitation will similarly determine the shape of their respective criminal law theories.

NOTES AND QUESTIONS

1. In an earlier part of his article, Moore taxonomizes theories about an area of law into descriptive, explanatory, and evaluative. Given his thesis that descriptive theories about criminal law are also in some sense evaluative theories, how can he maintain a distinction between the two kinds of theories?

2. Do such things as "functional kinds" exist? If so, how do they differ from "nominal kinds"?

3. Cannot things have functions without those who are judging what the functions are making some evaluation? What is the function of a hammer? A human heart? Dancing? Must we make some evaluations in order to answer these questions?

4. How does Moore (or Posner, for that matter) know which doctrines are *criminal law* doctrines in order to seek their function? Mustn't they already have in mind some structural criterion marking off criminal law from other areas of law in order to begin looking for criminal law's function?

5. Do you agree with Moore that a punishment is a punishment only if it serves a punishing purpose? Whose purpose counts here? What would Greenawalt say?

6. Do you agree with Moore that no retributive justice is achieved if an offender is punished for utilitarian reasons? Could we say, according to Moore, that such a person was *punished* at all? If the offender is punished no more than she deserves, but not *solely* because she deserves it, is no retributive justice achieved?

2.2 THE MORAL JUSTIFICATIONS FOR PUNISHMENT

2.2.1 Introduction

It is standard fare in the philosophy of punishment to give a laundry list of goods that punishment achieves. Such heterogeneous lists do little to aid the understanding of how punishment might be justified. We have accordingly organized the materials that follow into three pure types of punishment theories—the utilitarian, the retributive, and the rehabilitative—and a fourth type, generically called mixed theories of punishment because they mix two or more of the pure theories.

The primary organizing principle behind this taxonomy of punishment theories is to distinguish theories that treat punishment of deserving offenders as intrinsically good from theories that treat such punishment as only instrumentally good. That is, both the pure retributivist and the pure rehabilitationist regard punishment (or "involuntary treatment") as a matter of justice not in need of further justification. The practice is right because it is just, and that is the end of it. By contrast, the pure utilitarian regards punishment as justified only insofar as the practice causes to come into being other states of affairs that are intrinsically good; on this view, punishment as such is bad because it hurts people and can be (overall) good only because the good consequences it causes outweigh the harm it inflicts.

A secondary organizing principle is between two kinds of justice, retributive and distributive. Retributivists regard punishment as a forced suffering of those who deserve to suffer. Rehabilitationists regard punishment as a forced treatment of those who deserve the extra social resources it requires to give them this "benefit." Retributive desert is based on what the offender has done, and with what culpability; distributive desert is based on the special needs of the least advantaged members of society, whom offenders are assumed to be.

A third distinction is often confusingly introduced into punishment discussions, but it plays little role here once it is properly understood. This is the distinction between what are sometimes called "agent-relative" or "deontological" theories and those that are called "agent-neutral" or "consequentialist" theories. A deontological punishment theory would be one directing each of us not to fail to achieve (retributive or distributive) justice at any cost, including even the cost that more justice will fail to be done later if we do justice now. This is the well known "categorical" nature of morality of which Kant made so much. On this view a judge must not do injustice even if more injustice will be done later if she does not do a little now. By contrast, a consequentialist theory tells us to maximize intrinsically good things like the achievement of justice. A retributivist-consequentialist, for example, would forgo punishing a deserving offender now if so doing would allow more deserving offenders to receive their just deserts later.

The categorical force (or the lack of it) of the norms of a punishment theory is distinct from the content of those norms. What those norms regard as intrinsically good and right is not the same as the question of whether one must categorically seek such things or whether one should maximize such things. Moreover, once one separates this third distinction from the first, plainly the first is of greater interest in taxonomizing theories of punishment. It is more interesting to know about some theory whether it regards punishment as intrinsically right on its own or in need of causing further states of affairs that make it right than it is to know with what force each of us are obligated to punish. We have accordingly placed little emphasis on this last distinction as we have organized the differing theories of punishment below.

A Taxonomy of Purposes of Punishment
MICHAEL S. MOORE

The Prima Facie Justification of Punishment

There is by now a familiar list of prima facie reasons given to justify the institution of punishment. Such a list standardly includes incapacitation, special deterrence, general deterrence, denunciation, rehabilitation, and retribution. A word about each of these reasons is in order. Incapacitation is the simplest of theories, because, as the name suggests the good punishment achieves is that it incapacitates offenders by locking them up and preventing them from committing further crimes. Special deterrence has a similar aim: Punishing offenders deters them from committing further crime upon their release. Likewise, general deterrence aims at the prevention of crime by punishing offenders, except that those who are deterred are others in the general population rather than the offenders themselves. All three of these traditional theories of punishment share a common goal thought to justify punishment, namely, the reduction of crime.

The ideas captured in the theory labeled "denunciation," sometimes called the expressive theory of punishment, are somewhat more complicated. One strand of this theory urges that punishment must express society's condemnation because doing so educates citizens in the wrongfulness of the conduct that the criminal law attempts to discourage. So stated, the denunciation theory is no more than a somewhat broader form of the general deterrence theory: Both aim at the prevention of crime, one by scaring people out of it and the other by more subtle educational techniques. Another strand of the denunciation theory asserts that denouncing crime via symbolic blaming coupled with harsh treatment serves an end distinct from the prevention of future

From *Law and Psychiatry: Rethinking the Relationship* (Cambridge: Cambridge University Press, 1984), pp. 233–39.

criminal conduct. Theorists of this stripe urge that crime must be denounced by punishment, because doing so maintains a sense of social cohesion. If punishments are inflicted, then citizens do not have the sense that the social contract has been broken with impunity by others. The good achieved on this branch of the theory is not the prevention of future crimes; rather, it is thought that a sense of community is itself a good thing that punishment helps to achieve.

Rehabilitation is perhaps the most complex of the theories of punishment, because it involves two quite different ideals of rehabilitation that are usually confused. These two rehabilitative ideals can best be separated by thinking about two different ways of rendering offenders nondangerous. First, imagine that what is done is to place offenders in extraordinarily awful places of detention, with harsh treatment by inmates and guards. Here, nondangerousness is achieved because such offenders either become "penitent," or they are no longer willing to commit crimes because they are unwilling to risk again such awful treatment. For comparison, imagine that the same level of nondangerousness can be achieved if prisoners are placed in much nicer facilities, with kinder personnel (all of them softspoken, in white coats, and manifesting sincere concern), a place in which extensive therapy programs are undertaken. Imagine further that the second such program, although much more expensive than the first, not only make offenders nondangerous, but also makes them flourishing, happy, and self-actualizing members of our society.

The first sort of rehabilitative ideal is one that is achieved when we make criminals safe to return to the streets. This sort of rehabilitative theory justifies punishment, not by appeal to how much better off criminals will be at the end of the process, but rather by how much better off all of us will be if "treatment" is completed because the streets will be that much safer. Such a theory seeks to rehabilitate criminals only as a cost-effective means of shortening the expensive incarceration that would otherwise be necessary to protect us all against crime. The second sort of rehabilitative ideal, by way of contrast, is a paternalistic theory. It seeks to rehabilitate offenders not just so they can be returned safely to the streets, but so they can lead flourishing and successful lives. Such a theory justifies punishment, not in the name of all of us, but rather in the offenders' own name; since it does so in their name, but contrary to their own expressed wishes (few offenders want to be punished), this kind of rehabilitative theory is paternalistic in character.

This paternalistic type of rehabilitative theory has no proper part to play to any theory of punishment, even in the minimal sense of constituting a prima facie justification of punishment. There are three reasons why this is so. First, such a paternalistic reform theory allocates scarce societal resources away from other, more deserving groups that want them (such as retarded and autistic children or the poor) to a group that hardly can be said to deserve such favored status and, moreover, does not want such "benefits." As simple matter of distributive justice it is difficult to argue that criminals should be favored in the allocation of scarce social resources in these ways. Second, in any political theory according high value to liberty, paternalistic justifications are themselves to be regarded with suspicion. Criminals are not in the standard classes in society for which paternalistic state intervention is appropriate, such as the severely disordered, the young, or others whose capacity for rational choice is diminished; such a paternalistic theory is suspect on this ground alone. Third, such recasting of punishment in terms of "treatment" for the good of the criminal makes possible a kind of moral blindness that is dangerous in itself. As C. S. Lewis pointed out some years ago, adopting a "humanitarian" conceptualization of punishment makes it easy to inflict treatments and sentences that need bear no relation to the desert of the offender. We may do more to others "for their own good" than we ever allow ourselves to do when we see that it is really for our good that we act.

Retributivism, the final theory used to justify punishment, is the view that punishment is justified by the desert of the offender. The good that is achieved by punishing, in this view, has nothing to do with future states of affairs, such as the prevention of crime or the maintenance of social cohesion. Rather, the good that punishment achieves is that someone who deserves it gets it.

Retributivism is quite distinct from a view that urges that punishment is justified because a majority of citizens feel that offenders should be punished. Rather, retributivism is a species of objectivism in ethics that asserts that there is such a thing as desert and that the presence of such a (real) moral quality in a person justifies punishment of that person. What a populace may think or feel about vengeance on an offender is one thing; what treatment an offender deserves is another. And it is only this last notion that is relevant to retributivism.

Retributivism is also distinct from what is sometimes called "revenge utilitarianism." This is the view that the sate must punish because private citizens otherwise will take the law into their own hands and that such private vengeance leads to chaos and disorder. Punishment in such a view is justified by its ability to prevent these bad things. Retributivism has nothing to do with this essentially forward-looking justification. Moreover, this "prevention of private vengeance" theory is to my mind not even a prima facie justifying reason for punishment. The obvious thing to do if citizens are going to violate the law by taking it into their own hands is to deter those citizens by punishing them, not by punishing someone else. It places retributivism in an unnecessarily bad light to think that it justifies punishment only because of the shadow cast by a threat of illegal violence by vengeful citizens.

The Two Pure Theories of Punishment

It is common to reduce the survivors on this list of prima facie justifications of punishment to two general theories, the utilitarian theory and the retributive theory. To see how this is done, one need only consider the good state of affairs that is to be achieved by incarceration, special deterrence, general deterrence, and rehabilitation (to the extent that it is of the first sort of rehabilitative theory, and not the second). For all four of these rationales for punishment share the prevention of crime as the beneficial end that justifies punishment. In each case, the ultimate justification for inflicting the harm of punishment is that it is outweighed by the good to be achieved, namely, the prevention of future crimes by that offender or by others. This justification of an institution by the social welfare it will enhance make all such theories instances of the utilitarian theory of punishment.

Thus, the denunciation theory of punishment is a second kind of utilitarian theory of punishment, insofar as the good it seeks to achieve is not simply the prevention of crime. To the extent one grants intrinsic value to social cohesion, and does not regard that as a value only because it contributes to the maintenance of public order, the denunciation theory can be distinguished from the other utilitarian theories just considered by the differing social good it seeks to achieve. Nonetheless, it is still a utilitarian theory, since it outweighs the harm that is punishment by some form of net social gain that punishment achieves.

Both crime prevention and the maintenance of social cohesion are types of collective good. The general utilitarian theory of punishment is one that combines these and other forms of collective good that punishment might achieve, and calls them all a "social gain." Whenever the social gain outweighs the harm punishment causes to offenders or their families, such a theory would say that there is a net social gain. Such a vocabulary allows us a succinct definition of any form of utilitarian theory: Punishment is justified if and only if some net social gain is achieved by it.

A retributivist theory is necessarily nonutilitarian in character, for it eschews justifying punishment by its tendency to achieve any form of net social gain. Rather, retributivism asserts that punishment is properly inflicted because, and only because, the person deserves it. That some people deserve punishment in such a theory is both a necessary and a sufficient condition justifying criminal sanctions. A succinct definition of the retributivist theory of punishment, paralleling that given of the utilitarian theory, is that punishment is justified if and only if the persons receiving it deserve it.

The Mixed Theory of Punishment

Once one grants that there are two sorts of prima facie justifications of punishment— effecting a net social gain (utilitarian) and giving just deserts (retributivist)—one can also see that in addition to the two pure theories of punishment there can also be mixed theories. There are two logically possible mixed theories, although only one of these merits any serious attention. There is first of all the popular form of mixed theory that asserts that punishment is justified if and only if it achieves a net social gain and is given to offenders who deserve it. Giving just deserts and achieving a net social gain, in such a case, are each individually necessary but only jointly sufficient conditions justifying punishment. The second logically possible mixed theory would be one asserting that punishment is justified if and only if it achieves a net social gain, *or* if it is given to offenders who deserve it. Such a theory has no name, because there is no one, to my knowledge, who has ever adopted it. Such a theory is unnamed and unclaimed because it shares the defects of each of the pure theories, utilitarianism and retributivism. I shall accordingly put this "mixed theory" aside from further consideration.

The first kind of mixed theory itself has two branches. By far the most usual and popular form of the theory asserts that we do not punish people *because* they deserve it. Desert enters in, this theory further asserts, only as a limit on punishment: We punish offenders *because* some net social gain is achieved, such as the prevention of crime, but *only if* such offenders deserve it. It is, in other words, the achieving of a net social gain that justifies punishment, whereas the desert of offenders serves as a limiting condition on punishment but as no part of its justification. The alternative branch of the mixed theory is just the converse: One would urge that we punish *because* offenders deserve it, but *only if* some net social gain is achieved by doing so. In such a case, the roles of net social gain and desert are simply reversed: Giving offenders their just deserts serves as the justification of punishment, and the achieving of a net social gain as the limiting condition.

A cynic might view these two branches of the mixed theory as nothing more than an uncomfortable shuffle by mixed theorists. When accused of barbarism for punishing persons for retributivist reasons, they assert the first branch of the theory (they punish not because some persons deserve it, but because of a collective good that is achieved). When accused of immorality for imposing harsh treatment on someone as a means of making everyone else better off, such theorist shift to the other foot, and claim they do not punish someone to achieve a net social gain, but only to give offenders their just deserts. The cynic has a point here, because there is a sense in which the two branches of the theory are the same, namely, the sense that they justify exactly the same kinds of treatment for all cases. The only difference in theories is in the motivations of those who hold them. And while that may make a difference in our moral judgments of those who hold the different branches of the mixed theory of punishment, it does not make a difference in terms of the actual social institutions and judgments such theories will justify. I shall accordingly lump both of these branches together and call them the mixed theory of punishment.

2.2.2   Utilitarianism

Utilitarianism generally (and not just as a theory of punishment) is a moral and political theory with two components. The first is what might be called the maximizing component: if something is good, more of it is better. This is the "agent-neutral" or "consequentialist" aspect of utilitarianism. It postulates that an action or institution is right if it maximally achieves whatever are intrinsically good states of affairs while minimizing whatever are intrinsically bad states of affairs. The second component of utilitarianism is its distinctive theory of the good. Utilitarianism postulates that only one sort of thing is intrinsically good, which makes it a monistic theory rather than a pluralistic one. This one thing we may broadly label welfare, although different versions of utilitarianism will specify welfare differently—in terms of pleasure or happiness or preference-satisfaction.

As the selection from Benthan illustrates, a utilitarian will regard punishment as prima facie bad because it decreases welfare by causing displeasure to at least one person, namely, the one being punished. A utilitarian justification of punishment thus must emphasize other consequences of punishment that enhance welfare. The most obvious of such consequences is the prevention of the welfare loss that is crime.

Prima facie, surely utilitarianism is a plausible theory for both ethics and politics. After all, other things equal, is it not intuitively a good thing to augment human happiness? Other things equal, isn't it good for people to get what they want? The problem is that other things are not always equal, and punishment has often been used to show that. The selection from Michael Moore states the form of the argument against utilitarianism generally and against the utilitarian theory of punishment in particular. In general terms the argument is quite simple: the calculation of net social welfare that utilitarianism demands often cannot be equated with the intuitive demands of justice.

It is important to note that Moore gives voice to two versions of the justice objection. In one version, Moore assumes that it is unjust to punish the innocent and then argues that utilitarianism will sometimes demand the punishment of the innocent. In the other version, Moore assumes that it is unjust not to punish the guilty and then argues that utilitarianism (together with the mixed theory) will sometimes demand the exemption of the guilty from punishment.

Utilitarians have long been sensitive to this objection to their theory. They respond to the justice objection in two ways. First, they articulate a form of "indirect utilitarianism" when they distinguish two contexts in which a theory of punishment should operate: the legislative context of setting standards and the judicial context of applying standards to particular offenders. One might argue, as many utilitarians have, that the utilitarian calculus should be used to justify the general standards of the criminal law (including the entire practice of punishment itself) while the application of those standards should not be guided by the welfare calculus of utilitarianism. We shall encounter a version of this response in the selection from H. L. A. Hart in section 2.2.5 on the mixed theories of punishment.

Second, utilitarians often attempt to reconstrue what justice demands so that the conflict between justice and utilitarianism is less that it might seem. Military conscription, for example, is said not to be unjust, so surely sometimes an individual may be sacrificed to the general welfare.

An Introduction to the Principles of Morals and Legislation

JEREMY BENTHAM

I. The general object which all laws have, or ought to have, in common, is to augment the total happiness of the community; and therefore, in the first place, to exclude, as far as may be, everything that tends to subtract from that happiness: in other words, to exclude mischief.

From *An Introduction to the Principles of Morals and Legislation* (New York: Prometheus Books, 1988), pp. 170–71.

II. But all punishment is mischief: all punishment in itself is evil. Upon the principle of utility, if it ought at all to be admitted, it ought only to be admitted in as far as it promises to exclude some greater evil.[1]

III. It is plain, therefore, that in the following cases punishment ought not to be inflicted.

1. Where it is *groundless:* where there is no mischief for it to prevent; the act not being mischievous upon the whole.
2. Where it must be *inefficacious:* where it cannot act so as to prevent the mischief.
3. Where it is *unprofitable,* or too *expensive:* where the mischief it would produce would be greater than what is prevented.
4. Where it is *needless:* where the mischief may be prevented, or cease of itself, without it: that is, at a cheaper rate.

NOTES AND QUESTIONS

1. How would you justify the utilitarian principle that "the general object which all laws . . . ought to have . . . is to augment the total happiness of the community"? Can you justify your belief in the truth of such a principle any better than is often suggested about any other "first" or "supreme" principle (such as the Kantian principle that one should never treat another as a mere means but as an end in himself): "in the last resort we have to take a stand based on personal sentiment"?

2. As is well known, Bentham equated happiness with pleasure, turning the utilitarian calculus into the hedonic calculus of pleasure and pain. Do all pleasures stand

---

[1]What follows, relative to the subject of punishment, ought regularly to be preceded by a distinct chapter on the ends of punishment. But having little to say on that particular branch of the subject, which has not been said before, it seemed better, in a work, which will at any rate be but too voluminous, to omit this title. . . . A very few words, however, concerning the *ends* of punishment, can scarcely be dispensed with.

The immediate principal end of punishment is to control action. This action is either that of the offender, or of others: that of the offender it controls by its influence, either on his will, in which case it is said to operate in the way of *reformation;* or on his physical power, in which case it is said to operate by *disablement:* that of others it can influence no otherwise than by its influence over their wills; in which case it is said to operate in the way of *example.* A kind of collateral end, which it has a natural tendency to answer, is that of affording a pleasure or satisfaction to the party injured, where there is one, and, in general, to parties whose ill-will, whether on a self-regarding account, or on the account of sympathy or antipathy, has been excited by the offence. This purpose, as far as it can be answered *gratis* is a beneficial one. But no punishment ought to be allotted merely to this purpose, because (setting aside its effects in the way of control) no such pleasure is ever produced by punishment as can be equivalent to the pain. The punishment, however, which is allotted to the other purpose, ought, as far as it can be done without expense, to be accommodated to this. Satisfaction thus administered to a party injured, in the shape of a dissocial pleasure, may be styled a vindictive satisfaction or compensation: as a compensation, administered in the shape of a self-regarding profit, or stock of pleasure, may be styled a lucrative one. . . . Example is the most important end of all, in proportion as the *number* of the persons under temptation to offend is to *one.*

equal before the bar of justice and morality? Is pushpin as good as poetry if it is as pleasurable as poetry? Are our highest achievements judged to be such only because they are accompanied by —or because they cause—the most pleasure?

3. Are pleasure and happiness the same? Or is happiness the satisfaction of "higher" pleasure, such as that found in poetry, over "lower" pleasures, such as those of food and sex?

4. Are the pleasure/happiness/preferences of one person always of equal weight to anyone else's? Suppose your child is drowning, but so are two children of someone else, a stranger to you, someone who cares for each of her children as much as you care for yours. If you can save only one set of children, not both, and if you save your own child, have you done something morally bad? What would Bentham say? Even if you have done something bad (as judged on the utilitarian standard), would Bentham also have to think that you should be punished?

5. Suppose a child drowns in the following circumstances. Person A throws the child into a deep pond knowing that it cannot swim, whereas B, an Olympic gold metalist in freestyle swimming, sees the child in the pond, knows that it is drowning, and watches with indifference. Is there a difference in the moral blameworthiness between A and B? What would Bentham say?

6. As the earlier selection from Posner mentioned, it is common to assume that there is a declining marginal utility to money depending on the wealth of each person. That is, the marginal utility of money to any individual declines as that person's wealth increases, because each dollar matters less the more dollars one has. Assume that this is true. How much of your wealth should you distribute to the poor? What would Bentham say?

7. Bentham tells us to augment the *total* happiness of the community. Suppose a community has a "utility monster" in its midst, that is, a person who derives greater pleasure from the material goods of this earth than anyone else and for whom there is no declining marginal utility. In the initial allocation of entitlements for such a society, should the utility monster be assigned all material goods? All goods except those necessary for the survival of others?

8. One way for a utilitarian to respond to the "utility monster" objection is to modify the measure used in the utilitarian principle from *total* happiness to *average* happiness. Since "each is to count for one but only one," in Bentham's famous phrase, average happiness is not maximized by giving everything to the monster. Yet maximizing average utility leads to some puzzles of its own, for example, as regards population policy. In a society with the utility monster in it, is not the highest average happiness obtained by killing everyone else off?

9. "To consequences there is no end." If this statement is true, can it ever be determined whether any act or institution is good or bad? Mightn't the most heinous murder produce great happiness in the long run? The murder of Hitler's mother, for example? But isn't the only "long run" that ultimately counts the end of time, when all the happiness- and misery-producing consequences are in?

The Argument for Retributivism

MICHAEL S. MOORE

The Argument Against the Pure Utilitarian Theory

In exploring one's thoughts about punishment, it is perhaps easiest to start with some standard kinds of thought experiments directed against a pure utilitarian theory of punishment. A thought experiment is essentially a device allowing one to sort out one's true reasons for believing that certain propositions are true. To be successful, such a thought experiment need not involve any actual case or state of affairs, nor need the cases envisioned even be very likely; they only need be conceivable in order to test our own thoughts.

It is standard fare in the philosophy of punishment to assert, by way of several thought experiments, counterexamples to the utilitarian thesis that punishment is justified if and only if some net social gain is achieved. I mention only two such counterexamples: scapegoating and preventive detention. With regard to the first, it might be recalled that D. B. Cooper successfully skyjacked an aircraft some years ago, and that this successful, unsolved crime apparently encouraged the mass of skyjackings that have cost so much in terms of dollars, lives, and convenience. Cooper wore large sunglasses in his escapade, and there was accordingly only a very limited description available of him. Imagine that shortly after his skyjacking we had the benefit of the knowledge we now have by hindsight, and we decided that it would be better to punish someone who looked like Cooper (and who had no good alibi) in order to convince others that skyjacking did not pay. For a consistent utilitarian, there is a net social gain that would be achieved by punishing such an innocent person, and there is no a priori reason that the net social gain in such a case might not outweigh the harm that is achieved by punishing an innocent person;

The preventive detention kind of counterexample is very similar; Imagine that a psychiatrist discovers that a patient has extremely dangerous propensities. The patient is also the accused in a criminal trial. It turns out, however, that the accused is not guilty of the crime for which he is charged and in fact has committed no crime whatsoever. Should a judge who, we may suppose, is the only one who knows that the man is both dangerous and innocent find the accused guilty? Doing so will prevent the defendant's predicted criminal behavior because he will be incarcerated. In a utilitarian theory, it is difficult to see why such a judgment would not be perfectly appropriate, as long as the prediction is reliable enough, and as long as the crimes predicted are sufficiently serious that the good of their prevention outweighs the harm of punishing that person, even though he has committed no crime as yet.

From *Law and Psychiatry: Rethinking the Relationship* (Cambridge: Cambridge University Press, 1984), pp. 238–43.

The general form of the argument arising from these kinds of thought experiments is that of a reductio ad absurdum argument. The argument has three premises:

1. Punishment should be inflicted if and only if doing so achieves a net social gain.
2. A net social gain would be achieved in this case by the inflection of punishment.
3. Punishment should not be inflicted in this case.

Each of these premises corresponds to steps in both of the foregoing thought experiments. The first premise is simply a restatement of the utilitarian theory of punishment. The second premise presupposes that there are some cases where a net social gain can be achieved by punishing an innocent person and asserts that this is such a case. The third premise asserts our intuition that such persons ought not to be punished.

All three premises together yield a contradiction:

4. Punishment should not be inflicted and punishment should be inflicted.

The first two premises have as their joint conclusion that the person should be punished; this conclusion, when conjoined with the third premise, produces the contradictory conclusion.

The strongest possible form of a reductio ad absurdum argument is one that ends in a formal contradiction. To avoid the contradiction, there are only three possibilities, corresponding to each of the three premises. One could give up the third premise and simply admit that in such cases the persons should be punished despite their innocence. This move is a rather implausible one, inasmuch as it commits one to admitting that one will punish an entirely innocent person. The second possibility is to deny that there will be cases where there will be a net social gain from punishing an innocent person. This move is usually associated with the name of rule utilitarianism and involves the idea that one cannot make a general practice of punishing the innocent, because then the harm of so doing (in terms of demoralization costs in society and the like) will outweigh any possible good to be achieved, even the prevention of skyjacking. The problem with this response, popular as it is, is that it fails to deal fairly with the nature of the thought experiment. That is, suppose there are some risks of detection of punishment of innocent persons, and, thus, some risks of demoralization costs; such risk will only allow utilitarians to say that the number of cases in which punishment of the innocent will maximize utility is somewhat diminished. It does not foreclose as somehow impossible that there are such cases. Such cases are conceivable, and if in them one is still not willing to punish, one thereby shows oneself not to be a utilitarian about punishment.

This bring us to the third possibility: One can simply give up the first premise, that is, one can repudiate the utilitarian theory of punishment. Such thought experiments, I think, when clearly conceived and executed, show almost all of us that we are not pure utilitarians about punishment.

Arguments Against the Mixed Theory of Punishment

The arguments against the pure utilitarian theory of punishment do not by themselves drive one into retributivism. For one can alleviate the injustice of the pure utilitarian theory of punishment by adopting the mixed theory. Since under the mixed theory the desert of the offender is a necessary condition of punishment, it will follow from the mixed theory that in each of the kinds of counterexamples considered (where punishment is not deserved), punishment should not be given. No contradictions will be generated, because the premises are consistent:

1. Punishment should be inflicted if and only if doing so achieves both a net social gain and gives an offender his just deserts.
2. A net social gain would be achieved in this case by the infliction of punishment.
3. It is not the case that punishment would give an offender his just deserts in this case.
4. Punishment should not be inflicted.

From the first three of these premises, the conclusion is deducible that there should be no punishment. This is also what the fourth premise asserts, so that there is no contradiction when one substitutes the mixed theory for the utilitarian theory of punishment.

There is, nonetheless, another sort of thought experiment that tests whether one truly believes the mixed theory, or is in fact a pure retributivist. Such thought experiments are the kind that fill the editorial pages where outrage is expressed at the lightness of sentence in a particular case, or the lightness of sentencing generally in the courts of some communities. An example is provided by *State v. Chaney,* wherein the defendant was tried and convicted of two counts of forcible rape and one count of robbery. The defendant and a companion had picked up the prosecutrix at a downtown location in Anchorage. After driving the victim around in their car, the defendant and his companion beat her and forcibly raped her four times, also forcing her to perform an act of fellatio with the defendant's companion. During this same period of time, the victim's money was removed from her purse, and she only then was allowed to leave the vehicle after dire threats of reprisals if she attempted to report the incident to the police.

Despite this horrendous series of events,the trial judge imposed the minimum sentence on the defendant for each of the three counts and went out of his way to remark that he (the trial judge) was "sorry that the (military) regulations would not permit keeping (defendant) in the service if he wanted to stay because it seems to me that is a better setup for everybody concerned than putting him in the penitentiary." The trial judge also mentioned that as far as he was concerned, there would be no problem for the defendant to be paroled on the very first day of his sentence, if the parole board should so decide. The sentence was appealed by the state under a special Alaska procedure, and the attorney general urged the Alaska Supreme Court to disapprove the sentence.

The thought experiment such a case begins to pose for us is as follows: Imagine in such a case that after the rape but before sentencing the defendant has gotten into an accident so that his sexual desires are dampened to such an extent that he presents no further danger of rape; if money is also one of his problems, suppose further that he has inherited a great deal of money, so that he no longer needs to rob. Suppose, because of both of these facts, we are reasonably certain that he does not present a danger of either forcible assault, rape, robbery, or related crimes in the future. Since

Chaney is (by hypothesis) not dangerous, he does not need to be incapacitated, specially deterred, or reformed. Suppose further that we could successfully pretend to punish Chaney, instead of actually punishing him, and that no one is at all likely to find out. Our pretending to punish him will thus serve the needs of general deterrence and maintain social cohesion, and the cost to the state will be less than if it actually did punish him. Is there anything in the mixed theory of punishment that would urge that Chaney nonetheless should really be punished? I think not, so that if one's conclusion is that Chaney and people like him nonetheless should be punished, one will have to give up the mixed theory of punishment.

The argument structure is again that of a reductio and is as follows:

1. Punishment should be inflicted if and only if doing so both achieves a net social gain and gives an offender his just deserts.
2. A net social gain would not be achieved in this case by the infliction of punishment.
3. Punishment should be inflicted.

Again, these three premises generate a contradiction:

4. Punishment should not be inflicted and punishment should be inflicted.

From the first two premises, it follows that there should be no punishment; this contradicts the third premise that there nonetheless should be punishment.

One again has the choice of giving up one of the three premises of the argument. To give up the third premise is very unappealing to most people; doing so requires that people like Chaney should not be punished at all. Again, the tempting move is to assert that there will be no cases in which one will be sure enough that the danger is removed, or the ends of general deterrence served, that one can ever successfully assert the second premise. But as in the earlier case, this is simply to misunderstand the nature of the thought experiment. One only need think it conceivable that such dangers could be removed, or such ends of deterrence served, in order to test one's theory of punishment. And nothing in utilitarianism can guarantee that utility is always maximized by the punishment of the guilty. The only other way to avoid the contradiction is to give up the first premise. Yet this means that one would have to give up the mixed theory of punishment.

The Argument for Retributivism

If one follows the predicted paths through these thought experiments, the end result is that one finds oneself, perhaps surprisingly, to be a retributivist. We might call this an argument through the back door for retributivism, because the argument does not assert in any positive way the correctness of retributivism. It only asserts that the two theories of punishment truly competitive with retributivism, namely, the pure utilitarian theory and the mixed theory, are each unacceptable to us. That leaves retributivism as the only remaining theory of punishment we can accept.

It has seemed to some theorists that there is a limited amount of positive argument that can be given in favor of a retributivist theory and still have the theory remain truly retributivist. Hugo Bedau has recently reminded us, for example, that the retributivist faces a familiar dilemma:

> Either he appeals to something else—some good end—that is accomplished by the practice of punishment, in which case he is open to the criticism that he has nonretributivist, consequentialist justification for the practice of punishment. Or his justification does not appeal to something else, in which case it is open to the criticism that it is circular and futile.

In this respect, however, retributivism is no worse off than any other nonutilitarian theories in ethics, each of which seeks to justify an institution or practice not by the good consequences it may engender, but rather by the inherent rightness of the practice. The justification for any such theories is one that appeals to both our particular judgments and our more general principles, in order to show that the theory fits judgments that on reflection we are sure of, and principles that on reflection we are proud of.

NOTES AND QUESTIONS

1. Is there any benefit to performing the sort of "thought experiments" Moore envisions, where some of the imagined conditions are unlikely to be encountered in the real world (such as the condition of secrecy)?

2. What argument does Moore have against the dedicated utilitarian who will willingly punish the innocent, or willingly forgo punishment of the guilty, in the scenarios Moore imagines?

3. Should the utilitarian add a "publicity and honesty" condition that rules out both punishment of the innocent as if they were guilty and "only pretend" punishments of the guilty? How would such a publicity and honesty side constraint on the utilitarian calculation about punishability itself be justified? On strictly utilitarian grounds?

4. Is the utilitarian on safer ground if she restricts her use of the utilitarian calculus to the justification of the general rules under which offenders are punished? Is a general rule that licenses judges to punish some innocents, or to pretend-punish some guilty, so much less likely to be justified by the utilitarian calculus that the possibility that it might be so justified can be disregarded?

5. Even if one restricts the use of the utilitarian calculus to justifying general rules, what is a utilitarian judge to do in applying those rules to particular cases? Just apply the rules? Can or should a judge "just apply the rules" without regard to the policy that justified the rules to start with?

6. Kant's third formulation of his supreme principle of morality, the categorical imperative, was that persons "should always be treated as ends in themselves; not as

means." Can you put this idea in your own words? How would a natural rights theorist phrase such an idea?

7. Which of the two aspects of utilitarianism identified in the introduction to this section are implicated by the punishment of a (relatively) innocent person so as to serve the end of deterring others from crime? Is it the utilitarian theory of the good, which regards welfare as the only good thing (to the exclusion of other possible intrinsic goods, such as moral duties being kept and moral rights not being violated)? Or is it the consequentialist or maximizing aspect of the utilitarian theory, which demands that we take any action, no matter how evil, so long as we thereby prevent greater amounts of that same evil? Consider exemplary sentencing in well publicized cases. Presumably the offenders have right not to be punished more than they deserve, and all future victims of criminal violence have a right not to be subjected to it. Suppose that all such rights not being violated is an intrinsic good (thus leaving behind the utilitarian theory of the good) and moreover that nonviolation of each of such rights is equally good. Is it still troublesome to give the offenders exemplary sentences, or does the minimizing of *rights violations* (in substitution for the utilitarians' maximizing of *welfare*) eliminate the problem?

8. There would seem to be three levels of scapegoating:

a. Punishing an entirely innocent person so as to deter others.
b. Exemplary sentencing, where one adds an extra increment of punishment beyond what the offender deserves in order to deter others.
c. Sentencing within the limits of desert, where the offender is punished no more than he deserves but is punished not solely (or perhaps, at all) because he deserves it but rather because such punishment will deter others.

Are the justice objections to each of these all of the same type? Of the same strength?

9. How do you distinguish quarantines of those with communicable diseases, military conscription in wartime, and civil commitment of mentally ill persons on ground that they pose dangers to others, from scapegoating punishments of the innocent?

10. There is often a difficult factual issue to be resolved in applying the utilitarian calculus, even after the "infinite consequences worry" (see question 9 following the Bentham article) has been answered. This is the problem of calculating what consequences for welfare will flow from any given act or institution. It is common to raise this concern with respect to proof of the deterrent effect of punishment. Given the indeterminacy of the social sciences on the issue of how severity and certainty of punishments affect the crime level, is it rational or moral to punish people *for deterrent purposes*?

2.2.3 Retributivism

At the most general level of his political philosophy and his ethics a retributivist will necessarily disagree with at least one of the two essential tenets of utilitarianism. A retributivist will at least disagree with the utilitarian's monistic theory of the good, according to which the only intrinsically good things are the states of happiness, pleasure, or preference-satisfactions of sentient creatures. By contrast, a retributivist will hold other things to be intrinsically good besides welfare, including that moral duties be done, that moral rights not be violated, that moral virtue be instantiated. Since there are many moral duties, rights, and virtues, such a theory of the good may be quite pluralistic in its list of intrinsically good things.

A retributivist *may* (but need not) disagree with the consequentialist aspect of utilitarianism. To see the possibilities here, suppose we grant the retributivist his theory of the good, that is, that it is intrinsically good that guilty offenders be punished commensurate to their deserts. Now suppose a situation in which a guilty offender can be so punished but only at the cost of other, more numerous, but equally guilty offenders getting off scot-free. For example, the testimony of the first is needed to convict the others, yet the first will testify only if he is granted immunity. Should the retributivist judge punish the first offender anyway? A "deontological" or "agent-relative" retributivist will answer "yes", but an "agent-neutral" or "consequentialist" retributivist will not. Both are recognizable versions of retributivism because both are recognizable versions of more general theories of justice.

The readings included here give a small sampling of the burgeoning literature on retributivism, both pro and con. The selection from Kant is a classic. Kant warns us away from rummaging "around in the winding paths of a theory of happiness" in favor of a "categorical imperative" that the guilty be punished. In the ringing hyperbole familiar to every student of ethics, he counsels that it is better the heavens should fall and all humans perish than that justice not be done.

Herbert Morris argues that the retributive principle (that those who deserve punishment receive it) can be justified by a more general principle of fairness: it is unfair for criminals to reap the advantages of forgoing the mutual restraint exercised by the rest of us, and to deprive criminals of that unfair advantage requires that they be made to suffer, Michael Moore pursues a quite different justificatory strategy for retributivism. Moore seeks to show how our particular judgments—such as Kant's judgment that the last murderer on an island society about to disband should be punished despite the lack of any utilitarian reason to do so—need not reveal us to be blood-thirsty, resentful brutes. Instead, Moore argues, our retributive judgments can express the guilt moral persons feel whenever they hurt another in an immoral way. Moore argues that we must transfer the guilt we feel at our own transgressions to the moral outrage we should feel at similar transgressions by others.

David Dolinko (whose article is quoted extensively in the notes following the excerpts from Morris and Moore) will have none of this. He is worried that the likes of Morris and Moore have made retributivism intellectually respectable again, and he aims to take away that respectability. Dolinko takes Morris to task for failing to show what advantage or benefit criminals gain from their crimes. He also criticizes Morris for failing to fit a proper remedy to this obtaining of an unfair advantage by criminals; why not outlawing rather than legal punishment, Dolinko queries. Dolinko accuses Moore of using particularly violent crimes, such as the Yale murder case, to get the blood to the eyes of his readers and thereby "stacking the deck." More typical, Dolinko thinks, are less savage crimes that do not so strongly give rise to intuitions of deserved punishment. Dolinko also questions whether any general moral principle can be justified by showing how intuitively acceptable are its implications for particular cases.

The Metaphysical Elements of Justice
IMMANUEL KANT

Judicial punishment . . . is entirely distinct from natural punishment. . . . In natural punishment, vice punishes itself, and this fact is not taken into consideration by the legislator. Judicial punishment can never be used merely as a means to promote some other good for the criminal himself or for civil society, but instead it must in all cases be imposed on him only on the ground that he has committed a crime; for a human being can never be manipulated merely as a means to the purposes of someone else and can never be confused with the objects of the Law of things. . . . His innate personality (that is, his right as a person) protects him against such treatment, even though he may indeed be condemned to lose his civil personality. He must first be found to be deserving of punishment before any consideration is given to the utility of this punishment for himself or for his fellow citizens. The law concerning punishment is a categorical imperative, and woe to him who rummages around in the winding paths of a theory of happiness looking for some advantage to be gained by releasing the criminal from punishment or by reducing the amount of it—in keeping with the Pharisaic motto: "It is better that one man should die than that the whole people should perish." If legal justice perishes, then it is no longer worthwhile for men to remain alive on this earth. If this is so, what should one think of the proposal to permit a criminal who has been condemned to death to remain alive, if, after consenting to allow dangerous experiments to be made on him, he happily survives such experiments and if doctors thereby obtain new information that benefits the community? Any court of justice would repudiate such a proposal with scorn if it were sug-

From *The Metaphysical Elements of Justice* (1797), trans. John Ladd, (Indianapolis: Bobbs Merrill, 1965), pp. 120–22.

gested by a medical college, for [legal] justice ceases to be justice if it can be bought for a price.

What kind and what degree of punishment does public legal justice adopt as its principle and standard? None other than the principle of equality (illustrated by the pointer on the scales of justice), that is, the principle of not treating one side more favorably than the other. Accordingly, any undeserved evil that you inflict on someone else among the people is one that you do to yourself. If you vilify him, you vilify yourself; if you steal from him, you steal from yourself; if you kill him, you kill yourself. Only the Law of retribution *(jus talionis)* can determine exactly the kind and degree of punishment; if must be well understood, however, that this determination [must be made] in the chambers of a court of justice (and not in your private judgment). All other standards fluctuate back and forth and, because extraneous considerations are mixed with them, they cannot be compatible with the principle of pure and strict legal justice.

Now, it might seem that the existence of class distinctions would not allow for the [application of the] retributive principle of returning like for like. Nevertheless, even though these class distinctions may not make it possible to apply this principle to the letter, it can still always remain applicable in its effects if regard is had to the special sensibilities of the higher classes. Thus, for example, the imposition of a fine for a verbal injury has no proportionality to the original injury, for someone who has a good deal of money can easily afford to make insults whenever he wishes. On the other hand, the humiliation of the pride of such an offender comes much closer to equaling an injury done to the honor of the person offended; thus the judgment and Law might require the offender not only to make a public apology to the offended person but also at the same time to kiss his hand, even though he be socially inferior. Similarly, if a man of a higher class has violently attacked an innocent citizen who is socially inferior to him, he may be condemned, not only to apologize, but to undergo solitary and painful confinement, because by this means, in addition to the discomfort suffered, the pride of the offender will be painfully affected, and thus his humiliation will compensate for the offense as like for like.

But what is meant by the statement: "If you steal from him, you steal from yourself"? Inasmuch as someone steals, he makes the ownership of everyone else insecure, and hence he robs himself (in accordance with the Law of retribution) of the security of any possible ownership. He has nothing and can also acquire nothing, but he still wants to live, and this is not possible unless others provide him with nourishment. But, because the state will not support him gratis, he must let the state have his labor at any kind of work it may wish to use him for (convict labor), and so he becomes a slave, either for a certain period of time or indefinitely, as the case may be.

If, however, he has committed a murder, he must die. In this case, there is no substitute that will satisfy the requirements of legal justice. There is no sameness of kind between death and remaining alive even under the most miserable conditions, and consequently there is also no equality between the crime and the retribution unless the criminal is judicially condemned and put to death. But the death of the criminal must be kept entirely free of any maltreatment that would make an abomination of the humanity residing in the person suffering it. Even if a civil society were to dissolve itself by common agreement of all its members (for example, if the people inhabiting an island decided to separate and disperse themselves around the world), the last murderer remaining in prison must first be executed, so that everyone will duly receive what his actions are worth and so that the bloodguilt thereof will not be fixed on the people because they failed to insist on carrying out the punishment; for if they fail to do so, they may be regarded as accomplices in this public violation of legal justice.

NOTES AND QUESTIONS

1. Can you put in your own words what Kant finds objectionable about punishment being used "merely to promote some other good for the criminal himself or for civil society?"

2. Does Kant exclude entirely any role for utilitarian considerations in structuring or applying a scheme for punishment? If we punish someone no more than he deserves but only because it serves the ends of general deterrence, would Kant object?

3. What kind of an argument does Kant make to justify belief in his categorical imperative that punishment be imposed on a criminal "only on the ground that he has committed a crime"? Is his thought experiment of a civil society about to dissolve an argument? Would you punish the last murderer in such a situation?

4. Consider the force of Kant's categorical imperative:

a. If a dangerous experiment would not otherwise be performed except with a certain prisoner's consent, and if this experiment yields valuable medical knowledge preventing much human misery, do you agree that you may not induce the prisoner to consent promising a reduction in sentence being served?

b. If the punishment of five guilty persons can be obtained only by the testimony of a sixth such person, and if that testimony can be induced only by offering immunity from prosecution, do you agree that you may not offer such immunity?

5. What if you disagree with Kant on questions 4(a) and 4(b) (Kant presumably answers both in the negative); would this show that you were not a retributivist? Consider:

a. Would you ever justify a prima facie breach of a categorical obligation by a welfare gain? For example, would you lie to the would-be murderer who knocks on your door to inquire into the whereabouts of his intended victims? Would you torture an innocent person if that were the only way to induce a terrorist to reveal where a school bus full of children is buried?

b. Would you lie to a known perjurer if that were the only way to prevent many more lies by him? Would you torture the brother of a terrorist if that were the only way to prevent the torture of each inhabitant of a small village?

Can you answer any of the questions above affirmatively and still think the following?

a. It is intrinsically good that one keep one's promises and that one not torture, and this good

does not translate into the welfare of the actor, the victim, or anyone else.
b. Each of us is categorically enjoined to seek such intrinsic goods as keeping our promises and not torturing others even when our forgoing the seeking of such intrinsic goods would produce more of such goods in the long run.

6. Although we shall examine the "how much punishment" question later in these readings, preliminarily consider Kant's "principle of equality" in sentencing.

a. Is the "principle of returning like for like" part of retributivism or separate from it? Can you imagine punishing someone solely because they deserve it, without being committed to punishing them literally by returning like for like?
b. How literally does Kant intend his "like for like" principle to be interpreted? Death for murderers? Deprivation of property for thieves? Rape for rapists? Torture for torturers? If Kant does not intend the principle to be interpreted this literally, how else can you make sense of a punishment fitting the crime?

Persons and Punishment

HERBERT MORRIS

Let us suppose that men are constituted roughly as they now are, with a rough equivalence in strength and abilities, a capacity to be injured by each other and to make judgments that such injury is undesirable, a limited strength of will, and a capacity to reason and to conform conduct to rules. Applying to the conduct of these men [is] a group of rules, ones I shall label "primary," which closely resemble the core rules of our criminal law, rules that prohibit violence and deception and compliance with which provides benefits for all persons. These benefits consist of noninterference by others with what each person values, such matters as continuance of life and bodily security. The rules define a sphere for each person then, which is immune from interference by others. Making possible this mutual benefit is the assumption by individuals of a burden. The burden consists in the exercise of self-restraint by individuals over inclinations that would, if satisfied, directly interfere or create a substantial risk of interference with others in proscribed ways. If a person fails to exercise self-restraint even though he might have and gives in to such inclinations, he renounces a burden which others have voluntarily assumed and thus gains an advantage which others, who have restrained themselves, do not possess. This system, then, is one in which the rules establish a mutuality of benefit and burden and in which the benefits of noninterference are conditional upon the assumption of burdens.

Connecting punishment with violation of these primary rules, and making public the provision for punishment, is both reasonable and just. First, it is only reasonable

From *On Guilt and Innocence* (Los Angeles: University of California Press, 1976), pp. 33–36.

that those who voluntarily comply with the rules be provided some assurance that they will not be assuming burdens which others are unprepared to assume. Their disposition to comply voluntarily will diminish as they learn that others are with impunity renouncing burdens they are assuming. Second fairness dictates that a system in which benefits and burdens are equally distributed have a mechanism designed to prevent a maldistribution in the benefits and burdens. Thus, sanctions are attached to noncompliance with the primary rules so as to induce compliance with the primary rules among those who may be disinclined to obey. In this way the likelihood of an unfair distribution is diminished.

Third, it is just to punish those who have violated the rules and caused the unfair distribution of benefits and burdens. A person who violates the rules has something others have—the benefits of the system—but by renouncing what others have assumed, the burdens of self-restraint, he has acquired an unfair advantage. Matters are not even until this advantage is in some way erased. Another way of putting it is that he owes something to others, for he has something that does not rightfully belong to him. Justice—that is punishing such individuals—restores the equilibrium of benefits and burdens by taking from the individual what he owes, that is, exacting the debt. It is important to see that the equilibrium may be restored in another way. Forgiveness—with its legal analogue of a pardon—while not the righting of an unfair distribution by making one pay his debt is, nevertheless, a restoring of the equilibrium by forgiving the debt. Forgiveness may be viewed, at least in some types of cases, as a gift after the fact, erasing a debt, which had the gift been given before the fact, would not have created a debt. But the practice of pardoning has to proceed sensitively, for it may endanger in a way the practice of justice does not, the maintenance of an equilibrium of benefits and burdens. If all are indiscriminately pardoned less incentive is provided individuals to restrain their inclinations, thus increasing the incidence of persons taking what they do not deserve.

There are also in this system we are considering a variety of operative principles compliance with which provides some guarantee that the system of punishment does not itself promote an unfair distribution of benefits and burdens. For one thing, provision is made for a variety of defenses, each one of which can be said to have as its object diminishing the chances of forcibly depriving a person of benefits others have if that person has not derived an unfair advantage. A person has not derived an unfair advantage if he could not have restrained himself or if it is unreasonable to expect him to behave otherwise than he did. Sometimes the rules preclude punishment of classes of persons such as children. Sometimes they provide a defense if on a particular occasion a person lacked the capacity to conform his conduct to the rules. Thus, someone who in an epileptic seizure strikes another is excused. Punishment in these cases would be punishment of the innocent, punishment of those who do not voluntarily renounce a burden others have assumed. Punishment in such cases, then, would not equalize but rather cause an unfair distribution in benefits and burdens.

Along with principles providing defenses there are requirements that the rules be prospective and relatively clear so that persons have a fair opportunity to comply with the rules. There are, also, rules governing, among other matters, the burden of proof, who shall bear it and what it shall be, the prohibition on double jeopardy, and the privilege against self-incrimination. Justice requires conviction of the guilty, and requires their punishment, but in setting out to fulfill the demands of justice we may, of course, because we are not omniscient, cause injustice by convicting and punishing the innocent. The resolution arrived at in the system I am describing consists in weighing as the greater evil the punishment of the innocent. The primary function of the system of rules was to provide individuals with a sphere of interest immune from interference. Given this goal, it is determined to be a greater evil for society to interfere unjustifiably with an individual by depriving him of good than for the society to fail to punish those that have unjustifiably interfered.

Finally, because the primary rules are designed to benefit all and because the punishments prescribed for their violation are publicized and the defenses respected, there is some plausibility in the exaggerated claim that in choosing to do an act violative of the rules an individual has chosen to be punished. This way of putting matters brings to our attention the extent to which, when the system is as I have described it, the criminal "has brought the punishment upon himself" in contrast to those cases where it would be misleading to say "he has brought in upon himself," cases, for example, where one does not know the rules or is punished in the absence of fault.

To summarize, then: first, there is a group of rules guiding the behavior of individuals in the community which establish spheres of interest immune from interference by others; second, provision is made for what is generally regarded as a deprivation of some thing of value if the rules are violated; third, the deprivations visited upon any person are justified by that person's having violated the rules; fourth, the deprivation, in this just system of punishment, is linked to rules that fairly distribute benefits and burdens and to procedures that strike some balance between not punishing the guilty and punishing the innocent, a class defined as those who have not voluntarily done acts violative of the law, in which it is evident that the evil of punishing the innocent is regarded as greater than the nonpunishment of the guilty.

At the core of many actual legal systems one finds, of course, rules and procedures of the kind I have sketched. It is obvious, though, that any ongoing legal system differs in significant respects from what I have presented here, containing "pockets of injustice."

The Moral Worth of Retribution
MICHAEL S. MOORE

When we make a retributive judgment, we need not be motivated by the *ressentiment* emotions. Nor is the alternative some abstract. Kantian concern for justice, derived by reason alone and unsullied by any strong emotional origin. Our concern for ret-

From "The Moral Worth of Retribution," in Ferdinand Schoeman, ed., *Responsibility, Character and the Emotions* (Cambridge: Cambridge University Press, 1987), pp. 212–17.

ributive justice might be motivated by very deep emotions that are nonetheless of a wholly virtuous nature. These are the feelings of guilt we would have if we did the kinds of acts that fill the criminal appellate reports of any state.

The psychiatrist Willard Gaylin interviewed a number of people closely connected to the brutal hammering death of Bonnie Garland by her jilted boyfriend, Richard Herrin. He asked a number of those in a Christian order that had been particularly forgiving of Richard whether they could imagine themselves performing such an act under any set of circumstances. Their answer was uniformly "Yes." All of us can at least find it conceivable that there might be circumstances under which we could perform an act like Herrin's—not exactly the same, perhaps, but something pretty horrible. All of us do share this much of our common nature with the worst of criminals. (For those with a greater we-they attitude toward criminals, the thought experiment that follows must be run with a somewhat less horrible act than Richard's.)

Then ask yourself: What would you feel like if it was you who had intentionally smashed open the skull of a 23-year-old woman with a claw hammer while she was asleep, a woman whose fatal defect was a desire to free herself from your too clinging embrace? My own response, I hope, would be that I would feel guilty unto death. I couldn't imagine any suffering that could be imposed upon me that would be unfair because it exceeded what I deserved.

Is that virtuous? Such deep feelings of guilt seem to me to be the only tolerable response of a moral being. "Virtue" is perhaps an odd word in the context of extreme culpability, but such guilt seems, at the least, very appropriate. One ought to feel so guilty one wants to die. Such sickness unto death is to my mind more virtuous than the nonguilty state to which Richard Herrin brought himself, with some help from Christian counseling about the need for self-forgiveness. After three years in prison on an eight- to twenty-five-year sentence for "heat of passion" manslaughter, Richard thought he had suffered quite enough for the killing of Bonnie:

Herrin: I feel the sentence was excessive.

Gaylin: Let's talk about that a little.

Herrin: Well, I feel that way now and after the first years. The judge had gone overboard. . . .

Considering all the factors that I feel the judge should have considered: prior history of arrest, my personality background, my capacity for a productive life in society—you know, those kinds of things—I don't think he took those into consideration. He looked at the crime itself and responded to a lot of public pressure or maybe his own personal feelings. I don't know. I'm not going to accuse him of anything, but I was given the maximum sentence. This being my first arrest and considering the circumstances, I don't think I should have been given eight to twenty-five years.

Gaylin: What do you think would have been a fair sentence?

Herrin: Well, after a year or two in prison, I felt that was enough. . . .

Gaylin: How would you answer the kind of person who says, for Bonnie, it's her whole life; for you it's eight years. What's eight years compared to the more years she might have had?

Herrin: I can't deny that it's grossly unfair to Bonnie, but there's nothing I can do about it. . . .

She gone—I can't bring her back. I would rather that she had survived as a complete person, but she didn't. I'm not, again . . . I'm not saying that I shouldn't have been punished, but the punishment I feel is excessive, I feel I have five more years to go, and I feel that's just too much. There's no . . . I don't see any purpose in it. It's sad what happened, but it's even sadder to waste another life. I feel I'm being wasted in here.

Gaylin: But what about the people who say, Look, if you got two years, then someone who robs should get only two days. You know, the idea of commensurate punishment. If it is a very serious crime it has to be a very serious punishment. Are you saying two years of prison is a very serious punishment considering what you did?

Herrin: For me, yes.

Compared to such shallow, easily obtained self-absolution for a horrible violation of another, a deep sense of guilt looks very virtuous indeed.

To be sure, there is an entire tradition that regards guilt as a useless passion. For one thing, it is always backward-looking rather than allowing one to get on with life. For another, it betrays an indecision that Nietzsche among others found unattractive: "The bite of conscience is indecent," Nietzsche thought, because it betrays the earlier decision about which one feels guilty. Yet Nietzsche and his followers are simply wrong here. Guilt feelings are often a virtue precisely because they do look to the past. As Herbert Morris has argued, morality itself—including the morality of good character—has to take the past seriously. The alternative, of not crying over spilt milk (or blood), is truly indecent. A moral being *feels* guilty when he or she *is* guilty of past wrongs.

The virtue of feeling guilty is not raised so that punishment can be justified by its capacity to induce guilt. That is a possible retributive theory of punishment—a kind of moral rehabilitative theory—but it is not mine. Rather, the virtue of our own imagined guilt is relevant because of the general connection between the virtue of an emotion and its epistemic import. We should trust what our imagined guilt feelings tell us; for acts like those of Richard Herrin, that if we did them we would be so guilty that some extraordinarily severe punishment would be deserved. We should trust the judgments such imagined guilt feelings spawn because nonneurotic guilt, unlike *ressentiment,* comes with good epistemic credentials.

Next, we need to be clear just what judgment it is that our guilt feelings validate in this way. First and foremost, to *feel* guilty causes the judgment that we *are* guilty, in the sense that we are morally culpable. Second, such guilt feelings typically engender the judgment that we deserve punishment. I mean this not only in the weak sense of desert—that it would not be unfair to be punished—but also and more important in the strong sense that we *ought* to be punished.

One might think that this second judgment of desert (in either its weak or its strong sense) is uncalled for by our feelings of guilt, that the judgment to which our guilt feelings lead is the judgment that we ought to repair as best we can the damage we have done. Such a view would justify corrective justice theories of punishment, but not retributive theories. Yet I think that this puts too nice a face on our guilt feelings. They do not generate only a judgment that we ought to make amends in this compensatory way. Rather—and this is what troubles many critics of guilt as an emotion—to feel guilty is to judge that we must suffer. We can see this plainly if we imagine ourselves having made provisions for Bonnie's family, comforting them in any way possible, and then feeling that our debt for killing her has been paid. It is so clear that such corrective actions do *not* satisfy guilt that to feel that they do is not to have felt guilty to begin with.

Our feelings of guilt thus generate a judgment that we deserve the suffering that is punishment. If the feelings of guilt are virtuous to possess, we have reason to believe that this last judgment is correct, generated as it is by emotions whose epistemic import is not in question.

Last, we should ask whether there is any reason not to make the same judgment about Richard Herrin's actual deserts as we are willing to make about our own hypothetical deserts. If we experience any reluctance to transfer the guilt and desert *we* would possess, had we done what Richard Herrin did, to Herrin himself, we should examine that reluctance carefully. Doesn't it come from feeling more of a person than Richard? We are probably not persons who grew up in the barrio of East Los Angeles, or who found Yale an alien and disorienting culture. In any case, we certainly have never been subject to the exact same stresses and motivations as Richard Herrin. Therefore, it may be tempting to withhold from Richard the benefit each of us gives himself or herself: the benefit of being the subjective seat of a will that, although caused, is nonetheless capable of both choice and responsibility.

Such discrimination is a temptation to be resisted, because it is no virtue. It is elitist and condescending toward others not to grant them the same responsibility and desert you grant yourself. Admittedly, there are excuses the benefit of which others as well as yourself may avail themselves. Yet that is not the distinction invoked here. Herrin had no excuse the rest of us could not come up with in terms of various causes for our choices. To refuse to grant him the same responsibility and desert as you would grant yourself is thus an instance of what Sartre called bad faith, the treating of a free, subjective will as an object. It is a refusal to admit that the rest of humanity shares with us that which makes us most distinctively human, our capacity to will and reason—and thus to be and do evil. Far from evincing fellow feeling and the allowing of others to participate in our moral life, it excludes them as less than persons.

Rather than succumbing to this elitism masquerading as egalitarianism, we should ask ourselves what Herrin deserves by asking what *we* would deserve had we done such an act. In answering this question we should listen to our guilt feelings, feelings whose epistemic import is not in question in the same way as are those of *ressentiment.* Such guilt feelings should tell us that to do an act like Herrin's is to forfeit forever any lighthearted idea of going on as before. One should feel so awful that the idea of again leading a life unchanged from before, with the same goals and hopes and happiness, should appear revoltingly incomprehensible.[1]

---

[1]One may have noticed that the thought experiment just concluded has six steps to it. It is perhaps helpful to separate them explicitly: (1) The psychological presupposition that it is possible to engage in the thought experiment at all—that we can imagine we could do an act like Richard Herrin's; (2) the psychological question of what we would feel if we did such an action—guilty and deserving of punishment; (3) the moral question of the virtue of that feeling—that guilt is a virtuous emotion to feel when we have done such a wrongful act; (4) the psychological question of what judgments are typically caused by the emo-

It is admittedly not an easy task to separate the emotions one feels, and then in addition, discriminate which of them is the cause of one's retributive judgments. We can no more choose which emotion it will be that causes our judgments or actions than we can choose the reason for which we act. We can choose whether to act or not and whether to judge one way or another, but we cannot make it be true that some particular reason or emotion caused our action or our judgment. We must look inward as best we can to detect, but not to will, which emotions bring about our judgments; and here there is plenty of room for error and self-deception.

When we move from our judgments about the justice of retribution in the abstract, however, to the justice of a social institution that exists to exact retribution, perhaps we can gain some greater clarity. For if we recognize the dangers retributive punishment presents for the expression of resentment, sadism, and so on, we have every reason to design our punishment institutions to minimize the opportunity for such feelings to be expressed. There is no contradiction in attempting to make a retributive punishment system humane; doing so allows penitentiaries to be faithful to their names—places for penance, not excuses for sadism, prejudice, hatred, and the like.

Even the old biblical injunction—"Vengeance is mine, saith the Lord"—has something of this insight behind it. Retributive punishment is dangerous for individual persons to carry out, dangerous to their virtue and, because of that, unclear in its justification. But implicit in the biblical injunction is a promise that retribution will be exacted. For those like myself who are not theists, that cleansing function must be performed by the state, not God. If the state can perform such a function, it removes from retributive punishment, not the guilt, as Nietzsche and Sartre have it, but the *ressentiment*.

NOTES AND QUESTIONS

1. In a recent critique of both Morris and Moore, David Dolinko ("Some Thoughts about Retributions," *Ethics,* Vol. 101 [1991]) urges that every form of retributivism is "problematic."

---

tions of guilt—the judgments that we are guilty (culpable) and that we deserve to be punished; (5) the moral question of the correctness of the first-person judgment that we deserve to be punished—as an inference drawn from the virtue of the emotion of guilt that spawns such a judgment; (6) the moral question of the correctness of the third person judgment that Richard Herrin deserves to be punished—as an inference drawn from the fact that we would deserve to be punished if we had done the act that Herrin did. One might believe that the thought experiment requires a seventh step—namely, that the state ought to punish those who deserve it. And in terms of a complete justification of a retributive theory of punishment, this last step is a necessary one. My aim throughout this essay has been more limited: to validate particular judgments, such as that Stephen Judy deserved the death penalty. The thought experiment is designed to get us only this far, leaving for further argument (hinted at in the text that closes this section) that the state has the right and the duty to set up institutions which give persons their just deserts.

The claim is that punishment—which involves doing to wrongdoers things that we ordinarily think of as violating people's rights, like incarcerating them against their will
for years—is morally permissible because it is what wrongdoers deserve. Yet we do
not, in general, believe that treating a person in a way that would otherwise violate his
rights is automatically permissible simply because the person deserves this kind of
treatment.

Consider, for example, Lear, a rich man with two sons, Jeremy and Howard. Jeremy
truly loves Lear and has always treated him with affection and respect, even caring for
him (at great personal sacrifice) during Lear's final illness. Howard, on the other hand,
is a reprobate who has spent his time drinking, gambling, and chasing women, ne-
glecting his father (for whom, in truth, he feels little regard) almost completely.
Perversely, however, Lear has always felt a sneaking admiration for Howard while secretly despising Jeremy as a priggish, unimaginative, overly repressed bore. (This is
grossly inaccurate, and unfair to Jeremy, but Lear at some level always wished he himself could have boldly defied the constraints of propriety and convention, as he believes
Howard has.) Lear's will leaves Jeremy a comparative pittance and bequeaths the bulk
of the estate to Howard. Surely we might well agree that Jeremy deserved to inherit the
estate while Howard deserved to be cut out of the will. Yet the state, acting through its
judiciary, will not on that account set aside Lear's will and hand over to Jeremy that
which he, rather than Howard, deserves. To do so would violate Howard's *right* to the
estate, a right he possesses despite deserving to inherit nothing. As Joel Feinberg has
noted, "a person's desert of X is always a reason for giving X to him, but not always a
conclusive reason," because "considerations irrelevant to his desert can have overriding cogency in establishing how he ought to be treated on balance." (543–44)

Dolinko criticizes retributivism for treating desert as if it were a sufficient reason to punish, because there may be non-desert-related reasons not to punish that are
of greater importance. Yet is this not true of all justice-related reasons? Is giving people what they deserve as a matter of distributive justice, or giving them what they deserve as a matter of corrective justice, necessarily the strongest reason against all
possible competitors? If theorists of distributive or corrective justice need not mono-
maniacally pursue these forms of justice to the exclusion of other values, why must
a theorist of retributive justice claim any more?

2. The key notion for Morris is the idea of an *unfair advantage* that criminals
gain by their crimes. What is the advantage criminals gain? Why does Morris think
it unfair for them to gain it? One answer, explored by Dolinko, is that the unfair advantage

consists in the criminal's "indulging a (wrongful) self-preference," "permitting himself an excessive freedom in choosing," or "acting according to [his] tastes" instead of
exercising self-restraint. But then the advantage the criminal obtains from his crime
ought to be proportional to the burden of self-restraint that others carry but that he has
thrown off. And this in turn depends upon how great a temptation people generally feel
to commit the crime in question. Thus very serious crimes which most people feel little inclination to commit (e.g., murder) yield a lesser advantage—and hence deserve
a lesser punishment—than those (like speeding or tax evasion) that test most people's
self-restraint more severely. This, of course, is a most unwelcome result, which must
be avoided if Morris's approach is to be tenable. We need some better account of exactly what "unfair advantage" criminals derive from their misdeeds. (545–46)

Is it at all plausible that the degree of the advantage criminals gain is measured by the subjectively experienced temptations people generally feel to commit the crime in question, as Dolinko first construes it?

3. Dolinko considers a second construal of "unfair advantage," that of George Sher, who argues that the magnitude of the criminal's "benefit" from his crime is determined by "the strength of the moral prohibition he has violated." In Dolinko's words:

> Sher explains that
>
> > a person who acts wrongly does gain a significant measure of extra liberty: what he gains is freedom from the demands of the prohibition he violates. Because others take that prohibition seriously, they lack a similar liberty. And as the strength of the prohibition increases, so too does the freedom from it which its violation entails. Thus, even if the murderer and the tax evader do succumb to equally strong impulses, their gains in freedom are far from equal. Because the murderer evades a prohibition of far greater force . . . his net gain in freedom remains greater. And for that reason, the amount of punishment he deserves seems greater as well.
>
> Has Sher explained the criminal's "unfair advantage" in a way that makes Morris's version of retributivism plausible? I think not. First, Sher's discussion assumes that a crime necessarily involves the violation of a "moral prohibition," but this is in one sense false and in another useless for Sher's purposes. It is false if taken to mean that every crime involves behavior that is morally improper even prior to its legal proscription. Tax evasion, a crime Sher mentions, illustrates this point, since it involves behavior that would not be immoral at all absent a legal requirement to pay the tax in question. Driving on the left-hand side of the road, similarly, is in itself "morally neutral" conduct which can be thought immoral (in the United States, though not in the United Kingdom!) only insofar as it violates a law. Such crimes, to which the traditional epithet *malum prohibitum* applies, are distinguished from *malum in se* offenses, which involve behavior that would be immoral even in the absence of a legal prohibition: murder, rape, and robbery are examples. And Sher's criterion for the magnitude of a criminal's "unfair advantage"—"the strength of the moral prohibition he had violated"—breaks down for *malum prohibitum* offenses: we would be forced to conclude that none of these offenses results in "advantage" to the offender, so that no punishment for such offenses can be deserved.
>
> Sher might try to salvage his criterion by arguing that even *malum prohibitum* offenses do involve the breach of a moral prohibition—namely, the moral prohibition against breaking the law. Taken in this sense, however, the claim that every crime necessarily involves violation of a moral prohibition is useless for Sher, because every *malum prohibitum* offense will turn out to involve violation of the very same moral prohibition—"do not break the law." Hence, Sher's criterion would tell us that all such offenses yield the same "unfair advantage" and all deserve the same punishment—income tax evasion and big-time cocaine smuggling just as much as speeding or destroying birds' nests in a public cemetery.
>
> Sher's analysis is vitiated not only by the questionable assumption that a crime must involve a moral violation but even more fundamentally by the dubious status of its central claim—that one who breaks a law thereby "gains . . . freedom from the demands of the prohibition he violates. In what way does the lawbreaker "gain" this freedom? In one sense, the lawbreaker has perhaps revealed that he has a kind of "freedom" by exercising it—by demonstrating that he is able to violate the prohibition. In this sense, however, he must have been "free" from the prohibition even before his lawless act

(or he could not have committed it!), and presumably, many law-abiding citizens are equally "free" (in this sense) to violate the prohibition. In another sense, we may ask whether the criminal's wrongful act has released him from a constraint upon his actions which the prohibition imposes on the actions of his fellows. One would think the answer should be "no." Though the criminal has in fact done what is prohibited, this in no way dissolves or abrogates the obligation he, like everyone else, is under not to do that act. (Indeed, there would be no basis for deciding to punish the wrongdoer if his criminal act had somehow repealed the prohibition it is alleged to violate.) In a third sense, we may assert that by violating the prohibition, the criminal has manifested his disregard or contempt for that prohibition—has, we might say, shown that he regards himself as "free" from its demands. But it seems incorrect, if we are using "free" in this manner, to claim that the lawbreaker *gains* his freedom by breaking the law; rather, he breaks the law because he already regards himself as "free" to do so. Indeed, even people who in fact never violate a given prohibition—perhaps because the occasion never presents itself, perhaps because they fear being caught—could inwardly reject the prohibition's claim of authority over them and thus regard themselves as "free" to breach the prohibition. (546–48)

Is this objective measurement of advantage that Dolinko considers any better? Can one measure the advantage unfairly gained by the seriousness of the moral norm violated?

4. Dolinko worries that not all criminal prohibitions coincide with preexisting moral prohibitions. Tax evasion and driving on the left-hand side of the road are his examples. Do you agree with Dolinko that the only possible moral obligation one violates by either of these behaviors is the general obligation to obey a law just because it is a law? Or is there a third possibility, in addition to antecedently existing moral obligations and the general obligation to obey all laws, namely that we each have an obligation to solve coordination problems like these posed by traffic and tax cases?

5. Dolinko also worries that in no sense does the criminal gain freedom by violating norms the rest of us obey. Is freedom to do crime the benefit Morris had in mind, or is it rather the freedom from like treatment by others that a criminal unfairly gains?

6. Morris suggests that the reason criminal law recognizes excuses like youth, insanity, or epilepsy is because punishment of such persons would be "punishment of those who do not voluntarily renounce a burden others have assumed." Yet why should this matter to Morris? Do not such excused persons have to give back the property they steal? Why then should they not more generally disgorge any form of advantage accruing to them, however involuntarily, from their actions?

7. Dolinko also criticizes Morris's theory for failing to connect what we do by way of punishment to the disgorging of the benefits of crime. If the gravamen of all punishable crime is the obtaining of unfair advantage, should not a punishment that fit the crime be one whereby the advantage is disgorged? Does loss of liberty in prison accomplish this?

8. Consider the relationship between moral wrongdoing and retributive punishment. Does retributive justice demand punishment for all who break the law, even if the law they break prohibits morally neutral or even morally desirable behavior? To answer this question affirmatively, would one have to believe that all valid laws im-

pose obligations upon citizens to obey them, no matter how immoral the content of such laws? Consider in this regard the following from Dolinko:

> Moore, I suggest, has stacked the deck by giving us a group of especially savage murders and inviting us to generate, from these examples, an intuition that "criminals" as such ought to be punished (regardless of the consequences). No such intuition would likely arise from contemplating, say, an Englishman visiting Los Angeles who, in the dead of the night, with no other vehicles around, forgets for several minutes which side of the road he is required to drive on. Still less would we be likely to arrive at Moore's intuition by focusing on people who violate morally evil laws—for example, someone who violates an ordinance forbidding giving food to homeless persons. (557)

Dolinko seems to think that a retributivist is committed to punishing those who violate evil laws, such as an ordinance forbidding the giving of food to street bums (Dolinko's "homeless persons"). Is retributive justice served by punishing such legally prohibited but morally supererogatory acts? Suppose the answer is "no":

a. Should a judge nonetheless punish, for nonretributive reasons? What could such reasons be?
b. Should a legislator pass such criminal prohibitions initially, or repeal them if on the books?

9. Has Moore unfairly "stacked the deck," as Dolinko says, by appealing to our emotions with examples of particularly vicious crimes?

10. Dolinko also pursues a different worry when he complains about the bloodiness of Moore's examples:

> [W]hile Moore's retributivist claim applies to anyone who commits a crime, the "particular judgments" Moore adduces all involve a great deal more than simple violations of legally proscribed norms. They involve strikingly vicious murders—acts one might well judge deserving of punishment whether or not they constituted violations of law.
>   Moore's principal example, for instance, is the case of Steven Judy, who raped and murdered a stranded woman motorist, drowned her three small children, and later said he had not been "losing any sleep" over these deeds. Suppose that a member of a World War II Nazi extermination squad treated a Jewish woman and her children in the occupied Ukraine in this fashion, and later boasted similarly of his sound sleep. Suppose further that, under the laws applicable at that time and place, his deeds were not crimes at all. Wouldn't we nevertheless feel "an intuitive judgment that punishment (at least of some kind and to some degree) is warranted"—a judgment every bit as strong as that which Steven Judy's unambiguously criminal acts arouse? (556)

Dolinko supposes a morally horrible rape/murder that is not legally prohibited and asks whether a retributivist wouldn't be committed to punishing the killer. The Adolph Eichmann execution shows us that sometimes the answer will be "yes." But can a retributivist side-constrain the attainment of retributive justice by another demand of justice, namely, the principle of legality that forbids punishment absent prior statutory prohibition?

11. Dolinko also believes that he has detected an

> oddity of applying a coherence strategy at all to a problem like that of justifying punishment.
>   That problem arises only because we are calling into question an entire social prac-

tice. How, then, can we respond by appealing to particular instances of that practice, treating them as the datum whose "best explanation" we seek? Consider, as an analogy, a similar coherence justification for the view, say, that women are inferior to men, offered circa 1800 by one man to another. Someone has raised the question of whether it is really justifiable to treat women as inferior and is met with the response that, "Well, of course, we all have the intuition that in *this* situation we should discriminate against women, and likewise in *this* and *this;* now, the best way of accounting for these particular judgments is to suppose women to be morally and intellectually inferior to men." Wouldn't one feel that the crucial question is being begged? The coherence strategy for justifying retributivist punishment seems to me similarly flawed. (557–58)

Do coherence justifications in ethics always "beg the crucial question" when it is a general principle that is being called into question? Consider the general principle that it is unjust to punish anyone who is innocent, that is, who does not deserve it. Does our outrage in particular cases of such injustice count towards justifying the general principle?

12. Consider this final criticism of Morris and Moore by Dolinko:

Moore shares with many retributivists—Herbert Morris is a prominent example—the belief that his approach, unlike its rivals, treats criminal offenders with the respect that is their due as moral agents. Moore makes this belief explicit in discussing the case of Richard Herrin, a Yale student from a disadvantaged Latino background who beat his sleeping girlfriend to death with a hammer after she indicated she wanted to see other men. Appealing to the powerful guilt feelings we readers would feel if we imagined ourselves committing this crime, Moore asks "whether there is any reason not to make the same judgment about Richard Herrin's actual deserts as we are willing to make about our own hypothetical deserts," and concludes that there is not. Any reluctance we might feel to transfer to Herrin our hypothetical guilt and desert can only "come from feeling more of a person than Richard"—it is "elitist and condescending toward others not to grant them the same responsibility and desert you grant to yourself." The disturbing aspect of this argument is its potential for eliminating a salutary awareness of the costs and the limits of our practice of punishment.

Retributivists frequently complain that their consequentialist foes have no reason not to inflict punishment on innocent persons, if doing so would happen to have good consequences, and likewise no principled basis for rejecting torture and other barbaric punishments if these would maximize deterrence. Yet if we think that the point of punishment is to deter, we are likely to recognize that it has limits, imposed by rights that exist independently of our punishing practices. We can strive to achieve our deterrent goal only within the bounds that these rights demarcate. One who thinks retributively, on the other hand, like Moore, is apt to regard the whole punishment practice itself as an expression of "respect for persons." The sense of a tension between punishing offenders and respecting persons is lost, and it becomes all too easy to justify excesses and vindictiveness as "giving the criminal what he deserves" and thus respecting the wrongdoer, much as Moore shows his respect for Richard Herrin. (558–59)

Dolinko accurately depicts retributivists like Kant, Morris, and Moore to believe that criminals have a *right* to be punished. What sense can you assign to there being such a right, a right only retributivism protects?

2.2.4   Humanitarian or Scientific Alternatives to Punishment: The Rehabilitative Ideal

One of the problems in critically assessing rehabilitative approaches to punishment is the lack of clarity as to just what such approaches recommend. The selections below, from Karl Menninger and Fred Skinner, are no exception. Much of what they suggest seems driven by ordinary, garden-variety utilitarianism of the deterrence/crime-prevention variety. Yet there is a distinctive theory of punishment lurking in such readings, the essential tenets of which are as follows.

First, criminals are not to blame for what they do. Their behavior is fully determined, either by the Freudian unconscious that Menninger favors or by the environmental variables that Skinner favors. Such determination by factors outside the control of the criminal implies, for both Menninger and Skinner, that criminals are not blameworthy for their criminal behavior.

Secondly, the ideas of blameworthiness and retribution therefore have no application to the real world that scientists at least (if not lawyers) know we live in, a world where criminals do *not* choose to do crime of their free will. Therefore, we should replace these moral concepts with concepts of rehabilitation, cure, and behavioral alteration. The question raised by criminal behavior is thus not one of retributive justice and punishment but rather one of how to rehabilitate the criminal out of his condition.

Third, such rehabilitative treatment may involve devoting social resources to the betterment of criminals beyond those we would devote to them solely to prevent crime. Yet criminals should be given such extra social resources because they represent the least advantaged members of our society. In other words, it is distributive justice (of the liberal type), not utilitarianism, that justifies "punishment."

Fourth, criminals usually do not want the "benefit" of those extra social resources being devoted to them in the form of involuntary treatments or "punishment." Therefore, we have to be paternalistic: for their own good, even if against their own judgments about that good, we should coercively impose such treatments upon them.

It is important to see that this is not a crime-prevention theory of punishment, except incidentally. That is, the animating goal is that of distributive justice, to make the less well off better off; it happens that to do this is also to prevent them from engaging in crime, but that is because crime is their particular form of sickness. Still, the (utilitarian) benefits to society of crime prevention are incidental to a pure rehabilitative theory.

There are two directions from which to criticize a pure rehabilitative theory. The first is implicit in the materials on retributivism: the rehabilitationist ideal is not harsh enough in its recommended treatment of criminals, since the last thing criminals deserve is extra social resources. To make this criticism is to join issue with the rehabilitationists' denial that criminals have free will and with their assertion that without free will no one is responsible.

The second direction of criticism is that rehabilitationists are too harsh to criminals. The seemingly kind, compassionate concern for the mental and moral health of offenders may simply be the velvet glove over a very steely fist. This is the direction from which C. S. Lewis's criticism proceeds.

The Crime of Punishment

KARL MENNINGER

The Scientific Position

I propose in this book to examine this strange paradox of social danger, social error, and social indifference. I shall do so from the standpoint of one whose life has been spent in scientific work.

Scientists are not illusion-proof. We are not always or altogether objective. We are not oracles. But we have been trained in a way of observing and interpreting things that has produced rich harvests for the civilized world. This is the systematic collection of certain facts, the orderly arrangement of those facts, and the drawing of tentative conclusions from them to be submitted to further investigation for proof or disproof. These conclusions often contradict and revise "commonsense" solutions which were the best we could do—until we learned better. People no longer have to rely upon common sense for traveling. The commonsense way is to walk, or to ride an animal. Science has discovered better ways by the use of *uncommon* sense. The commonsense time to go to bed is when it gets dark; the uncommon sense of artificial illumination has changed all that. Crime problems have been dealt with too long with only the aid of common sense. Catch criminals and lock them up; if they hit you, hit them back. This is common sense, but it does not work.

Now there *is* a science of criminology and there is a broader spectrum of social sciences. Psychiatry is only one of these. But sciences are all related, and social scientists all share a faith in the scientific method as contrasted to obsolete methods based on tradition, precedent, and common sense.

I am a psychiatrist. But do not think of me as one of those "alienists" called to the witness stand to prove some culprit "insane" and "irresponsible" and hence "not guilty." I abhor such performances worse than you, dear reader, possibly can.

Think of me as a doctor to whom people come to talk about their troubles, and talk very frankly. They may spend most of their time talking about the acts and attitudes of other people, people with whom they interact.

Think of me as a doctor who has worked for years with fellow scientists—physicians, neurologists, surgeons, psychiatrists, psychoanalysts, sociologists, anthropol-

From *The Crime of Punishment* (New York: Viking Press, 1969), pp. 4-6, 10–12, 17–18, 26.

ogists, psychiatric social workers, nurses, therapists—to try to alleviate painful situations. Our common objective has been to obtain a better understanding of why some people do certain things that hurt themselves or other people. We have tried to use this understanding to improve situations—sometimes by changing the particular subject of our study or getting him to change himself, and sometimes by trying to effect changes in his surroundings. Frequently, not always, we have been successful: the undesirable behavior ceased; the patient "got well," and he and his family and neighbors gave thanks. We rejoiced then, not merely in the pride of successful achievement and in human sympathy, but in the satisfaction of having our basic scientific working hypotheses confirmed as "true." This is the crowning reward of the scientist.

When, therefore, we turn our eyes or ears toward the great cry for help arising from the crime situation (better called the social safety problem), we tend to think in terms of the basic postulates and procedures that have guided us in responding to these other forms of human distress.

. . .

"Justice"

We justify the perpetuation of this social anachronism by reference to the holy principle of justice. I am told that Justice Oliver Wendell Holmes was always outraged when a lawyer before the Supreme Court used the word "justice." He said it showed he was shirking his job. The problem in every case is what should be done in *this* situation. It does not advance a solution to use the word *justice*. It is a subjective emotional word. Every litigant thinks that justice demands a decision in his favor.

I propose to demonstrate the paradox that much of the laborious effort made in the noble name of justice results in its very opposite. The concept is so vague, so distorted in its applications, so hypocritical, and usually so irrelevant that it offers no help in the solution of the crime problem which it exists to combat but results in its exact opposite—injustice, injustice to everybody. Socrates defined justice as the awarding to each that which is due him. But Plato perceived the sophistry of this and admitted that justice basically means power, "the interest of the stronger," a clear note that has been repeated by Machiavelli, Hobbes, Spinoza, Marx, Kalsem, on down to Justice Holmes.

Contrast the two ways in which the word is commonly used. On the one hand, we want to obtain justice for the unfairly treated; we render justice to an oppressed people, we deal justly with our neighbor. (Cf. Micah.) We think of justice in terms of fair dealing and the rescue of the exploited and we associate it with freedom and social progress and democracy.

On the other hand, when justice is "meted out,"justice is "served," justice is "satisfied" or "paid." It is something terrible which somebody "sees to it" that somebody else gets; not something good, helpful, or valuable, but something that hurts. It is the whiplash of retribution about to descend on the naked back of transgressors. The end of justice is thus to give help to some, pain to others.

What is it that defeats and twists the idea of justice in its legal applications? Is it our trial court system? We would like to think of our courts as reflections of our civilization, bulwarks of public safety, tribunals for the insurance of fair and objective judgment. Should we revert to some earlier process of investigation of the alleged offender? Or is it that people confuse justice with the elimination of dangerousness from human misbehavior? Is protection from violence something obtained with the *aid* of justice or *in spite* of it?

. . .

Justice in Science

The very word *justice* irritates scientists. No surgeon expects to be asked if an operation for cancer is just or not. No doctor will be reproached on the grounds that the dose of penicillin he has prescribed is less or more than *justice* would stipulate.

Behavioral scientists regard it as equally absurd to invoke the question of justice in deciding what to do with a woman who cannot resist her propensity to shoplift, or with a man who cannot repress an impulse to assault somebody. This sort of behavior has to be controlled; it has to be discouraged; it has to be *stopped.* This (to the scientist) is a matter of public safety and amicable coexistence, not of justice.

I do not mean that science discards value systems. Doctors do not like to be beaten up or robbed or cheated any more than lawyers do. But the question doctors might ask is not what would be *just* to do to this dangerous fellow, this dishonest woman, but, as in the case of a patient with compulsions, what would be effective in deterring them! That he or she has broken the law gives us a technical reason for acting on behalf of society to try to do something that will lead him to react more acceptably, and which will protect the environment in the meantime. And this is exactly what the present system based on the concepts of justice and precedent *fails* to do.

What *is* this system of justice that does its job so poorly, after all these years of trial and error? (No pun intended.) Who is responsible for the continuation of an ineffective, expensive, "unjust," and barbarous method of dealing with delinquency that produces only more delinquency? Where are our lawyers? They know how wretched it is. Where are our judges? They wrestle with its creaking machinery daily. Where are our scientists, who ought to be offering some remedies? Are they really trying to help the lawyers or do they disdainfully ignore them as hopelessly argumentative or scholastic? And the responsible, intelligent press—is it really indifferent to the abuses and failures of the system? Or has it become cynical about the possibility of any constructive change?

The lawyers, the judges, the scientists, the editors—all of these are honorable men. All are intelligent men. They know the system is rotten and they know it is not working. Many of them want to see it change, Many of them are working to bring this about. But they encounter great difficulty, on the one hand, from rigidities in state constitutions, and even greater rigidities in the attitude of the public.

. . .

In the eyes of the law all [criminal] acts are of a kind, with but one motive—the wish to break the law. Why the wish to do so becomes so powerful as to elude all the existing controls, internal and external, is of no interest to the law or the representatives of the law. What various forces combine to determine a particular antisocial, illegal act—this is no concern of the law. What internal pressures and external events led up to the criminal act as a logical link in a continuing chain of behavior and adaptation—this is not a legal question nor a legal concern. The law is concerned only with the fact that its stipulations were *broken,* and the one who breached them—provided he can be convicted—must pay the penalty. Having erred, he must be officially and socially hurt—"punished." Then everything will be all right again. "Justice" will have been done.

On the other hand, science, represented by psychiatry, looks at all such instances of lawbreaking as pieces in a total pattern of behavior. It asks, Why? What was behind the discovered act which brought the matter to our attention? What pain would drive a man to such a reaction, such a desperate outbreak, and such a deliberate gamble?

Could not a better way be found for dealing with despair and ignominy and poverty and frustration and bitterness than to let pressures mount until they result in social aggression and irreversible tragedy?

Beyond Freedom and Dignity

B. F. SKINNER

It should be possible to design a world in which behavior likely to be punished seldom or never occurs. We try to design such a world for those who cannot solve the problem of punishment for themselves, such as babies, retardates, or psychotics, and if it could be done for everyone, much time and energy would be saved.

. . .

The defenders of freedom and dignity object to solving the problem of punishment that way. Such a world builds only automatic goodness. T. H. Huxley saw nothing wrong with it: "If some great power would agree to make me always think what is true and do what is right, on condition of being some sort of a clock and wound up every morning before I got out of bed, I should close instantly with the offer." But Joseph Wood Krutch refers to this as the scarcely believable position of a "proto-modern," and he share T. S. Eliot's contempt for "systems so perfect that no one will need to be good."

The trouble is that when we punish a person for behaving badly, we leave it up to him to discover how to behave well, and he can then get credit for behaving well. But if he behaves well for the reasons we have just examined, it is the environment that must get the credit. At issue is an attribute of autonomous man. Men are to behave well only because they are good. Under a "perfect" system no one needs goodness.

There are, of course, valid reasons for thinking less of a person who is only automatically good, for he is a lesser person. In a world in which he does not need to work hard, he will not learn to sustain hard work. In a world in which medical science has alleviated pain, he will not learn to take painful stimuli. In a world which promotes automatic goodness, he will not learn to take the punishments associated with be-

From *Beyond Freedom and Dignity* (New York: Knopf, 1971), pp. 62–63, 67–69, 70–71, 76–77.

having badly. To prepare people for a world in which they cannot be good automatically, we need appropriate instruction, but that does not mean a permanently punitive environment, and there is no reason why progress toward a world in which people may be automatically good should be impeded. The problem is to induce people not to be good but to behave well.

. . .

Many of the issues of punitive control arc raised by the concept of responsibility, an attribute which is said to distinguish man from the other animals. The responsible person is a "deserving" person. We give him credit when he behaves well, in order that he will continue to do so, but we are most likely to use the term when what he deserves is punishment. We *hold* a person responsible for his conduct in the sense that he can be justly or fairly punished. This is again a matter of good husbandry, of a judicious use of reinforcers of "making the punishment fit the crime." More punishment than necessary is costly and may suppress desirable behavior, while too little is wasteful if it has no effect at all.

The legal determination of responsibility (and justice) is in part concerned with facts. Did a person, indeed, behave in a given way? Were the circumstances such that the behavior was punishable under the law? If so, what laws apply, and what punishments are specified? But other questions seem to concern the inner man. Was the act intentional or premeditated? Was it done in the heat of anger? Did the person know the difference between right and wrong? Was he aware of the possible consequences of his act? All these questions about purposes, feelings, knowledge, and so on, can be restated in terms of the environment to which a person has been exposed. What a person "intends to do" depends upon what he has done in the past and what has then happened. A person does not act because he "feels angry"; he acts *and* feels angry for a common reason, not specified. Whether he deserves punishment when all these conditions are taken into account is a question about probable results: will he, if punished, behave in a different way when similar circumstances again arise? There is a current tendency to substitute controllability for responsibility, and controllability is not so likely to be regarded as a possession of autonomous man, since it explicitly alludes to external conditions.

The assertion that "only a free man can be responsible for his conduct" has two meanings, depending upon whether we are interested in freedom or responsibility. If we want to say that people are responsible, we must do nothing to infringe their freedom, since if they are not free to act they cannot be held responsible. If we want to say they are free, we must hold them responsible for their behavior by maintaining punitive contingencies, since if they behaved in the same way under conspicuous nonpunitive contingencies, it would be clear that they were not free.

Any move toward an environment in which men are automatically good threatens responsibility. In the control of alcoholism, for example, the traditional practice is punitive. Drunkenness is called wrong, and ethical sanctions are imposed by a persons's peers (the condition generated being felt as shame), or it is classified as illegal and subject to governmental sanctions (the condition generated being felt as guilt), or it is called sinful and punished by religious agencies (the condition generated being felt as a sense of sin). The practice has not been conspicuously successful, and other controlling measures have been sought. Certain medical evidence appears to be relevant. People differ in their tolerances to alcohol and their addictive dependencies. Once a person has become an alcoholic, he may drink to relieve severe withdrawal symptoms which are not always taken into account by those who have never experienced them. The medical aspects raise the question of responsibility: how fair is it to punish the alcoholic? From the point of view of husbandry, can we expect punishment to be effective against the opposing positive contingencies? Should we not rather treat the medical condition? (Our culture differs from the Erewhon of Samuel Butler in imposing no punitive sanctions on illness.) As responsibility diminishes, punishment is relaxed.

. . .

The real issue is the effectiveness of techniques of control. We shall not solve the problem of alcoholism by increasing a sense of responsibility. It is the environment which is "responsible" for the objectional behavior, and it is the environment, not some attribute of the individual, which must be changed. We recognize this when we talk about the punitive contingencies in the natural environment. Running head-on into a wall is punished by a blow to the skull, but we do not hold a man responsible for not running into walls nor do we say that nature holds him responsible. Nature simply punishes him when he runs into a wall. When we make the world less punishing or teach people how to avoid natural punishments, as by giving them rules to follow, we are not destroying responsibility or threatening any other occult quality. We are simply making the world safer.

The concept of responsibility is particularly weak when behavior is traced to genetic determiners. We may admire beauty, grace, and sensitivity, but we do not blame a person because he is ugly, spastic, or color blind. Less conspicuous forms of genetic endowment nevertheless cause trouble. Individuals presumably differ, as species differ, in the extent to which they respond aggressively or are reinforced when they effect aggressive damage, or in the extent to which they engage in sexual behavior or are affected by sexual reinforcement. Are they, therefore, equally responsible for controlling their aggressive or sexual behavior, and is it fair to punish them to the same extent? If we do not punish a person for a club foot, should we punish him for being quick to anger or highly susceptible to sexual reinforcement? The issue has recently been raised by the possibility that many criminals show an anomaly in their chromosomes. The concept of responsibility offers little help. The issue is controllability. We cannot change genetic defects by punishment; we can work only through genetic measures which operate on a much longer time scale. What must be changed is not the responsibility of autonomous man but the conditions, environmental or genetic, of which a person's behavior is a function.

. . .

Under punitive contingencies a person appears to be free to behave well and to deserve credit when he does so. Nonpunitive contingencies generate the same behavior, but a person cannot then be said to be free, and the contingencies deserve the credit when he behaves well. Little or nothing remains for autonomous man to do and receive credit for doing. He does not engage in moral struggle and therefore has no chance to be a moral hero or credited with inner virtues. But our task is not to encourage moral struggle or to build or demonstrate inner virtues. It is to make life less punishing and in doing so to release for more reinforcing activities the time and energy consumed in the avoidance of punishment. Up to a point the literatures of free-dom and dignity have played a part in the slow and erratic alleviation of aversive fea-tures of the human environment, including the aversive features used in intentional control. But they have formulated the task in such a way that they cannot now accept the fact that all control is exerted by the environment and proceed to the design of better environments rather than of better men.

The Humanitarian Theory of Punishment

C. S. LEWIS

In England we have lately had a controversy about Capital Punishment. I do not know whether a murderer is more likely to repent and make a good end on the gallows a few weeks after his trial or in the prison infirmary thirty years later. I do not know whether the fear of death is an indispensable deterrent. I need not, for the purpose of this article, decide whether it is a morally permissible deterrent. Those are questions which I propose to leave untouched. My subject is not Capital Punishment in partic-ular, but that theory of punishment in general which the controversy showed to be al-most universal among my fellow-countrymen. It may be called the Humanitarian the-ory. Those who hold it think that it is cold and merciful. In this I believe that they are seriously mistaken. I believe that the "Humanity" which it claims is a dangerous il-lusion and disguises the possibility of cruelty and injustice without end. I urge a re-turn to the traditional or Retributive theory not solely, not even primarily, in the in-terests of society, but in the interests of the criminal.

According to the Humanitarian theory, to punish a man because he deserves it, and as much as he deserves, is mere revenge, and, therefore, barbarous and immoral. It is maintained that the only legitimate motives for punishing are the desire to deter others by example and to mend the criminal. When this theory is combined, as fre-quently happens, with the belief that all crime is more or less pathological, the idea of mending tails off into that of healing or curing, and punishment becomes thera-peutic. Thus it appears at first sight that we have passed from the harsh and self-righteous notion of giving the wicked their deserts to the charitable and enlightened one of tending the psychologically sick. What could be more amiable? One little point which is taken for granted in this theory needs, however, to be made explicit. The things done to the criminal, even if they are called cures, will be just as compulsory as they were in the old days when we called them punishments. If a tendency to steal can be cured by psychotherapy, the thief will no doubt be forced to undergo the treat-ment. Otherwise, society cannot continue.

From *Crime and Justice,* Vol. 2, *The Criminal in the Arms of the Law,* Leon Radzinowicz and Marvin E. Wolfgang, eds. (New York: Basic Books, 1971), 43–45, 46–48.

My contention is that this doctrine, merciful though it appears, really means that each one of us, from the moment he breaks the law, is deprived of the rights of a human being.

The reason is this. The Humanitarian theory removes from Punishment the concept of Desert. But the concept of Desert is the only connecting link between punishment and justice. It is only as deserved or undeserved that a sentence can be just or unjust. I do not here contend that the question "Is it deserved?" is the only one we can reasonably ask about a punishment. We may very properly ask whether it is likely to deter others and to reform the criminal. But neither of these two last questions is a question about justice. There is no sense in talking about a "just deterrent" or a "just cure." We demand of a deterrent not whether it is just but whether it will deter. We demand of a cure not whether it is just but whether it succeeds. Thus when we cease to consider what the criminal deserves and consider only what will cure him or deter others, we have tacitly removed him from the sphere of justice altogether; instead of a person, a subject of rights, we now have a mere object, a patient, a "case."

The distinction will become clearer if we ask who will be qualified to determine sentences when sentences are no longer held to derive their propriety from the criminal's deservings. On the old view the problem of fixing the right sentence was a moral problem. Accordingly, the judge who did it was a person trained in jurisprudence; trained, that is, in a science which deals with rights and duties, and which, in origin at least, was consciously accepting guidance from the Law of Nature, and from Scripture. We must admit that in the actual penal code of most countries at most times these high originals were so much modified by local custom, class interests, and utilitarian concessions, as to be very imperfectly recognizable. But the code was never in principle, and not always in fact, beyond the control of the conscience of the society. And when (say, in eighteenth-century England) actual punishments conflicted too violently with the moral sense of the community, juries refused to convict and reform was finally brought about. This was possible because, so long as we are thinking in terms of Desert, the propriety of the penal code, being a moral question, is a question on which every man has the right to an opinion, not because he follows this or that profession, but because he is simply a man, a rational animal enjoying the Natural Light. But all this is changed when we drop the concept of Desert. The only two questions we may now ask about a punishment are whether it deters and whether it cures. But these are not questions on which anyone is entitled to have an opinion simply because he is a man. He is not entitled to an opinion even if, in addition to being a man, he should happen also to be a jurist, a Christian, and a moral theologian. For they are not questions about principle but about matter of fact; and for such *cuiquam in sua arte credendum.* Only the expert "penologist" (let barbarous things have barbarous names), in the light of previous experiment, can tell us what is likely to deter: only the psychotherapist can tell us what is likely to cure. It will be in vain for the rest of us, speaking simply as men, to say, "but this punishment is hideously unjust, hideously disproportionate to the criminal's deserts." The experts with perfect logic will reply, "but nobody was talking about deserts. No one was talking about *punishment* in your archaic vindictive sense of the word. Here are the statistics proving that this treatment deters. Here are the statistics proving that this other treatment cures. What is your trouble?"

The Humanitarian theory, then, removes sentences from the hands of jurists whom the public conscience is entitled to criticize and places them in the hands of technical experts whose special sciences do not even employ such categories as rights or justice. It might be argued that since this transference results from an abandonment of the old idea of punishment, and, therefore, of all vindictive motives, it will be safe to leave our criminals in such hands. I will not pause to comment on the simple-minded view of fallen human nature which such a belief implies. Let us rather remember that the "cure" of criminals is to be compulsory; and let us then watch how the theory actually works in the mind of the Humanitarian. The immediate starting point of this attitude was a letter I read in one of our Leftist weeklies. The author was pleading that a certain sin, now treated by our laws as a crime, should henceforward be treated as a disease. And he complained that under the present system the offender, after a term in gaol, was simply let out to return to his original environment where he would probably relapse. What he complained of was not the shutting up but the letting out. On his remedial view of punishment the offender should, of course, be detained until he was cured. And of course the official straighteners are the only people who can say when that is. The first result of the Humanitarian theory is, therefore, to substitute for a definite sentence (reflecting to some extent the community's moral judgment on the degree of ill desert involved) an indefinite sentence terminable only by the word of those experts—and they are not experts in moral theology nor even in the Law of Nature—who inflict it. Which of us, if he stood in the dock, would not prefer to be tried by the old system?

It may be said that by the continued use of the word punishment and the use of the verb "inflict" I am misrepresenting Humanitarians. They are not punishing, not inflicting, only healing. But do not let us be deceived by a name. To be taken without consent from my home and friends; to lose my liberty; to undergo all those assaults on my personality which modern psychotherapy knows how to deliver; to be re-made after some pattern of "normality" hatched in a Viennese laboratory to which I never professed allegiance; to know that this process will never end until either my captors have succeeded or I have grown wise enough to cheat them with apparent success—who cares whether this is called Punishment or not? That it includes most of the elements for which any punishment is feared—shame, exile, bondage, and years eaten by the locust—is obvious. Only enormous ill desert could justify it; but ill-desert is the very conception which the Humanitarian theory has thrown overboard.

. . .

It is, indeed, important to notice that my argument so far supposes no evil intentions on the part of the Humanitarian and considers only what is involved in the logic of his position. My contention is that good men (not bad men) consistently acting upon that position would act as cruelly and unjustly as the greatest tyrants. They might in some respects act even worse. Of all tyrannies a tyranny sincerely exercised for the good of its victims may be the most oppressive. It may be better to live under robber barons than under omnipotent moral busybodies. The robber baron's cruelty may sometimes sleep, his cupidity may at some point be satiated: but those who torment us for our own good will torment us without end for they do so with the approval of their own conscience. They may be more likely to go to Heaven yet at the same time likelier to make a Hell of earth. Their very kindness stings with intolerable insult. To be "cured" against one's will and cured of states which we may not regard as disease is to be put on a level with those who have not yet reached the age of reason or those who never will; to be classed with infants, imbeciles, and domestic animals. But to be punished, however severely, because we have deserved it, because we "ought to have known better," is to be treated as a human person made in God's image.

In reality, however, we must face the possibility of bad rulers armed with a Humanitarian theory of punishment.. . . . [W]isdom and virtue are not the only or the commonest qualifications for a place in the government. The practical problem . . . is . . . that of living as innocently as we can . . . under . . . rulers who will never be perfectly wise and good and who will sometimes be very wicked and very foolish. And when they are wicked, the Humanitarian theory of punishment will put in their hands a finer instrument of tyranny than wickedness ever had before. For if crime and disease are to be regarded as the same thing, it follows that any state of mind which our masters choose to call "disease" can be treated as crime; and compulsorily cured. It will be vain to plead that states of mind which displease government need not always involve moral turpitude and do not therefore always deserve forfeiture of liberty. For our masters will not be using the concepts of Desert and Punishment but those of disease and cure. We know that one school of psychology already regards religion as a neurosis. When this particular neurosis becomes inconvenient to government, what is to hinder government from proceeding to "cure" it? Such "cure" will, of course, be compulsory; but under the Humanitarian theory it will not be called by the shocking name of Persecution. No one will blame us for being Christian, no one will hate us, no one will revile us. The new Nero will approach us with the silky manners of a doctor, and though all will be in fact as compulsory as the *tunica molesta* or Smithfield or Tyburn, all will go on within the unemotional therapeutic sphere where words like "right" and "wrong" or "freedom" and "slavery" are never heard. And thus when the command is given, every prominent Christian in the land may vanish overnight into Institutions for the Treatment of the Ideologically Unsound, and it will rest with the expert gaolers to say when (if ever) they are to re-emerge. But it will not be persecution. Even if the treatment is painful, even if it is life-long, even if it is fatal, that will be only a regrettable accident; the intention was purely therapeutic. Even in ordinary medicine there were painful operations and fatal operations; so in this. But because they are "treatment," not punishment, they can be criticized only by fellow-experts and on technical grounds, never by men as men and on grounds of justice.

This is why I think it essential to oppose the Humanitarian theory of punishment, root and branch, wherever we encounter it. It carries on its front a semblance of mercy which is wholly false. That is how it can deceive men of good will. The error began, perhaps, with Shelley's statement that the distinction between mercy and justice was invented in the courts of tyrants. It sounds noble, and was indeed the error of a noble mind. But the distinction is essential. The older view was that mercy "tempered" justice, or (on the highest level of all) that mercy and justice had met and kissed. The essential act of mercy was to pardon; and pardon in its very essence involves the recognition of guilt and ill desert in the recipient.

If crime is only a disease which needs cure, not sin which deserves punishment, it cannot be pardoned. How can you pardon a man for having a gumboil or a club foot? But the Humanitarian theory wants simply to abolish Justice and substitute

Mercy for it. This means that you start being "kind" to people before you have considered their rights, and then force upon them supposed kindnesses which they in fact had a right to refuse, and finally kindnesses which no one but you will recognize as kindnesses and which the recipient will feel as abominable cruelties. You have overshot the mark. Mercy, detached from Justice, grows unmerciful. That is the important paradox. As there are plants which will flourish only in mountain soil, so it appears that Mercy will flower only when it grows in the crannies of the rock of Justice; transplanted to the marshlands of mere Humanitarianism, it becomes a man-eating weed, all the more dangerous because it is still called by the same name as the mountain variety. But we ought long ago to have learned our lesson. We should be too old now to be deceived by those humane pretensions which have served to usher in every cruelty of the revolutionary period in which we live. These are the "precious balms" which will "break our heads."

There is a fine sentence in Bunyan: "It came burning hot into my mind, whatever he said, and however he flattered, when he got me home to his house, he would sell me for a slave." There is a fine couplet, too, in John Ball:

> Be ware ere ye be woe
> Know your friend from your foe.

One last word. You may ask why I send this to an Australian periodical. The reason is simple and perhaps worth recording: I can get no hearing for it in England.

NOTES AND QUESTIONS

As previewed in the introduction to this section, the rehabilitative ideal in criminal law is a blend of a faith in science, incompatibilist metaphysics between scientific determinism and moral responsibility, and the egalitarian (but not libertarian) branch of liberal politics. Consider each aspect of the ideal below.

1. The traditional tasks of science are the truth-seeking tasks of describing, explaining, and predicting phenomena. A science of human behavior, including criminal behavior, presumably shares this goal of all science. As even the short excerpts from Menninger and Skinner illustrate, they each had surprising confidence in the explanatory power of their respective theories of human behavior. One question, which these readings cannot raise adequately, is whether the dynamic psychiatry of Menninger or the behavioral psychology of Skinner actually gives more accurate descriptions, explanations, and predictions of criminal behavior than the commonsense psychology presupposed by the criminal law. Neither the repressed unconscious of Freudian psychiatry nor the strictly environmental stimuli of Skinnerian behaviorism have fared well as scientific theories in recent decades. Yet for our purposes it almost does not matter. Criminal lawyers are regularly berated for scientific naïveté by what-

ever science of human behavior is fashionable, and the intellectual demise of Freud and Skinner betoken no end to the parade of scientific theories challenging the criminal law in this way. These days the challenges come more from cognitive psychology, artificial intelligence, physiological psychology, genetics, ethology, and biological psychiatry than from the older psychologies represented by Menninger and Skinner. Although it is always in point to question the *truth* of any of such theories, more pertinent here is to question the *relevance* of such sciences to the theory of punishment. For that issue, the challenges of Menninger and Skinner are still illustrative.

2. Neither Skinner nor Menninger are content to explain why people engage in criminal behavior. They also regard the criminal justice system as a failure from the scientific viewpoint. Is this a scientific question? What is the goal they assign to the criminal justice system that it fails to achieve and which they claim their sciences could better achieve? Is that assignment of a goal by them itself a scientific enterprise?

3. Are the ways of thinking of the sciences of human behavior incompatible with the conceptualizations of the criminal law (in terms of voluntariness, intentionality, excuse, responsibility, rights, justice, and the like)? Consider:

a. Skinner's claim that "questions about purposes, feelings, knowledge, and so on can be restated in terms of the environment to which a person has been exposed." Is Skinner claiming that we can *translate* statements like "Jones intended to kill Smith" into statements about what Jones "has done in the past and what has then happened"? Can we *translate* "Jones feels angry" into "Jones is acting in a certain manner, one often described as angrily"? This would make Skinner what is called a "logical behaviorist," one who thinks all of the commonsense psychological talk of the criminal law is simply a sloppy way of referring to behavioral reinforcers and behavioral tendencies.

b. Or is Skinner making the much more challenging claim of the "methodological behaviorist," that is, that a good scientific explanation of why Jones killed Smith will make no mention of causally efficacious mental states of intention, belief, or emotion but only of the contingencies of reinforcement that were the true causes of Jones's act?

c. For Skinner, is "responsibility" itself just a misleading way of referring to "the environment that must get the credit"?

d. For Menninger, does "justice" similarly have no place in a scientific explanation of human behavior? Is that because "the concept is so vague, so distorted in its applications, so hypocritical, and usually so irrelevant" that the concept is a useless one? Can you make sense of Menninger's statement that use of such a concept results in "injustice, injustice to everybody"? Can *in*justice be a useful concept if justice is not? Or is Menninger referring to different kinds of justice, one useful (distributive justice) and one not (retributive justice)?

4. Suppose we had a complete science of human behavior, in the sense that we could explain and predict every person's every action. Suppose further that the factors doing the explaining and the predicting in such a science were not beliefs, intentions, and emotions—the mental states of the commonsense psychology presupposed by the criminal law; rather, these factors are unconscious, subliminal desires; or environmental stimuli; or genetically transmitted and survival-selected traits; or complicated firing patterns of two-valued switches—in short factors over which our conscious will has no ability to control. Is no one then morally responsible because

lacking in freedom? Would such suppositions show that there are no selves, no agents, no "autonomous man" to even be responsible? Consider some explanations we do have, and ask if they have this effect:

a. Person A has a known propensity to tell the same old boring joke if he thinks of it, and he thinks of it by associating to the word "Truman." You say the word to him, and, sure enough, he tells the same old boring joke. You caused him to do so, but is his doing so not an exercise of his agency for which he is responsible?

b. Exposure to good parenting and educational opportunities of a certain rarefied kind are essential to becoming a successful symbolic logician. When such a logician discovers a new proof, should we nonetheless praise *her* for *her* discovery?

c. Most of our beliefs are nonwilled, in the sense that we cannot wish to believe and therefore perform a procedure that results in our so believing. The same is true ultimately for our desires—we do not desire to desire what we desire, and even when we do, we do not create such second-order desires by executing third-order desires. Yet suppose Jones killed Smith *because* (1) Jones desired to inherit Smith's wealth; and (2) Jones believed that (given what he believed about Smith's will) if Jones killed Smith, he would inherit Smith's wealth. Is Jones' killing not his responsibility because caused by unwilled states of belief and desire? Is the causation of Jones' behavior in any relevant way different than that proposed by Menninger and Skinner?

5. Menninger at one point asks us what the state should do with "a woman who cannot resist her propensity to shoplift, or with a man who cannot repress an impulse to assault somebody." What does Menninger mean by "cannot"? Is it simply that these agents *cannot* do other than shoplift or assault in the sense that it is determined that they *will* shoplift or assault? Is there a more relevant "cannot" that is stronger than this contra-causal sense? What about a kleptomaniac who shoplifts items for which she has no need, or the assaulter with an obsession about a certain person—do these give rise to some stronger sense of "*cannot* do otherwise?"

6. Is it our fault (i.e., the fault of the noncriminal part of society) that there are criminals? Is one of Menninger's points that it is our fault and therefore that we lack the *right* to punish?

7. Are criminals drawn from the least advantaged classes in society, those least advantaged in terms of wealth, health, intelligence? Are criminals the only members of those classes? Do such disadvantages justify Menninger's argument for therapeutic state concern even if such concern were not necessary on crime prevention grounds?

8. If we put responsibility and justice aside as reasons to punish, must we also, as Lewis suggests, put them aside as reasons not to punish? Does it depend on why Menninger, Skinner et al., urge us to put them aside?

9. What sense would Lewis make of the idea that all criminals possess a "right to be punished"? Should criminals value such a right?

10. Skinner's utopian politics tell him he would "instantly close" with Huxley's offer to be programmed so that not doing good was not a possibility for him. Would Lewis? Would you? Is there some virtue or other benefit in the resisting of temptation that such programming would eliminate?

2.2.5 Attempts to Integrate the Divergent Theories of Punishment

The existence of problems with each of the three pure theories of punishment suggest that perhaps mixed theories could combine the strengths of each of the pure theories while avoiding the problems. The question is which of the pure theories should go into the mix, and how should they be combined? It will not do (as the Hart reading below reminds us) to return to the common but sloppy analysis that blithely asserts that deterrence, reform, incapacitation, and retribution are all part of the justification of punishment, and simply leave it at that. Repeating this old mantra does not align theories of punishment within the larger categories of political theory generally (utilitarianism and deontological justice theories of either the egalitarian or libertarian kinds); nor does the mantra give any hints at how such disparate factors as deterrence and retribution are to be combined.

The selection below from H. L. A. Hart attempts to mix utilitarian theories with retributive theories. Left out of such a mix is the rehabilitative ideal. In addition to space constraints, there are three reasons we have omitted any other kinds of mixed theories from this discussion. First, the best known attempts to mix pure theories are those that attempt to mix utilitarianism and retributivism. The best developed literature on "mixing" is thus to be found here, not with the rehabilitative theory. Second, while the rehabilitative theory has often been combined with utilitarianism, that mixed reform-deterrence theory itself has to be qualified by retributivism if it is to be at all plausible. Such mixing of all three theories is more complicated than we need. Third, the decline in the acceptance of the rehabilitative ideal means that there is less contemporary concern about possible mixed theories of punishment in which the rehabilitative ideal figures.

Also omitted from the selections below, as from the literature on punishment generally, is any discussion of what we shall call *dysjunctively* mixed theories of punishment. These would be theories that assert, for example, that *either* the moral desert of the offender *or* the social utility gained by punishing someone is a sufficient reason to punish. (These might be called the "Blondie" mixed theories, after the punk rocker of the 1980s whose hit single was that she was "going to get you, one way or the other.") The motivation for adopting mixed theories of punishment is to avoid the problems of the pure theories; dysjunctively mixed theories suffer from the problems of each of the pure theories mixed and thus do not eliminate problems but multiply them.

The typical mixed theories are always conjunctival mixed theories, in the sense that both utility and desert are necessary to justify an overall scheme of punishment. How such mixing takes place nonetheless differs considerably between different kinds of mixed theories. For some theorists, the mixture is by modal assignment: utilitarianism deals with moral necessity, whereas retributivism deals with logical necessity (i.e., one cannot be said to be *punished* unless the punishment is given because one deserves it). For Hart, by contrast, utilitarianism and retributivism are both moral theories, not logical definitions; yet the first applies to justify the general institution of punishment, whereas the second applies to justify the application of that practice of punishing to individual offenders. For yet other mixed theorists, neither of these jurisdictional modes of combining utilitarianism and retributivism will do, requiring as they do the carving out of an exclusive jurisdiction where each sort of reason may operate without the interference of the other. Rather, a better mixed theory is one that operates solely with moral necessity, not logical necessity, and that operates at one level, not two. Take the level of justifying the general practice of punishing; the giving of just deserts and the increasing of utility are both morally necessary for the institution of punishment to be justified.[1]

[1] A good representative of this kind of mixed theory is Andrew von Hirsch, *Doing Justice: The Choice of Punishments* (New York: Hill and Wang, 1976), pp. 46–55.

Punishment and Responsibility

H. L. A. HART

Many are now troubled by the suspicion that the view that there is just one supreme value or objective (e.g. Deterrence, Retribution or Reform) in terms of which *all* questions about the justification of punishment are to be answered, is somehow wrong; yet, from what is said on such occasions no clear account of what the different values or objectives are, or how they fit together in the justification of punishment, can be extracted. . . .

. . . It is likely that in our inherited ways of talking or thinking about punishment there is some persistent drive towards an over-simplification of multiple issues which require separate consideration. To counter this drive what is most needed is *not* the simple admission that instead of a single value or aim (Deterrence, Retribution, Reform or any other) a plurality of different values and aims should be given as a conjunctive answer to some *single* question concerning the justification of punishment. What is needed is the realization that different principles (each of which may in a sense be called a "justification") are relevant at different points in any morally acceptable account of punishment. What we should look for are answers to a number of different questions such as: What justifies the general practice of punishment? To whom may punishment be applied? How severely may we punish? In dealing with these and other questions concerning punishment we should bear in mind that in this, as in most other social institutions, the pursuit of one aim may be qualified by or pro-

From *Punishment and Responsibility* (Oxford: Oxford University Press, 1962), pp. 2–4, 6–13.

vide an opportunity, not to be missed, for the pursuit of others. Till we have developed this sense of the complexity of punishment (and this prolegomenon aims only to do this) we shall be in no fit state to assess the extent to which the whole institution has been eroded by, or needs to be adapted to, new beliefs about the human mind.

Justifying Aims and Principles of Distribution

There is, I think, an analogy worth considering between the concept of punishment and that of property. In both cases we have to do with a social institution of which the centrally important form is a structure of *legal* rules, even if it would be dogmatic to deny the names of punishment or property to the similar though more rudimentary rule-regulated practices within groups such as a family, or a school, or in customary societies whose customs may lack some of the standard or salient features of law (e.g., legislation, organized sanctions, courts). In both cases we are confronted by a complex institution presenting different interrelated features calling for separate explanation; or, if the morality of the institution is challenged, for separate justification. In both cases failure to distinguish separate questions or attempting to answer them all by reference to a single principle ends in confusion. Thus in the case of property we should distinguish between the question of the *definition* of property, the question why and in what circumstance it is a *good* institution to maintain, and the questions in what ways individuals may become *entitled* to acquire property and *how much* they should be allowed to acquire. These we may call questions of *Definition, General Justifying Aim,* and *Distribution,* with the last subdivided into questions of *Title* and *Amount.*

The Nature of an Offence

Before we reach any question of justification we must identify a preliminary question to which the answer is so simple that the question may not appear worth asking; yet it is clear that some curious "theories" of punishment gain their only plausibility from ignoring it, and others from confusing it with other questions. This question is: Why are certain kinds of action forbidden by law and so made crimes or offences? The answer is: To announce to society that these actions are not to be done and to secure that fewer of them are done. These are the common immediate aims of making any conduct a criminal offence and until we have laws made with these primary aims we shall lack the notion of a "crime" and so of a "criminal." Without recourse to the simple idea that the criminal law sets up, in its rules, standards of behaviour to encourage certain types of conduct and discourage others we cannot distinguish a punishment in the form of a fine from a tax on a course of conduct. This indeed is one grave objection to those theories of law which in the interests of simplicity or uniformity obscure the distinction between primary laws setting standards for behaviour and secondary laws specifying what officials must or may do when they are broken. Such theories insist that all legal rules are "really" directions to officials to exact "sanctions" under certain conditions, e.g., if people kill. Yet only if we keep alive the distinction (which such theories thus obscure) between the primary objective of the law in encouraging or discouraging certain kinds of behaviour, and its merely ancillary sanction or remedial steps, can we give sense to the notion of a crime or offence.

It is important however to stress the fact that in thus identifying the immediate aims of the criminal law we have not reached the stage of justification. There are indeed many forms of undesirable behaviour which it would be foolish (because ineffective or too costly) to attempt to inhibit by use of the law and some of these may be better left to educators, trades unions, churches, marriage guidance councils, or other nonlegal agencies. Conversely there are some forms of conduct which we believe cannot be effectively inhibited without use of the law. But it is only too plain that in fact the law may make activities criminal which it is morally important to promote and the suppression of these may be quite unjustifiable. Yet confusion between the simple immediate aim of any criminal legislation and the justification of punishment seems to be the most charitable explanation of the claim that punishment is *justified* as an "emphatic denunciation by the community of a crime." Lord Denning's dictum that this is the ultimate justification of punishment can be saved . . . only if it is treated as a blurred statement of the truth that the aim not of punishment, but of criminal legislation is indeed to denounce certain types of conduct as something not to be practised. Conversely the immediate aim of criminal legislation cannot be any of the things which are usually mentioned as justifying punishment: for until it is settled what conduct is to be legally denounced and discouraged we have not settled from what we are to *deter* people, or who are to be considered *criminals* from whom we are to exact *retribution,* or on whom we are to wreak *vengeance,* or whom we are to *reform.*

Even those who look upon human law as a mere instrument for enforcing "morality as such" (itself conceived as the law of God or Nature) and who at the stage of justifying punishment wish to appeal not to socially beneficial consequences but simply to the intrinsic value of inflicting suffering on wrong-doers who have disturbed by their offence the moral order, would not deny that the aim of criminal legislation is to set up types of behaviour (in this case conformity with a preexisting moral law) as legal standards of behaviour and to secure conformity with them. No doubt in all communities certain moral offences—e.g., killing—will always be selected for suppression as crimes and it is conceivable that this may be done not to protect human beings from being killed but to save the potential murderer from sin; but it would be paradoxical to look upon the law as designed not to discourage murder at all (even conceived as sin rather than harm) but simply to extract the penalty from the murderer.

General Justifying Aim

I shall not here criticize the intelligibility or consistency or adequacy of those theories that are united in denying that the practice of a system of punishment is justified by its beneficial consequences and claim instead that the main justification of the practice lies in the fact that when breach of the law involves moral guilt the application to the offender of the pain of punishment is itself a thing of value. A great variety of claims of this character, designating "Retribution" or "Expiation" or "Reprobation" as the justifying aim, fall in spite of differences under this rough general description. Though in fact I . . . [think] that these all either avoid the question of justification altogether or are in spite of their protestations disguised forms of Utilitarianism, I shall assume that Retribution, defined simply as the application of the pains of punishment to an offender who is morally guilty, may figure among the conceivable justifying aims of a system of punishment. Here I shall merely insist that it is one thing to use the word Retribution *at this point* in an account of the principle of punishment in order to designate the General Justifying Aim of the system, and quite another to use it to secure that to the question "To whom may punishment be applied?" (the question of Distribution), the answer given is "Only to an offender for an offence." Failure to distinguish Retribution as a General Justifying Aim from retribution as the simple insistence that only those who have broken the law—and voluntarily broken it—may be punished, may be traced in many writers. . . . We shall distinguish the latter from Retribution in General Aim as "retribution in Distribution." Much confusing shadow-fighting between utilitarians and their opponents may be avoided if it is recognized that it is perfectly consistent to assert *both* that the General Justifying Aim of the practice of punishment is its beneficial consequences *and* that the pursuit of this General Aim should be qualified or restricted out of deference to principles of Distribution which require that punishment should be only of an offender for an offence. Conversely it does not in the least follow from the admission of the latter principle of retribution in Distribution that the General Justifying Aim of punishment is Retribution though of course Retribution in General Aim entails retribution in Distribution.

We shall consider later the principles of justice lying at the root of retribution in Distribution. Meanwhile it is worth observing that both the old-fashioned Retributionist (in General Aim) and the most modern sceptic often make the same (and, I think, wholly mistaken) assumption that sense can only be made of the restrictive principle that punishment be applied only to an offender for an offence if the General Justifying Aim of the practice of punishment is Retribution. The sceptic consequently imputes to all systems of punishment (when they are restricted by the principle of retribution in Distribution) all the irrationality he finds in the idea of Retribution as a General Justifying Aim; conversely the advocates of the latter think the admission of retribution in Distribution is a refutation of the utilitarian claim that the social consequences of punishment are its Justifying Aim.

The most general lesson to be learnt from this extends beyond the topic of punishment. It is, that in relation to any social institution, after stating what general aim or value its maintenance fosters we should enquire whether there are any and if so what principles limiting the unqualified pursuit of that aim or value. Just because the pursuit of any single social aim always has its restrictive qualifier, our main social institutions always possess a plurality of features which can only be understood as a compromise between partly discrepant principles. This is true even of relatively minor legal institutions like that of a contract. In general this is designed to enable individuals to give effect to their wishes to create structures of legal rights and duties, and so to change, in certain ways, their legal position. Yet at the same time there is need to protect those who, in good faith, understand a verbal offer made to them to mean what it would ordinarily mean, accept it, and then act on the footing that a valid contract has been concluded. As against them, it would be unfair to allow the other party to say that the words he used in his verbal offer or the interpretation put on them did not express his real wishes or intention. Hence principles of "estoppel" or doctrines of the "objective sense" of a contract are introduced to prevent this and to qualify the principle that the law enforces contracts in order to give effect to the joint wishes of the contracting parties.

Distribution

This as in the case of property has two aspects: (i) Liability (Who may be punished?) and (ii) Amount. In this section I shall chiefly be concerned with the first of these.

From the foregoing discussions two things emerge. First, though we may be clear as to what value the practice of punishment is to promote, we have still to answer as a question of Distribution "Who may be punished?" Secondly, if in answer to this question we say "only an offender for an offence," this admission of retribution in Distribution is not a principle from which anything follows as to the severity or amount of punishment; in particular it neither licenses nor requires, as Retribution in General Aim does, more severe punishments than deterrence or other utilitarian criteria would require.

The root question to be considered is, however, why we attach the moral importance which we do to retribution in Distribution. Here I shall consider the efforts made to show that restriction of punishment to offenders is a simple consequence of whatever principles (Retributive or Utilitarian) constitute the Justifying Aim of punishment.

The standard example used by philosophers to bring out the importance of retribution in Distribution is that of a wholly innocent person who has not even unintentionally done anything which the law punishes if done intentionally. It is supposed that in order to avert some social catastrophe officials of the system fabricate evidence on which he is charged, tried, convicted and sent to prison or death. Or it is supposed that without resort to any fraud more persons may be deterred from crime if wives and children of offenders were punished vicariously for their crimes. In some forms this kind of thing may be ruled out by a consistent sufficiently comprehensive utilitarianism.[1] Certainly expedients involving fraud or faked charges might be very difficult to justify on utilitarian grounds. We can of course imagine that a negro might be sent to prison or executed on a false charge of rape in order to avoid widespread lynching of many others; but a *system* which openly empowered authorities to do this kind of thing, even if it succeeded in averting specific evils like lynching, would awaken such apprehension and insecurity that any gain from the exercise of these powers would by any utilitarian calculation be offset by the misery caused by their existence. But official resort to this kind of fraud on a particular occasion in breach of the rules and the subsequent indemnification of the officials responsible might save many lives and so be thought to yield a clear surplus of value. Certainly vicarious punishment of an offender's family might do so and legal systems have occasionally though exceptionally resorted to this. An example of it is the Roman *Lex Quisquis* providing for the punishment of the children of those guilty of *majestas*. In extreme cases many might still think it right to resort to these expedients but we should do so

---

[1] See J. Rawls, "Two Concepts of Rules," *Philosophical Review* (1955), pp. 4–13.

with the sense of sacrificing an important principle. We should be conscious of choosing the lesser of two evils, and this would be inexplicable if the principle sacrificed to utility were itself only a requirement of utility.

Similarly the moral importance of the restriction of punishment to the offender cannot be explained as merely a consequence of the principle that the General Justifying Aim is Retribution for immorality involved in breaking the law. Retribution in the Distribution of punishment has a value quite independent of Retribution as Justifying Aim. This is shown by the fact that we attach importance to the restrictive principle that only offenders may be punished, even where breach of this law might not be thought immoral. Indeed even where the laws themselves are hideously immoral as in Nazi Germany—e.g., forbidding activities (helping the sick or destitute of some racial group) which might be thought morally obligatory—the absence of the principle restricting punishment to the offender would be a further *special* iniquity; whereas admission of this principle would represent some residual respect for justice shown in the administration of morally bad laws.

NOTES AND QUESTIONS

1. State in your own words Hart's distinction between the General Justifying Aim of a practice and the Principles of Distribution under that practice. Consider a formerly communist state trying to decide: (1) whether to permit private property, (2) who should be assigned initial property entitlements, and (3) how much property each entitled person should receive. How would Hart allocate these questions between the answers given by the General Justifying Aim and those given by the Principles of Distribution of property?

2. What is the parallel between the legislative role versus the judicial role, on the one hand, and the General Justifying Aim and the Principles of Distribution, on the other?

3. What reason does Hart give us to assign utilitarianism to the General Justifying Aim of punishment and retributivism to the Principles of Distribution? What reason does Hart give us to assign each of the two theories *exclusive* jurisdiction within its domain, so that retributive reasons cannot enter into the General Justifying Aim of punishment and utilitarian considerations cannot enter into the principles that determine the distribution of punishment?

4. Does Hart think that it is intrinsically good for the guilty to get their due in the way of punishment? If not, in what sense is he at all a retributivist? In what sense does retributivism enter into his mixed theory of punishment?

5. If Hart rejects the idea that it is intrinsically good for the guilty to be punished, what is the good achieved by requiring guilt in the distribution of punishment? Is it that the (utilitarian-justified) rules defining the general practice of punishment by their terms require punishment when they are literally violated and forbid punish-

ment when they are not? Or does Hart also eschew such literalism or formalism and have in mind some nonutilitarian, nonretributivist third sort of intrinsic good to govern how punishment should be distributed within a utilitarian-justified general practice of punishment? Can you think of any plausible candidates for such a third sort of value? What does bother you about punishing someone who is innocent of violating any statutory prohibition even when utility would be enhanced by such punishment?

6. To the extent that Hart is simply a literalist about rule application in his principles of distribution, in what sense would such literalism be properly called "retributivist"? Is such literal application of a practice defensible? If one is a utilitarian about why we have any punishment institutions, why would the utilitarian point to the practice not penetrate that practice (in the sense of guiding interpretations and applications of that practice to particular cases)?

2.3 WHAT TO PUNISH

2.3.1 Getting at the Question and Its Possible Answers

An answer to the question of what should be prohibited by the criminal law we shall call a theory of criminal legislation. As the selection from Joel Feinberg below sets forth, the question is one addressed to an ideal legislator. It is only secondarily and incidentally a question a court might ask in reviewing that legislator's work. Further, as Feinberg also explores, the question is not one seeking a full set of reasons justifying the numerous prohibitions of any criminal code. Rather, the question asked is whether there are any principled limits an ideal legislator should observe as she considers what behaviors to criminalize. Which considerations are proper, and which improper, as the motivations justifying criminal prohibitions?

The preliminary discussion of this question by Feinberg gives one way of taxonomizing possible answers to this question. Feinberg, building on John Stuart Mill, taxonomizes his answers in terms of harms. There are four major principles potentially justificatory of criminal legislation, corresponding to four kinds of harms such legislation would seek to prevent: (1) the harm principle, which states that it is always a valid reason to prohibit behavior criminally if that behavior causes physical or economic injury to individuals other than the harm causer(s); (2) the offense principle, which finds such reasons in the moral or aesthetic offense or other psychic injury experienced by individuals at the behavior of others; (3) the paternalism principle, which finds such reasons in the physical, economic, moral, or psychic injury caused to the actor himself by the behavior to be prohibited; (4) the legal moralist principle, which finds such reasons in the immorality of the conduct in question even if such conduct causes harm to no one.

One of the virtues of Feinberg's taxonomy is its fit within the traditional categories of political theory and thus its fit with the three pure theories of punishment. Feinberg's first two principles can be combined and reformulated in a way that makes them a statement of the general principle of utility definitive of utilitarianism. (Mill's own version of the harm principle, which makes physical or economic injury to others *necessary* as well as sufficient for criminal legislation, is usually viewed as an expression of utilitarianism side-constrained by the nonutilitarian value of liberty.) The paternalism principle looks much like the Rehabilitative Ideal, both in the paternalism of each and in the distributive justice ideal that underlies both. The legal moralist principle seemingly goes hand in hand with the retributivist theory of punishment, for retributive justice seemingly is achieved only when moral wrongdoing is punished, not when morally innocent behavior is punished. (We say "seemingly" because this last connection would not hold if one thought that all laws obligate citizen obedience, even if in content such laws are immoral.)

Harm to Others

JOEL FEINBERG

The Basic Question of the Book

This book is an attempt to find a general answer, albeit a complicated one, to the question: What sorts of conduct may the state rightly make criminal? . . .

Our question can be understood as one posed for an ideal legislature in a democratic country. It is not my purpose to try to specify what such a body *would* choose to include in its ideally wise and useful penal code, but rather what it *may* include, if it chooses within the limits that morality places on its legislative decisions. This . . . work, then, is an account of the moral constraints on legislative action. As such, it is an extended essay in applied moral philosophy. Even though it incidentally considers the rationale of various crimes, it does not provide detailed answers to legislative questions. Rather it attempts to provide a coherent and plausible set of moral principles to guide the legislator by locating the moral constraints that limit his options. The book will not consider the further questions of cost-benefit analysis that must guide the legislator in his choices among those alternatives that do fall within the recommended moral limits. Within the proper limits a legislator must consider the social utility of his various options, their likely effects on various private and public interests, constituent desires and pressures, even the demands of "politics" in a narrow sense (log-rolling, compromising, political debt-paying, etc.). Our primary question,

From *Harm to Others* (New York: Oxford University Press, 1984), pp. 3–15.

however, is not one about social utility and practical wisdom. I do not offer suggestions here about what it would be "a good idea" to legislate within the scope of what *may* be legislated. This book is a quest not for useful policies but for valid principles. . . .

The Concept of Moral Legitimacy

A basic distinction presupposed by this work, then, is that between criminal statutes that are *legitimized* by valid moral principles and those that are *justified* on balance as being both legitimate *and* useful, wise, economical, popular, etc. I have no intention of undertaking a deep philosophical analysis of the basic idea of moral legitimacy. That would be difficult, distracting, and because of that notion's intuitive familiarity, quite unnecessary. The idea of legitimacy is not an invention of arcane philosophy. It is part of the conceptual equipment of every man and woman "on the street." Consider an illustration of its every day use.

If a red-headed stranger stops me as I am strolling north along Fifth Avenue and demands that I tell him where I am going, my first reaction will be to ask, in return, why he wishes to know. I will be genuinely curious, and also disposed to be polite and accommodating if he should have a good reason for his question. But if he brushes off my request and demands peremptorily that I answer his questions or else "face the consequences," my mood will change abruptly. "Where I am going," I will say, "is *my business,* not yours. I am not answerable to you. You are not my owner, or my master, or a policeman. You have no authority over me of any kind, direct or delegated. Now stand out of my way."

If the stranger nevertheless persists in blocking my path and preventing me from proceeding in a northward direction, his interference with my liberty is *illegitimate, improper,* or *morally illicit.* These predicates, it should be noticed, are not legal or political terms. If the law gave all red-headed men the power to question and forcibly restrain all balding brunettes, that very legal authority would be morally illegitimate, and the statute conferring it would be morally unjustified, whatever its legal or constitutional status. The same would be true of a statute that simply outlawed walking in a northerly direction by specifying a criminal punishment and conferring enforcement power on policemen instead of civilians. It is *not the business of the state,* we might complain, to determine for no good reason the direction in which pedestrians may walk. Even if the constitution gave the legislature the right to make such a law, it would be *wrong* for the legislature to exercise its constitutional authority in such an arbitrary fashion. . . .

The Idea of a Liberty-limiting Principle

We can also formulate the basic question of these volumes as one about the moral limits of individual liberty, understanding "liberty" simply as the absence of legal coercion. When the state creates a legal statute prohibiting its citizens from doing X on pain of punishment, then the citizens are no longer "at liberty" to do X. The credible threat of punishment working directly on the citizens' motives makes X seem substantially less eligible than before for their deliberate doing. We can think of every possible act as so related to a penal code that it must either be (1) required (a duty), (2) merely permitted (one we are "at liberty" to do or forbear doing), or (3) prohibited (a crime). Where coercive law stops, there liberty begins. The citizen's zone of liberty, therefore, corresponds to the second class, since (1) and (3) are alike in directing coercive threats at him. When we are required to do X (a duty), we are prohibited, under pain of penalty, from omitting to do X; when we are prohibited from doing Y we are required, under threat of penalty, to omit doing Y. The goal of this work then is to trace the contours of the zone in which the citizen has a moral claim to be at liberty, that is, free of legal coercion. . . .

While it is easy to overemphasize the value of liberty, there is no denying its necessity, and for that reason most writers on our subject have endorsed a kind of "presumption in favor of liberty" requiring that whenever a legislator is faced with a choice between imposing a legal duty on citizens or leaving them at liberty, other things being equal, we should leave individuals free to make their own choices. Liberty should be the norm; coercion always needs some special justification. That "presumption" together with its justifying reasons we can call the "presumptive case for liberty." We shall not pause long to try to make the case here. . . . Suffice it to say that the person deprived of a liberty will think of its absence as a genuine personal loss, and when we put ourselves in his shoes we naturally share his assessment. Moreover, loss of liberty both in individuals and societies entails loss of flexibility and greater vulnerability to unforeseen contingencies. Finally, free citizens are likelier to be highly capable and creative persons through the constant exercise of their capacities to choose, make decisions, and assume responsibilities. Perhaps these simple truisms, by no means the whole of the case for liberty, are nevertheless sufficient to establish some presumption in liberty's favor, and transfer the burden of argument to the shoulders of the advocate of coercion who must, in particular instances, show that the standing case for liberty can be overridden by even weightier reasons on the other side of the scales.

Thus, still another way of posing this work's basic question suggests itself: what kinds of reasons can have weight when balanced against the presumptive case for liberty? Answers to this question take the form of what I shall call "liberty-limiting principles" (or equivalently, "coercion-legitimizing principles"). A liberty-limiting principle is one which states that a given type of consideration is always a morally relevant reason in support of penal legislation even if other reasons may in the circumstances outweigh it. So conceived, the diverse liberty-limiting principles proposed by various philosophers, while distinct and separate, are nonetheless not rivals. More than one, and even all of them, could be true. As formulated here they do not contradict one another. . . .

Commonly Proposed Liberty-Limiting Principles

About the propriety of one class of crimes there can be no controversy. Willful homicide, forcible rape, aggravated assault, and battery are crimes (under one name or another) everywhere in the civilized world, and no reasonable person could advocate their "decriminalization." Almost as noncontroversial as these serious "crimes against the person" are various serious "crimes against property": burglary, grand larceny, and various offenses involving fraud and misrepresentation. The common element in crimes in these two categories is the direct production of serious harm to individual persons and groups. Other kinds of properly prohibited behavior, like reckless driving and the reckless discharging of lethal weapons, are banned not because they necessarily cause harm in every case, but rather because they create unreasonable risks of harm to other persons.

Still other crimes that have an unquestioned place in our penal codes are kinds of conduct that rarely cause clear and substantial harm to any specific person or group, but are said to cause harm to "the public," "society," "the state," public institutions or practices, the general ambience of neighborhoods, the economy, the climate, or the environment. Typical of crimes in this general category are counterfeiting, smuggling, income tax evasion, contempt of court, and violation of zoning and antipollution ordinances. The harms produced by such crimes can be labeled "public" as opposed to "private" harms provided it is kept in mind that the public is composed of private individuals standing in complex social and legal relations to one another. In some cases of public harm—for example the poisoning of a city's water supply or the undermining of a government's currency—the harm to many or all private citizens is direct and serious. In other cases—for example, a single instance of tax evasion—the harm to any given individual is highly dilute and unnoticeable. Crimes of the latter sort do have a tendency, of course, to weaken public institutions in whose health we all have a stake, and if they were allowed to become general, the institutions in question would be undermined to our great collective loss.

Generalizing then from the clearest cases of legitimate or proper criminalization, we can assert tentatively that it is legitimate for the state to prohibit conduct that causes serious private harm, or the unreasonable risk of such harm, or harm to important public institutions and practices. In short, state interference with a citizen's behavior tends to be morally justified when it is reasonably necessary (that is, when there are reasonable grounds for taking it to be necessary as well as effective) to prevent harm or the unreasonable risk of harm to parties other than the person interfered with. More concisely, the need to prevent harm (private or public) to parties other than the actor is always an appropriate *reason* for legal coercion. This principle which we have tentatively extracted from the clearest cases of legitimate interference, can be called "the harm to others principle" or "the harm principle" for short, and recommended to legislatures as part of a moral guide to the limits of their proper activity. John Stuart Mill argued in effect that the harm principle is the *only* valid principle for determining legitimate invasions of liberty, so that no conduct that fails to satisfy its terms can properly be made criminal. We would be better advised, however, to begin in a cautious way with the claim that the harm principle is *a* valid legislative principle (though not necessarily the *only* one), and then, applying it hypothetically to the difficult and controversial areas case by case, try to determine to what extent, if any, it must be modified or supplemented to achieve moral adequacy.

The harm principle then is a useful starting place for our inquiry, but it could hardly be advanced, at this stage in the argument, as our final conclusion without begging some of the most controversial questions of public policy. Moreover, in its present form, the principle is too vague to be of any potential use at all. Clearly not every kind of act that causes harm to others can rightly be prohibited, but only those that cause avoidable and substantial harm. Since the effect of legal coercion may itself be harmful to the interests of the actor it restrains, one would think that only the prevention of still more serious harms to others could justify its infliction. So the harm principle must be made sufficiently precise to permit the formulation of a criterion of "seriousness," and also, if possible, some way of grading types of harms in terms of their seriousness. Without these further specifications, the harm principle may be taken to invite state interference without limit, for virtually every kind of human conduct can affect the interests of others for better and worse to *some* degree, and thus would properly be the state's business.

So far, despite such misgivings, we have endorsed the view that considerations of harm prevention are always relevant reasons in support of coercion. The more radical view of Mill's that such considerations are the only relevant reasons cannot be evaluated until the classes of reasons put forth by other candidate principles have been examined. Most writers would accept at least some additional kinds of reasons as equally legitimate. Three others, in particular, have won widespread support. It has been held (but not always by the same person) that it is always a good and relevant reason in support of penal legislation that: (1) it is reasonably necessary to prevent hurt or offense (as opposed to injury or harm) to others (the *offense principle*); (2) it is reasonably necessary to prevent harm to the very person it prohibits from acting, as opposed to "others" (*legal paternalism*); (3) it is reasonably necessary to prevent inherently immoral conduct whether or not such conduct is harmful or offensive to anyone (*legal moralism*). An especially interesting position, and one which deserves separate discussion, is that formed by the intersection of moralism and paternalism which holds that a good reason for restricting a person's liberty is that it is reasonably necessary to prevent moral (as opposed to physical or economic) harm to that person himself. This view, which provides one of the leading rationales for the prohibition of pornography, can be labeled *moralist paternalism.*

The liberty-limiting principles listed above, since they do not purport to specify necessary conditions for legitimate state coercion, are not mutually exclusive. It is logically open to us to hold only one of them, rejecting all the others (as Mill did), or to hold two or more of them at once, even all of them together, and it is possible to deny all of them (as an anarchist might). Our strategy here will be to begin by accepting the harm principle and then examine controversial classes of crimes not legitimized by that principle, to determine whether the harm principle requires supplementation by one or more of the others.

The alternative principles suggest an orderly classification of the various categories of criminal statutes that are the objects of current controversy. The *offense principle,* for example, could provide reasons for creating such "morals offenses" as open lewdness, solicitation, and indecent exposure and for criminalizing the distribution or sale of pornography, activities and materials offensive to religious or patriotic sensibilities, and racial and ethnic slurs. *Legal paternalism* would provide support for criminal prohibition of self-mutilation, suicide, euthanasia, drunkenness, possession and use of psychoactive drugs, and various forms of gambling, as well as requirements, enforced by criminal sanctions, that hunters wear red caps and motorcyclists wear crash helmets, that motorists use seat belts, that doctors' prescriptions be required for the purchase of various medicines, and so on. *Legal moralism* provides grounding for statutes prohibiting deviant sexual activities—homosexual or extramarital sexual intercourse and "perversions" especially shocking to the legislators, even when performed in private by consenting adults—adultery, bigamy, prostitution even when discreetly arranged, and live sex shows or bloody gladiatorial contests presented by voluntary performers before consenting audiences.

NOTES AND QUESTIONS

1. Why does Feinberg frame his question "as one posed for an ideal legislature in a *democratic* country?" Why does it matter if the system is a democratic one? Is it harder or easier to justify principled limits on what may be prohibited by criminal legislation if the law-making body is democratically selected?

2. Is Feinberg's question a question of political morality or a question of simple rationality? Is the basic duty that limits a democratic legislature a duty to enact criminal legislation for *some reason?* Is that the basis of a correlative right of each citizen to have his behavior regulated only by those coercive laws that have some reason behind them?

3. What is the role of liberty in this? Is the "presumption of liberty" a rational presumption or a moral one? If it is moral, then one would be saying that it is a good that individuals not be coerced, no matter the moral status of the behavior they are coerced out of. Why is it good to not be coerced out of murder, rape, mayhem, theft? Is there any value in being "at liberty" to do immoral actions?

4. Like many others, Feinberg notes that "virtually every kind of human conduct can affect the interests of others for better or worse to *some* degree, and thus would properly be the state's business" under Mill's harm principle. How does Feinberg prevent such a collapse of Mill's principle? As an alternative answer, distinguish the *effects* of action from the *motives* of those who would prohibit it: if all behavior has effects on others, need those effects be the motive of legislators prohibiting such behaviors? If not, which is the harm principle concerned with? Does it matter to the answer of this question who is applying the harm principle, a legislator or a court reviewing that legislator's work?

2.3.2 The "Soft Harm" of Psychic or Moral Offense as a Justification of Criminal Legislation

Offense to Others

JOEL FEINBERG

There is a limit to the power of abstract reasoning to settle questions of moral legitimacy. The question raised by this chapter is whether there are any human experiences that are harmless in themselves yet so unpleasant that we can rightly demand legal protection from them even at the cost of other persons' liberties. The best way to deal with that question at the start is to engage our imaginations in the inquiry, consider hypothetically the most offensive experiences we can imagine, and then sort them into groups in an effort to isolate the kernel of the offense in each category. Accordingly, this section will consist of a number of vividly sketched imaginary tales, and the reader is asked to project himself into each story and determine as best he can what his reaction would be. In each story the reader should think of himself as a passenger on a normally crowded public bus on his way to work or to some important appointment in circumstances such that if he is forced to leave the bus prematurely, he will not only have to pay another fare to get where he is going, but he will probably be late, to his own disadvantage. If he is not exactly a captive on the bus, then, he would nevertheless be greatly inconvenienced if he had to leave the bus before it reached his destination. In each story, another passenger, or group of passengers, gets on the bus, and proceeds to cause, by their characteristics or their conduct, great offense to *you*. The stories form six clusters corresponding to the kind of offense caused.

Affronts to the Senses

> Story 1. A passenger who obviously hasn't bathed in more than a month sits down next to you. He reeks of a barely tolerable stench. There is hardly room to stand elsewhere on the bus and all other seats are occupied.
> Story 2. A passenger wearing a shirt of violently clashing orange and crimson sits down directly in your forward line of vision. You must keep your eyes down to avoid looking at him.
> Story 3. A passenger sits down next to you, pulls a slate tablet from his brief case, and proceeds to scratch his fingernails loudly across the slate, sending a chill up your spine and making your teeth clench. You politely ask him to stop, but he refuses.
> Story 4. A passenger elsewhere in the bus turns on a portable radio to maximum volume. The sounds it emits are mostly screeches, whistles, and static, but occasionally some electronically amplified rock and roll music blares through.

From *Offense to Others* (New York: Oxford University Press, 1985), pp. 10–22.

Disgust and Revulsion

Story 5. This is much like story 1 except that the malodorous passenger in the neighboring seat continually scratches, drools, coughs, farts, and belches.

Story 6. A group of passengers enters the bus and shares a seating compartment with you. They spread a table cloth over their laps and proceed to eat a picnic lunch that consists of live insects, fish heads, and pickled sex organs of lamb, veal, and pork, smothered in garlic and onions. Their table manners leave almost everything to be desired.

Story 7. Things get worse and worse. The itinerant picnickers practice gluttony in the ancient Roman manner, gorging until satiation and then vomiting onto their table cloth. Their practice, however, is a novel departure from the ancient custom in that they eat their own and one another's vomit along with the remaining food.

Story 8. A coprophagic sequel to story 7.

Story 9. At some point during the trip the passenger at one's side quite openly and nonchalantly changes her sanitary napkin and drops the old one into the aisle.

Shock to Moral, Religious, or Patriotic Sensibilities

Story 10. A group of mourners carrying a coffin enter the bus and share a seating compartment with you. Although they are all dressed in black, their demeanor is by no means funeral. In fact, they seem more angry than sorrowful, and refer to the deceased as "the old bastard" and "the bloody corpse." At one point they rip open the coffin with hammers and proceed to smash the corpse's face with a series of hard hammer blows.

Story 11. A strapping youth enters the bus and takes a seat directly in your line of vision. He is wearing a T-shirt with a cartoon across his chest of Christ on the cross. Underneath the picture appear the words "Hang in there, baby!"

Story 12. After taking the seat next to you a passenger produces a bundle wrapped in a large American flag. The bundle contains, among other things, his lunch, which he proceeds to eat. Then he spits into the star-spangled corner of the flag and uses it first to clean his mouth and then to blow his nose. Then he uses the main striped part of the flag to shine his shoes.

Shame, Embarrassment (Including Vicarious Embarrassment) and Anxiety

Story 13. The passenger who takes the seat directly across from you is entirely naked. On one version of the story, he or she is the same sex as you; on the other version of the story, he or she is the opposite sex.

Story 14. The passenger in the previous story proceeds to masturbate quietly in his or her seat.

Story 15. A man and woman, more or less fully clothed to start, take two seats directly in front of you, and then begin to kiss, hug, pet, and fondle one another to the accompaniment of loud sighs and groans of pleasure. They continue these activities throughout the trip.

Story 16. The couple of the previous story, shortly before the bus reaches their destination, engage in acts of mutual masturbation, with quite audible instructions to each other and other sound effects.

Story 17. A variant of the previous story which climaxes in an act of coitus, somewhat acrobatically performed as required by the crowded circumstances.

Story 18. The seat directly in front of you is occupied by a youth (of either sex) wearing a T-shirt with a lurid picture of a copulating couple across his or her chest.

Story 19. A variant of the previous story in which the couple depicted is recognizable (in virtue of conventional representations) as Jesus and Mary.

Story 20. The couple in stories 15–17 perform a variety of sadomasochistic sex acts with appropriate verbal communications ("Oh, that hurts so sweet! Hit me again! Scratch me! Publicly humiliate me!")

Story 21. The two seats in front of you are occupied by male homosexuals. They flirt and tease at first, then kiss and hug, and finally perform mutual fellatio to climax.

Story 22. This time the homosexuals are both female and they perform cunnilingus.

Story 23. A passenger with a dog takes an aisle seat at your side. He or she keeps the dog calm at first by petting it in a familiar and normal way, but then petting gives way to hugging, and gradually goes beyond the merely affectionate to the unmistakably erotic, culminating finally with oral contact with the canine genitals.

Annoyance, Boredom, Frustration

Story 24. A neighboring passenger keeps a portable radio at a reasonably low volume, and the sounds it emits are by no means offensive to the senses. Nor is the content of the program offensive to the sensibilities. It is, however, a low-quality "talk show" which you find intensely boring, and there is no possible way for you to disengage your attention.

Story 25. The two seats to your left are occupied by two persons who put on a boring "talk show" of their own. There is no way you can avoid hearing every animated word of their inane conversation, no way your mind can roam to its own thoughts, problems, and reveries.

Story 26. The passenger at your side is a friendly bloke, garrulous and officious. You quickly tire of his conversation and beg leave to read your newspaper, but he persists in his chatter despite repeated requests to desist. The bus is crowded and there are no other empty seats.

Fear, Resentment, Humiliation, Anger (from Empty Threats, Insults, Mockery, Flaunting, or Taunting)

> Story 27. A passenger seated next to you reaches into a military kit and pulls out a "hand grenade" (actually only a realistic toy), and fondles and juggles it throughout the trip to the accompaniment of menacing leers and snorts. Then he pulls out a (rubber) knife and "stabs" himself and others repeatedly to peals of maniacal laughter. He turns out to be harmless enough. His whole intent was to put others in apprehension of harm.
>
> Story 28. A passenger sits next to you wearing a black arm band with a large white swastika on it.
>
> Story 29. A passenger enters the bus straight from a dispersed street rally. He carries a banner with a large and abusive caricature of the pope and an anti-Catholic slogan. (You are a loyal and pious Catholic.)
>
> Story 30. Variants of the above. The banner displays a picture of a black according to some standard offensive stereotype (Step 'n Fetchit, Uncle Tom, etc.) with an insulting caption; or a picture of a sneering, sniveling, hook-nosed Fagin or Shylock, with a scurrilous anti-Jewish caption; or a similar offensive denunciation or lampooning of groups called "Spicks," "Dagos," "Polacks," etc.
>
> Story 31. Still another variant. A counter-demonstrator leaves a feminist rally to enter the bus. He carries a banner with an offensive caricature of a female and the message, in large red letters: "Keep the bitches barefoot and pregnant."

I have tried to make a number of different points by telling these bloodcurdling tales: that there are at least six distinguishable classes of offended states that can be caused by the blamable conduct of others; that to suffer such experiences, at least in their extreme forms, is an evil; but that to the normal person (like the reader) such experiences, unpleasant as they are, do not cause or constitute harm. It is very important that the reader put himself on the bus and imagine his own reactions, for no amount of abstract argument can convince him otherwise that the represented experiences are in principle of a kind that the state can legitimately make its business to prevent. . . .

It should be clear . . . that despite the miscellaneous character of "offended states" they have some important characteristics in common. They are at the very least unpleasant to the one who suffers them, though the mode of displeasure varies from case to case. With the exception of irritations to the senses, and only some of these, they are complex states whose unpleasantness is in part a function of the tension between conflicting elements. And, most importantly from the legislative point of view, they are nuisances, making it difficult for one to enjoy one's work or leisure in a locality which one cannot reasonably be expected to leave in the circumstances. In extreme cases, the offending conduct commandeers one's attention from the outside, forcing one to relinquish control of one's inner state, and drop what one was doing in order to cope, when it is greatly inconvenient to do so.

NOTES AND QUESTIONS

1. Why does Feinberg invite you to take a ride on his bus? Do you agree with Feinberg that "no amount of abstract argument can convince [one] that the represented experiences are in principle of a kind that the state can legitimately make its business to prevent"? Do these stories differ in their epistemic roles from the thought experiments we encountered in the theory of punishment? What would Dolinko, for example, think of this form of "argument" by Feinberg?

2. Might someone who is not on the bus be as offended as those who are? Suppose the passengers on the bus are all doing one or more of the activities Feinberg describes; the rest of us outside the bus only know what is going on inside. Could our offense, disgust, or distress justify state intervention? Why does the ease of avoidance of the distressed person matter to Feinberg? What about true busybodies with uncontrollably vivid imaginations—can they avoid being distressed by what is going on in the bus even if they are not on it?

3. Feinberg recognizes that our sensibilities can change over time. Should the offense principle take people's sensibilities as they are or as they ought to be? If the latter, by what standard do we judge whether something ought to offend or disgust people? Consider a well publicized bit of behavior by Jane Fonda with her first husband, Roger Vadim: because they believed that people should not be embarrassed at bodily functions, they installed a glass-walled bathroom. Were Roger and Jane right about our scatological taboos? Is it the sort of thing about which they could be right?

4. Should the offense principle distinguish between what Feinberg calls "lower order sensibilities" and "moral, religious and patriotic sensibilities?" How is *that* discrimination to be justified? In terms of sheer amount of disgust, cannot one be as disgusted at another's eating of a wriggling sea slug as at another's oral copulating with a dog?

5. By the general notion of liberty Feinberg articulated in the earlier selection, each of the actors on the bus would seem to be "at liberty" to do what they do. Is there some other, stronger sense of liberty that gives some of these actors more of a right to do what they do? Why, for example, might it matter if the behavior in question itself has cognitive content? Why might it matter if the behavior in question relates to self-definition or other important interests? Why might it matter if the behavior in question could not, as it happens, be performed in private?

6. Do you think that criminal laws prohibiting public heterosexual intercourse, indecent exposure, abuse of a corpse, and pornographic films are justified? If so, are they necessarily justified by an offense principle, or can some other principle be used to justify them?

7. If offense is ever a reason to criminalize behavior, how does one limit such a principle? As long as enough people are offended enough, could not any behavior be criminalized?

2.3.3   The Paternalistic Concern about Harm to the Actors Whose Behavior Is Prohibited

Paternalism

GERALD DWORKIN

Neither one person, nor any number of persons, is warranted in saying to another human creature of ripe years, that he shall not do with his life for his own benefit what he chooses to do with it.

—Mill

I do not want to go along with a volunteer basis. I think a fellow should be compelled to become better and not let him use his discretion whether he wants to get smarter, more healthy or more honest.

—General Hershey

I take as my starting point the "one very simple principle" proclaimed by Mill in *On Liberty* . . . "That principle is, that the sole end for which mankind are warranted, individually or collectively, in interfering with the liberty of action of any of their number, is self-protection. That the only purpose for which power can be rightfully exercised over any member of a civilized community, against his will, is to prevent harm to others. He cannot rightfully be compelled to do or forbear because it will be better for him to do so, because it will make him happier, because, in the opinion of others, to do so would be wise, or even right."

   This principle is neither "one" nor "very simple." It is at least two principles; one asserting that self-protection or the prevention of harm to others is sometimes a sufficient warrant and the other claiming that the individual's own good is *never* a sufficient warrant for the exercise of compulsion either by the society as a whole or by its individual members. I assume that no one, with the possible exception of extreme pacifists or anarchists, questions the correctness of the first half of the principle. This essay is an examination of the negative claim embodied in Mill's principle—the objection to paternalistic interferences with a man's liberty.

By paternalism I shall understand roughly the interference with a person's liberty of action justified by reasons referring exclusively to the welfare, good, happiness, needs, interests or values of the person being coerced. One is always well-advised to illustrate one's definitions by examples, but it is not easy to find "pure" examples of paternalistic interferences. For almost any piece of legislation is justified by several

From "Paternalism," in Richard Wasserstrom, ed., *Morality and the Law* (Belmont, Calif.: Wadsworth, 1971), pp. 107–08, 113–19.

different kinds of reasons and even if historically a piece of legislation can be shown to have been introduced for purely paternalistic motives, it may be that advocates of the legislation with an anti-paternalistic outlook can find sufficient reasons justifying the legislation without appealing to the reasons which were originally adduced to support it. Thus, for example, it may be that the original legislation requiring motorcyclists to wear safety helmets was introduced for purely paternalistic reasons. But the Rhode Island Supreme Court recently upheld such legislation on the grounds that it was "not persuaded that the legislature is powerless to prohibit individuals from pursuing a course of conduct which could conceivably result in their becoming public charges," thus clearly introducing reasons of a quite different kind. . . .

. . .

I shall begin for dialectical purposes by discussing Mill's objections to paternalism and then go on to discuss more positive proposals.

An initial feature that strikes one is the absolute nature of Mill's prohibitions against paternalism. It is so unlike the carefully qualified admonitions of Mill and his fellow Utilitarians on other moral issues. He speaks of self-protection as the *sole* end warranting coercion, of the individual's own goals as never being a sufficient warrant. Contrast this with his discussion of the prohibition against lying in *Utilitarianism:*

> Yet that even this rule, sacred as it is, admits of possible exception, is acknowledged by all moralists, the chief of which is where the with-holding of some fact . . . would save an individual . . . from great and unmerited evil.

The same tentativeness is present when he deals with justice:

> It is confessedly unjust to break faith with any one: to violate an engagement, either express or implied, or disappoint expectations raised by our own conduct, at least if we have raised these expectations knowingly and voluntarily. Like all the other obligations of justice already spoken of, this one is not regarded as absolute, but as capable of being overruled by a stronger obligation of justice on the other side.

This anomaly calls for some explanation. The structure of Mill's argument is as follows:

1. Since restraint is an evil the burden of proof is on those who propose such restraint.
2. Since the conduct which is being considered is purely self-regarding, the normal appeal to the protection of the interests of others is not available.
3. Therefore we have to consider whether reasons involving reference to the individual's own good, happiness, welfare, or interests are sufficient to overcome the burden of justification.
4. We either cannot advance the interests of the individual by compulsion, or the attempt to do so involves evils which outweigh the good done.
5. Hence the promotion of the individual's own interests does not provide a sufficient warrant for the use of compulsion.

Clearly the operative premise here is (4), and it is bolstered by claims about the status of the individual as judge and appraiser of his welfare, interests, needs, etc.:

> With respect to his own feelings and circumstances, the most ordinary man or woman has means of knowledge immeasurably surpassing those that can be possessed by any one else.

He is the man most interested in his own well-being: the interest which any other person, except in cases of strong personal attachment, can have in it is trifling, compared to that which he himself has.

These claims are used to support the following generalizations concerning the utility of compulsion for paternalistic purposes.

The interferences of society to overrule his judgment and purposes in what only regards himself must be grounded on general presumptions; which may be altogether wrong, and even if right, are as likely as not to be misapplied to individual cases.

But the strongest of all the arguments against the interference of the public with purely personal conduct is that when it does interfere, the odds are that it interferes wrongly and in the wrong place.

All errors which the individual is likely to commit against advice and warning are far outweighed by the evil of allowing others to constrain him to what they deem his good.

Performing the utilitarian calculation by balancing the advantages and disadvantages we find that: "Mankind are greater gainers by suffering each other to live as seems good to themselves, than by compelling each other to live as seems good to the rest." Ergo, (4).

This classical case of a utilitarian argument with all the premises spelled out is not the only line of reasoning present in Mill's discussion. There are asides, and more than asides, which look quite different and I shall deal with them later. But this is clearly the main channel of Mill's thought and it is one which has been subjected to vigorous attack from the moment it appeared—most often by fellow Utilitarians. The link that they have usually seized on is, as Fitzjames Stephen put it in *Liberty, Equality, Fraternity,* the absence of proof that the "mass of adults are so well acquainted with their own interests and so much disposed to pursue them that no compulsion or restraint put upon them by any others for the purpose of promoting their interest can really promote them." Even so sympathetic a critic as H. L. A. Hart is forced to the conclusion that:

In Chapter 5 of his essay [*On Liberty*] Mill carried his protests against paternalism to lengths that may now appear to us as fantastic . . . No doubt if we no longer sympathise with this criticism this is due, in part, to a general decline in the belief that individuals know their own interest best.

Mill endows the average individual with "too much of the psychology of a middle-aged man whose desires are relatively fixed, not liable to be artificially stimulated by external influences; who knows what he wants and what gives him satisfaction or happiness; and who pursues these things when he can."

Now it is interesting to note that Mill himself was aware of some of the limitations on the doctrine that the individual is the best judge of his own interests. In his discussion of government intervention in general (even where the intervention does not interfere with liberty but provides alternative institutions to those of the market) after making claims which are parallel to those just discussed—e.g., "People understand their own business and their own interests better, and care for them more, than the government does, or can be expected to do." He goes on to an intelligent discussion of the "very large and conspicuous exceptions" to the maxim that:

Most persons take a juster and more intelligent view of their own interest, and of the means of promoting it than can either be prescribed to them by a general enactment of the legislature, or pointed out in the particular case by a public functionary.

Thus there are things

of which the utility does not consist in ministering to inclinations, nor in serving the daily uses of life, and the want of which is least felt where the need is greatest. This is peculiarly true of those things which are chiefly useful as tending to raise the character of human beings. The uncultivated cannot be competent judges of cultivation. Those who most need to be made wiser and better, usually desire it least, and, if they desired it, would be incapable of finding the way to it by their own lights.

. . . A second exception to the doctrine that individuals are the best judges of their own interest, is when an individual attempts to decide irrevocably now what will be best for his interest at some future and distant time. The presumption in favor of individual judgment is only legitimate, where the judgment is grounded on actual, and especially on present, personal experience; not where it is formed antecedently to experience, and not suffered to be reversed even after experience has condemned it.

The upshot of these exceptions is that Mill does not declare that there should never be government interference with the economy but rather that

. . . in every instance, the burden of making out a strong case should be thrown not on those who resist but on those who recommend government interference. Letting alone, in short, should be the general practice: every departure from it, unless required by some great good, is a certain evil.

In short, we get a presumption, not an absolute prohibition. The question is why doesn't the argument against paternalism go the same way?

I suggest that the answer lies in seeing that in addition to a purely utilitarian argument Mill uses another as well. As a Utilitarian, Mill has to show, in Fitzjames Stephen's words, that: "Self-protection apart, no good object can be attained by any compulsion which is not in itself a greater evil than the absence of the object which the compulsion obtains." To show this is impossible; one reason being that it isn't true. Preventing a man from selling himself into slavery (a paternalistic measure which Mill himself accepts as legitimate), or from taking heroin, or from driving a car without wearing seat-belts may constitute a lesser evil than allowing him to do any of these things. A consistent Utilitarian can only argue against paternalism on the grounds that it (as a matter of fact) does not maximize the good. It is always a contingent question that may be refuted by the evidence. But there is also a noncontingent argument which runs through *On Liberty*. When Mill states that "there is a part of the life of every person who has come to years of discretion, within which the individuality of that person ought to reign uncontrolled either by any other person or by the public collectively," he is saying something about what it means to be a person, an autonomous agent. It is because coercing a person for his own good denies this status as an independent entity that Mill objects to it so strongly and in such absolute terms. To be able to choose is a good that is independent of the wisdom of what is chosen. A man's "mode of laying out his existence is the best, not because it is the best in itself, but because it is his own mode." It is the privilege and proper condition of a human being, arrived at the maturity of his faculties, to use and interpret experience in his own way.

As further evidence of this line of reasoning in Mill, consider the one exception to his prohibition against paternalism.

> In this and most civilised countries, for example, an engagement by which a person should sell himself, or allow himself to be sold, as a slave, would be null and void; neither enforced by law nor by opinion. The ground for thus limiting his power of voluntarily disposing of his own lot in life, is apparent, and is very clearly seen in this extreme case. The reason for not interfering, unless for the sake of others, with a person's voluntary acts, is consideration for his liberty. His voluntary choice is evidence that what he so chooses is desirable, or at least endurable, to him, and his good is on the whole best provided for by allowing him to take his own means of pursuing it. But by selling himself for a slave, he abdicates his liberty; he foregoes any future use of it beyond that single act. He therefore defeats, in his own case, the very purpose which is the justification of allowing him to dispose of himself. He is no longer free; but is thenceforth in a position which has no longer the presumption in its favour, that would be afforded by his voluntarily remaining in it. The principle of freedom cannot require that he should be free not to be free. It is not freedom to be allowed to alienate his freedom.

Now leaving aside the fudging on the meaning of freedom in the last line, it is clear that part of this argument is incorrect. While it is true that *future* choices of the slave are not reasons for thinking that what he chooses then is desirable for him, what is at issue is limiting his immediate choice; and since this choice is made freely, the individual may be correct in thinking that his interests are best provided for by entering such a contract. But the main consideration for not allowing such a contract is the need to preserve the liberty of the person to make future choices. This gives us a principle—a very narrow one—by which to justify some paternalistic interferences. Paternalism is justified only to preserve a wider range of freedom for the individual in question. How far this principle could be extended, whether it can justify all the cases in which we are inclined upon reflection to think paternalistic measures justified, remains to be discussed. What I have tried to show so far is that there are two strains of argument in Mill—one a straightforward Utilitarian mode of reasoning and one which relies not on the goods which free choice leads to but on the absolute value of the choice itself. The first cannot establish any absolute prohibition but at most a presumption and indeed a fairly weak one, given some fairly plausible assumptions about human psychology; the second, while a stronger line of argument, seems to me to allow on its own grounds a wider range of paternalism than might be suspected. I turn now to a consideration of these matters.

We might begin looking for principles governing the acceptable use of paternalistic power in cases where it is generally agreed that it is legitimate. Even Mill intends his principles to be applicable only to mature individuals, not those in what he calls "non-age." What is it that justifies us in interfering with children? The fact that they lack some of the emotional and cognitive capacities required in order to make fully rational decisions. It is an empirical question to just what extent children have an adequate conception of their own present and future interests but there is not much doubt that there are many deficiencies. For example, it is very difficult for a child to defer gratification for any considerable period of time. Given these deficiencies and given the very real and permanent dangers that may befall the child it becomes not only permissible but even a duty of the parent to restrict the child's freedom in various way. There is however an important moral limitation on the exercise of such parental power which is provided by the notion of the child eventually coming to see the correctness of his parent's interventions. Parental paternalism may be thought of as a wager by the parent on the child's subsequent recognition of the wisdom of the restrictions. There is an emphasis on what could be called future-oriented consent—on what the child will come to welcome, rather than on what he does welcome.

The essence of this idea has been incorporated by idealist philosophers into various types of "real-will" theory as applied to fully adult persons. Extensions of paternalism are argued for by claiming that in various respects, chronologically mature individuals share the same deficiencies in knowledge, capacity to think rationally, and the ability to carry out decisions that children possess. Hence in interfering with such people we are in effect doing what they would do if they were fully rational. Hence we are not really opposing their will, hence we are not really interfering with their freedom.

NOTES AND QUESTIONS

1. When characterizing a proposed piece of criminal legislation as paternalistic or not, are we looking to the effects of the passage of the legislation that might *justify* it, or are we looking only to those of its predicted effects that *motivated* the lawmakers? Which does Dworkin care about? Consider his example of the Rhode Island statute prohibiting the riding of motorcycles without a helmet: if the legislature was motivated to criminalize such behavior because of the harms to helmetless riders, but it also turns out that most injured helmetless riders are underinsured so that their injuries impose economic costs on others besides themselves, should we still consider the statute paternalistic in character?

2. What is the difference between a paternalistic and a utilitarian justification for criminal legislation? If the paternalistic principle criminalizes behaviors only when the discounted value of the harm to the actor is greater than the pleasure or other benefit of doing the activity to the actor, is there any difference? Should a utilitarian calculate the punishment costs, that is, the amount of unhappiness caused by those punishments necessary to induce the desired behavior in others? Should the paternalist?

3. Why might a thoroughgoing utilitarian reject the paternalistic principle? How does such a utilitarian rejection compare with Mill's more absolute rejection of the

paternalistic principle? Could a utilitarian agree with Mill's argument that interfering with a person's liberty in the interests of the good of the individual whose behavior is being regulated is *never* an acceptable reason for criminal regulation? Dworkin construes Mill to be constraining utilitarianism with a separate value of autonomy. Could a utilitarian agree that autonomy is not a side constraint on calculations of utility but rather a presupposition of people having preferences worth summing in a utilitarian calculus?

4. What animates the paternalistic principle? Why should we expend state resources to prevent behavior that harms only the actor? Is there some notion of distributive justice according to which the state should act like a concerned friend?

5. In his article, Dworkin frames his own limited acceptance of paternalistic legislation in terms of the hypothetical consent of the actor. Why should such purely hypothetical consent matter when there is not only an absence of consent but actually a protest to interference? In forcible rape, where the woman not only does not consent but protests, should it matter if it could be shown that she would have consented had she been asked nicely?

6. Apparently hypothetical consent matters to Dworkin in the context of justifying legislation because the situations in which it does work are precisely situations when the actor is in some sense absent, so that both his protests and the lack of any real consent aren't to be taken seriously. "It isn't really him that is protesting or failing to consent," we might say. Assess how true this is of young children, the insane, the person who refuses to wear seat belts, the smoker, the person who believes he will float upward if he jumps out of a window, the duelist, the suicide.

7. To the extent that there are cases in which the actor is in some sense absent, where is he? Less metaphorically, what theory of the self must you or Dworkin have to say of that self that it is absent in some or all of the foregoing cases? What qualities have to be present before that self is all here?

8. Dworkin has later characterized his hypothetical consent paternalism as "soft paternalism." "Hard paternalism" is state interference even when the (fully present) actor would not consent. Do you agree with Dworkin that even certain instances of hard paternalism can be justified? Which ones—seat belts, motorcycle helmets, life preservers, slavery contracts?

2.3.4   Using the Criminal Law to Punish or Prevent Moral Wrongdoing

Harmless Wrongdoing

JOEL FEINBERG

In restricting the list of valid liberty-limiting principles to the harm and offense principles, liberalism, as we have seen, denies that the need to protect a free, informed, and competent actor from the harmful consequences of his own voluntary conduct is ever a good reason for restricting his liberty. That is to say that "liberalism," as I am using the term, rejects the legitimizing principle called "legal paternalism." But the liberal view also denies that the need and opportunity to prevent any class of evils other than harms and offenses can ever be a good reason for criminal prohibitions. An alternative to the liberal view, then, can be put in the following very general way: "It can be morally legitimate for the state, by means of the criminal law, to prohibit certain types of action that cause neither harm nor offense to anyone, on the grounds that such actions constitute or cause evils of other kinds." This straightforward but vague denial of liberalism we can call "legal moralism in the broad sense."

· · ·

. . . What would . . . a case [for legal moralism] look like? Let me suggest that it would take as its general principle that it is always right, other things being equal, to prevent evils; that the need to prevent evils of any description is a good kind of reason in support of a legal prohibition. That appears at first sight to be as plausible a principle as that which makes the need to prevent one particular kind of evil, namely the loss of liberty, a presumptively good reason against legal coercion. If we then add to the legal moralist's case the proposition that there are kinds of evils that are neither harms in themselves nor the causes of harm or offense, his presumptive case is complete, and "the score of the game before it starts" is even, unless or until it can be shown that one of the conflicting presumptive cases is a great deal stronger than the other.

In conceding, however grudgingly, that there is a standing presumptive case for moralistic legislation, the liberal abandons his opposition to legal moralism as we have defined it in these volumes. If legal moralism is the principle that it is always a *relevant reason* of at least minimal cogency in support of penal legislation that it will prevent genuine evils other than harm and offense, *and* if the prevention of evils, any evils at all, is a point in favor of any course of action however preponderant the reasons against it, then it follows logically that legal moralism so defined is correct. Although the word "evil" is vague, it seems plausible to claim that it is better that evils not exist; that their existence is always to be regretted; and that their eradication and prevention are always reasons for action. Even the liberal, then, must acknowledge that legal moralism is, in principle, a valid liberty-limiting principle. What then is left of the liberal position? I think the liberal can salvage almost everything he orig-

From *Harmless Wrongdoing* (New York: Oxford University Press, 1988), pp. 3–6, 17–25, 40–43, 124–33.

inally meant to protect by insisting that while the prevention of evils as such is a reason, nevertheless as reasons go it is not much of one, typically putting only a modest weight on the balancing scales, rarely if ever enough to offset the presumptive case for liberty. The liberal then will have to argue this afresh for each main category of nonharmful evils posited by the moralist, and he must be prepared to admit that some of the moralist's evils may be weightier than others, even though few of them amount to very much as reasons for coercion. Many liberals will deny that there are any genuine evils at all other than harm and offense, but these liberals, if they follow the tack I suggest, will insist that even if there are (or were) such evils, they would have very little weight, as a class, when compared with harms and (even) offenses. In specific cases of proposed legislation then, liberals, despite their grudging concession, can nearly always oppose moralistic statutes.

We can now resume our discussion of the sorts of evils the criminal law might be designed to eliminate or . . . , depending on the liberty-limiting principles legislators might adopt.

Not everyone will agree that all or even most of the items on the following list are genuine evils. I do not even make that claim myself, but I submit (a) that most readers will acknowledge that at least one of them is plausibly held to be an evil in the legislative genus and (b) that it will be very difficult to claim sincerely of any given item so acknowledged to be an evil that it is also a personal harm, offense, or exploitative injustice.

Violations of taboos. It has been said that all known human societies, primitive and advanced, have incest rules. In characterizing these rules as taboos, anthropologists mean that they are absolutely unconditional prohibitions applying without exception, whose violation not only cannot be justified, but cannot be excused either by any of the normal exculpating appeals (mistake, duress, etc.). A taboo is a prohibition whose form "puts the demand for reason out of place"; it is thought to be inviolate and sacrosanct, and such that anyone who feels bound by it will think of it as underived from reasons, in any usual way, but rather something as basic and underivative as the process of giving reasons itself. Not that a given taboo cannot be supported by reasons. An isolated instance of brother-sister incest could lead to genetic abnormalities; isolated instances of parent-child incest would be clear cases of the sexual abuse of children and likely to cause severe emotional damage to the victims; widespread violation of the rules would undermine, for better or worse, traditional social institutions like the nuclear family. But the incest rules do not function simply to prevent injustices or inutilities. They have a powerful grip on us even when such reasons do not apply. After all, contraceptives and sterilization can prevent genetic disasters; intercourse in private can prevent offense and contagious example; and incestuous relations between consenting adults might be exempt from the objection based on child abuse. In the words of Graham Hughes: "It is hard to see what reason there is to declare it a heinous crime for a thirty-five-year-old man and his thirty-year-old sister to decide to go to bed together." One reason why Hughes is right about this (though it is not his reason) is that criminal sanctions are hardly necessary to enforce a genuine taboo; crime statistics do not show a rash of brother-sister incest crimes. But leaving the question of criminal enforcement aside, how many of us can calmly consider, without flinching, the example of a contraceptively protected, privately performed, and genuinely consensual sexual act between a thirty-eight-year-old father and a twenty-year-old daughter, or (even more unthinkable to many) a thirty-eight-year-old mother and a twenty-year-old son? If such discreet and private acts are "evils," it cannot be simply because they harm or offend.

Conventional "immoralities" when discreet and harmless. I have in mind here the usual list of so-called morals offenses when performed in private between consenting adults. They include all extramarital and homosexual intercourse, and perhaps solitary masturbation as well. Not many sophisticated persons will regard all these forms of conduct as "evils," but it is worth pointing out nonetheless that if they are evils they are often harmless and (since unobserved) inoffensive ones. It is more difficult to think of examples under this heading that do not pertain to sexual conduct, but the following contrived one might do. Imagine that a death in a family occasions not the usual public funeral and period of mourning but rather a secret family banquet at which the body of the deceased, hacked into pieces and baked in a garlic and mushroom sauce, is consumed by the survivors, having earlier secured the consent of the deceased while he was still alive. Our prevailing morality would certainly condemn such conduct, even through no interests were harmed or endangered by it, and no sensibilities offended. . . .

If there are acceptable examples of free-floating evils, either from the above list or elsewhere, then legal moralism begins to assume a plausible shape, for an evil is something we are well rid of, and if criminal prohibitions seem both necessary and effective means of eliminating it, that would seem to be a reason, of at least some weight, in favor of them. When that evil is something other than harm of offense . . . then it follows that there is a kind of minimal case for legal moralism. That case is simple, but not obviously simplistic. It is not conceptually muddled, nor defeated in its own formulation. Neither does legal moralism (in its "pure" versions) have to ride on the coattails of one or more of the other liberty-limiting principles. So we must give at least this much of a grudging nod to its credentials. The question now is whether the minimal case for legal moralism, even in principle, is strong enough to give any but minuscule support to proposals for criminalization. How much weight, at a maximum, are non-grievance evils capable of putting on the scales to be weighed against liberty? . . .

Unlike the moral conservative, the strict legal moralist honors morality for its own sake, not simply because of its central place in a group's traditional way of life. The morality he wishes to enforce by law then must be *true morality,* a collection of governing principles thought to be "part of the nature of things," critical, rational, and correct. True morality, so understood, provides the standards and principles by which to judge the actual institutions of any given society, including its *conventional morality*—the rules and principles actually established in that society, for better or worse. That a given rule, standard, or customary practice is part of the established morality of a group is not a good reason for enforcing it by means of the criminal law, on this view, unless it is also a correct rule of morality, capable of satisfying a transcultural critical standard. On the other hand, if the established rule does satisfy such a test, then that is a very good reason, on this view, for enforcing it.

Even the liberal can be a "strict legal moralist," as the latter view has been so far defined, provided he holds that there is and can be *no harmless wrongdoing*. For if all wrongdoing necessarily harms or endangers the interests and violates the rights of others, then there is a perfect coincidence between what is "truly immoral" and what is "harmful" in the liberal's sense. Anthony Woozley, to mention only one distinguished writer, expresses the prefect coincidence view when he boldly maintains that "a question of [true] morality is a question about there being a harm, or risk of harm, or intended harm to somebody which is produced or manifested in conduct of such and such a kind." Since Woozley denies that there can be any (true) immoralities that do not cause or threaten harm, it is no surprise that he further holds that there can be no immoral conduct "from which the law should a priori be excluded," a conclusion that sounds, paradoxically, like that of the strict legal moralist. Clarity would be served, then, if we added to our definition of strict legal moralism the tenet that there *are* harmless immoralities as determined by a "natural" or correct standard. That condition would not be satisfied by Woozley's view, which we can therefore exclude from the scope of the present discussion. On the other hand, I have grudgingly acknowledged that some behavior can involve or produce evils—"free-floating evils"—that are subject to adverse criticism by "correct" standards, even though they harm (wrong) no one in particular (though as a group these evils are much less significant than genuine grievance evils). We can concede this point to the strict moralist, however, while denying his central claim that free-floating moral evils can rightly be prevented by the criminal law.

The strict legal moralist takes free-floating moral evils much more seriously. (Oddly, some of the samples that he characteristically takes *most* seriously, like sexual deviance, do not strike many liberals as intuitively evil at all, much less as "true immoralities.") Typically, the true immoralities, as the strict moralist conceives them, even when private and harmless, are such evident and odious evils that they should be forbidden on the ground of their evil alone. As we have seen, the argument has a perfect simplicity; a single premise yields a single conclusion. Such and such activities are inherently immoral; therefore they should be prohibited even when private and harmless to individuals.

More often than not, strict moralism also deploys a version of the retributive theory of punishment. Not only should the criminal law prevent true immoralities, including the more odious of the free-floating ones, but it is an end in itself that the wrongdoer, even when his wrongdoing is victimless, should suffer the pains of punishment. The full theory of strict moralism, then, has three tenets: (1) true moral evils may rightly be prohibited by the criminal law even when they are free-floating; (2) some of the more serious true moral evils *are* free-floating; (3) it is an end in itself that moral wrongdoers, even when their misdeeds wrong no one, should be punished.

Strict legal moralism as we have defined it comes very close to the description Bertrand Russell gives of what he calls "puritanism"—

> We may define a Puritan as a man who holds that certain kinds of acts, even if they have no visible bad effects upon others than the agent, are inherently sinful, and being sinful, ought to be prevented by whatever means is most effectual—the criminal law if possible . . . This view is of respectable antiquity; indeed it was probably responsible for the origin of criminal law. But originally it was reconciled with a utilitarian basis of legislation by the belief that certain crimes roused the anger of the gods against

communities which tolerated them, and were therefore socially harmful. . . . But nowadays even Puritans seldom adopt this point of view. . . . The laws in question can, therefore, only be justified by the theory of vindictive punishment, which holds that certain sins, though they may not injure anyone except the sinner, are so heinous as to make it our duty to inflict pain upon the delinquent.

The puritanical position on legally enforcing the ban on certain nonharmful immoralities, as Russell describes it, has become a steadily more *pure* kind of strict moralism. In the beginning, harmless immoralities had to be prevented and punished not only because they were true immoralities but also, given the precedent of Sodom and Gomorrah, because they endangered the community. But in more recent times the argument frequently stands unbolstered by further appeals to social harm and danger, and the appeal is to strict moralism through and through.

. . .

The most characteristic argument for the strict moralistic position in its pure form involves the imaginative use of examples. The strict moralist must find actual or hypothetical examples of actions or states of affairs that are not only "evil in the generic sense" but *morally* evil as judged by "natural" objective standards, and perfectly free-floating, that is not evil simply because harmful (in the liberal's sense), offensive, or exploitatively unfair, but *evil in any case*. Then, if the example is such that the liberal, reacting spontaneously, would be embarrassed to have to oppose criminal prohibition, the example has telling probative impact. Indeed, such arguments, while technically ad hominem in form, have as much force as can normally be expected in ethical discourse. This strategy requires that the strict moralist cite some plausible (though admittedly uncharacteristic) free-floating moral evils that are such great evils that the need to prevent them *as such* is likely to be accepted by the reader as a weightier reason than the case for individual liberty on the other side of the scales. All the legal moralist can do at this point is present relevant examples in a vivid and convincing way, pointedly reminding the reader of certain principles of critical morality that he holds in common with the legal moralist and takes equally seriously. The relative "weight" of acknowledged reasons is not otherwise amenable to proof. More exactly, the legal moralist offers *counterexamples* to the liberal thesis that personally harmless transactions between consenting adults in private cannot be evils of sufficient magnitude to justify preventive coercion. . . .

Vicarious sexual pleasures of a "depraved" sort are not the only examples of private enjoyments found repugnant by some legal moralists. Professional boxing matches are another case in point. Here some of the liberals themselves are among the most denunciatory. The *New York Times* published an editorial demanding the abolition of professional boxing altogether shortly after the bloody first Frazier-Ali fight. One of the many indignant letters to the editor that followed denounced the *New York Times,* in turn, on familiar liberal principles.:

> Ali and Frazier fought of their own free choice. Neither of them has complained that he was forced to submit to brutal and dehumanizing treatment. Those who paid money to see the fight did so willingly and most of them thought they got their money's worth. . . . [W]hat was immoral about this fight? No rights were transgressed. Those who disapprove of professional boxing were not forced to watch.

... The parallel to declining civilizations of the past referred to in your editorial is without any basis in fact. The contestants in the cruel sports that were practiced in the dying days of the Roman Empire, for example, were not free men with free choice. ...

The liberal author of that letter is set up for the last of the ingenious moralistic counterexamples to be considered here. Irving Kristol has us consider the possibility of gladiatorial contests in Yankee Stadium before consenting adult audiences, of course, and between well-paid gladiators who are willing to risk life or limb for huge stakes. The example is not far-fetched. We can imagine that, with closed circuit television, the promoter could offer twenty million dollars to the winners and ten million to the estates of the losers. How could we advocate legal prohibition without abandoning the liberal position that only the harm and offense principles can provide reasons of sufficient strength to override the case for liberty? Kristol has no doubts that the liberal is stuck with his huge free-floating evil and can urge prohibition only at the cost of hypocrisy:

> I might also have [used the word] ... "hypocritical." For the plain fact is that none of us is a complete civil libertarian. We all believe that there is some point at which the public authorities ought to step in to limit the "self-expression" of an individual or a group even where this might be seriously intended as a form of artistic expression, and even where the artistic transaction is between consenting adults. A playwright or theatrical director might, in this crazy world of ours, find someone willing to commit suicide on the stage, as called for by the script. We would not allow that—any more than we would permit scenes of real physical torture on the stage, even if the victim were a willing masochist. And I know of no one, no matter how free in spirit, who argues that we ought to permit gladiatorial contests in Yankee Stadium, similar to those once performed in the Colosseum of Rome—even if only consenting adults were involved.

The example of the gladiatorial show, at first sight, satisfies the requirements for argumentative cogency. Almost anyone would concede that the bloody contest would be an evil, and most would be willing to concede (at least at first) that the evil would be in the non-grievance category, since in virtue of the careful observance of the *Volenti* maxim, there would be no aggrieved victim. Moreover, the evil involved, in all of its multiple faces, would be a moral one. It is morally wrong for thousands of observers to experience pleasure at the sight of maiming and killing. It is an obscenely immoral spectacle they voluntarily observe, made even worse by their bloodthirsty screams and vicarious participation. If we reserve the term "immoral," as some have suggested, for *actions,* then the immoralities are compounded and multiplied, for the promoter acts immorally in arranging the contest, advertising it, and selling tickets; each gladiator acts immorally by voluntarily participating; and millions of voluntary spectators share the guilt. If all these individual moral failings can be coherently combined, they add up to a social evil of great magnitude indeed. And yet it seems at first sight that the evil is a non-grievance one, since no one can complain in a personal grievance that he has been wronged.

From liberals who are determined to avoid hypocrisy, Kristol's examples will elicit at least three types of reply. First, Kristol is entirely too complacent about the problem of determining genuine "willingness" and "voluntary consent." The higher the risk of harm involved, the stricter must be the standards, one would think, for voluntariness. When it is a person's very life that is at issue, the standards would have to be at their strictest, especially when the life involved is clearly of great value to its possessor, unlike the life of the would-be suicide suffering from a painful terminal illness. Perhaps, as we have seen, the state would have the right, on liberal principles, to require such things as psychiatric interviews, multiple witnessing, cooling-off periods, and the like, before accepting a proffered consent as fully voluntary. Kristol talks glibly of finding "willing" public suicides in "this crazy world of ours," not noticing that an agreement is hardly consensual if one of the parties is "crazy." To exploit a crazy person in the way he describes is not distinguishable from murder and equally condemned by the harm principle. On the other hand, we must admit that a self-confident and powerful gladiator need not be "crazy" to agree to risk his life before the howling mobs for twenty million dollars. There could be a presumption that such a person doesn't fully understand what he is doing, or is not fully free of neurotic influences on his choice, but these hypotheses are rebuttable in principle, and in some cases that we can easily imagine, with only minor difficulty and expense rebuttable in fact. The liberal's second and third responses (below), then, are the more pertinent ones.

In conceding to the legal moralist that the wholly voluntary contest *is* an "evil" we are not making that judgment primarily because of the injury or death, the utterly "defeated interest," of the losing contestant. That result is an "evil," one might say, because it is regrettable that anyone had to be injured in that way, but so long as we adhere to the doctrine of the absolute priority of personal autonomy that sort of evil is always more than counterbalanced (indeed it is as if cancelled out) by prior consent to the risk. The primary evil relied upon by the legal moralist is not that anyone was harmed (i.e., injured *and* wronged), for no one was, and not that anyone was injured even without being wronged, since that "otherwise evil" is nullified by consent, and there would be an even greater evil, indeed a wrong, if consent were overruled. The fatal maiming of the loser was an "evil" (regrettable state) that he had an absolute right to risk. In reaffirming that right we are making it clear that we are not backtracking on our opposition to paternalism. The acknowledged evil that makes this case a hard one for the liberal is apparently a free-floating one, an evil not directly linked to human interests and sensibilities. That evil consists in the objective regrettability of millions deriving pleasure from brutal bloodshed and others getting rich exploiting their moral weakness. The universe would be an intrinsically better place, the strict legal moralist insists, if that did not occur, even though no one actually was wronged by it, and there is no one to voice a personal grievance at it.

The liberal who is sensitive to the charge of hypocrisy may, in the end, have to reply as follows. Gladiatorial contests and "voluntary" submission to torture are among the most extreme hypothetical examples of non-grievance evils that the legal moralist's imagination can conjure. There seems little likelihood that they will ever occur, as least in the foreseeable future. Yet they seem to be convincing hypothetical examples of very great evils. A liberal might treat them as the limiting case. . . . The need to prevent them would be, in his view, one of the very weightiest reasons for coercion that one could plausibly imagine from the category of (merely) free-floating evils. He could then concede that the question of whether they could legitimately be prevented by state coercion is a difficult and close one, and admit this without hypocrisy or inconsistency. He would still hesitate to resort to legal coercion even to prevent the greatest of free-floating evils, simply because he cannot say who is *wronged* by the evils. At any rate, he can concede that the case is close. But the actual examples that people quarrel over: pornographic films, bawdy houses, obscene books, homosexuality, prostitution, private gambling, soft drugs, and the like, are at most very minor free-floating evils, and at the least, not intuitively evils at all. The liberal can continue to oppose legal prohibitions of them, while acknowledging that the wildly improbable evils in the hypothetical examples of Buckley and Kristol are other kettles of fish. The liberal position least vulnerable to charges of inconsistency and hypocrisy would be the view that the prevention of free-floating evils, while always a relevant reason for coercion, is nevertheless a reason in a generally inferior category, capable of being weighed on the same scale as the presumptive case for liberty only in its most extreme—and thus far only hypothetical—forms.

The preceding paragraph describes a rather uncomfortable fallback position for the liberal who wishes to preserve without hypocrisy what he can of his liberal principles in the face of Kristol's vivid counterexample. Before he settles in to that position, however, he would be well advised to look more carefully at the complex of images and associations we experience when we ponder the example that is supposed to appeal to our "intuitions." What exactly is it about that example that we are responding to when it inclines us toward Kristol's conclusion? Inevitably, I think, we import into the example a nightmare of unconsented-to indirect harms. We naturally set the example in a brutal society full of thugs and bullies who delight in human suffering, whose gladiatorial rituals concentrate and reenforce their callous insensitivity and render it respectable. We cannot hold an image of these wretches in our minds without recoiling, for each of them alone will seem threatening or dangerous, and thousands or millions of them together will be downright terrifying. It is highly difficult, if not plain impossible, to think of widespread indifference to suffering as a mere private moral failing unproductive of further individual and social harm. And so we move quickly (too quickly) in the direction of Kristol's conclusion, ready to endorse with enthusiasm his judgment that the gladiatorial contest would be a huge evil, and to accept uncritically at the same time that the evil would be free-floating.

The immorality of the participants in Kristol's story, then, is not like that of the solitary taboo-breakers or other harmless wrongdoers who can righteously rebuff our interference with the claim that what they do is none of our business. Rather it is an inseparable component of our spontaneous reaction to the story that the wrongdoing and "wrongfeeling" in it powerfully threaten basic human interests and are therefore quite assuredly everybody's business. I have insisted that moral corruption as such is not a relevant ground for preventive criminalization, but when the moral dispositions that are corrupted include concern about the sufferings of others, then the interests of others become vulnerable, and the corrupting activity can no longer be thought to be exclusively self-regarding. Nor are we considering here the mere "speculative tendency" of actions to endanger others, short of a clear and present danger that they will. When the bloody maiming and slaughtering of a human being is considered so thrilling and enjoyable that thousands will pay dearly to witness it, it would seem to follow that thousands are already so brutalized that there is a clear and present danger that some innocent parties (identities now unknown) will suffer at *their* hands. Indeed, it may be too late, in Kristol's gladiator example, to prevent such harms by prohibiting the show. If seventy thousand people will fill Yankee Stadium and enough others will attend closed television showings in theaters to permit the producer to pay thirty million dollars (my example) to the gladiators and still make a profit, then we are as a people already brutalized, and legal coercion, at best, can only treat the symptoms and slow their spread.

Kristol might reply to the above argument as follows. "*I* am writing the story," he might say, "in order to make *my* point. And in *my* version of the story, the spectators, for all their love of gory thrills, are not dangerous to other people. None of them would ever be likely to commit battery, mayhem, or homicide. Perhaps providing them with an orderly outlet for their savage passions makes them even less dangerous than they would otherwise be." In any case, he might say, they resemble in their motives and actions the dutiful wife of the dying invalid who secretly welcomes his sufferings but would never do anything to cause them herself or the honorable bigot who values whites more than blacks but would never intentionally violate the rights of a black. The participating spectators then are, *ex hypothesi,* harmless to others. They all witness the spectacle voluntarily, and the gladiators themselves participate voluntarily, and no third parties are endangered or directly offended, so no one has a grievance. Yet it remains a monstrous moral evil that people should get pleasure in this way from the suffering of others, an evil whose prevention justifies prohibition, even though it is free-floating.

So might Kristol rejoin. But then the liberal reader might reply: "I never thought to interpret your example in *that* way. Indeed, it is highly unlikely that one could cultivate genuine joy at others' suffering without himself becoming more of a danger to others, and it is wildly improbable that hundreds and thousands of spectators could come to be bloodthirsty without constituting a threat to at least *some* of the rest of us. Perhaps what you ask us to assume is psychologically impossible. But never mind; I agree that it is at least *logically* possible that people should be capable of such de-compartmentalization in their responses. So have it your way. But now my problem is that the original intuition to which you appealed, that the gladiator show is a sufficiently great evil to counterbalance autonomous liberty on the scales, is now substantially weakened. I can still acknowledge that it *is* a free-floating evil that a person derives pleasure from the suffering of others, while now denying that it is the business of the law to interfere." The example of a free-floating evil is now a purer one, but what it has gained in purity it has lost in intuitive forcefulness.

NOTES AND QUESTIONS

1. What motivates the legal moralist principle? Is it the simple intuition that if some action or state of affairs is evil, then that (legislative) action that prevents it is good? Or is it the "puritanical" (in Bertrand Russell's terminology) idea that if an ac-

tion is evil the (legislative) action that makes possible its punishment is a good? Can a legal moralist find both prevention of future evils and punishment of past evils to be good?

2. Feinberg juxtaposes the prima facie desirability of preventing and punishing human-created evils with the prima facie desirability of being at liberty from state coercion. He assumes we are to balance these two prima facie goods to decide whether to legislate. There can be a balancing of such goods only if they can conflict, and they can conflict only if some liberty is lost when evil actions are coercively prohibited. Is there any valuable liberty in the freedom to do evil?

3. Why is it important for Feinberg to establish that there are evils that are "non-grievance" or "free-floating?" What if there were not, so that the only moral evils there were were harm to people other than the actor—how would legal moralism differ from a traditional liberalism that restricted justification of criminal legislation to the harm principle?

4. What is the best liberal argument against criminalizing fornication between consenting, sane, unmarried adults in private: (1) that the behavior is not immoral or (2) that the immorality of the conduct is no reason to criminalize it? Should liberals usually prefer the second form of argument?

5. Why does Feinberg recommend that the legal moralist legislator eschew reliance on conventional morality as he considers what behavior is immoral? If conventional morality were used to define what is immoral behavior, and if conventional morality is constituted by what most people believe is immoral, how would a legal moralism that relied on such conventional morality differ from the offense principle? From preference-utilitarianism generally?

6. Does legal moralism commit one to thinking that there is a true morality? Is such moral realism the only metaethical alternative to relativism and conventionalism?

7. Do you agree with Feinberg that there are free-floating evils? How about defamation of a dead person? The soaking of a cat in gasoline and setting it afire? The sadistic enjoyment of another's suffering?

8. What sort of argument does Feinberg construct for the legal moralist out of "the imaginative use of examples"? Can such intuitively satisfactory applications of the legal moralist principle constitute an argument for the truth of that principle? Consider in this regard David Dolinko's criticism of the thought experiment methodology of Michael Moore in the preceding section.

9. So how about modern-day gladiatorial contests in Yankee Stadium between well-paid, willing, sane adults—may anyone but a legal moralist honestly prohibit them? Is Feinberg's own, non-fallback argument on behalf of his liberalism itself honest? Could we not think that each of us well-socialized, nondangerous human beings has within us enough sadism to enjoy such a contest without becoming "a brutal society full of thugs and bullies who are delighted in human suffering"? Freud and Nietzsche certainly thought so. Even if we, like Feinberg, think otherwise, is it this potential for brutalizing our society that motivates us to prohibit such contests, or is

it the moral sickness of the soul that enjoyment of such spectacles expresses, without regard to any further evil effects?

10. Consider statutes prohibiting cruelty to animals. In order to prohibit torturing cats, must we believe either that cat torturers tend to become person torturers, or that cats have legal interests protected by the harm principle, or that cat torturing in private will inevitably become known and then offend many people? Would we be more honest to say that it is the inherent evil that justifies criminalizing this behavior even if there is no other harm or offense caused by it?

A Theory of Criminal Law Theories

MICHAEL S. MOORE

On the legal moralist theory of proper legislative aim, morally wrong action ought to be prohibited by the doctrines of the special part of the criminal law. Saying this, and saying what morally wrongful actions are, tells only half the story needed by a conscientious legislator. The other half is what else (besides the evil of moral wrongness going unpunished) counts in deciding what behavior should be criminalized.

I below mention four other considerations that should restrain a legislator from legally prohibiting every act that is morally wrong to perform. Depending on the weight attached to such considerations, the result could be a legislative program that is quite liberal in its content even though illiberal in its theory of proper legislative aim.

Limits of Fair Notice

Despite my refusal to *define* criminal law in terms of the harshness of its sanctions, it remains true that criminal sanctions are on average harsher than normal civil sanctions. This fact about punishment heightens the importance of the rule-of-law virtue of predictability, because citizens' inability to predict the application of criminal sanctions chills liberty and unfairly surprises more than inability to predict the application of civil sanctions.

The upshot of this heightened importance of predictability is the kind of formal constraint it imposes on legislators vis-à-vis *criminal* legislation. Lon Fuller's justly famous eight desiderata of legislation—generality, publicity, prospectivity, stability,

From "A Theory of Criminal Law Theories," *Tel Aviv University Studies in Law,* Vol. 10 (1990), pp. 181–83.

clarity, consistency, fidelity, congruency (of official with lay interpretation)—*are* desiderata because they enhance law's action-guiding potential. They thus dictate a form for criminal legislation where concern for such action-guiding potential is heightened.

Limits of Autonomy

Even if the function of criminal law is backward-looking—to punish those who deserve it—one of its predictable effects gives legislators a forward-looking reason to restrain their enacting every moral wrong into a criminal prohibition. Sanction-backed criminal norms coerce conforming behavior out of those not otherwise inclined to so act. This coercive effect of criminal law (as opposed to its educative effect) necessarily impairs our autonomy. An old example is gift-giving. Assume we are all morally obligated to give a certain percentage of our income to those less fortunate. Criminal legislation coercing us to give that amount cuts into the ability of each of us to choose autonomously to give. Indeed, the moral worth of those "givings" motivated solely by fear of sanctions seems very small when compared to true charity (autonomous giving).

Autonomy can be a value of very great weight. Suppose one thinks that those members of the human species that are potential persons—fetuses—ought not to be killed, and that therefore abortion is a moral wrong. The decision about whether to bear a child is nonetheless the kind of intimate and personal decision that autonomy should strongly protect. Coercive sanctions prohibiting abortion would severely diminish the possibility of autonomous decision, and on this ground alone the conscientious legislator might well refrain from criminalizing this (assumed *arguendo*) wrongful action.

Limits of Convenience

There are well-charted evils attendant upon use of the criminal sanction to prohibit certain kinds of behaviors even if one is confident such behaviors are morally wrong. Behavior that is usually done in private, that has limited impact upon others (except perhaps via their own imaginations of what the actors are doing), and that is so deeply motivated that if prohibited it will be done anyway, is very costly to criminalize. The costs include invasion of privacy (true privacy, not constitutional "privacy," which is autonomy) through the enforcement techniques required to enforce such prohibitions; the creation of a "crime tariff," making the activities much more profitable than they would otherwise be; the potential for discriminatory enforcement of laws that cannot be comprehensively enforced; and the disrespect for law in general engendered by having laws that cannot or will not be enforced. A conscientious legislator has to balance the values disserved by criminalizing this class of behavior against the goodness of punishing culpably done wrongful action. The result in many cases should be that such behavior is not criminalized even though it is morally wrongful.

Epistemic Limits

Anyone who believes that there are right answers to moral questions like, "what actions are morally wrongful?" also should have some epistemic modesty about his own grasp of what those right answers are. After all, whatever one can be right about, one can also be wrong about. The true implication, thus, of realism about morality is not some self-righteous attitude that motivates one at every opportunity to cram one's own view of the good and the right down other people's throats. Rather, the attitudinal implication is one of humility in the face of hard moral questions, a humility accompanied by a curiosity about the differing answers to those hard moral questions discovered by others.

Some moral questions are not difficult to resolve. That murder is wrong, rape is wrong, deceiving one's friends is wrong, and homosexual sex is not wrong are moral conclusions easy to reach. But some moral questions are neither easy nor are answers to them uncontroversial. Euthanasia and torturing terrorists in order to extract lifesaving information are in this category. About such questions a legislator might well hesitate to enact her own best theory of moral wrongdoing into law, for to do so shuts off that experiment in seeking the good that each intelligent life represents.

NOTES AND QUESTIONS

1. Is Moore pretending to be a liberal? Can a moral realist/retributivist/legal moralist be a liberal? Or is liberalism best defined so as to exclude adherence to the former views? How might one alternatively define "liberalism" so that there could be a legal moralist liberal? (Put aside Feinberg's suggestion that morality itself may be liberal in content, prohibiting only actions that cause harms to others.)

2. What does Moore mean by autonomy? Is he, like Feinberg, committed to finding some good of autonomy even when that autonomy is exercised to do evil actions? Is a fully autonomously chosen murder in any sense "better" than a murder less fully autonomously chosen? Or is this beside the point—is the better question the one that asks whether an autonomously chosen nonmurder is better than a murder not done only because of fear of criminal sanctions?

3. Will Moore's "limits of convenience" roughly track the traditional liberal limits on criminal legislation in terms of Mill's harm principle? What assumptions must Moore make about the strength of the immorality of conduct that is barred from being prohibited by these limits of convenience?

4. If the legal moralist like Moore is also a deontologist, as is likely, can he resort to those practical consequences to justify not doing his duty as a legislator, which is to prevent or punish immorality? (Recall our earlier query about this in the introductory section to this chapter.)

5. How does one know whether one knows enough about the morality of a given type of conduct to legislate against it? Should a legal moralist legislator stay her hand only when she cannot decide whether the conduct is immoral? Or should she stay her hand even when she believes the conduct is immoral but she recognizes a genuine possibility that she could be in error in this judgment? Does the sensible person hold the last attitude about all personal moral judgments?

6. What role should the legal moralist legislator accord to the fact that other intelligent and well-meaning people disagree with his judgment about the immorality of some bit of conduct? Should he defer at all to diverging opinion, and if so, should he do so on grounds of democracy or of epistemic modesty?

3

Principal Liability

3.1 INTRODUCTION

Since the seminal work of Glanville Williams, it has become customary to divide Anglo-American criminal law between a "general part" and a "special part." The special part probably corresponds to what most laypersons think of when they think of substantive (i.e., nonprocedural) criminal law. It consists of the do's and don'ts of the criminal law. It is the secular version of the Ten Commandments, considerably enlarged and elaborated upon. The religious and moral prohibitions against killing, for example, have their criminal law analogues in the now considerable body of homicide law. Despite their complexity, such doctrines as those defining heat-of-passion killings, premeditated killings, and the like, all belong to the special part, because they are not general doctrines throughout the criminal law. Rather, they define the parameters of only one kind of crime, homicide.

By contrast, the general part of criminal law is, as the name suggests, general in the sense that the doctrines and principles making up this part of the criminal law apply across the board, to all crimes. One can think of the general part as a kind of overlay on the special part, so that the doctrines of the latter are modified by, and interpreted in light of, the doctrines of the general part.

The principles of the general part are not only general, but they have their roots deep in the history of Western morality. If one reads Chapter 1, Book 3 of Aristotle's *Nichomachean Ethics,* for example, one will find many of the principles of Anglo-American law described as principles of moral blameworthiness. Because of this history, the comparative unchangingness of the principles of the general part, and the moral compellingness and generality of applications of these principles, it is the general part that makes up the bulk of an introductory course in substantive criminal law in American law schools. For similar reasons, we have focused on the general part in these readings.

Within the general part of Anglo-American criminal law there are four ways in which an individual can become liable to criminal punishment. The most common way, and the way on which the other three are conceptually dependent, is to become liable for causing some legally prohibited state of affairs by one's own actions or omissions. The usual name for this is *principal liability*. In a subsequent part of the readings we shall explore the three alternative modes of criminal liability: liability for helping another to cause some legally prohibited state of affairs (*accomplice liability*); liability for trying to cause (or, in some cases, risking the causation of) some legally prohibited state of affairs (*attempt liability* or its risk-creation analogue); or liability for agreeing with another that one of the group will cause some legally prohibited state of affairs (*conspiracy liability*). It is important at the outset to see why conspiracy, complicity, and attempt are not just three substantive crimes whose doctrines ought rather to be allocated to the special part. Properly understood, these doctrines articulate three alternative ways in which a person can be criminally liable for any of the states of affairs prohibited by the offenses of the special part. These doctrines thus very much belong to the general part, along with those doctrines defining the conditions of that conceptually primary liability, principal liability.

Why should Anglo-American criminal law have conceptualized criminal liability into these four compartments? Since under some punishment schemes at least, *which* theory of liability is used does *not* matter for degree of punishability, why does our law divide the pie in this way? Central to answering this question is understanding the role of causation in criminal liability. The central idea behind this fourfold taxonomy of liability is that it matters to one's moral blameworthiness whether one's own act(s) caused some bad state of affairs to come into being or whether one only helped another, tried but failed, or agreed to cause but did not oneself cause that bad state of affairs to come into being.

A central, preliminary question about the general part is thus to ask whether causation does or should matter this much. Why should it matter to an offender's blameworthiness if, for example, he shoots at another, intending to kill him, but he misses, or only wounds him? Why should it matter to an offender's blameworthiness if he intends to kill, whether he executes that intention through his own action or through the actions of others?

The readings in this introduction section of the chapter are designed to explore such questions. Sanford Kadish states the Kantian view: it does not matter morally that one causes a bad state of affairs. What matters is what Kant called the "inner wickedness" of the offender, namely, that he intended (or perhaps tried) to bring such a state of affairs into existence.

The selection from Michael Moore defends the traditional view of the morality that underlies the fourfold organization of criminal law's general part. Moore seeks to show how we cannot accept the Kantian view and have any notion of moral responsibility left at all.

In the organization of these readings, we have adopted the traditional view of the matter represented by Moore. This is not because all of the editors agree with this view (although it is a safe bet that one of them does); rather, it is our belief that we do a better job of exploring the underpinnings and theoretical assumptions of Anglo-American criminal law better the closer we hew to its own organization. We have therefore not adopted the highly reformatory implications of the Kantian view to organize these readings. Despite that organizational choice, the issue is very much a live one, with much to be said for each side. We invite the reader to explore it in the readings that follow.

The Criminal Law and the Luck of the Draw

SANFORD H. KADISH

I propose to consider what to make of a doctrine of the criminal law that seems to me not rationally supportable notwithstanding its near universal acceptance in Western law, the support of many jurists and philosophers, and its resonance with the intuitions of lawyers and lay people alike. This is the doctrine—the harm doctrine, I'll call it—that reduces punishment for intentional wrongdoers (and often precludes punishment for negligent and reckless wrongdoers) if by chance the harm they intended or risked does not occur. I will also consider a corollary of the harm doctrine which offers a full defense if it so happens that, unbeknownst to the defendants, the harm they intended could not possibly have been done.

Whether the harm doctrine can be justified is, as George Fletcher has said, a "deep, unresolved issue in the theory of criminal liability." Indeed, a German scholar, Björn Burkhardt, recently concluded his comparative review of the law on this subject with the sobering words that "little progress has been made toward a solution of this issue in the last two hundred years." He continued: "The arguments of the past still dominate contemporary discussion. . . . [H]ardly anything of substance has been added." And he concluded: "In the final analysis, it is questionable whether a compelling and rational argument on this issue is possible." That may well be so. The debate over the issue remains unresolved notwithstanding the earnest attention of generations of scholars. But though the ground is well trod, the subject continues to have

From *Journal of Criminal Law and Criminology,* Vol. 84 (1994), pp. 679–82, 688–90.

a fascination for those of us who worry about the criminal law (perhaps just because it has defied successful resolution), and I am not immune to its attraction.

I should explain at the start what I mean by saying that the harm doctrine is not rationally supportable. I mean that it is a doctrine that does not serve the crime preventive purposes of the criminal law and is not redeemed by any defensible normative principle. Suppose, for example, the law provided that any crime committed during the night of a half-moon may not be punished with more than one-half the punishment appropriate on all other occasions. This distinction is patently irrelevant to any crime preventive purpose of the criminal law. Yet it might still be rationally supportable if it could be justified by moral principle. But no such principle can relate guilt or desert to the phases of the moon. Here, then, we would have an extreme instance of a rationally indefensible doctrine. One qualification: sometimes the law must defer to people's irrationalities to maintain the acceptance needed to govern. This might possibly be the case even with my half-moon doctrine of punishment. The doctrine, however, would still be rationally indefensible, even though its adoption by the law would not be.

Of course our criminal law has for centuries included many irrational doctrines— whole Augean stables full. Some of them were that way from the start. Others got that way when changed conditions made them anomalous, like the murder rule requiring the victim to have died within a year and a day of the injury. But these differ from the harm doctrine in that they are widely recognized as insupportable, and their long persistence in the law is simply evidence that the law is slow to change. The harm doctrine is special (although, as we will see, not singular) in that large segments of the legal and lay community regard it as sound.

I will begin by setting out the law that most clearly exhibits the harm doctrine at work. This is the law governing the punishment of failed efforts to do some prohibited harm (the law of attempts) and of actions that create the risk of the harm without producing it (the law of culpable risk creation). These rules are well known and I will only sketch them briefly.

First, the law of attempts. Consider the case of a man who stabbed his son in anger, pleaded guilty, and was convicted of a crime equivalent for our purposes to attempted murder. After serving several months of a two-year sentence, he was paroled. However, three months later his son, who had been hospitalized since the attack, took a turn for the worse and died, whereupon the prosecutor, quite within the law, charged the father with murder, a crime punishable with life imprisonment or death.

What did the father do in jail or on parole that merited the greater punishment? Not a thing. If a good constitution or a good surgeon had saved the son, the father could not have been further punished. The occurrence of the resulting death alone raises the crime and the punishment. In most jurisdictions this same principle operates for all crimes, not just homicidal crimes. In California, for example, an attempt to commit a crime is punishable with half the punishment for the completed crime. Thus, the reward for failing, no matter how hard you try to succeed or how close you come, is a lesser punishment.

Now consider crimes of culpable risk creation—crimes in which a person is punished, not for attempting a harm, but for culpably risking it. The punishment of these crimes is also made to depend on chance. Take the case of Mr. Malone. He and his friend decided to play a game of Russian Roulette in which each took turns spinning the chamber of a revolver, with one round in it, and firing at the other. When Malone's turn came to pull the trigger the gun fired and killed his friend. Malone was convicted of second degree murder, based on the egregious risk to life he needlessly created.

That sounds fair enough. But suppose instead, that the bullet only inflicted a flesh wound, or that the bullet was not in the firing chamber when Malone pulled the trigger. Could Malone then have been convicted of any crime? Perhaps he could have been convicted of some ad hoc statutory offense concerning firearms, but such an offense would carry nothing like the penalty for murder. And if there had been no special statute of this kind, he could not be convicted of any crime at all, since traditionally just recklessly endangering another was itself not criminal—except in specific contexts, like driving a car. Some jurisdictions have in recent years made it criminal to recklessly endanger another person in all situations, but even these statutes treat the offense as a minor one.

. . .

My argument to this point has been that attributing legal significance to the chance happening of harm either undercuts or is irrelevant to the crime prevention purposes of criminal punishment. Even so, as I said at the outset, a practice may be justified by some relevant principle of justice. Now I take the principle that limits punishment to what the offender deserves to be such a principle, and one which those subscribing to the harm doctrine would want to rely on. The question, then, is whether wrongdoers deserve less punishment (or none at all) because the harm they intended or culpably risked happens not to occur, or could not have occurred, for reasons unknown to them.

Isn't desert the same whether or not the harm occurs? It is commonly accepted that punishment is deserved if persons are at fault, and that fault depends on their choice to do the wrongful action, not on what is beyond their control. Reconsider my attempt cases. Would the father who stabbed his son deserve less punishment if a skillful doctor had been available to save the son's life? Would the Russian Roulette player deserve less punishment if the bullet happened to be in another chamber when he fired?

. . .

While in principle it's difficult to find good reasons for making desert turn on chance, here's the rub: most of us do in fact make judgments precisely of this kind. Doesn't it seem natural for a parent to want to punish her child more for spilling his milk than for almost spilling it, more for running the family car into a wall than for almost doing so? That's the way our unexamined intuitions run. The sight of the harm arouses a degree of anger and resentment that far exceeds that aroused by apprehension of the harm. What Adam Smith observed of his time is still largely true of ours:

> Our resentment against the person who only attempted to do a mischief, is seldom so strong as to bear us out in inflicting the same punishment upon him, which we should have thought due if he had actually done it. In the one case, the joy of our deliverance alleviates our sense of the atrocity of his conduct; in the other, the grief of our misfortune increases it.

Since he believed that the real demerit is the same in both cases, the person's intentions and actions being equally culpable, Smith concluded that in this respect there is "an irregularity in the sentiments of all men, and a consequent relaxation of discipline in the laws of . . . all nations, of the most civilized, as well as of the most barbarous."

What should we make of this paradox? Is there something to be said after all for the popular sentiment that fortuitous results do have a bearing on blameworthiness, something that is missed by treating it simply as an irregularity? Can attributing punishment significance to the occurrence of harm be justified in terms of the desert principle?

Obviously, the foundation of my argument against making punishment turn on the chance happening of harm rests on the incompatibility of luck and desert. But perhaps this assumption is mistaken. A distinguished philosopher, Thomas Nagel, has advanced the paradoxical notion of "moral luck." His point is that we do commonly make and defend judgments of moral desert despite the presence of substantial elements of chance. So if the harm principle is irrational because it makes moral desert turn on chance, then so are many of our considered moral judgments.

Nagel instances four situations in which moral desert turns on chance. Two of the four are based on a determinist premise; namely, that you may be lucky or unlucky in the antecedent factors that determine the kind of person you turn out to be and in how you choose to exercise your will. True enough if one accepts determinism. But, first, that explanation of human action is highly contestable, and second, the criminal law, with its concepts of personal responsibility and desert, plainly rejects it.

A third instance Nagel gives of moral luck is that you may be lucky or not in whether circumstances present you with an occasion to make a moral choice that will reveal your moral shortcomings; for example, luck in whether you are ever presented with the need to choose to betray a friend or break a promise. But I don't believe that this threatens our sense of justice in blaming in the same way that luck in the fortuitous outcome of an action (the harm doctrine) threatens it. The settled moral understanding is that what you deserve is a function of what you choose. It may be that you would not have had occasion to make a choice that revealed your badness if you had better luck. Nonetheless, you did make a choice—nobody made you—and it is that choice for which you are blamed. It is a different matter, however, to say that chance occurrences that follow after you have made your choice determine what you deserve, for that is to rest desert upon factors other than what you chose to do. Fortuity prior to choice, therefore, may be accommodated to our notions of just desert; fortuity thereafter cannot. As I see it, that leaves the harm doctrine, Nagel's fourth instance of moral luck, as the one deep challenge to the desert principle, the singular paradox which Adam Smith early identified.

NOTES AND QUESTIONS

1. What does Kadish mean by a doctrine being, or not being, "rationally supportable"? Why does Kadish accept only two sorts of rational support? Why two

rather than one? Based his idea of what is "rationally supportable," can you guess what must be Kadish's theory of punishment?

2. Kadish briefly adverts to Tom Nagel's important classification of kinds of moral luck. Three of those kinds are: *constitutive luck,* which is the luck of being constituted in the way we are so that we are not tempted to do more immoral acts than we do; *opportunity luck,* which is the luck of *not* having the opportunities to do all the immoral things we might be disposed to do; and *result luck,* which is the luck of failing to cause all the evil states of affairs which we try to cause or risk causing by our actions. Does Kadish think that constitutive luck and opportunity luck exist, even though he clearly rejects the idea of result luck? How would he defend such a distinction? How would you? Is there any difference in the degree of an agent's control over what traits of character make him the person that he is, what opportunities present themselves to him that would allow him to exercise the bad features of his character, and what results follow from his actions?

3. Do you agree with Kadish that determinism—the idea that human behavior is part of the natural world and caused like all other events—is "highly contestable"? What reason do we have to think that human actions can cause other events to occur while being themselves uncaused? How would such "first causes" differ from God?

4. Do you agree with Kadish that "the criminal law, with its concepts of responsibility and desert, plainly rejects [determinism]"? What must Kadish think of the compatibility of these two statements: (1) human actions are caused like all other events; and (2) human actors are morally responsible for their actions?

5. If one were to put aside Kadish's libertarian and incompatibilist metaphysics, how would one distinguish constitutive moral luck from result moral luck?

6. With regard to opportunity moral luck, why does Kadish think that "fortuity prior to choice . . . may be accommodated to our notions of just desert; fortuity thereafter cannot"? Do you agree with Kadish that the would-be armored-car robber who does not get the chance to rob the car because it changes its route is morally lucky, in the sense that he is not as morally responsible as he would have been had he found the car and robbed it?

The Independent Moral Significance of Wrongdoing

MICHAEL S. MOORE

If one were to adopt the standard educated view about the moral irrelevance of results, a large range of other judgments of responsibility would be affected. Indeed, as I shall argue in this section, the range of judgments affected would be so large that the notion of desert (or responsibility) would disappear entirely. One should thus view the argument that follows in two ways: first, as an incremental argument against the standard educated view, the increments being measured by the variety of other particular judgments about responsibility that both seem intuitive and yet would be overturned by the implications of the standard educated view; and, secondly, as a reductio ad absurdum argument, the absurd conclusion to which the standard educated view leads being that no one is responsible for anything.

The discussion which follows is organized in descending order of generality: as more and more of the judgments discussed have to be given up because of the standard educated view, we approach closer and closer to the demise of responsibility in toto. The discussion is also organized psychologically: as we move temporally backwards in the causal antecedents of those simplest bodily movements by virtue of which we do wrongs, judgments about the moral significance of volitions, of intentions, of motivations, of character, and of the factors (of environment and genetic endowment) that determine character, become challenged by the standard educated view. Again, ultimately the argument will be that none of these causal antecedents of action has moral significance if consequences do not, so that responsibility—even in its sense as culpability alone—disappears.

Our Limited Capacities/Opportunities to Effectuate Choices, Intentions, and Plans

Suppose one took the view that because one cannot control all factors influencing a bullet's flight into a vital organ of an intended victim, the death of that victim is not something that increases the deserts of the shooter. This same feature—of control of all factors—is present in the more immediate effectuation of one's choices. On my view of actions and the mental states that cause them, behind the movement of an actor's trigger finger are:

1. The volition or willing to move the finger;
2. The intention, plan, or choice (to kill the victim) that is executed by the more specific volition;

From *Journal of Contemporary Legal Issues,* Vol. 1 (1994), pp. 271–78.

3. The set of beliefs and desires, the content of which form a valid practical syllogism, that are executed by one's intentions;
4. The more general traits of character which cause one to have the beliefs and desires that motivate one on particular occasions.

My hypothetical shooter may be the kind of greedy, heartless person who desires to inherit his uncle's money, believes that if he kills his uncle, he will inherit his money, and because of this belief/desire set he decides to kill his uncle, which decision (or intention) is executed by willing the movement of his finger on the trigger of the gun pointed at the victim.

Just as a number of events could intervene between the movement of the trigger finger and the death of the victim that would rob the bullet of its normal capacity to kill, so a number of events could intervene between each of these mental states and their normal effects so as to rob them of their normal causal power. Despite their similarity, I shall separately discuss the four antecedent mental states in two pairs, corresponding to the causal fortuities occurring before and after choice. In this section I deal with the causal fortuities necessary for choice to issue in executory bodily movements, and in the next, with the causal fortuities necessary for character to result in those choices that are "in character" for the agent.

One final organizational preliminary: it is common to distinguish two different ways in which something can lose its normal ability to bring about a certain result. We often distinguish defects in equipment from lack of any chance to use perfectly operating equipment. We call the first, diminished capacity, and the second, lack of opportunity. Failures of our intentions to issue in the movements needed to execute them may occur because of either mental incapacities or lack of the opportunity to use perfectly adequate capacities.

Suppose I intend to kill Jones by shooting him and thus know that I at some point will need to will the movement of my finger on the trigger of a gun pointed at Jones. Having formed the intent, I may lack the opportunity to execute it. I may, for example, discover that Jones is never alone; or that he has removed himself from the jurisdiction; or that when I reach for my gun, finding Jones alone and vulnerable I discover that my pocket has just been picked by some thief; or that in a hundred different ways, none of which I have any control over, I never get the chance to shoot Jones.

Alternatively, I may have the opportunity to shoot and kill Jones—he is before me, alone, in the right circumstance, I have a loaded gun in my hand—but I suffer a sudden incapacitation. For example, as I raise the gun before I have willed my trigger finger to move, someone who is a dead-ringer for my long dead friend appears, the sight of which so startles and distracts me that I forget about my intention to kill Jones long enough for Jones to escape. Alternatively, such sudden loss of capacity can occur between my willing and my finger movement: I get so excited at having the opportunity to kill Jones at last (recognizing how utterly fortuitous it is that I have such opportunity, see above) that my fingers tremble and shake so much that I can't will my trigger finger to move in the required way.

I have no control whatsoever over these extraneous factors intervening between my intention and my bodily motion, no more than I have such control over wind speeds, bullet firing capacities, and the like that can intervene after I have moved my trigger finger. The possibility of there being such intervening factors—the necessity that there not be such intervening factors present for me to succeed—equally rule out any moral distinction between the one who intends to kill Jones and doesn't, and the one who intends to kill Jones and succeeds, on the standard educated view. The focus of my responsibility, in other words, must on the standard view be on my intention to kill Jones, *all* that happens after that (including those mental states of volition) being morally irrelevant.

There are two possible responses for one holding the standard educated view: admit the reductio but deny that it is to an absurdity or deny that there is any reduction. To adopt the first response is to say that intention alone is all that counts morally. That is easy enough to admit about the second sort of lack of capacity case, for there at least the agent does the last mental act (of willing) needed to kill Jones. In the other cases, we either have not gotten the opportunity to try (because we can't find the victim, etc.) or we had the opportunity but were incapacitated from trying to execute our intention to kill Jones (because we were distracted at the wrong moment, etc.). Insofar as one finds *trying* to be of some moral salience, beyond simply *intending,* these cases should be troublesome.

That leaves the other response, which is to find some grounds to distinguish the cases. One possibility would be to draw the line between those factors that prevent success by occurring before bodily movement is initiated, and those that do so by occurring after bodily movement is initiated. Yet this line is surely arbitrary vis-à-vis the degree of control exercisable by an agent over the possible factors occurring on either side of this temporal line. Just because factors intervening before movement is initiated have to operate through my mind does not give me greater control over them. I need have no more control over whether I am distracted, startled, or excited, in the situation imagined, than I do over whether my finger, unbeknownst to me is not on the trigger I think it is on. I have no more control over the brain and nerve events necessary for my intentions to cause the appropriate volitions, or for my volitions to cause the appropriate bodily movements, than I do over the wind on my bullets once I have sent them on their way.

A more plausible line would be built around the notion of mental trying: when I have the opportunity and the capacities to execute my intention to kill Jones down to the level of mental trying (volitions), that is sufficient morally, i.e., nothing that happens after that is relevant to my deserts. Yet how do I have any greater control over the factors that can prevent my having either the opportunity or the capacity to mentally try to kill Jones? Glitches can occur in my processes of inference (from intending to willing) as they can in the wind, and I equally control neither; the victim's movements that can prevent me from having any opportunity to try to kill him are no more under my control than are the movements of the wind that can deflect my bullet. How, then, can one distinguish—by degrees of control over possibly disrupting factors—these cases of failure of *internal* execution from the case of failure of *external* execution about which the standard educated view makes so much?

I conclude that there is no plausible line to be found that divides intervening factors (between the controlled and the uncontrolled) and that also saves the judgment that mental trying matters morally to one's deserts. Yet the latter is a strong intuition, in that it seems to matter whether one actually tried to execute one's intention to kill or not. One of the costs of the standard educated view about consequences is that one must give up this intuition.

Our Limited Capacities/Opportunities to Make Choices

One might not have been too disturbed at having to give up the notion that mental tryings have any relevance to desert, given the uncontrollable fortuities involved in making or executing such volitional tryings. After all, one could hold the line at intentions, plans, and choices. Those at least, can be of moral significance because those are fully under an actor's control. Yet this is not true either, as I propose to show in this section.

Again, we should distinguish failures to form a culpable intention due to lack of opportunity to do so, from those failures due to diminished capacity to do so. On the opportunity side, imagine that Smith is a vicious, violent individual who very much resents Jones for having taken his (Smith's) job. Smith's character in general, and his desires in particular, are thus very much pro the death of Jones. Given more time, Smith would have formed the firm intention to kill Jones, given Smith's character and his motivations. As it happens, Smith never got the chance to intend to kill Jones, because: Jones died of natural causes; Jones got fired from the job about which Smith was so envious; Smith became injured so that he couldn't accept the job about which he was so envious, even if it were offered to him on the death of Jones; etc. None of these are factors over which Smith has any control, yet whether Smith forms his culpable intention to kill Jones depends on whether such factors occur.

Likewise, Smith may get the opportunity to choose to kill Jones, but he may lack the capacity to make such a choice. To adopt an example of Joel Feinberg's, every time Smith begins to think of Jones having the job Smith wanted, specks of dust throw Smith into sneezing fits that prevent any envious rage from developing. Alternatively, at the point when Smith is raging and is right on the verge of forming his intention to kill Jones, he is distracted by a loud noise which lasts long enough to dissipate the anger which otherwise would have led Smith to intend to kill Jones. Such extraneous dust motes and noises are not within the control of Smith, yet whether they occur determines whether Smith forms the culpable intention.

Feinberg's conclusion about these cases is the right one: "in whatever sense legal responsibility for external states can be contingent on factors beyond one's control and therefore a matter of luck, in precisely the same sense can 'moral' responsibility for inner states also be contingent and a matter of luck." As before, the standard educated view has two possible responses here: to accept Feinberg's conclusion, which is to admit that intention and choice are without any moral significance, or to deny Feinberg's conclusion by denying that the lack of control over factors preventing choice from being made is the same as the lack of control over factors preventing choice from being realized in action.

The first sort of response is a much less palatable one here than it was in the previous section, for there, the fallback position was to the moral significance of intentions. The fallback position once one gives up on the moral significance of intentions has to be to character. This would be the view that our just deserts are determined exclusively by our character, that is, by what sort of a person we are in general. What we did, what we tried to do, and what we choose to do, would on this view have no more than evidentiary status vis-à-vis our deserts; only insofar as these items reflect good or bad character would they have any moral significance whatever.

This is not an attractive moral view. Its unattractiveness does not lie in the proposition that we are in some sense responsible for being the sort of person that we are, for we do have a responsibility for our characters (even if not a *punishable* responsibility). Rather, the rub comes with saying that this is the only independent desert-basis there is. When we choose to do a wrongful act that is out of character for us, try to do it, and then do it, how can that have no bearing on our just deserts? The weakness of the character view lies precisely in its inability to deal with our momentary lapses from who, in general, we are. This would make immorality like the proverbial "one-free-bite" rule in tort law (according to which a dog gets one bite without liability by its owner): a generally good person can do no evil, so long as he does it infrequently enough that such choosings are not in character for him.

This leaves the standard educated view with the other response, one that denies that the lack of control over factors producing intentions is the same as the lack of control over factors executing intentions into actions. Sanford Kadish adopts this line of defense:

> [Y]ou may be lucky or not in whether circumstances present you with an occasion to make a moral choice that will reveal your moral shortcomings; for example, luck in whether you are ever presented with the need to choose to betray a friend or break a promise. But I don't believe that this threatens our sense of justice in blaming in the same way that luck in the outcome of an action (the harm doctrine) threatens it. The settled moral understanding is that what you deserve is a function of what you choose. It may be that you would not have had occasion to make a choice that revealed your badness if you had better luck. Nonetheless, you did make a choice—nobody made you—and it is that choice for which you are blamed. It is a different matter, however, to say that chance occurrences that follow after you have made your choice determine what you deserve, for that is to rest desert upon factors other than what you chose to do. Fortuity prior to choice, therefore, may be accommodated to our notions of just desert; fortuity thereafter cannot.

It is easy to understand (and agree with) the intuition that motivates Kadish here: choosing is central to our "settled moral understanding" of desert, in the sense that choosing is central to at least one of the two bases for desert. Thus it is very tempting to draw the line in the sand here, and to say that fortuities prior to choice do not matter even though the fortuities occurring after choice do. Yet a fortuity is a fortuity. Certain factors over which one had no control were determinative of whether or not the bullet found its target; yet certain other factors, over which one had no more control, were equally determinative of whether or not one chose to try to kill another with the bullet. With no more control by the actor, and no less determination of the relevant event, how are the second sort of factors to be distinguished from the first?

Of course, it is true that "nobody made you" make the choice to shoot; the fortuitously occurring or not-occurring factors necessary for you to choose to shoot did not *make* you so choose. But it is equally true that no one made the bullet do exactly what you intended it to do when you put the gun against your victim's head; the absence of wind, of defective bullets, etc., did not *make* the bullet do what it did either. Nor did these factors make *you* do what you did, which was to kill. Nobody made you either choose to kill, try to kill, or kill, even though there had to be a number of factors present for any of these events to occur, and over none of those factors did you have any control.

The blunt fact is that we have no more control over all the factors necessary in order to choose to kill than we do over all the factors necessary for us to kill. Choice is thus not a line that can be used here. We have to go in one of two directions. Either we keep regressing, to motivations, to character, to factors that cause character, in the search for something of which we are in full control; this as we shall see is a fruitless quest, so that ultimately no one can be responsible because no one can have such complete control over anything that can plausibly be identified with his moral agency. Or we give up this odd notion of control so that we can say that we are in control (in our new and better sense) of our choices because they are our choices—even though causally dependent on factors that are themselves unchosen. And this starts us back from whence we have come, for in this sense of control we also control whether or not we execute our general choices with volitions, and in this sense of control we control our bodily movements when we will them with our volitions. Further, in this sense of control we control the gun in our hand, and we control the bullet, its impact on the victim, and his death; we chose each of these events as means and we tried to rule out the extraneous factors as best we could at all levels. It is, in this sense of control, ludicrous to deny that we controlled whether or not we killed when we put a gun at our intended victim's head and blew his brains out.

Thus, the standard educated view cannot stop the slide from choice to chosen results. If we control the first, we control the second—in any relevant sense of control.

NOTES AND QUESTIONS

1. In a part of his article not included here, Moore seeks to infer from the felt emotions of resentment and guilt the truth of the moral proposition that results are pertinent in determining the degree of one's responsibility. Are the emotions relevant guides to moral truth? How about our many hatreds, prejudices, jealousies—do these lead to moral insight?

2. Moore qualifies his view by arguing that only *virtuous* emotions are reliable indicators of moral truth. Is this circular? Is the virtue of an emotion just the ability of such an emotion to generate true moral judgments?

3. Is it virtuous to resent the wrongdoings of others? Would it be more virtuous to forgive those who trespass against us?

4. Is it virtuous to feel guilty over our own misdeeds? Or should we recognize that we cannot undo the past and thus should get on with our lives without the crip-

pling effects of guilt? What sort of advice would you give to a guilty friend? Would you think better or worse of such a friend if he or she got over the guilt easily?

5. Moore also argues from the forward-looking experience of choosing what to do in the face of a moral dilemma. Yoda, the old master in *The Empire Strikes Back,* advises his charge, "Do not try; do." As forward-looking advice, this might be right: we try harder if we aim to succeed rather than just aim to make a good effort. Yet does the backward-looking judgment of there being a greater responsibility for successful wrongdoing then follow?

6. Moore's reductio argument depends on our not having any greater control over any of the following:

a. Whether features of the environment intervene to prevent my bodily movements from having their normal and intended effects in the world;
b. Whether I have the opportunity or capacity to get my willings of certain movements of my body, to actually cause those bodily movements;
c. Whether I have the opportunity or capacity to execute my evil intention into those willings of those bodily movements necessary to effectuate my evil intention;
d. Whether I have the opportunity or capacity to form my evil intention from my evil desires and the beliefs I have about how to effectuate those desires in action;
e. Whether I have the opportunity or capacity to form my evil desires out of my generally evil character;
f. Whether I have the opportunity or capacity to form my generally evil character out of those genetic and environmental factors that cause me to be who I am;
g. Whether I have the opportunity or capacity to shape those genetic and environmental factors that cause me to have the evil character that I do.

What do you think? Do we have more control over possible interferences with some of these causal links than others?

7. If Moore is right that we have no more control at any level, is the proper conclusion to be drawn that no one is ever really responsible for anything? Or is Moore's conclusion correct—that we are more responsible for causing bad results than for merely trying to do so?

3.2   ACTS AND OMISSIONS

Crimes generally prohibit the bringing about of a prohibited state of affairs, be it death, the disappearance of another's property, or unwanted sexual intercourse. Often it is possible to bring about that state of affairs either by an *act* or by an *omission,* either by actively precipitating it or by passively letting it happen. The law generally punishes only the former. But that requires that the law draw a fairly strict distinction between acts and omissions. Is it possible to draw such a distinction? And why is it desirable to draw it anyway? Those are the questions addressed in the excerpts by Leo Katz and Shelly Kagan.

The act-omission distinction is merely one perennial question surrounding the concept of an act. The excerpt from the introduction to Michael Moore's book *Act and Crime* reviews some of the various other questions that arise and sketches out the doctrines the law has generated to resolve them.

Crimes of Omission
LEO KATZ

If omissions are treated so much more leniently than acts, that makes it important to be able to distinguish the two. Some cases are easily classified. To fail to help Kitty Genovese is an omission; to stab Kitty Genovese is an act. But a disconcertingly large number of cases dumbfound one's intuitions. A man is riding his spring cart. Instead of holding the horse's reins in his hands, he lets them rest on its back. As the horse is trotting down a hill, a child passes in front of it, is knocked down, and dies. Had the man held the reins, he could have pulled the horse up. Did the passing cart's careless driver kill the child or merely fail to prevent its death? A pharmacist repeatedly sells a patient some highly toxic medication. The first time the patient has a prescription, on subsequent occasions he does not. The patient dies. Is the pharmacist guilty of an act or an omission? A manufacturer permits unsterilized Chinese goathair to be worked into cloth as a result of which several employees die of an infection. Act or omission? A man picks up his inebriated friend at a local tavern. They have a quarrel, and the man abandons his friend at some dangerous spot, so that in attempting to make it home on his own he stumbles into a pond and drowns. Act or omission? A child, chased by a wild dog, runs toward the open door of a nearby villa. The malicious owner slams the door in his face, and the dog tears the child to pieces. Act or omission?

The need to distinguish between acts and omissions is not confined to the criminal law and neither is the difficulty in articulating the distinctions. Among the most pivotal Supreme Court decisions of recent times is *Immigration and Naturalization Service v. Chadha*. At issue was one of the most basic provisions of the Constitution, the requirement that every law be passed by both houses of Congress and not disapproved by the president (unless Congress overrides his veto). Beginning in the 1930s Congress saw the need to create more and more administrative agencies to oversee the implementation of increasingly complex pieces of legislation: that is how the Immigration and Naturalization Service, the Internal Revenue Service, the Federal Trade Commission, and the Environmental Protection Agency were born. Congress soon discovered that it could not possibly anticipate the infinitude of problems these agencies would have to address and as a result drafted its laws very loosely, giving

From *Bad Acts and Guilty Minds: Conundrums of the Criminal Law* (Chicago: University of Chicago Press, 1987), pp. 140–45.

the agencies extensive power to "fill them out" with more specific rules and regulations of their own. Then it began to have second thoughts. What if it disapproved of some of the regulations passed by the agencies? Would it have to amend the law formally so as to nullify regulations it did not like? That seemed terribly cumbersome. Instead Congress gave the agencies only a conditional grant of power. They were free within very broad limits to pass the regulations they saw fit. These regulations would become effective within a specified amount of time unless one of the houses of Congress found them abhorrent, in which case it could just veto the regulation by a simple majority vote, and it would never become effective.

Chadha argued that this scheme was unconstitutional. The merits of his case hinged on the distinction between acts and omissions. Chadha pointed out that under the congressional scheme one house of Congress could all by itself act to overturn a regulation and thereby remake the law without getting the approval of the other house or the president.

But there is another way to look at the congressional scheme. One might view the house's veto as an *omission* rather than an *act*. By vetoing the regulation, one might argue, the house is not really *acting* to change the law but *omitting* to change the law: After all, it is keeping a new regulation off the books. And when a house is omitting to change the law rather than acting to change it, clearly the approval of the other house or the president is not required. That, of course, raises the question: If the new regulation is itself a change in the law, why isn't the president, like the two houses, free to veto it? But, in fact, he is. As head of the executive branch of government, he can simply tell the administrative agency not to propose the regulation in the first place. Alas, the Supreme Court did not see things this way. It decided the "one-house veto" was an act rather than an omission and held it unconstitutional. But whether the Court was right is far from obvious.

These many hard cases are alarming. True, any distinction has its borderline cases. But are these merely borderline cases or do they betoken the lack of any analytical substance to the distinction between acts and omissions? A man in Brazil is committing suicide. Were we to fly to Brazil and try to dissuade him, he would not kill himself. We view this as a clear-cut case of omission. King fires a bullet into Davis's chest. We view this as a clear-cut case of an act. Nevertheless: But for our staying in America and minding our own business, the man in Brazil would still be alive. But for King's firing a bullet into Davis's chest, he would still be alive. Thus presented, the two cases seem virtually identical. Why are we so sure that they exemplify two very different concepts?

Some have suggested that acts involve bodily movements and omissions do not. But the man who stays in America and busies himself with his own affairs instead of setting out for Brazil is a paragon of physical agitation. He is nonetheless guilty of no more than an omission.

More intriguing is a suggestion made by the philosopher Jonathan Bennet. Bennet was confronted by the need to develop a basis for the distinction between act and omission in the course of investigating the following hypothetical: "A woman in labor will certainly die unless an operation is performed in which the head of her unborn child is crushed or dissected, while if it is not performed, the child can be delivered, alive, by post-mortem caesarean section." Unless the obstetrician operates and crushes the baby's skull, the mother will die. Many people in this context, a group Bennet dubs "the conservatives," would rigidly adhere to the credo: It is always wrong to kill an innocent human, whatever the consequences of not doing so. They would prohibit the doctor from operating. In this case, Bennet pointed out, not killing one human being seems to involve killing another human being. Why do "conservatives" not see it that way? Why do they see the mother's death as the consequence of an act? Why do they not call the doctor who sits down to write up his medical report instead of crushing the baby's skull to save the mother a killer, but do so label the doctor who chooses to save the mother? Bennet can only see one reason. The doctor who writes up his lab notes is taking one of many possible actions that would result in the mother's death. The doctor who crushes the baby's skull is taking the only action that would result in the baby's death. In short, the difference between death-producing omissions and death-producing acts is that in the former the actor engages in one of many death-producing activities whereas in the latter he engages in one out of a very few death-producing activities. Bennet concludes that this distinction is morally irrelevant. Others have thought it highly relevant. It shows, they point out, that our "reluctance to penalize omissions is justified by the fact that to prohibit an act . . . leaves the subject free to do many, many alternative acts; prohibiting an omission leaves him free to do only one act, the act which he is forbidden to omit. This is a more severe burden to place on the citizen than if he is merely forbidden to perform the act."

The validity of Bennet's test has been seriously questioned. Suppose Cooper stands surrounded by a lynch mob. Miller gives him the coup de grace. But it is clear that if not Miller, someone else would certainly have killed him. According to Bennet's criterion, Miller is merely guilty of an omission. Our intuition tells us he is guilty of an act. Or suppose Jones and Smith are spies who have been captured by the enemy. They have been wired to each other so that a movement by one would electrocute the other. Jones moves and kills Smith. Here all of Jones's actions but one—sitting still—would have resulted in Smith's death. Jones took one of those actions. Under Bennet's criterion he is guilty merely of an omission. According to our intuition that's far from clear.

The true test for whether something is an act or an omission I believe to be the following: If the defendant did not exist, would the harmful outcome in question still have occurred in the way it did? This test certainly gives us the right answer to our easy cases. If the witnesses to Kitty Genovese's murder had not existed, she would still have died. But if her assailant had not existed, she would not have died. If you did not exist, the man in Brazil would still have committed suicide. But if Miller had trampled Cooper to death, his death would have occurred in a somewhat different manner: someone other than Miller would have finished Cooper off. The test helps us to treat satisfactorily some cases where our intuition hesitated. It would pronounce the man who rode his spring cart so recklessly guilty of an act. It is evidence, however, that the test captures our intuitions well, that it yields equivocal results in the very cases that cause our intuitions to equivocate most strongly. What would have happened if the pharmacist who refilled the patient's outdated prescription had not existed? Are we to assume another pharmacist would have filled his prescription the first time around? Are we to assume that pharmacist to be careful or negligent? We can't tell. What would have happened if the manufacturer who permitted the use of unsterilized goathair had not existed? Would his factory exist? Would somebody more or less careful run it? We can't tell. What if the man who picked up his inebriated friend at the tavern did not exist? Would the drunk then have awaited sobriety before he left the tavern and not drowned in the pond? We can't tell. What if the owner who slammed the door in the fleeing child's face had not existed? Would a more benevolent owner occupy his place? Would the villa exist at all? We can't tell.

It is a problem of many counterfactual assumptions that they are inherently ambiguous. Because of this ambiguity contradictory results can often be deduced from them. Assume for a moment that New York City is located in Georgia. What follows from that? Arguably it follows that New York is located south of the Mason-Dixon line. Arguably it follows that Georgia extends north of the Mason-Dixon line. The source of the problem is this. There are three true facts: (1) New York City is not located in Georgia. (2) Georgia lies south of the Mason-Dixon line. (3) New York is north of the Mason-Dixon line. We are asked to assume the opposite of 1. To be in a consistent world we now have to assume the opposite of either 2 or 3. If we assume the opposite of 2, we conclude that Georgia extends north of the Mason-Dixon line. If we assume the opposite of 3, we conclude that New York is south of the Mason-Dixon line. But the counterfactual assumption does not tell us whether 2 or 3 is to be negated. Hence a question based on the assumption is unavoidably ambiguous. This same problem plagues the counterfactual question: Would X have occurred in the same manner if the defendant had not existed? It lies at the heart of our hitherto mysterious inability to classify some occurrences as acts or omissions.

Having settled the nature of omissions, the question remains: Why do omissions strike us as morally less offensive than acts? Why do we loathe the indifferent onlookers of Kitty Genovese's stabbing less than her assailant?

Many of our reasons for not prosecuting the callous bystander are practical rather than moral. A law requiring bystanders to help is very difficult to draft. What is such a law to do, for instance, with the wealthy man who refuses to give alms to the starving beggar? Is he obligated to give away his money to starving beggars until he has no more to give? One statutory proposal seeks to avoid this undesirable possibility by providing: "The circumstances placing a person in a position to act [must be] purely fortuitous." Under this rule the wealthy man need not give any money to the starving beggar because the beggar is without funds, "If the rich man [passing by the beggar] had food with him, he might be required to share it, for the presence of food would be purely fortuitous. But he is not required to share his money, because a man's wealth is not a fortuity." Unfortunately, this restriction rests on the hazy concept of fortuity. Why isn't a man's wealth a fortuity? What if he just won it in the lottery?

Another practical reason for not prosecuting callous bystanders is that such prosecutions might be counterproductive. Many people might stay away from places where they could be called upon to help. Others would be less willing to help, because help has become mandatory rather than voluntary.

Yet another practical reason for not prosecuting bystanders is that the consequences of an omission are generally less certain than those of an act. Holding somebody's head under water is more likely to kill him than not throwing him a life vest.

But there is a deeper, moral, reason why killing-by-omission offends us less than killing-by-commission. Compare these two situations. (1) Bert will die unless Berta gives him one of her kidneys. Berta is ailing and doesn't want to risk an operation. So she lets Bert die. (2) Berta will die unless Bert gives her his only kidney. She kills Bert and takes his kidney. In both 1 and 2 Berta brings about Bert's death to assure her own survival; in 1 she does it by an omission, in 2 by an act. Why are we less offended by her conduct in 1 than in 2? Because in 1 she simply holds on to her own kidney, whereas in 2 she appropriates somebody else's kidney. We value personal autonomy and Berta's conduct in 2 offends against that value, while her conduct in 1 doesn't. Our sentiments about very other case of omission can be understood by analogizing it to these two cases. The person who fails to prevent harm that would occur even if he didn't exist simply fails to give away something he owns. The person who brings about harm that wouldn't occur if he didn't exist takes away something owned by someone else. Both persons may be callous, but only the latter offends our sense of personal autonomy.

Interfering

SHELLY KAGAN

[It might seem that what makes doing harm worse than allowing harm to happen is that in the former case one is] interfering with the welfare of another.

Intuitively, the idea is this: often agents step into the causal flow in such a manner as to alter the outcome of processes which were already under way. This is in contrast to cases where the agent simply lets the ongoing process continue. In the former case, but not the latter, the agent can be said to *interfere:* he makes a difference in a way that he does not when he merely refrains from altering the causal flow.

Obscure as the notion of on-going processes may be, the concept of interfering certainly seems to point to *something* of importance. When I bring about harm to another, he is worse off because of me; I interact with the causal nexus in such a way that it would have been better for him had I not interacted at all. The relevant processes which were under way would have sustained his well-being. But I step in, alter them, and interfere: and he is the worse for it. Had I simply left him alone—indeed, had I never even existed—he would have been better off. When I merely allow harm, however, I do *not* interfere with the well-being of another: I simply permit the processes which were already under way to take their course. That I do not alter the processes is brought out by the fact that had I never even existed he would have been no worse off. This suggests a rough intuitive test of whether an agent has interfered with another, thus falling foul of the constraint against doing harm. It is a counterfactual test: we ask whether the victim would have been better off had the agent not existed: if the answer is "yes," then the agent has interfered; if the answer is "no," then he has not.

From *The Limits of Morality* (Oxford: Clarendon Press, 1989), pp. 94–99.

Our intuitions about interfering seem to discriminate correctly between my hold-ing Basil's head under water until he drowns, and my mere failure to save Maude when she is struggling with the waves. Basil is worse off for my being in the world: had I never existed, the harm would not have befallen him. I have interfered with his life. But Maude can make no such complaint. She is none the worse for my existence; had I never existed, she would still be drowning. I have not interfered with *her* life. . . .

The rough counterfactual test works well with standard cases: if I fail to send famine relief, and some individual dies of starvation, I have not interfered, for he would have been no better off had I never existed. If I send poison to some unsus-pecting stranger, however, I *have* interfered: he would have been better off had I not existed. In the latter case, but not the former, I violate the constraint against doing harm.

Now in fact the counterfactual test as I have described it won't quite do. There are gimmicky cases for which the test gives what is intuitively the wrong answer about whether the agent has interfered. Suppose a King slits the throat of his oldest son, so that the second oldest may inherit the throne. Surely the father has interfered with the welfare of the poor boy, violating the constraint against doing harm. Yet the King might exclaim that had he never existed the *son* would not have existed, and so the victim would have been no better off. Thus the counterfactual test yields the intu-itively incorrect result that the King has not interfered. Qualms about whether the dead son might not actually have been better off never having been born at all just don't seem to the point: the test, as I've stated it, excuses too much.

As a second gimmicky case, suppose that after the coronation of the second son, the third son squanders his lesser inheritance and—dying of starvation— comes be-fore his older brother, begging for food. But the second son is as ruthless as his fa-ther, and allows his younger brother to starve to death. He is ruthless, yes. But intu-itively we feel that the second son has not *interfered* with the welfare of the third. Yet (the ghost of) the third son might exclaim that had the second son never existed the third son himself would have inherited the kingdom and would not have starved; so the victim would have been better off had the agent never existed. Thus the counter-factual test yields the intuitively incorrect result that the ruthless son has interfered with his younger brother. Therefore the test, as I've stated it, condemns too much.

These are, as I say, gimmicky cases. [Our] response to them is undoubtedly that they show only that the counterfactual test would need to be made a bit more precise in order to capture adequately the notion of interfering. Our intuition is quite clear that the test has gone wrong in these cases; and it may not be worth the trouble to de-scribe the test more accurately.

In fact, however, it is not at all clear whether the counterfactual test can be ade-quately repaired. To see this, let's ask how we might revise the test so as to handle the first case, where the King cuts the throat of his oldest son. The King truthfully ob-serves that since the son owes his very existence to his father, had the King never ex-isted the son would have been no better off. The problem with the test seems to be this: since we are wondering whether the King interferes when he cuts the throat of his son, our focus is too broad if we imagine the King's never having existed at all. The relevant question seems to be not, would the son have been better off had the King never existed, but rather, would the son have been better off had the King not existed at the time he was cutting his son's throat. To the latter question the answer is obviously yes. This suggests that the proper counterfactual test for interference is to ask whether the victim would have been better off had the agent not existed at the time of the reaction in question.

Intuitively, an agent can interfere with an ongoing process even though the existence and nature of that process is not altogether independent of the agent's existence. In particular, an agent can interfere with a process at a given time even though the process would not exist at that time were it not for the *previous* existence of the agent. Since the original, rough counterfactual test asked what would have happened if the agent had never existed *at all,* the change it asked us to imagine was too drastic. The test altered too much. What was needed was a more fine-grained approach, and this is provided by the suggested revision. Furthermore, not only does the revised counterfactual test give us the intuitively correct answer for the gimmicky case of the King, it continues to provide the intuitively appropriate answers in the more standard cases as well. (It must be admitted, however, that the revised test still *condemns* inappropriately in the second gimmicky case, in which the second son allows his younger brother to starve.)

Unfortunately, however, even the suggested revision is still too crude. Imagine that while dining alone with the Queen, the King confesses his ill treatment of their son. Stunned by the news, the Queen begins to choke on her food and is in danger of choking to death. The King rushes to her side, pounds her back with his left hand until the food is dislodged, and the Queen's life is saved; at the same time, however, he deliberately stabs her in the leg with the dagger in his right hand, causing the Queen to limp for the rest of her days. Having saved the Queen's life is, of course, commendable. But surely the King's stabbing the Queen interferes with her welfare and violates the constraint against doing harm. Yet the King may exclaim anew that had he not existed at the time of the stabbing, the Queen would have died and so would not have been better off than she is (with her limp). Thus even the revised test excuses too much, yielding the intuitively incorrect result that the King has not interfered.

Apparently we need to focus the counterfactual test even more narrowly. The original test altered too much in asking whether the victim would have been better off had the agent never existed at all. Although the revised test is an improvement, it seems that in asking what would have happened had the agent not existed at the time of the act in question, it still changes too much. We need to focus on the act itself, and see whether *its* existence alters the outcome of the ongoing processes. This suggests the following refinement of the counterfactual test: the agent interferes by reacting in a given way if the victim would have been better off had the given reaction not occurred. Since the Queen would have been better off had the King not stabbed her, the King's stabbing the Queen interferes with her well-being. Here, at last, we have a test that does not seem to excuse too much.

But if this latest version of the test does not excuse too much, this is at least in part because it condemns far too much. Not only does the test still fail on the second gimmicky case, involving the death of the youngest son, even in *standard* cases where we want to say that the agent has not interfered, the test no longer gives the intuitively correct answers. If I stand back idly and watch Maude drown, for example, I have not interfered with her. Yet consider my reaction of refusing to jump in and rescue her:

had that reaction not occurred, I would have reacted differently; in particular, it seems, I would not have refused to jump in. But had I jumped in, we can suppose, Maude would not have drowned. So in failing to jump in—the test now tells us—I *do* interfere with Maude's life. Similarly, in failing to send money to famine relief I interfere with the life of some stranger who dies of starvation, for had my reaction not occurred—had I sent money—someone's life would have been saved. And so on. Furthermore, if we stick to the suggestion that the moral offensiveness of doing harm should be located in interference, it now turns out that all of the cases we want to classify as cases of merely allowing harm are nonetheless cases of interfering, and so are just as offensive. Thus the justification for the constraint against *doing* harm (as opposed to merely allowing harm) disappears.

Rather than accepting this consequence, it seems more plausible . . . to insist that the latest version of the counterfactual test is grossly inadequate as a test of whether an agent has interfered or not. Our intuitive picture of interference is that of an agent stepping into the causal flow and altering it. That notion has not been captured by any test that yields the result that failure to step into the causal flow is itself a way of stepping in.

So the latest version of the test needs to be rejected as well. Indeed, the most vivid way of bringing out the inadequacy of that version is that it accuses the agent of interfering, even in cases where the victim would have been no better off had the agent never existed at all! But this, of course, brings us back to the original version of the counterfactual test, whose own shortcomings we have already noted.

It does seem that in our successive revisions of the counterfactual test we have ended up with a version that has largely lost contact with the notion of interference it was meant to capture. But this still leaves us with the question of whether the test can be salvaged after all. . . . I do not know of any more promising ways to sharpen the test so as to get around gimmicky cases (while at the same time, of course, preserving our judgments in the standard cases); nor do I know of any more promising alternatives to the counterfactual test.

NOTES AND QUESTIONS

1. Shelly Kagan offers some powerful counterexamples to the counterfactual omissions test Katz adopts. Katz seems not unaware of these difficulties but is not seriously bothered by them. Why not?

2. Judith Jarvis Thomson has famously employed something very much akin to the act-omission distinction to justify abortion. She does so with the following ingenious hypothetical case:

> You wake up in the morning and find yourself back to back in bed with an unconscious violinist—a famous, unconscious violinist. He has been found to have a fatal kidney

ailment, and the Society of Music Lovers has canvassed all the available medical records and found that you alone have the right blood type to help. They have therefore kidnapped you, and last night the violinist's circulatory system was plugged into yours, so that your kidneys can be used to extract poisons from his blood as well as your own. The director of the hospital now tells you, "Look, we're sorry the Society of Music Lovers did this to you—we would never have permitted it if we had known. But still, they did it, and the violinist now is plugged into you. To unplug you would be to kill him. But never mind, it's only for nine months. By then he will have recovered from his ailment and can safely be unplugged from you." [Are you morally obligated to go along?]

How then, Thomson proceeds to ask, is this different from the relationship of the mother to her fetus? Is she right?

3. If we wanted to rid ourselves of the act-omission distinction, it would be a remarkably difficult thing to do. As Leo Katz writes elsewhere:

The act-omission distinction has a way of proving its sturdiness by appearing again and again in different contexts and guises. Actually, the very critics who belittle it have themselves been unable to do without it. Ask them what they do when they are uncertain about some issue. For that matter, ask yourself what you do if you cannot make up your mind whether to believe X or its opposite. Usually you will find it advisable to remain agnostic. What you will not do is to say: "I might as well believe both X and not-X. Although I am certain to be wrong about one of them, I am also certain to be right about the other. So it's a wash." Your not saying this indicates that errors of commission weigh more heavily than errors of omission. . . . [It is also worth noting what happens to the act-omission distinction when we dole out praise. Here the distinction] seems to apply with, if anything, greater force than in the realm of blame. Those who merely stand by and do not prevent important work from going forward, though they could if they were determined to, are felt to deserve significantly less glory than those who actually carry out the mission or the discovery. Indeed the notion of an award would become meaningless if all noninterferors, all "omitters," were viewed as on a par with the "actor."[1]

---

[1]Leo Katz, *Ill-Gotten Gains: Evasion, Blackmail, and Kindred Puzzles of the Law* (Chicago: University of Chicago Press, 1996) 46, 201.

Act and Crime

MICHAEL S. MOORE

There are three sorts of doctrine [relating to acts] in Anglo-American criminal law. The first is that there can be no criminal offence without the doing of a voluntary act. The second is that all crimes consist not only of a *mens rea* requirement but also a requirement of *actus reus*. The third is that no one should be prosecuted or punished more than once for the same crime. The first is commonly called the voluntary-act requirement, the second, the *actus reus* requirement, and the third, the double-jeopardy requirement. . . .

Unfortunately, the important unifying functions of these three general doctrines has become obscured by the pall of scepticism that has descended upon them. In criminal law scholarship there is little agreement about what any of these requirements come to, or about how they are related. About *actus reus,* to begin with, Jerome Hall once complained about the "considerable confusion" introduced into criminal law theory by the differing concepts other writers have employed. Similarly, Josh Dressler, apparently influenced by Hall, finds "the phrase [*actus reus*] has no single accepted criminal law meaning." Meir Dan-Cohen also finds that "no single . . . definition prevails nor is the term used uniformly among lawyers." Because "the term comprises a set of elements with no obvious common denominator other than . . . that they do not include the offender's state of mind," Dan-Cohen concludes that "it is impossible to give a comprehensive affirmative definition of the *actus reus";* he therefore settles for "a residual definition: the *actus reus* designates all the elements of the criminal offence except the *mens rea.*" As Glanville Williams shows in detail, this negative definition simply lumps a number of disparate items together.

The voluntary-act requirement is thought to be in even worse shape. There are three levels of scepticism here: doctrinal, moral, and metaphysical. To begin with, a number of criminal law theorists deny that Anglo-American criminal law has an act requirement. Dan-Cohen urges that this is a "requirement" that is "honored mainly in the breach," as does Douglas Husak. They refer to crimes of status, omission, or possession as obvious counter-examples to any supposed act requirement. A somewhat different denial of there being any act requirement comes from Mark Kelman. On Kelman's view, one can always find, or not find, an act on which to predicate criminal liability, depending on how narrowly or broadly one frames the time period during which one looks; any act "requirement" thus becomes illusory for Kelman.

A second version of this doctrinal scepticism charges that if there is an act requirement in Anglo-American criminal law, it is not *an* act requirement; rather, there are several, because there are several concepts of act at work. As George Fletcher asks, "An act as opposed to what? Sometimes the concept of a human act is contrasted

From *Act and Crime: The Implications of the Philosophy of Action for the Criminal Law* (Oxford: Oxford University Press, 1993), pp. 239–44.

with an 'omission'; sometimes with a status or condition; sometimes with acting involuntarily as in cases of hypnotism and sleepwalking." And, as Fletcher does not add, but others do, sometimes "act" is fourthly opposed to mental states like wishes and intentions. The sceptical conclusion is that "the" act requirement is in reality four separate requirements: the requirement that there be more than a pure omission, more than a mere status or condition, more than in involuntary bodily movement, and more than a mental state. These four requirements may be united by a common name but little else.

This fractionating of the act requirement may go even further. Some have thought that even when we consider each of these four act requirements, one at a time, there may be only an illusory unity. J. L. Austin famously talked about "excluder" words, words like "real" or "free" (his examples) that seem to name something but actually are used to exclude the application of words like "illusion" or "coercion". Hart argued that "voluntary" was an excluder word, so that if one focused on the supposedly univocal requirement that bodily movement be *voluntary* to be an act, what really was being said was that a heterogeneous range of conditions was being excluded, conditions like unconsciousness, hypnotic states, sleep, etc. In which case the supposed requirement of a voluntary act (versus involuntary movement) was in reality a large number of different requirements: the requirement that the actor not be asleep, not be unconscious, not be hypnotized, not be suffering a reflex movement, etc.

J. L. Austin thought that even this might not be a finely enough grained approach to action. As Austin noted, the general phrase "doing an action" is an abstract expression only philosophers and lawyers use; ordinary people talk of killings, letter-postings, telephonings, etc. Austin queried whether we do not "oversimplify metaphysics" by assuming that all actions share some essential feature(s). We come easily to think that "all 'actions' are, as actions (meaning what?), equal, composing a quarrel with striking a watch, winning a war with sneezing." To pursue Austin's query very far would be to dissolve any general act requirement running throughout the criminal law into the special act requirement of each statute that prohibits actions of mayhem, rape, arson, etc.

The moral criticisms of the act requirement focus on the moral justifiability of punishing people for their acts. Sometimes the criticism is that the act requirement is *over*-inclusive in what it makes eligible for punishment, the argument being that persons with disadvantaged social backgrounds, certain mental instabilities, and the like do not freely choose to do wrong even if formally they satisfy the act requirement. As often the criticism of the act requirement is that it is *under*-inclusive. With regard to situations where the actor possesses the ability easily to prevent some harm but intentionally omits to do so, the argument is that such an actor is just as culpable as is the actor who, by his acts, causes the condition of peril to start with. What is the moral difference, this argument asks, between the actor who omits to turn on the respirator with the intention that the patient die, and the actor who acts to turn off the respirator with the intention that the patient die? Do not both actors freely *choose* both that the patient die and that their own behaviour is such that that death is sure to occur?

Even more radical scepticism about the moral justifiability of the act doctrine stems from the insight that morality is concerned with much besides our acts. We judge ourselves and others morally by who we are—what character and emotions we possess—as well as by what we *do*. Indeed, this insight leads some to conclude that bad acts are only moral proxies for what really matters to morality, bad character. A well-conceived criminal code, accordingly, would reduce the act requirement to a kind of evidentiary status: bad acts are usually good evidence of bad character, but their presence is not sufficient to infer bad character and their absence is not sufficient to infer good character. A criminal code that treats acts as sufficient in these two directions is to be criticized for sacrificing a closer fit with morality in the name of administrative convenience.

Apart from these scepticisms about there being any doctrinally coherent or morally justifiable act requirement, there is also some scepticism about the existence of acts themselves. On this view even if criminal law has an act requirement, there are no items in the world to answer to it. Herbert Hart, for example, once urged that the verbs of action did not refer to anything because the utterances in which such verbs were used were not descriptive utterances; rather, such sentences were used to ascribe responsibility so that action verbs expressed the conclusion that the "actor" was responsible but did not describe a ground for responsibility. As Patrick Fitzgerald once put Hart's point here, "in ordinary speech the word 'act', together with such allied expressions as 'A did it,' is used not so much to describe what has happened, as to ascribe responsibility." On this view, one might as well look in the world for "ouches," "dints," and "sakes," as for acts, since all such words do not refer to things but have other functions in our language.

A more currently fashionable way of denying that acts even exist is part of what I have called the "interpretive turn." On this view, whether we call something an act depends on the interpretive stance we, the observers, take to it. It does not depend on anything instrinsic to it. Critical legal-studies types like Kelman often believe this, but even mainstream criminal-law theorists such as George Fletcher have imbibed some of this *verstehen* view. In understanding action, Fletcher tells us, we must eschew the "causal understanding" appropriate to natural events like avalanches, and focus on the "interdependence of human subjects and modes of understanding that arise from human interaction." In this "perception of human acting as a form of intersubjective understanding" we interpret something to be an action only when "we can perceive a purpose in what he or she is doing." It is *our* perception of a purpose that *is* the difference between action and non-action, for Fletcher.

Not surprisingly, the supposed muddiness of the criminal law's act and *actus reus* requirements entails that the relationship between the two requirements is also unclear. Some assume that the act requirement and the *actus reus* requirement are one and the same thing. Others urge that the act requirement is part of the *actus reus* requirement, but that the latter has other necessary features as well. Yet others have thought that the two requirements have almost nothing to do with each other.

The double-jeopardy requirement is also often thought to be in poor shape with respect to its doctrinal coherence, its moral point, and its metaphysical presuppositions. In the United States there are several different doctrinal tests: the 'same evidence' test, the 'same intent' test, the 'same act or transaction' test, etc. In addition, there are four different authoritative sources for these doctrines: the federal constitution, most state constitutions, a variety of state statutes, and the common-law merger doctrine. In addition, with respect to any of these sources and doctrines, there are three different contexts of application where the doctrines are differently applied; the same-evidence test, for example, means one thing when the issue is multiple *punishments* for multiple counts tried in a single trial but it has a different meaning when the issue is multiple *prosecutions* for multiple charges brought in successive trials. Some conclude from these characteristics of American double-jeopardy doctrine that there is no coherent double-jeopardy requirement in the American legal system.

Some sceptics go further and explain the doctrinal incoherence of American double-jeopardy law in terms of the lack of any unitary moral point to the double-jeopardy prohibitions. Because of the differing policies behind separable applications of the clause, Peter Westen, for example, urges:

> in order to decide what the words of the fifth amendment mean, one must first ascertain what purposes they serve. When one does, one will discover . . . that the purposes are "separate," and, accordingly, that the meanings of the constituent terms change in accord with the several purposes for which they are invoked.

Such policy-based scepticism extends to there being any univocal meaning to double jeopardy's crucial concept of the "same offence":

> To try to formulate a single definition of "same offence" for these three separate purposes would produce a statement of such abstract generality as to be of no usefulness in resolving actual cases.

In addition to these doctrinal and moral doubts, many think that there can be no coherent double-jeopardy requirement because metaphysically there are no definite identity conditions to either actions or offences. To apply any double-jeopardy prohibition, in other words, requires that one be able to say when two somewhat differently worded offences are none the less "the same" for double-jeopardy purposes, and it requires that one be able to say when two differently described acts done on some occasion by an accused are in reality "the same." Yet the first of these sameness enquiries requires us to be able to individuate types of actions (offences), which requires us to individuate universals—which (in the famous characterization of certain critics of the Scholastics in the Middle Ages) is like counting how many angels can dance on the head of a pin. Moreover, the second of these sameness enquiries requires us to be able to individuate particular acts. The sceptical thought here is that acts have no natural boundaries, that whether one sees one act or several depends on the eye of the beholder. J. L. Austin expressed such a scepticism when he queried: "What is *an* or *one* or *the* action? For we can generally split up what might be called one action in several distinct ways, into different *stretches* or *phases* or *stages.*" Many legal theorists have followed Austin's sort of scepticism here. Thus, John Salmond urged that "an act has no boundaries any more than an event or place has. Its limits must be artificially defined for the purpose in hand for the time being. . . . To ask what act a man has done is like asking in what place he lives." Similarly, Larry Simon concludes (citing and relying upon Austin) that "any sequence of conduct can be defined as an 'act'. . . . Whether any span of conduct is an act depends entirely upon the verb in the question we ask."

I thus assume that the act, *actus reus,* and double-jeopardy requirements can use some clarification and resuscitation. If we use the above summarized sceptical assaults on the three requirements as our guide, we can usefully separate the questions any theory of action suitable for criminal-law purposes should ask and answer. Some of these are questions about criminal-law doctrines and their coherence, some are about the moral point justifying such doctrines, and some are about the things such doctrines purport to require, namely, acts and actions. I begin with the act requirement:

1a. Does the criminal law have an act requirement as a prerequisite to liability to punishment?
 b. If so, is it one requirement, several requirements, or as many requirements as there are different verbs of action used in the particular prohibitions of the special part of the criminal law?
2a. Should the criminal law make acting a prerequisite to criminal liability?
 b. To the extent that it should not do so—as, for example, about certain kinds of omissions—how can such departures from the act requirement be justified if the requirement itself is justified?
3a. If there is and should be a univocal act requirement as part of the definition of all crimes, do things called acts actually exist in the world such that the requirement could be satisfied?
 b. If so, what is the nature of such acts? Are they, for example, events of a certain kind, and if so are they mental events, bodily movements, or even events in the physical world like the death of a person (when caused by a stabbing, say)?

There is a parallel set of questions to be asked of the *actus reus* requirement:

1a. Does the criminal law have an *actus reus* requirement as a prerequisite to liability to punishment?
 b. If so, is it one requirement, several, or as many different requirements as there are different verbs of action used in the particular prohibitions of the special part of the criminal law?
2. Should the criminal law make the doing of some complex action that instantiates some complex action description contained in some statute in force at the time the act was done a prerequisite of criminal liability?
3a. If there is and should be a univocal *actus reus* requirement, do things actually exist in the world (let us provisionally call them "complex actions") such that the requirement could be satisfied?
 b. If so, what is the nature of such complex actions? Are they, for example, events of a certain kind, and if so, how do such events relate to other events like the movements of human bodies?

Once we have answered these two sets of questions, we should be in a position also to answer the parallel questions about the double-jeopardy requirement:

1a. Does the criminal law have a double-jeopardy requirement?
 b. If so, is it one requirement, several, or as diverse as the actions or offences that might be said to be "the same"?
2a. Should the criminal law prohibit being punished twice or even prosecuted twice for acts or offences that are in some sense "the same"?

b. If so, do the values that justify such a prohibition have sufficient commonality that they justify one doctrinal prohibition, several, or many?

3. If there is and should be a univocal double-jeopardy requirement, are the identity conditions of both actions and the offences that prohibit them sufficiently precise to allow the requirement to be nonarbitrarily applied?

There are other questions we could ask in a philosophical theory of action, but the above are the most relevant to the criminal lawyer. Answering such questions may help us to rediscover the potential for elegance and intellectual integrity that a criminal code may possess, a potential that so charmed our forebears in legal philosophy. I shall begin with the questions about the criminal law's act requirement, the morality that justifies such a requirement, and the metaphysical nature of the acts which it requires.

NOTES AND QUESTIONS

1. How does the act-omission distinction fit with Moore's three basic doctrines? According to the criminal law scholars Moore discusses? According to Moore himself?

2. What is the relationship between the various skepticisms Moore discusses and Shelly Kagan's discussion of the counterfactual test for the act-omission distinction?

3.3 CAUSATION

As we have seen, causation is a watershed element in criminal liability, for whether an offender is liable as a *principal* (versus as an accomplice) for a *completed* crime (versus as an attemptor or a risker) depends on whether that offender *caused* some legally prohibited state of affairs. It is the notion of causation that distinguishes the major theories of criminal liability.

Given the crucial role played by the concept in theorizing about criminal liability, it is remarkable that a long tradition of scholarship has abandoned the analysis of causation to torts scholars. Causation certainly plays a pivotal role in torts law too, but no more so than in the criminal law. Moreover, it is not clear that the concepts of causation employed in the two areas of law are the same. (If they were, criminal law could simply borrow from tort law here.) The reasons for requiring causation as a prerequisite of liability differ for tort and criminal law, and it is certainly possible (on some but not all of the concepts of causation that are introduced below) that those different reasons require different concepts.

Criminal law thus needs its own analysis of causation. Yet the notion of causation has proved to be remarkably resistant to the efforts of scholars to unpack it, be they philosophers, economists, or legal scholars. The upshot has been a bewildering array of proposed analyses, many of them having some authority in the law. Even worse, courts have often not even acknowledged the distinctions between the differing theories of causation; they have adopted what might be called the "stew theory" of causation, which is to throw *all* proposed theories in the pot together, stir well, and leave the issue to some poor jury.

We thus need to spend some time here sorting out the questions asked about causation and sorting out the competing answers to those questions. Let us start with the questions. All theorists focus on the nature of the causal relation. When we say "X caused Y," what do we mean by "caused"? Only secondarily should we be concerned with what might be called the "ontology of causation." This is the question as to *what* can be a cause of *what*—that is, between what sort of entities can the causal relation exist? Events only? States too? Types of events or states? Facts about them? Persons or other objects as causes?

There is a close relationship between our primary question, "what is causation?" and this secondary question, "what can be a cause?" Yet most theorists assume that the relational question is primary: understand what that relation is, and you are a long ways toward understanding which sorts of entities can stand in that relation.

There are actually two causal relations on which we need to focus as we approach the issues of causation. The first is standardly called the "singular causal relation." When we say, "A's striking of the spark caused the fire," we typically mean to describe a singular causal relation between one event-particular, A's action, and another event-particular, the fire. Contrast such statements with this one: "Striking sparks causes fires." The latter statement describes a causal generalization that holds between one *type* of event, spark strikings, and another *type* of event, fires. Such statements do not refer to any particular event but rather generalize about classes of events. The relation is thus not a singular causal relation but rather a causal generalization.

In the criminal law, as in torts, we are interested in knowing whether a defendant's particular action caused some particular state of affairs to exist. For example, did Jones's shooting of the gun cause the death of Smith? We are thus interested in singular causal relations. Our interest in causal generalizations is relegated to a mode of proof of the existence of such singular causal relations. Nonetheless, it is crucial to distinguish the two relations, because the failure to do so can easily lead one astray.

It may surprise some to see no distinction being drawn between "cause in fact" and "proximate cause" in this focus on singular causal relations. This is because how one answers the question about singular causal relations determines whether this familiar doctrinal distinction is viable. Many theorists analyze singular causal relations in a way that either eliminates the distinction or relegates it to a very minor role. What matters, according to such theorists, is the existence of a singular causal relation, and that relation is so discriminating in what it picks out as a cause that there is little or no work to be done by any notion of "proximate cause." It is only those theorists who analyze the singular causal relation as being much less discriminating that have need for a test of proximate causation in addition to cause in fact. Such theorists join skeptics about the existence of singular causal relations in adding a second test, one of policy that is misleadingly labeled in terms of ("proximate" or "legal") causation.

We have thus focused this discussion on the enquiry into the nature of singular causal relations, suspending any concern about dividing up this question into two distinct doctrinal niches. What should be distinguished are ten distinct answers to the question about the nature of singular causal relations. A useful way of taxonomizing these ten distinct answers is around what might be called discriminating versus nondiscriminating notions of cause.

Discriminating theories hold causation to be a real relation capable of limiting criminal liability in an appropriate way without supplementation. Nondiscriminating theories either hold causation not to be a real relation at all or hold it to lack enough discriminating power that it cannot serve to limit criminal liability unless it is supplemented with policy tests. Using this distinction, we may group the theories as follows:

A. Nondiscriminating Theories of Causation
   1. Nonskeptical Theories: sine qua non and the counterfactual (or necessity) test
   2. Skeptical Theories
      a. Humean Skepticism
      b. More Radical Skepticism
B. Noncausal, Policy-oriented, Supplemental Tests of "Proximate Causation"
   1. Ad Hoc Policy Balances on a Case-by-Case Basis
   2. Foreseeability
   3. Harm within the Risk
C. Discriminating Theories of Causation
   1. Mechanistic Causation
   2. Direct Causation
   3. Aspect Causation
   4. Substantial Factor Causation

1. Counterfactual View

We begin with the dominant view of causation in the law, the counterfactual view.[1] On this view, there is such a thing as a causal relation, and its nature is given by counterfactuals of the form, "if A had not struck the spark, the fire would not have oc-

---

[1]Adopted, for example, by the American Law Institute's Model/Penal Code §2.03(1). For a sophisticated philosophical treatment of counterfactual analyses of causation, see David Lewis, "Causation," *Journal of Philosophy,* Vol. 70 (1973), pp. 557–67. For criticism of the counterfactual analyses, see Michael Moore, *Act and Crime: The Implications of the Philosophy of Action for the Criminal Law* (Oxford: Clarendon Press, 1993, pp. 267–274. For a defense, see Richard Wright, "Causation, Responsibility, Risk, Probability, Naked Statistics and Proof: Pruning the Bramble Bush by Clarifying the Concepts," *Iowa Law Review,* Vol. 73 (1988), pp. 1032–42.

curred." If this dominant view of causation were accepted, it would make causation a very nondiscriminating relation. That means some supplemental test would have to be added to the sine qua non test, most often a supplemental test of policy (even though misleadingly called "proximate causation"). Thus the counterfactual view of causation requires the criminal law to add some second, more discriminating test to this one.

2. Humean Skepticism

We next examine two skeptical views, both of which deny that there is any such thing as a singular causal relation. The first of these views, stemming from David Hume, asserts that the only causal relation that exists is the relation we earlier called causal generalizations.[2] On this view, when people talk of singular events causing other singular events to occur, they are misleadingly referring to types of events and the causal generalizations that hold between them. There is one obvious problem for Hume: how can Hume distinguish mere temporal succession from causation? Those (rather numerous) economists who equate causal relations to probability functions simply repeat in modern garb Hume's kind of skepticism about the existence of singular causal relations.

3. More Radical Skepticism

The second skeptical view is that of some American legal realists and of critical legal studies.[3] These are more radical skepticisms, for they view both singular causal relations and causal generalizations as empty of factual content. Needed, on this view, are policy analyses justifying liability, albeit not on any "causal" grounds.

4. Ad Hoc Policy

The fourth view we should distinguish is a view about causation only in the loosest sense. On this view, "proximate cause" is a label we put on a balance of competing policies that have nothing to do with actual causation. In other words, is the label we put on the conclusion about liability, not a reason for reaching this conclusion.[4]

---

[2]David Hume, "Liberty and Necessity," in *Enquiry Concerning Human Understanding* (Oxford: Clarendon Press, 1902), pp. 80–83. See also Moritz Schlick, "Causality in Everyday Life and in Recent Science," *University of California Publications in Philosophy,* Vol. 15 (1932), pp. 99–125. For criticism of this view, see David Lewis, "Causation," *Journal of Philosophy,* Vol. 70 (1973), pp. 556–57. Hume's view is shared today by economists and others who equate probabilistic linkage with causation. On this, see R. Wright, "Actual Causation versus Probabilistic Linkage: The Bane of Economic Analysis," *Journal of Legal Studies,* Vol. 14 (1985), pp. 435–39, 455–56.

[3]For a representative sample, see Wex S. Malone, "Ruminations on Cause-in-Fact," *Stanford Law Review,* Vol. 9 (1956), pp. 60–99; Mark Kelman, "The Necessary Myth of Objective Causation Judgments in Liberal Political Theory," *Chicago-Kent Law Review,* Vol. 63 (1987), pp. 579–637. For criticism of the latter view, see Michael Moore, "Thomson's Preliminaries About Causation and Rights," *Chicago-Kent Law Review,* Vol. 63 (1987), pp. 503–5.

[4]The best representative of ad hoc policy balancing is still Henry Edgerton, "Legal Cause," *University of Pennsylvania Law Review,* Vol. 72 (1924), pp. 211–244, 343–375. Some of the law and economics literature on causation shares Edgerton's view.

5. Foreseeability

The fifth view of causation, the foreseeability view, asks a deceptively simple question: was the harm that in fact resulted from the defendant's action foreseeable to him when he acted? This question is not as simple as it appears, because of problems in fixing upon a description of the harm about which we ask, "was *that* foreseeable?"[5] Preliminarily, however, one should see how foreseeability fits in with the other tests. Notice that the foreseeability test also makes no pretense of being a causal test; foreseeability is a matter of average cognitive capacities applied to the information base possessed by the actor in question. Reasons of policy, such as fairness or deterrence, have to enter in to justify use of this test. Notice secondly that this test applies only in conjunction with some nondiscriminating notion of causation, usually the counterfactual notion. Foreseeability is thus one of those supplemental tests, like the explicit policy test, use of which makes sense only when conjoined to some other test of factual causation.

6. Harm within the Risk

The sixth view of causation is the version usually called "harm within the risk." The idea is simple enough: ask whether the harm that was caused by the defendant's action was an instance of one of those types of harm that made his behavior negligent or reckless to start with (or, in the case of crimes with intent as the mens rea, ask whether the harm was within the type of harm defendant intended). The Model Penal Code largely adopts this test (see, e.g., §§2.03(2) and 2.03(3)). Notice that, like both the foreseeability and the policy tests, the harm-within-the-risk test is explicitly not causal. Notice also that this test too is supplemental to some other (causal) analysis, usually the counterfactual one.

7. Aspect Causation View

The seventh view is what we shall call the "aspect causation" view.[6] This does purport to be a causal test, not a noncausal test justified on policy grounds; and this purports to give us a very discriminating view of causation, so that no other test need be used. Despite these two differences with the harm-within-the-risk test, the aspect-cause test is very similar: first isolate that aspect of the defendant's action that made his conduct risky (or that he intended, for crimes of intent), and ask whether, counterfactually, the harm that occurred would not have occurred had the defendant's action not had that aspect to it.

---

[5]For an examination of this problem, see Michael Moore, "Foreseeing Harm Opaquely," in S. Shute, J. Gardner, and J. Horder, eds., *Action and Value in Criminal Law* (Oxford: Clarendon Press, 1993), pp. 125–30, 143–52.

[6]Despite their differences, the two best representatives of this view are Robert Keeton, *Legal Cause in the Law of Torts* (Columbus: Ohio State University Press, 1963); and Richard Wright, "Causation in Tort Law," *California Law Review,* Vol. 73 (1985), pp. 1737–1828.

8. *Mechanistic Causation*

The eighth analysis of causation seeks to show that the singular causal relation is a sufficiently discriminating one that it can do all the work demanded of the causal requirements of the criminal law. This is a mechanistic approach to causation, whereby the relation is conceived in terms of forces, collisions, and matter in motion.[7] The spatiotemporal closeness required by these mechanistic notions is what promises the discriminating analysis of the causal relation.

9. *Direct Causation*

Hart and Honore, the only selection included below, defend a ninth view of causation. They also seek to vindicate a discriminating concept of causation, one that should be seen as a version of the direct cause conception of proximate causation. Causes, they tell us, are to be distinguished from mere background conditions. While such background conditions may be necessary for a certain harm to come about, causes are quite another matter. Here we must look to voluntary human actions and those abnormal conjunctions of natural events we call "acts of God" or "coincidences." These two types of events are both picked out as causes, and should one of them intervene between a first event and a second, their intervening existence makes impossible that the first event should be a cause of the second. Such an intervened-upon first event is then relegated to being a background condition, not a cause, even if that first event is a voluntary human action.

10. *Substantial Factor Causation*

The last view of causation we should distinguish is epistemically, but not metaphysically, skeptical. According to this view, causation is epistemically primitive, meaning that no other concept can be used to analyze it. The causal relation is quite real; we just cannot say anything about it.[8] If one adds to this the idea that the causal relation is a scalar affair, so that there can be more and less of it, then one has a well-known test for causation: ask whether a substantial amount of this primitive causal relation existed between defendant's action and the legally prohibited state of affairs.[9] Such a "substantial factor" test, partially adopted by the Restatement of Torts, promises a quite discriminating notion of causation, depending on how rigorously the word "substantial" is read.

---

[7]Two well-known representatives of this approach are Joseph Beale, "The Proximate Consequences of an Act," *Harvard Law Review,* Vol. 33 (1920), pp. 633–58, and Richard Epstein, "A Theory of Strict Liability," *Journal of Legal Studies,* Vol. 2 (1973), pp. 151–204. For a recent attempt to show that something like this view of causation is the one presupposed by criminal law, see Michael Moore, "Causation and Responsibility," forthcoming, *Social Philosophy and Policy,* Vol. 16, No. 2 (1999).

[8]See Richard Taylor, *Action and Purpose* (Englewood Cliffs, N.J.: Prentice-Hall, 1966), p. 39.

[9]Jeremiah Smith, "Legal Cause in Actions of Torts," *Harvard Law Review,* Vol. 25 (1911), pp. 103–28, 223–52, 303–27.

Causation in the Law
H. L. A. HART AND A. M. HONORÉ

Responsibility in Law and Morals

We have so far traced the outline of a variety of causal concepts the diversity of which is to be seen in such familiar examples of the use of causal language as the following: "The explosion of gas caused the building to collapse," "He made him hand over his money by threatening to shoot," "The consequence of leaving the car unlocked was that it was stolen," "The strike was the cause of the drop in profits."

The main structure of these different forms of causal connection is plain enough, and there are many situations constantly recurring in ordinary life to which they have a clear application; yet it is also true that like many other fundamental notions these have aspects which are vague or indeterminate; they involve the weighing of matters of degree, or the plausibility of hypothetical speculations, for which no exact criteria can be laid down. Hence their application, outside the safe area of simple examples, calls for judgment and is something over which judgments often differ. Even the type of case which is most familiar, and most nearly approximates to Mill's model for "cause and effect," where causal connection between a physical event and some earlier initiating event or human action is traced through a series of physical events, involves an implicit judgment on such imprecise issues as the *normal* condition of the thing concerned and the *abnormality* of what is identified as the cause. Very often, in particular where an omission to take common precautions is asserted to be the cause of some disaster, a speculation as to what *would have* happened had the precaution been taken is involved. Though arguments one way or another over such hypothetical issues may certainly be rational and have more or less "weight," there is a sense in which they cannot be conclusive. When such areas of dispute are reached, the decision whether to describe the facts of a case in the terms of some given form of causal connection will be influenced very much by factors connected with the context and purpose of making the causal statement.

Hitherto we have discussed only one principal purpose for which causal language is used: i.e., when an explanation is sought or provided of some puzzling or unusual occurrence. But as well as this explanatory context, in which we are concerned with what *has* happened, there are many others. Our deliberations about our own conduct often take the form of an inquiry as to the future consequences of alternative actions; here causal connections are *ex hypothesi* bounded by the horizon of the foreseeable. But even if we confine ourselves to causal statements about the past there are still different contexts and purposes to be discriminated. Thus it would be wrong to think of

From *Causation in the Law,* 2d ed. (Oxford: Clarendon Press, 1985), pp. 62–63, 68–83.

the historian as using causal notions only when he is explaining. The movement of his thought is not always from the later problematic event to something earlier which explains it and in using causal language he is not always engaged in diagnosis. His thought very often takes the contrary direction; for in addition to providing explanations (answers to the question "why?") he is also concerned to trace the outcome, the results, or the consequences of the human actions and omissions which are his usual starting points, though he may also work out the "effects" of natural events. So he will discuss the consequences of a king's policy or the effects of the Black Death. This is so because the narrative of history is scarcely ever a narrative of brute sequence, but is an account of the roles played by certain factors and especially by human agents. History is written to satisfy not only the need for explanation, but also the desire to identify and assess contributions made by historical figures to changes of importance; to triumphs and disasters, and to human happiness or suffering. This assessment involves tracing "consequences," "effects," or "results," and these are more frequently referred to than "causes" which has a primarily diagnostic or explanatory ring. In one sense of "responsibility" the historian determines the responsibility of human beings for certain types of change; and sometimes he does this with an eye to praising or blaming or passing other forms of moral judgment. But this need not be so; the historian, though concerned to trace the consequences of human action, need not be a moralist.

. . .

Tracing Consequences

"To consequences no limit can be set": "Every event which would not have happened if an earlier event had not happened is the consequence of that earlier event." These two propositions are not equivalent in meaning and are not equally or in the same way at variance with ordinary thought. They have, however, both been urged sometimes in the same breath by the legal theorist and the philosopher: they are indeed sometimes said by lawyers to be "the philosophical doctrine" of causation. It is perhaps not difficult even for the layman to accept the first proposition as a truth about certain physical events; an explosion may cause a flash of light which will be propagated as far as the outer nebulae; its effects or consequences continue indefinitely. It is, however, a different matter to accept the view that whenever a man is murdered with a gun his death was the consequence of (still less an "effect" or of "caused by") the manufacture of the bullet. The first tells a perhaps unfamiliar tale about unfamiliar events; the second introduces an unfamiliar, though, of course, a possible way of speaking about familiar events. it is not that this unrestricted use of "consequence" is unintelligible or never found; it is indeed used to refer to bizarre or fortuitous connections or coincidences: but the point is that the various causal notions employed for the purposes of explanation, attribution of responsibility, or the assessment of contributions to the course of history carry with them implicit limits which are similar in these different employments.

It is, then, the second proposition, defining consequence in terms of "necessary condition," with which theorists are really concerned. This proposition is the corollary of the view that, if we look into the past of any given event, there is an infinite number of events, each of which is a necessary condition of the given event and so, as much as any other, is its cause. This is the "cone" of causation, so called because, since any event has a number of simultaneous conditions, the series fans out as we go back in time. The justification, indeed only partial, for calling this "the philosophical doctrine" of causation is that it resembles Mill's doctrine that "we have no right to give the name of cause to one of the conditions exclusive of the others of them." It differs from Mill's view in taking the essence of causation to be "necessary condition" and not "the sum total" of the sufficient conditions of an event.

Legal theorists have developed this account of cause and consequence to show what is "factual," "objective," or "scientific" in these notions: this they call "cause in fact" and it is usually stressed as a preliminary to the doctrine that any more restricted application of these terms in the law represents nothing in the facts or in the meaning of causation, but expresses fluctuating legal policy or sentiments of what is just or convenient. Moral philosophers have insisted in somewhat similar terms that the consequences of human action are "infinite": this they have urged as an objection against the Utilitarian doctrine that the rightness of a morally right action depends on whether its consequences are better than those of any alternative action in the circumstances. "We should have to trace as far as possible the consequences not only for the persons affected directly but also for those indirectly affected and to these no limit can be set." Hence, so the argument runs, we cannot either inductively establish the Utilitarian doctrine that right acts are "optimific" or use it in particular cases to discover what is right. Yet, however vulnerable at other points Utilitarianism may be as an account of moral judgment, this objection seems to rest on a mistake as to the sense of "consequence." The Utilitarian assertion that the rightness of an action depends on its consequences is not the same as the assertion that it depends on all those later occurrences which would not have happened had the action not been done, to which indeed "no limit can be set." It is important to see that the issue here is not the linguistic one whether the word "consequence" would be understood if used in this way. The point is that, though we could, we do not think in this way in tracing connections between human actions and events. Instead, whenever we are concerned with such connections, whether for the purpose of explaining a puzzling occurrence, assessing responsibility, or giving an intelligible historical narrative, we employ a set of concepts restricting in various ways what counts as a consequence. These restrictions colour *all* our thinking in causal terms; when we find them in the law we are not finding something invented by or peculiar to the law, though of course it is for the law to say when and how far it will use them and, where they are vague, to supplement them.

No short account can be given of the limits thus placed on "consequences" because these limits vary, intelligibly, with the variety of causal connection asserted. Thus we may be tempted by the generalization that consequences must always be something intended or foreseen or at least foreseeable with ordinary care: but counter-examples spring up from many types of context where causal statements are made. If smoking is shown to cause lung cancer, this discovery will permit us to describe past as well as future cases of cancer as the effect or consequence of smoking even though no one foresaw or had reasonable grounds to suspect this in the past. What is common and commonly appreciated and hence foreseeable certainly controls the scope

of consequences in certain varieties of causal statement but not in all. Again the voluntary intervention of a second person very often constitutes the limit. If a guest sits
down at a table laid with knife and fork and plunges the knife into his hostess's breast,
her death is not in any context other than a contrived one thought of as caused by, or
the effect or result of the waiter's action in laying the table; nor would it be linked
with this action as its consequence for any of the purposes, explanatory or attributive,
for which we employ causal notions. Yet as we have seen, there are many other types
of case where a voluntary action or the harm it does are naturally treated to the consequence of to some prior neglect of precaution. Finally, we may think that a simple
answer is already supplied by Hume and Mill's doctrine that causal connection rests
on general laws asserting regular connection; yet, even in the type of case to which
this important doctrine applies, reference to it alone will not solve our problem. For
we often trace a causal connection between an antecedent and a consequent which
themselves very rarely go together: we do this when the case can be broken down into
intermediate stages, which themselves exemplify different generalizations, as when
we find that the fall of a tile was the cause of someone's death, rare though this be.
Here our problem reappears in the form of the question: When can generalizations be
combined in this way?

We shall examine first the central type of case where the problem is of this last-
mentioned form. Here the gist of the causal connection lies in the general connection
with each other of the successive stages; and is not dependent on the special notions
of one person providing another with reasons or exceptional opportunities for actions.
This form of causal connection may exist between actions and events, and between
purely physical events, and it is in such cases that the words "cause" and "causing"
used of the antecedent action or event have their most obvious application. It is convenient to refer to cases of the first type where the consequence is harm as cases of
"causing harm," and to refer to cases where harm is the consequence of one person
providing another with reasons or opportunities for doing harm as cases of "inducing" or "occasioning" harmful acts. In cases of the first type a voluntary act, or a conjunction of events amounting to a coincidence, operates as a limit in the sense that
events subsequent to these are not attributed to the antecedent action or event as its
consequence even though they would not have happened without it. Often such a limiting action or coincidence is thought of and described as "intervening": and lawyers
speak of them as "superseding" or "extraneous" causes "breaking the chain of causation." To see what these metaphors rest on (and in part obscure) and how such factors operate as a limit we shall consider the detail of three simple cases.

(i) A forest fire breaks out, and later investigation shows that shortly before the
outbreak A had flung away a lighted cigarette into the bracken at the edge of the forest, the bracken caught fire, a light breeze got up, and fanned the flames in the direction of the forest. If, on discovering these facts, we hesitate before saying that A's action caused the forest fire this would be to consider the alternative hypothesis that in
spite of appearances the fire only succeeded A's action in point of time, that the
bracken flickered out harmlessly and the forest fire was caused by something else. To
dispose of this it may be necessary to examine in further detail the process of events
between the ignition of the bracken and the outbreak of fire in the forest and to show

that these exemplified certain types of continuous change. If this is shown, there is no longer any room for doubt: A's action *was* the cause of the fire, whether he intended it or not. This seems and is the simplest of cases. Yet it is important to notice that even in applying our general knowledge to a case as simple as this, indeed in regarding it as simple, we make an implicit use of a distinction between types of factor which constitute a limit in tracing consequences and those which we regard as mere circumstances "through" which we trace them. For the breeze which sprang up after A dropped the cigarette, and without which the fire would not have spread to the forest, was not only subsequent to his action but entirely independent of it: it was, however, a common recurrent feature of the environment, and, as such, it is thought of not as an "intervening" force but as merely part of the circumstances in which the cause "operates." The decision so to regard it is implicitly taken when we combine our knowledge of the successive stages of the process and assert the connection.

It is easy here to be misled by the natural metaphor of a causal "chain," which may lead us to think that the causal process consists of a series of single events each of which is dependent upon (would not have occurred without) its predecessor in the "chain" and so is dependent upon the initiating action or event. In truth in any causal process we have at each phase not single events but complex sets of conditions, and among these conditions are some which are not only subsequent to, but independent of the initiating action or event. Some of these independent conditions, such as the evening breeze in the example chosen, we classify as mere conditions in or on which the cause operates; others we speak of as "interventions" or "causes." To decide how such independent elements shall be classified is also to decide how we shall combine our knowledge of the different general connections which the successive stages exemplify, and it is important to see that nothing *in* this knowledge itself can resolve this point. We may have to go to science for the relevant general knowledge before we can assert with proper confidence that A's action did cause the fire, but science, though it tells us that an air current was required, is silent on the difference between a current in the form of an evening breeze and one produced by someone who deliberately fanned the flames as they were flickering out in the bracken. Yet an air current in this deliberately induced form is not a "condition" or "mere circumstance" through which we can trace the consequence; its presence would force us to revise the assertion that A caused the fire. Conversely if science helped us to identify as a necessary factor in producing the fire some condition or element of which we had previously been totally ignorant—e.g., the persistence of oxygen—this would leave our original judgment undisturbed if this factor were a common or pervasive feature of the environment or of the thing in question. There is thus indeed an important sense in which it is true that the distinction between cause and conditions is not a "scientific" one. It is not determined bylaws or generalizations concerning connections between events.

When we have assembled all our knowledge of the factors involved in the fire, the residual question which we then confront (the attributive question) may be typified as follows: Here is A's action, here is the fire: can the fire be attributed to A's action as its consequence given that there is also this third factor (the breeze or B's intervention) without which the fire would not have happened? It is plain that, both in raising questions of this kind and in answering them, ordinary thought is powerfully influenced by the analogy between the straightforward cases of causal attribution (where the elements required for the production of harm in addition to the initiating action are all "normal" conditions) and even simpler cases of responsibility which we do not ordinarily describe in causal language at all but by the simple transitive verbs of action. These are the cases of the direct manipulation of objects involving changes in them or their position: cases where we say "He pushed it," "He broke it," "He bent it." The cases which we do confidently describe in causal language ("The fire was caused by his carelessness," "He caused a fire") are cases where no other human action or abnormal occurrence is required for the production of the effect, but only normal conditions. Such cases appear as mere long-range or less direct versions or extensions of the most obvious and fundamental case of all for the attribution of responsibility: the case where we can simply say "He did it." Conversely in attaching importance to thus causing harm as a distinct ground of responsibility and in taking certain kinds of factors (whether human interventions or abnormal occurrences), without which the initiating action would not have led to harm, to preclude the description of the case in simple causal terms, common sense is affected by the fact that here, because of the manner in which the harm eventuates, the outcome cannot be represented as a mere extension of the initiating action; the analogy with the fundamental case for responsibility ("He did it") has broken down.

When we understand the power exerted over our ordinary thought by the conception that causing harm is a mere extension of the primary case of doing harm, the interrelated metaphors which seem natural to lawyers and laymen, in describing various aspects of causal connection, fall into place and we can discuss their factual basis. The persistent notion that some kinds of event required in addition to the initiating action for the production of harm "break the chain of causation" is intelligible, if we remember that though such events actually *complete* the *explanation* of the harm (and so *make* rather than *break* the causal explanation) they do, unlike mere normal conditions, break the *analogy* with cases of simple actions. The same analogy accounts for the description of these factors as "new actions" (*novus actus*) or "new causes," "superseding," "extraneous," "intervening forces": and for the description of the initiating action when "the chain of causation" is broken as "no longer operative," "having worn out," *functus officio.* So too when the "chain" is held not to be "broken," the initiating action is said to be still "potent," "continuing," "contributing," "operative," and the mere conditions held insufficient to break the chain are "part of the background," "circumstances in which the cause operates," "the stage set," "part of the history."

(ii) A throws a lighted cigarette into the bracken which catches fire. Just as the flames are about to flicker out, B, who is not acting in concert with A, deliberately pours petrol on them. The fire spreads and burns down the forest. A's action, whether or not he intended the forest fire, was not the cause of the fire: B's was.

The voluntary intervention of a second human agent, as in this case, is a paradigm among those factors which preclude the assimilation in causal judgments of the first agent's connection with the eventual harm to the case of simple direct manipulation. Such an intervention displaces the prior action's title to be called the cause and, in the persistent metaphors found in the law, it "reduces" the earlier action and its immediate effects to the level of "mere circumstances" or "part of the history." B in this case was not an "instrument" through which A worked or a victim of the circumstances A has created. He has, on the contrary, freely exploited the circumstances and brought about the fire without the cooperation of any further agent or any chance coincidence. Compared with this, the claim of A's action to be ranked the cause of the fire fails. That this and not the moral appraisal of the two actions is the point of comparison seems clear. If A and B both intended to set the forest on fire, and this destruction is accepted as something wrong or wicked, their moral wickedness, judged by the criterion of intention, is the same. Yet the causal judgment differentiates between them. If their moral guilt is judged by the outcome, this judgment though it would differentiate between them cannot be the source of the causal judgment; for it presupposes it. The difference just is that B has caused the harm and A has not. Again, if we appraise these actions as good or bad from different points of view, this leaves the causal judgments unchanged. A may be a soldier of one side anxious to burn down the enemy's hide-out: B may be an enemy soldier who has decided that his side is too iniquitous to defend. Whatever is the moral judgment passed on these actions by different speakers it would remain true that A had not caused the fire and B had.

There are, as we have said, situations in which a voluntary action would not be thought of as an intervention precluding causal connection in this way. These are the cases discussed further below where an opportunity commonly exploited for harmful actions is negligently provided, or one person intentionally provides another with the means, the opportunity, or a certain type of reason for wrongdoing. Except in such cases a voluntary intervention is a limit past which consequences are not traced. By contrast, actions which in any of a variety of different ways are less than fully voluntary are assimilated to the means by which or the circumstances in which the earlier action brings about the consequences. Such actions are not the outcome of an informed choice made without pressure from others, and the different ways in which human action may fall short in this respect range from defective muscular control, through lack of consciousness or knowledge, to the vaguer notions of duress and of predicaments, created by the first agent for the second, in which there is no "fair" choice.

In considering examples of such actions and their bearing on causal judgments there are three dangers to avoid. It would be folly to think that in tracing connections through such actions instead of regarding them, like voluntary interventions, as a limit, ordinary thought has clearly separated out their non-voluntary aspect from others by which they are often accompanied. Thus even in the crude case where A lets off a gun (intentionally or not) and startles B, so that he makes an involuntary movement of his arm which breaks a glass, the commonness of such a reaction as much as its compulsive character may influence the judgment that A's action was the cause of the damage.

Secondly, we must not impute to ordinary thought all the fine discriminations that could be made and in fact are to be found in a legal system, or an equal willingness to supply answers to complex questions in causal terms. Where there is no precise system of punishment, compensation or reward to administer, ordinary men will not often have faced such questions as whether the injuries suffered by a motorist who collides with another in swerving to avoid a child are consequences attributable to the neglect of the child's parents in allowing it to wander on to the road. Such questions courts have to answer and in such cases common judgments provide only a general, though still an important indication of what are the relevant factors.

Thirdly, though very frequently non-voluntary actions are assimilated to mere conditions or means by which the first agent brings about the consequences, the assimilation is never quite complete. This is manifested by the general avoidance of many causal locutions which are appropriate when the consequences are traced (as in the first case) through purely physical events. Thus even in the case in which the second agent's role is hardly an "action" at all—e.g., where A hits B, who staggers against a glass window and breaks it—we should say that A's blow made B stagger and break the glass, rather than that A's blow caused the glass to break, though in any explanatory or attributive context the case would be *summarized* by saying that A's action was the cause of the *damage.*

In the last two cases where B's movements are involuntary in the sense that they are not part of any action which he chose or intended to do, their connection with A's action would be described by saying that A's blow *made* B stagger or *caused* him to stagger or that the noise of A's shot *made* him jump or *caused* him to jump. This would be true, whether A intended or expected B to react in this way or not, and the naturalness of treating A's action as the cause of the ultimate damage is due to the causal character of this part of the process involving B's action. The same is, however, true where B's actions are not involuntary movements but A is considered to have made or caused B to do them by less crude means. This is the case if, for example, A uses threats or exploits his authority over B to make B do something—e.g., knock down a door. At least where A's threats are of serious harm, or B's act was unquestionably within A's authority to order, he too has made or forced or (in formal quasi-legal parlance) "caused" B to act.

Outside the area of such cases, where B's will would be said either not to be involved at all, or to be overborne by A, are cases where A's act creates a predicament for B *narrowing* the area of choice so that he has either to inflict some harm on himself or others, or sacrifice some important interest or duty. Such cases resemble coercion in that A narrows the area of B's choice but differ from it in that this predicament need not be intentionally created. A sets a house on fire (intentionally or unintentionally): B to save himself has to jump from a height involving certain injury, or to save a child rushes in and is seriously burned. Here, of course, B's movements are not involuntary; the "necessity" of his action is here of a different order. His action is the outcome of a choice between two evils forced on him by A's action. In such cases, when B's injuries are thought of as the consequence of the fire, the implicit judgment is made that his action was the lesser of two evils and in this sense a "reasonable" one which he was obliged to make to avoid the greater evil. This is often paradoxically, though understandably, described by saying that here the agent "had no choice" but to do what he did. Such judgments involve a comparison of the importance of the respective interests sacrificed and preserved, and the final assertion that A's action was the cause of the injuries rests on evaluations about which men may differ.

Finally, the ground for treating some harm which would not have occurred without B's action as the consequence of A's action may be that B acted in ignorance of or under a mistake as to some feature of the situation created by A. Poisoning offers perhaps the simplest example of the bearing on causal judgments of actions which are less than voluntary in this Aristotelian sense. If A intending B's death deliberately poisons B's food and B, knowing this, deliberately takes the poison and dies, A has not, unless he coerced B into eating the poisoned food, caused B's death: if, however, B does not know the food to be poisoned, eats it, and dies, A has caused his death, even if he put the poison in unwittingly. Of course only the roughest judgments are passed in causal terms in such cases outside law courts, where fine degrees of "appreciation" or "reckless shutting of the eyes" may have to be discriminated from "full knowledge." Yet, rough as these are, they indicate clearly enough the controlling principles.

Though in the foregoing cases A's initiating action might often be described as "the cause" of the ultimate harm, this linguistic fact is of subordinate importance to the fact that, for whatever purpose, explanatory, descriptive, or evaluative, consequences of an action are traced, discriminations are made (except in the cases discussed later) between free voluntary interventions and less than voluntary reactions to the first action or the circumstances created by it.

(iii) The analogy with single simple actions which guides the tracing of consequences may be broken by certain kinds of conjunctions of physical events. A hits B who falls to the ground stunned and bruised by the blow; at that moment a tree crashes to the ground and kills B. A has certainly caused B's bruises but not his death: for though the fall of the tree was, like the evening breeze in our earlier example, independent of and subsequent to the initiating action, it would be differentiated from the breeze in any description in causal terms of the connection of B's death with A's action. It is to be noticed that this is not a matter which turns on the intention with which A struck B. Even if A hit B inadvertently or accidentally, his blow would still be the cause of B's bruises: he would have caused them, though unintentionally. Conversely even if A had intended his blow to kill, this would have been an attempt to kill but still not the cause of B's death, unless A knew that the tree was about to fall just at that moment. On this legal and ordinary judgments would be found to agree; and most legal systems would distinguish for the purposes of punishment an attempt with a fatal upshot, issuing by such chance or anomalous events, from "causing death"—the terms in which the offences of murder and manslaughter are usually defined.

Similarly the causal description of the case does not turn on the moral appraisal of A's action or the wish to punish it. A may be a robber and a murderer and B a saint guarding the place A hoped to plunder. Or B may be a murderer and A a hero who has forced his way into B's retreat. In both cases the causal judgment is the same. A had caused the minor injuries but not B's death, though he tried to kill him. A may indeed be praised or blamed but not for causing B's death. However intimate the connection between responsibility and causation, it does not determine causal judgments in this simple way. Nor does the causal judgment turn on a refusal to attribute grave consequences to actions which normally have less serious results. Had A's blow killed B outright and the tree, falling on his body, merely smashed his watch we should still treat the coincidental character of the fall of the tree as determining the form of causal statement. We should then recognize A's blow as the cause of B's death but not the breaking of the watch.

The connection between A's action and B's death in the first case would naturally be described in the language of *coincidence*. "It was a coincidence: it just happened that, at the very moment when A knocked B down, a tree crashed at the very place where he fell and killed him." The common legal metaphor would describe the fall of the tree as an "extraneous" cause. This, however, is dangerously misleading, as an analysis of the notion of coincidence will show. It suggests merely an event which is subsequent to and independent of some other contingency, and of course the fall of the tree has both these features in relation to A's blow. Yet in these respects the fall of the tree does not differ from the evening breeze in the earlier case where we found no difficulty in tracing causal connection. The full elucidation of the notion of a coincidence is a complex matter for, though it is very important as a limit in tracing consequences, causal questions are not the only ones to which the notion is relevant. The following are its most general characteristics. We speak of a coincidence whenever the conjunction of two or more events in certain spatial or temporal relations (1) is very unlikely by ordinary standards and (2) is for some reason significant or important, provided (3) that they occur without human contrivance, and (4) are independent of each other. It is therefore a coincidence if two persons known to each other in London meet without design in Paris on their way to separate independently chosen destinations; or if two persons living in different places independently decide to write a book on the same subject. The first is a coincidence of time and place ("It just happened that we were at the same place at the same time"), and the second a coincidence of time only ("It just happened that they both decided to write on the subject at the same time").

Use of this general notion is made in the special case when the conjunction of two or more events occurs in temporal and/or spatial relationships which are significant, because, as our general knowledge of causal processes shows, this conjunction is required for the production of some given further event. In the language of Mill's idealized model, they form a necessary part of a complex set of jointly sufficient conditions. In the present case the fall of the tree just as B was struck down within its range satisfies the four criteria for a coincidence which we have enumerated. First, though neither event was of a very rare or exceptional kind, their conjunction would be rated very unlikely judged by the standards of ordinary experience. Secondly, this conjunction was causally significant for it was a necessary part of the process terminating in B's death. Thirdly, this conjunction was not consciously designed by A; had he known of the impending fall of the tree and hit B with the intention that he should fall within its range B's death would not have been the result of any coincidence. A would certainly have caused it. The common-sense principle that a contrived conjunction cannot be a coincidence is the element of truth in the legal maxim (too broadly stated even for legal purposes) that an intended consequence cannot be too "remote." Fourthly, each member of the conjunction in this case was independent of the other; whereas if B had fallen against the tree with an impact sufficient to bring it down on him, this sequence of physical events, though freakish in its way, would not be a coincidence and in most contexts of ordinary life, as in the law, the course of events would be summarized by saying that in this case, unlike that of the coincidence, A's act was the cause of B's death, since each stage is the effect of the preceding stage. Thus, the blow forced the victim against the tree, the effect of this was to make the tree fall and the fall of the tree killed the victim.

One further criterion in addition to these four must be satisfied if a conjunction of events is to rank as a coincidence and as a limit when the consequences of the action are traced. This further criterion again shows the strength of the influence which the analogy with the case of the simple manipulation of things exerts over thought in causal terms. An abnormal *condition* existing at the time of a human intervention is distinguished both by ordinary thought and, with a striking consistency, by most legal systems from an abnormal event or conjunction of events subsequent to that intervention; the former, unlike the latter, are not ranked as coincidences or "extraneous" causes when the consequences of the intervention come to be traced. Thus A innocently gives B a tap over the head of a normally quite harmless character, but because B is then suffering from some rare disease the tap has, as we say, "fatal results." In this case A has caused B's death, though unintentionally. The scope of the principle which thus distinguishes contemporaneous abnormal conditions from subsequent events is unclear; but at least where a human being initiates some physical change in a thing, animal, or person, abnormal physical states of the object affected, existing at the time, are ranked as part of the circumstances in which the cause "operates." In the familiar controlling imagery these are part of "the stage already set" before the "intervention."

Judgments about coincidences, though we often agree in making them, depend in two related ways on issues incapable of precise formulation. One of these is patent, the other latent but equally important. Just how unlikely must a conjunction be to rank as a coincidence, and in the light of what knowledge is likelihood to be assessed? The only answer is: "very unlikely in the light of the knowledge available to ordinary men." It is, of course, the indeterminacies of such standards, implicit in causal judgments, that make them inveterately disputable, and call for the exercise of discretion or choice by courts. The second and latent indeterminacy of these judgments depends on the fact that the things or events to which they relate do not have pinned to them some uniquely correct description always to be used in assessing likelihood. It is an important pervasive feature of all our empirical judgments that there is a constant possibility of more or less specific description of any event or thing with which they are concerned. The tree might be described not simply as a "tree" but as a "rotten tree" or as a "fir tree" or a "tree sixty feet tall." So too its fall might be described not as a "fall" but as a fall of a specified distance at a specified velocity. The likelihood of conjunctions framed in these different terms would be differently assessed. The criteria of appropriate description like the standard of likelihood are supplied by consideration of common knowledge. Even if the scientist knew the tree to be rotten and could have predicted its fall with accuracy, this would not change the judgment that its fall at the time when B was struck down within its range was a coincidence; nor would it make the description "rotten tree" appropriate for the assessment of the chances involved in this judgment. There are other controls over the choice of description derived from the degree of specificity of our interests in the final outcome of the causal process. We are concerned with the fall of an object sufficient to cause "death" by impact and the precise force or direction which may account for the detail of the wounds is irrelevant here.

Opportunities and Reasons

Opportunities. The discrimination of voluntary interventions as a limit is no longer made when the case, owing to the commonness or appreciable risk of such harmful intervention, can be brought within the scope of the notion of providing an opportunity, known to be commonly exploited for doing harm. Here the limiting principles are different. When A leaves the house unlocked, the range of consequences to be attributed to this neglect, as in any other case where precautions are omitted, depends primarily on the way in which such opportunities are commonly exploited. An alternative formulation of this idea is that a subsequent intervention would fall within the scope of consequences if the likelihood of its occurring is one of the reasons for holding A's omission to be negligent.

It is on these lines that we would distinguish between the entry of a thief and of a murderer; the opportunity provided is believed to be sufficiently commonly exploited by thieves to make it usual and often morally or legally obligatory not to provide it. Here, in attributing consequences to prior actions, causal judgments are directly controlled by the notion of the risk created by them. Neglect of such precautions is both unusual and reprehensible. For these reasons it would be hard to separate the two ways in which such neglect deviates from the "norm." Despite this, no simple identification can be made of the notion of responsibility with the causal connection which is a ground for it. This is so because the provision of an opportunity commonly taken by others is ranked as the cause of the outcome independently of the wish to praise or blame. The causal judgment may be made simply to assess a contribution to some outcome. Thus, whether we think well or ill of the use made of railways, we would still claim that the greater mobility of the population in the nineteenth century was a consequence of their introduction.

It is obvious that the question whether any given intervention is a sufficiently common exploitation of the opportunity provided to come within the risk is again a matter on which judgments may differ, though they often agree. The courts, and perhaps ordinary thought also, often describe those that are sufficiently common as "natural" consequences of the neglect. They have in these terms discriminated the entry of a thief from the entry of a man who burnt the house down, and refused to treat the destruction of the house as a "natural" consequence of the neglect.

We discuss later the argument that this easily intelligible concept of "harm within the risk," overriding as it does the distinctions between voluntary interventions and others, should be used as the general test for determining what subsequent harm should be attributed for legal purposes to prior action. The merits of this proposal to refashion the law along these simple lines are perhaps considerable, yet consequences of actions are in fact often traced both in the law and apart from it in other ways which depend on the discrimination of voluntary interventions from others. We distinguish, after all, as differing though related grounds of responsibility, causing harm by one's own action, and providing opportunities for others to do harm, where the guiding analogy with the simple manipulation of things, which underlies causal thought, is less close. When, as in the examples discussed above, we trace consequences through the non-voluntary interventions of others our concern is to show that certain stages of the process have a certain type of connection with the preceding stages, and not, as when the notion of risk is applied, to show that the ultimate outcome is connected in some general way with the initiating action. Thus, when A's shot makes B start and break a glass, it is the causal relationship described by the expression "made B start" that we have in mind and not the likelihood that on hearing a shot someone may break a glass. Causal connection may be traced in such cases though the initiating action and the final outcome are not contingencies that commonly go together.

Apart from these conceptual reasons for distinguishing these related grounds for responsibility, it is clear that both in the law and apart from it we constantly treat harm as caused by a person's action though it does not fall "within the risk." If, when B broke the glass in the example given above, a splinter flew into C's eye, blinding him, A's action is indeed the cause of C's injury though we may not always blame him for so unusual a consequence.

Reasons. In certain varieties of interpersonal transactions, unlike the case of coercion, the second action is quite voluntary. A may not threaten B but may bribe or advise or persuade him to do something. Here, A does not "cause" or "make" B do anything: the strongest words we should use are perhaps that he "induced" or "procured" B's act. Yet the law and moral principles alike may treat one person as responsible for the harm which another free agent has done "in consequence" of the advice or the inducements which the first has offered. In such cases the limits concern the range of those actions done by B which are to rank as the consequence of A's words or deeds. In general this question depends on A's intentions or on the "plan of action" he puts before B. If A advises or bribes B to break in and steal from an empty house and B does so, he acts in consequence of A's advice or bribe. If he deliberately burns down the house, this would not be treated as the consequence of A's bribe or advice, legally or otherwise, though it may in some sense be true that the burning would not have taken place without the advice or bribe. Nice questions may arise, which the courts have to settle, where B diverges from the detail of the plan of action put before him by A.

NOTES AND QUESTIONS

1. Hart and Honoré distinguish three contexts in which we use the words of causal relation, words like "consequence," "effect," and "cause": explanatory contexts, attributions of moral responsibility, and construction of intelligible historical narratives. They tell us that in all of these nonlegal contexts "we employ a set of concepts restricting in various ways what counts as a consequence." Suppose as an historian we were explaining the defeat of the Spanish Armada by Drake's squadron. Would the presence of timber in Scotland (from which Drake's ships were built) be a cause? Could Drake have defeated the Armada without ships? What would Hart and Honore say?

2. Consider a slightly different case, one where the condition necessary to the production of some event is simultaneously present with that event (rather than being in the distant past). For example, a fire breaks out in a warehouse. An insurance investigator is sent to discover "the cause" of the fire. He reports back: "the presence

of oxygen in the air." What, if anything, is inappropriate about the investigator's report? Would Hart and Honore say he had found *the* cause, or even *a* cause, of the fire?

3. Hart and Honoré spend a great deal of their efforts to show us how we pick causes from conditions either simultaneously present or linked in a temporal chain or "cone" of causation. Do they tell us what the basic relation is that isolates causal candidates for us? Is it Hume's regularity analysis? Some kind of counterfactual test? Some unsayable primitive?

4. With regard to temporally ordered chains of causation (the subject of the lawyers' concern with proximate cause), Hart and Honore say that two kinds of conditions can intervene to break an otherwise unbroken chain of causation, relegating every item prior to such intervention to the status of "background conditions" rather than "cause." These two intervening causes are voluntary human actions and that abnormal conjunction of natural events we colloquially call "coincidences." Why should these two items be a barrier through which causation cannot be traced? Is this based on a libertarian metaphysics, to the effect that human choices and "acts of God" cannot be caused? Or is this based on our practical interests in just those explanations as are framed in terms either of our fellow humans' doings or of extraordinary (and thus interesting) natural events? Can Hart and Honoré be analyzing *causation* if the basis for their analysis is the latter rather than the former?

5. Consider the Hart and Honoré analogy between causing harm and doing something harmful. Is it their thesis that descriptions like "A caused B's death" are appropriate if and only if it is appropriate to say, "A killed B?" Is the development of English verbs of action relevant to our analysis of causation? Does the language itself (and not just its use by historians, scientists, and moralists) evidence a distinction between cause and mere conditions?

6. What do Hart and Honoré mean by "voluntary," as used in their thesis that voluntary interventions by second actors break causal chains and relieve the first actor from being a cause of the harm? Should "voluntary" be defined as whatever is not "*in*voluntary?" If so, does "involuntary" include the following situations: lack of an action by the second agent, as when his body is shoved through a plate glass window; ignorance or mistake by the second agent, as when he hands tea to the victim not knowing that it is poisoned; duress on the second actor by the first, as when the latter tells the former to hit another or else his own family will be killed; the compulsion of natural circumstance, as where the victim of a defendant's negligently set fire finds himself trapped on the roof of a tall building and jumps (to his injury) in order to avoid being burned to death?

7. Now consider the second of Hart and Honoré's intervening causes, that of coincidence. A coincidence, as they define it, is an after-arising, significant, uncontrived, and independent event that is unusual (or abnormal) in its conjunction with the later event it causes. By this test, if I see a tree falling, and I push Jones under it so that he will be killed, is Jones's death a coincidence? If I push Jones against a rotten

tree (which I do not know to be rotten), and the support of Jones on the tree causes the tree to fall on him and kill him, have I caused Jones's death?

8. What is the difference between describing an intervening event to be "abnormal" and describing it as being "unforeseeable?"

9. Consider the case where the defendant stabs victim V with a wound that is mortal only if V does not receive medical treatment. As it happens, medical treatment is available, but V refuses it on religious grounds and thereafter dies. Did the defendant cause V's death? Is V's choice a subsequent voluntary action, breaking the causal chain, or is her choice but the manifestation of a prior condition (of religious belief) that is not eligible to be an *intervening* cause?

10. Hart and Honoré seem to except the provision of opportunities from their analysis of when a voluntary human action constitutes an intervening cause. Is this right? If you leave the keys in your unlocked car and a thief steals it and runs down victim V, have you *caused* V's injuries? Are you (should you be) responsible, morally and legally, for V's injuries even if you did *not* cause them? Would this be (like) omission liability, *viz.,* liability for failing to prevent rather than for causing?

11. You and I have a colleague who served in the Carter administration. Such service was the highlight of her life, and with little or no encouragement she will tell the same boring story about her accomplishments within the administration. We test at lunch what it takes to bring on the story—I say, "Carter went to Korea." She tells the story. Did I cause the story to be told? Did I tell the story? Am I responsible (for boring my colleagues at lunch with the same old story) even if I did not cause it to be told?

3.4 LEGALITY

To have done something legally wrong within Anglo-American criminal law systems is to do more than perform a voluntary action that causes a harmful or otherwise immoral state of affairs to exist. In addition to the voluntary act and causation requirements, Anglo-American criminal law requires that something called the legality requirement be satisfied. Exactly what are the doctrinal expressions of that requirement and what values are served by imposing such a requirement on criminal liability are explored in the readings to follow. The first selection, from Michael Moore, gives an overview of the doctrines making up the principle of legality and of the values such doctrines serve. The larger selection from John Jeffries examines in greater depth three such doctrines and three such values.

The Principle of Legality

MICHAEL S. MOORE

The principle of legality is in reality a mixture of four values that jointly justify a wide variety of criminal-law doctrines. The values are those of fairness, liberty, democracy, and equality, which are unpacked as follows. It is *unfair* to surprise citizens with liability to criminal sanctions when they reasonably relied on their actions not being criminal at the time they were done. It impedes *liberty* if citizens cannot know the content of the criminal law well enough to take into account the possibilities of penal liability in planning their actions. The value of *democratic decision-making* requires that elected legislatures decide what is and what is not criminal, and (not electorally responsive) courts would frustrate that value if they were to take it upon themselves to make conduct criminal without statutory authorization. *Equality* dictates that those who are in all morally relevant respects alike be treated alike, and this requires that neither legislatures nor judges single individuals out for arbitrarily different treatment.

In Anglo-American law the doctrinal expressions of these values are numerous, and many of such doctrines are over-determined by more than one of the four values just described. The main doctrines are nine in number:

1. The prohibition against "common-law crimes," or "crimes by analogy," holds that courts are without power to create new crimes, either from whole cloth or by analogy to crimes already prohibited by statute. The primary value furthered by this doctrine is democracy, because the justification for restricting criminal law-making to legislatures is largely due to the more democratic selection of legislatures over judges. However, fairness and liberty are also served by courts refusing to use (retroactively applicable) adjudication as the occasion on which to announce new crimes.
2. The doctrine that ex post facto laws are unconstitutional plainly serves the values of fairness and liberty. Retroactive criminal laws would both unfairly disappoint reliance on an activity not being criminal when it is done, and chill liberty by the fear that such surprise might be forthcoming.
3. The constitutional (due process) prohibition of retroactive judicial enlargement of criminal liability, like the ex post facto limitation on legislation, plainly serves the values of fairness and liberty. For the purposes of these values, it does not matter whether the surprise comes from law-making by a court or by a legislature.
4. The void-for-vagueness doctrine requires legislatures to frame acts with sufficient clarity that they can be understood by those to whom they are directed. Such failure of understanding can occur not only because of vagueness in some statutory predicate, but also because of ambiguity in the predicate; inconsistency between

From *Act and Crime: The Implications of the Philosophy of Action for the Criminal Law* (Oxford: Oxford University Press, 1993), pp. 239–44.

this statutory provision and some other; inability of most citizens to be able to verify factually whether the behaviour they contemplate will or will not have the characteristics the statute prohibits. Any of these inabilities to understand makes a criminal statute "void-for-vagueness" under the due process clause. The main values served here are fairness and liberty, but the equality value is also served by not allowing vague statutes to grant such discretion to enforcement officials that discriminatory application is made possible.

5. The prohibition against bills of attainder also serves the equality value by requiring of criminal legislation that it be general in the sense that it apply to some *class* of persons. Such generality is the first step towards equal treatment, because such generality precludes the numerical distinctness of persons being used to single individuals out for criminal punishment. Because bills of attainder are also retroactive in effect, the prohibition also serves the values of fairness and liberty.

6. The common-law maxim that criminal statutes must be strictly construed serves the values of fairness and liberty by disallowing prosecution in the vague penumbra of some statute's *actus reus* prohibition. Such a maxim gives citizens the benefit of the doubt in the interpretation of criminal statutes, so that any reasonable mistakes of interpretation due to the vagueness of the statutory language do not result in criminal liability.

7. Mistake of law by an accused is allowed as a defence when that defendant's mistake was induced by his reliance on (mis)-advice about the law received from some governmental official. Here the value is mostly fairness, because the defendant is unfairly whipsawed between one governmental agency (which gave the advice) and another (the court trying him).

8. Some state constitutions require that criminal statutes be in English, again with the plain rationale that citizens must be able to find out what is punishable in advance. The values served are again fairness and liberty.

9. Mistake of law is also a defence to criminal prosecution in situations where the law making an act criminal was not publicly promulgated. The doctrine also has as its rationale the values of fairness and liberty. What isn't publicly available cannot be known, so that when applied such a statute unfairly surprises, and the potential for such surprise chills the liberty of those not knowing whether their act is secretly criminal.

The four values, as they converge to jointly justify these nine doctrines, are what is misleadingly referred to as "the" principle of legality. Such principle prohibits punishment except for actions prohibited by some public, prospective, general, clear, consistent, verifiable, strictly construed, legislatively created law.

NOTES AND QUESTIONS

1. If the principle of legality is really a cluster of nine legal doctrines serving four values, in what sense is there *a* requirement of legality? Why are these doctrines

clustered together? The philosopher Ludwig Wittgenstein once imagined a rope made of many smaller strands, no one of which ran the entire length of the rope. Cross sections of the rope at different locations would thus show very different combinations of strands. Is it, he queried, still one rope? Is legality still one requirement?

2. Moore distinguishes the values of liberty from fairness. Suppose a statute is too vague to be understood; a defendant who tried to understand it but failed is convicted. Which value is disserved? Suppose a statute seems clear on its face, and a given defendant reads it in the seemingly obvious way. The court that tries her, however, gives the statute an unforeseeable interpretation enlarging liability and convicting this defendant. Which value is disserved?

3. Could a drunk-driving statute, which defines drunk driving as driving while one's blood alcohol by weight is over 0.1 percent, be held void-for-vagueness? Would the complaint about such a statute be that it contains too much precision in defining exactly what is forbidden?

Legality, Vagueness, and the Construction of Penal Statutes

JOHN JEFFRIES

Justifications for *nulla poena sine lege,* the vagueness doctrine, and the rule of strict construction cluster around three kinds of arguments. The first concerns the association of popular sovereignty with legislative primacy and the consequent illegitimacy of judicial innovation. In contemporary constitutional discourse, this sort of assertion is called "separation of powers." The second contention is based on the perceived unfairness of punishing conduct not previously defined as criminal. "Notice" and "fair warning" describe claims of this sort. Finally, a third kind of argument involves the potential for arbitrary and discriminatory enforcement of the penal law and the resort to legal formalism as a constraint against unbridled discretion. Many terms are used to state such ideas, but they are perhaps most familiar as appeals to the "rule of law." Each type of justification is examined below.

Separation of Powers

Enlightenment theoreticians decreed that liberty is most secure where political power is fractured and separated. As adapted to a representative democracy, this idea meant

From *Virginia Law Review,* Vol. 71 (1985), pp. 201–19, 223–24, 226–34.

that the legislative, executive, and judicial functions should be separate, if interactive. Lawmaking was the legislative province. As the branch most directly accountable to the people, only the legislature could validate the surrender of individual freedom necessary to formation of the social contract. The legislature, therefore, was the only legitimate institution for enforcing societal judgments through the penal law. Judicial innovation was politically illegitimate.

. . .

Notice

A second plausible rationale for legality and related doctrines is the requirement of notice. Notice is essential to fairness. Crimes must be defined in advance so that individuals have fair warning of what is forbidden: lack of notice poses a "trap for the innocent" and "violates the first essential of due process of law."

This sort of talk has strong intuitive appeal. At least within the political tradition of liberal democracy, the essentiality of notice seems obvious, and the perceived unfairness of punishment without warning requires no explication. Moreover, the rationale of notice is nicely comprehensive. It is a theme shared by legality, vagueness, and strict construction, uniting all three doctrines in a common front against unfair surprise. Thus, judicial crime creation is bad because it is retrospective; notice of illegality may effectively be denied. Similarly, indefinite statutes are objectionable because they are uninformative; it is difficult to tell what conduct is proscribed. And when the statute is not vague but only ambiguous, strict construction steps in to restrict its meaning to that which should have been foreseen; laws that in general give fair warning are conformed in detail to the warning given.

In these and other respects, the notice rationale is very satisfying. It charts a coherent progression from legality to vagueness to strict construction, relates these doctrines to other constitutional pronouncements in an intelligible way, and seems, at least superficially, to explain the law as it stands. A look beneath the surface, however, is distinctly unsettling. The rhetoric of fair warning is plausible and comprehensive, but in many contexts it is also shallow and unreal. Its explanatory value at the level of doctrinal rationalization is purchased at the cost of unusual disparity with actual practice. In essence, the rhetoric of fair warning is used to justify (perhaps even to obscure) practices that, on reflection, seem to have little or no relation to a notice rationale.

Consider the vagueness doctrine. The invalidation of indefinite laws is routinely justified on grounds of notice. Other reasons are also given, but the requirement of fair warning is always included and usually given pride of place. Yet the actual administration of the vagueness doctrine belies this rationale. For one thing, the kind of notice required is entirely formal. Publication of a statute's text always suffices; the government need make no further effort to apprise the people of the content of the law. In the context of civil litigation, where notice is taken seriously, publication is a last resort; more effective means must be employed wherever possible. It may be objected that no more effective means is possible where the intended recipient of the information is the entire populace or some broad segment thereof, rather than in identifiable individual or entity. But this argument at most explains why publication should sometimes suffice; it does not explain why no further obligation is ever considered. Nor does it explain why publication in some official document, no matter how inaccessible, is all that is required. In short, the fair warning requirement of the vagueness doctrine is not structured to achieve actual notice of the content of the penal law.

A more telling point concerns the permissible sources of specificity in the penal law. Among many disputed aspects of the vagueness doctrine, one settled rule is that the precision required of a criminal statute need not appear on its face. Facial uncertainty may be cured by judicial construction. Indeed, judicial specification will be accepted as sufficient even where it amounts to a wholesale rewriting of the statutory text. Thus, the "fair warning" that the law regards as the "first essential of due process" may be discoverable only by a search of the precedents. As every first-year law student knows (and has not had time to forget), this process of research and interpretation is anything but easy. For the trained professional, the task is time-consuming and tricky; for the average citizen, it is next to impossible. Where there is a lawyer at hand, this kind of notice may be meaningful. But in the ordinary case, the notice given must be recovered from sources so various and inaccessible as to render the concept distinctly unrealistic.

And what if notice fails? What if an individual acts in honest ignorance of the law's commands or in the mistaken belief that his conduct is lawful? The answer, of course, is that we punish him anyway. *Ignorantia juris neminem excusat* states that the entrenched policy of the penal law. In some jurisdictions, a defense of estoppel bars prosecution where the government has affirmatively misled the individual, but where the government is not responsible for the error, ignorance of the law is no excuse. The assumption seems to be that most such claims are fraudulent. Doubtless that is true, but in other areas the law is concerned, indeed preoccupied, with separating the wheat from the chaff. Why not here? If notice of illegality is an essential prerequisite to the fairness of punishment, how can the law be indifferent to claims of honest and reasonable mistake? One would think that a system organized around the requirement of fair warning would have to take into account cases where, through no fault of the accused, such warning was not received.

One explanation might be that *ignorantia juris* creates an incentive to know the law and justifies punishment despite mistake as an appropriate sanction for error. There are things to be said both for and against this approach, but for present purposes one need only note that it is surely inconsistent with the premises underlying the notice rationale. That requirement imposes on the state the obligation to give fair warning of what is forbidden. The underlying assumption must be that what is not expressly prohibited is allowed—that the individual is presumptively free to do as he or she pleases, and that in doubtful cases the burden of proof (so to speak) lies on the government. But if unawareness of illegality is itself the wrong to be punished, this assumption is reversed, and the individual bears the risk of not knowing the law. Unless the conduct is plainly authorized, one acts at one's own risk; and where the law is opaque or inaccessible, the risk may be very great. From the actor's point of view, this approach to notice amounts to a virtual presumption of illegality. Of course, such talk runs directly counter to the rhetorical tradition of the "presumption of innocence" and to the libertarian political assumptions evoked by that phrase. No doubt that is why one never hears *ignorantia juris* described in this way.

It is unnecessary to say here whether the policy of *ignorantia juris* leads inevitably to such unwelcome conclusions of whether some more palatable explanation exists. For now it is enough to show that *ignorantia juris* is radically inconsistent with a concern for actual notice and places that rationale in an exceedingly ironic light. To my mind, the continuing strength of "ignorance of the law is no excuse" is telling evidence of the abstracted and artificial character of the rhetoric of "fair warning."

The same points can be made about strict construction. Just as the concern for notice would require invalidation of laws that give no fair warning, it would also imply that remaining ambiguities be resolved against the state. Otherwise, the interpretation of penal statutes would threaten that same unfair surprise against which the vagueness doctrine more generally guards. In effect, strict construction strips away from the criminal law those potential applications for which fair warning was not clearly given. In this respect, the rule of strict construction is thought to implement the principle of legality and to reinforce the prohibition against indefinite laws.

Again, however, judicial administration of the rule belies any real concern for fair warning. Pronouncements in ancient precedent are taken to have resolved statutory ambiguity, no matter how unlikely it may be that the accused has had access to such discussions. Mistake is irrelevant. Even where the defendant shows actual reliance on an interpretation of law and further shows that such reliance was prudent and reasonable, the law does not care. The individual must get it right, and no amount of good faith or due diligence is exculpatory. The converse is also true: strict construction may be invoked without regard to the defendant's actual expectation or belief. Uncertainty in coverage is said to threaten unfair surprise, even where there is no plausible claim that the actor relied on any view of the law.

Thus, neither the vagueness doctrine nor the rule of strict construction makes much sense in terms of notice. Although both are conventionally aligned with the rhetoric of fair warning, neither is administered in a manner congruent with that rationale. That is not to say that there are not good reasons for these results, but only that those reasons must be sought elsewhere. Considered solely as means of ensuring effective notice of illegality, the array of conventional doctrines governing judicial innovation in the penal law is fundamentally unintelligible.

It would be wrong, however, to think that the idea of notice is entirely empty or that the concern for fair warning is merely a rhetorical charade. In fact, there is a core concept of notice as a requirement of fairness to individuals that is, and should be, taken very seriously. It does not depend, however, on whether a trained professional, given access to the appropriate sources and the time to consider them, would have foreseen the application of the law. The issue, in other words, is not the hypothetical construction of "lawyer's notice." The concern is, rather, whether the ordinary and ordinarily law-abiding individual would have received some signal that his or her conduct risked violation of the penal law. Punishment for conduct that the average citizen would have had no reason to avoid is unfair and constitutionally impermissible. That, at any rate, is the teaching of *Lambert v. California*. The meaning of that case is subject to infinite disputation, but to me it stands for the unacceptability in principle of imposing criminal liability where the prototypically law-abiding individual in the actor's situation would have had no reason to act otherwise.

That this proposition is rarely tested does not make it any less fundamental. The fact that plausible claims of this sort are so seldom encountered is further evidence that the rhetoric of notice and fair warning has been extended far beyond the circumstances that give it force. In the great generality of cases, notice is not a persuasive rationale for the constraints surrounding judicial behavior in the penal law.

Rule of Law

The most important concern underlying *nulla poena sine lege* and the vagueness doctrine is the so-called "rule of law." Unfortunately, use of this phrase is treacherous. On the one hand, it has degenerated into a political slogan of remarkable plasticity. Too often the rule of law is equated with the rule of good law, so that it becomes an indiscriminate claim of virtue in a legal system. On the other hand, philosophers and legal theorists have refined and explicated the concept in ways that are, for my purposes, prohibitively elaborate.

My own meaning is limited and quite conventional. The rule of law signifies the constraint of arbitrariness in the exercise of government power. In the context of the penal law, it means that the agencies of official coercion should, to the extent feasible, be guided by rules—that is, by openly acknowledged, relatively stable, and generally applicable statements of proscribed conduct. The evils to be retarded are caprice and whim, the misuse of government power for private ends, and the unacknowledged reliance on illegitimate criteria of selection. The goals to be advanced are regularity and evenhandedness in the administration of justice and accountability in the use of government power. In short, the "rule of law" designates the cluster of values associated with conformity to law by government.

NOTES AND QUESTIONS

1. Jeffries considers three criminal law doctrines and three policies behind them. The first doctrine he calls "legality," or sometimes *nulla poena sine lege* (no punishment without law). In the Anglo-American system, this doctrine is a doctrine denying courts the power to make conduct criminal by common law decision. In our system, criminal law is statutory law. This is often put as the slogan, "there are no common law crimes." How should such a doctrine apply to the following sorts of situations:

a. A state legislature repeals the entire criminal code. The courts step in to declare various types of conduct criminal or not criminal as it arises in particular cases. The courts state they are guided in this task by the natural law. They therefore convict someone of the crime of not keeping a promise.

b. The thirteen original colonies had little criminal law of their own in 1776. After declaring their independence from England, each of the legislatures of the former colonies passes a reception statute, which receives into their law the common law of crimes as it existed in England on July 4, 1776. One of those crimes was being a common scold, defined by Blackstone as a noisy and quarrelsome woman who is a nuisance to her neighbors. Two hundred and some odd years later, may a woman be convicted of being a common scold in one of the thirteen original states with reception statutes still in their codes?

c. A state legislature passes a statute making it criminal to conspire to commit any crime, but also making it criminal to conspire to do any immoral act. If it is not a crime to publish a directory of prostitutes, but it is immoral, can one be convicted for agreeing with another to publish such a directory?

2. The main value served by the doctrine barring common law crimes, Jeffries asserts, is the political ideal of the separation of powers. Is it intrinsically good that political power be divided? Or is it good only because such division causes to come about other things that are intrinsically good. If the latter, what are those other goods? Consider:

a. The prevention of tyranny by checks and balances.
b. Efficiency of governance by assigning tasks to institutions whose structural features make them best able to perform those tasks.
c. The good of democracy, according to which elected representatives should make the major social choices and the less representative institutions should implement but not second-guess such choices.

Which of the goods are served by separating a judicial power from the legislative? Which by barring the courts from declaiming conduct to be criminal?

3. One of the benefits of the common law has long been thought to be its ability to change with society and to fill in wherever gaps or loopholes appear. Tort and contract law have both been benefited in this way by their common law history. Why is criminal law different? Is the creation of criminal law inherently more a legislative prerogative than is the creation of tort or contract law?

4. A second value supporting the bar on common law crimes, Jeffries says, is that of notice. Why is giving citizens notice of the content of the criminal law good? Jeffries argues that the good served by notice is fairness, it being unfair to punish citizens without notice that the conduct for which they are being punished is criminal. What if a certain class of persons are indifferent to the content of the criminal law, in the sense that they plan to do what they want even if it is criminal—is it unfair to punish them for this conduct even if they lacked notice? Or is some other good achieved by reversing their conviction because of the lack of notice by the state?

5. What can citizens fairly be expected to consult in ascertaining what conduct is criminal? Published statutes? Codified statutes with an index? Case reports? Blackstone and ancient treatises? Legislative history? Commonly perceived moral duties?

6. Jeffries complains that our notice requirement is only a formal, technical one, what he calls lawyer's notice, and not effective notice. Conceding that most people most of the time cannot have a lawyer research the legality of their proposed conduct, is there still any value to be found in a legal system being constructed in such a way

that anyone dedicated to finding out whether some bit of conduct was criminal could do so?

7. What is the relation between mistake-of-law doctrines and the notice requirement? If mistake of law were more generally an excuse, would we need a void-for-vagueness doctrine, for example?

8. What does Jeffries mean by the "rule of law"? Is it a law of rules, as Justice Scalia once put it? If so, why is it good for judges, police, and other officials to be guided by rules as they administer the criminal justice system? For separation-of-powers reasons? For notice reasons? Because without a rule to guide them their decision would be arbitrary in the sense of being without reason, a matter of whim or caprice? Because without a rule one couldn't hold officials accountable, because we couldn't know if they were deciding without reason? Are these all the same?

9. Jeffries says that "there is no necessary connection between the formal requirements of the rule of law and any substantive notion of equality," giving as his example rigorous, nonarbitrary enforcement of the rules of apartheid. Yet is one of the aspects of the rule of law what is sometimes called "principled generality," namely, the requirement that each rule be extended to cover as many persons and situations as bear no morally relevant difference to other persons and situations covered by the rule? Yet isn't such principled generality nothing but the demand for equality, that cases alike in all morally relevant respects must be treated alike?

10. Does the existence and rigorous enforcement of rules promote principled generality? Doesn't that depend on the content of the rules? Do mandatory sentencing rules, for example, increase or decrease the treatment of like cases alike? Might not such rules prevent the treating of like cases alike because their categories are too narrow to capture all the morally relevant differences between offenders?

11. Should we trust police and prosecutors less than judges to seek to apply truly equal treatment to offenders? Is that why unexceptionally enforced rules are better than broad mandates, selectively enforced?

3.5 MENTAL STATES

Human beings are practical reasoners. They have desires and beliefs and form intentions to act on the basis of those desires and beliefs. If you have a desire to learn about the foundations of criminal law (for whatever reason) and believe that reading this book will help you to achieve that goal, that desire/belief set explains why you formed the intention to read this book and are doing so now. Indeed, we believe that reasons for action and consequent intentions are genuine causes of action, as opposed to mere "rationalizations." Rules for conduct—whether moral, prudential, or legal—are clearly variables that produce beliefs and desires and thus are influential in guiding conduct. The ability to use rules is an essential part of practical reasoning.

The human ability to form reason-based intentions that cause our conduct is the foundation for our self-conception as potentially rational and autonomous creatures. This potential in turn is the foundation for our normative evaluation of conduct. As we know from ordinary experience, the evaluation of both the morality and prudence of conduct is based largely on the mental states that accompany conduct. An entirely accidental homicide is evaluated quite differently from an intentional homicide, even though a person has been killed in both cases. Furthermore, evaluations of the same acts committed with the same mental state depend on the desire/belief sets that motivate agents to form the mental state and act on it. A person who kills intentionally to save her own life in reaction to a potentially fatal, wrongful attack by the victim is treated quite differently from a person who kills intentionally to collect the victim's life insurance.

The account of human beings as practical reasoners and the importance of mental states to the normative evaluation of conduct are commonplaces, the "standard" view, but they are philosophically controversial. Some philosophers and social scientists believe that reasons for action, intentions, and the rest of our mental paraphernalia are not genuinely causal and are only rationalizations. For such thinkers, human beings are simply among the more complicated biophysical contraptions within the animal and vegetable kingdoms. Rationality and autonomy, according to this view, are illusory bases for believing that human beings are "different" from other creatures in normatively important ways. If one believes this alternative account of human behavior, moral and political conclusions different from those suggested by the commonplace account follow. Moral evaluation of mental states is improper if those states play no genuine causal role in human conduct.

Although there are substantial theoretical objections to the standard account, the criminal law has implicitly adopted this account. Substantive criminal law is a set of rules that are meant to guide conduct by being used in the practical reasoning of the citizens to whom they apply. Moreover, as the previous chapter disclosed, failure to obey the rules of the criminal law warrants moral condemnation according to all justifications of punishment, except for the rare, pure consequentialist. Except for anomalous strict liability crimes, the definition of all crimes therefore includes the requirement that the prohibited conduct be accompanied by a specific mental state, a mens rea, such as intent or knowledge. Moreover, affirmative defenses are usually based on the reasons—the motives—for the defendant's conduct. The selections that follow explore in greater detail the justification for the requirement of mental states in the definition of crime. The first selection challenges the standard view that intentions have causal efficacy, that reasons matter, which is a foundation of our jurisprudence. The selection is difficult but important because the challenge to the standard view is perhaps the most fundamental that philosophy can present to the law's view of the person. The second selection considers why mental states, including both mens rea and the motives that justify application of the affirmative defenses, are important. (Chapter 5 specifically addresses affirmative defenses, those doctrines of justification and excuse that exculpate a defendant even though the agent satisfied all the definitional elements of a crime, including the mental state element.)

The Explanation of Human Action
ALEXANDER ROSENBERG

We can divide human activities roughly into two classes: those we count as "mere" behavior and those we view as actions. Mere behavior includes what happens inside our bodies, like the beating of our hearts and the opening and closing of the eye's iris. Action is behavior that does not just happen to us, but that somehow we "control."

. . .

How then do we go about explaining human actions? Long before the self-conscious attempts of the social scientist, common sense had provided us all with a theory about the behavior of our fellow human beings. It is a theory that we use every day to form our expectations about the behavior of one another and to explain our own behavior to one another. This implicit theory, often given the label "folk psychology" by philosophers, has always been the natural starting place for explanations social scientists have given. In fact to the extent that social scientists, like historians, expound no explicit explanatory theory at all for the human actions they explain, they refrain from doing so because they have taken over folk psychology without even noticing. . . .

. . . Human actions are explained by identifying the beliefs and desires that lead to them. Often, such explanations are elliptical, or abbreviated, or proceed by making tacit assumptions that most people can be expected to share. If we explain why someone moved his king in a chess game, simply by saying he did it to avoid a check, the explanation works because it assumes that the player wanted to avoid check and believed that moving his king was a way of doing so. If we don't mention his desire, but simply attribute a purpose (to avoid check), and don't make it explicit that he believed that moving the king would attain this purpose, that is because these features of commonsense explanations "go without saying." . . .

Therefore, when we explain an action we do so by identifying the desires and beliefs that give rise to it. It is typical of philosophers to go beyond this point on which all agree, to ask *why*, that is, why is citing the desires and the beliefs *explanatory?* What connection obtains between the desires and the beliefs and the action they explain that makes them *relevant* to the behavior, that enables them to satisfy our curiosity about the behavior?

. . .

Naturalistic philosophers will justify the question of their connection by pointing out that only if we can identify the link between beliefs and desires on the one hand and action on the other will we be able to *improve* upon folk psychology's explanations of human action. Otherwise perhaps we should seek the explanation of action elsewhere. Interpretationalists will argue that only by identifying this link can we convince misguided social scientists that understanding human action is not a species of casual

From *Philosophy of Social Science* (Boulder, Colo.: Westview Press, 1988), pp. 22–49.

inquiry. Both sides to the dispute about the progress of the social sciences agree that we cannot ignore the question of what enables beliefs and desires to explain actions.

What we need in order to show how particular desires and beliefs work together to explain actions is some general theory about desires, beliefs, and actions. . . .

. . . We need some sort of general connection between desires, beliefs, and actions, and once we have identified this generalization, we will want to know how it enables the two former to explain the latter. Will the connection be more like a mathematical definition or a general law? Or will it be different from either in its explanatory power? On our answer will hinge the proper research strategy for social science: Should it be more like natural science, focused on observation and experiment in order to discover laws, or more like mathematics, focused on logical connections and the meanings of its concepts; or should it be different from either?

Something like the following oversimplified general statement seems to lie behind our ordinary explanations of human action, our predictions about how people will behave in the future, and explanations in social science that trade on folk psychology:

> [L] Given any person x, if x wants d and x believes that a is a means to attain d, under the circumstances, then x does a.

This then is the leading explanatory principle folk psychology offers us.

. . .

[L] must be understood either as embodying a pretty strong "other things being equal," or ceteris paribus clause, or else as an approximation for some more precise general law that can be expected to replace it. Why is this? Because as it stands, [L] is false.

Consider how easy it is to construct exceptions to it. Suppose that x wants d, but x wants something else (d') even more strongly than he wants d. If the actions required to secure d and to secure d' are incompatible, x will not undertake action a, but some other action (a') required to attain d'. Or suppose x believes that a is a means of attaining d, but not the best, or most efficient, or most enjoyable, or cheapest means of attaining it. Then x won't do a, even if he wants d, has no overriding incompatible wants, and believes a is a means of attaining d. Things can get even worse for [L]. Even if x believes that a is the best means of securing d, x may not know how to do a, or knowing how, may be unable to do it.

We can of course "improve" [L] by adding clauses to it covering each of these problems. The result will be a much more complex statement. . . . But instead of adding clauses to [L], we could simply argue that these exceptions are rare and treat [L] as bearing an "other things being equal" clause that implicitly excludes each of the exceptions. . . . However, an unremovable ceteris paribus clause, requiring that other things be equal when the desire for d and the belief about a lead to doing a, opens up [L] to a potentially serious charge of vagueness. The scope of a ceteris paribus clause must in the long run be reduced, if not eliminated. . . .

Now that we have identified a general statement (with or without a ceteris paribus clause) that connects beliefs and desires to actions and thus can serve to underwrite our explanations, both ordinary and social scientific, we need to ask what kind of a general claim this is. [L] certainly looks like one that identifies the *causes* of actions and thus bids fair to be a law, or at least to be an important precursor to a law, in the natural scientists' sense of the term, of human action. . . .

For simplicity hereafter, we will use the word "causal" to mean law governed. What is crucial is the insistence that scientific explanation requires laws, whether causation is really always law governed or not.

However, . . . unlike (other) causes, beliefs and desires are also *reasons* for action: They justify it, show it to be rational, appropriate, efficient, reasonable, correct. They render it intelligible. So, perhaps explanations in ordinary life and social science work by showing that actions are reasonable, efficient, appropriate, or rational in the light of the agent's beliefs and desires. In this case, [L] will certainly not work like a law or the precursor to one. For causal laws don't provide intelligibility. Rather, [L] will reflect the fact that beliefs and desires justify or sanction some action as reasonable. If this is how [L] works, then the fundamental explanatory strategy in social science is not that of revealing brute causation. The aim is instead one of making the action *rationally intelligible.* If [L] also mentions causes, then this is a secondary by-product that it will provide derivatively.

In fact, [L] has often been identified as a *principle of rationality.* . . . Thus, far from being a contingent law describing the causes of actions, [L] turns out to be a definition, implicit or explicit, of what it means to be rational. And the social sciences that exploit [L] are not inquiries into the causation of various actions. Rather, they are investigations into the rationality of these actions.

This is a crucial contrast that every account of the explanation of human action must face. This difference between reasons and causes is sometimes difficult to keep clear, especially if, as most social scientists hold, beliefs and desires are *both* reasons for actions *and* their causes.

But if they are both, then why distinguish between reasons and causes? We do it because we need to identify where the explanatory power of action explanations lies. . . .

So, what *is* the difference between reasons and causes? It's easier illustrated than expressed: Suppose we ask a jogger why she jogs 10 kilometers a day. She replies, "because it's good for me." There is a fair amount left unsaid in this typical explanation: First, it's not just that jogging is good for her, it's that she *believes* it is; second, she *wants* to do things that are good for her; third, she believes that jogging won't prevent her from doing other things equally good for her. Doubtless there are other things she wants and believes that are "understood" in this explanation. All these things *justify* her jogging 10 kilometers a day. They make it seem intelligible, reasonable, rational: If we were in her shoes, that is, had her beliefs and desires, we'd jog that much too.

But suppose the "real reason" she jogs every day is that physiological changes in her body over the years addicted her to it, so that if she doesn't jog, she feels lousy all day. Though she never notices this correlation, it keeps her jogging by physiologically punishing her for skipping a day and rewarding her with a "runner's high" when she does jog. this is a typical behaviorist's explanation, and the scare quotes around "real reason" are there because if this is what explains her jogging, then clearly it does so not by *justifying* it but by causing it in virtue of some *contingent causal law.* In this case, reasons do not explain behavior—causes do. . . .

Of course, most social science proceeds on the supposition that the desires and beliefs that explain behavior are both reasons for it and its causes. . . .

Now, explaining human actions requires us to identify their "real reasons." And the crucial question for social science is whether the "real reasons" are connected to actions in virtue of some logically necessary principle of reasoning or in virtue of some contingent causal law. As we can see, this is a question about [L]. For [L] is what connects someone's real reasons, his beliefs and desires, with his actions. Does [L] underwrite our explanations of actions because it describes causal relations—that is, lawlike connections— in virtue of which actions are determined by beliefs and desires? Or does [L] underwrite these explanations because it helps us identify the reasons that make a particular action justified, intelligible, rational, meaningful, or somehow significant to us?

Of course, it is just possible that [L] does both: helps us identify the causes for actions and the reasons for them. . . . But as we shall now see, this happy reconciliation is not on the cards. . . .

. . . The problem of progress is (1) the difficulty facing attempts to improve [L] into a general theory of human behavior with increasing explanatory unity and predictive precision; and (2) the question of why no replacement for [L] has so far been found. To see this, let us try to apply [L] to the *causal* explanation of a particular action. . . .

Scientifically explaining a particular human action presumably involves deriving a statement describing the action from [L] and a set of statements about the agent's desires and beliefs. Let's take a prosaic example: Smith is carrying an umbrella as he goes to work. Why? Here is an explanation:
Initial conditions:

1. Smith wants d, to stay dry today.
2. Smith believes that a, carrying an umbrella, is the best way for him to d, stay dry today.

Law:

3. for any agent x, if x wants d, and x believes that doing a is the best way for him to secure d, then x does a.

Therefore:

4. Smith does a, carries an umbrella today.

This explanation may be a little stilted and unnecessarily cluttered. But it is what stands behind the briefer explanation "Smith thinks it's gonna rain." Now, how good a scientific explanation is this?

What if someone challenged it, demanding evidence to show that the initial conditions actually obtained? For all we know, Smith might be a British merchant banker, who always carries an umbrella because it's part of the required uniform, rain or shine.

. . .

How do we find out exactly what people believe and desire? The most convenient way is of course to ask them. Failing that, we can experiment: We try to arrange their circumstances so that their behavior will reveal their beliefs and desires. But usually the only way to discern the desires and beliefs of others is to observe their behavior. One thing we cannot do is read their minds. Now all three methods, asking, experimenting, observing, are really aspects of the same strategy: All three involve inferring back from action to desire and belief. Sometimes in the case of asking this fact escapes our notice. We are tempted to think that asking a question is a direct approach to what someone believes or wants.

But a little reflection reveals that asking is just a version of arranging subjects' circumstances and then watching their actions. After all, speech is itself intentional action. . . .

But this means that the *easiest* way to establish what someone believes and wants is fearfully complex. And what is more, establishing what a person wants and believes requires that we make further assumptions about other beliefs and desires of theirs, and it requires us to employ [L] itself. But this raises a brace of serious methodological problems.

The first is a regress problem in identifying initial conditions: In order to explain an action we need to identify the beliefs and desires that produced it in accordance with [L]. In order to identify these beliefs and desires, we need to make assumptions about other beliefs and desires. But our original problem was that of determining exactly what people believe and want. If to do this, we already need to know many of their other desires and beliefs, then our original problem faces us all over again. We have made little progress in answering the challenge to our original explanation. In ordinary circumstances we don't face this problem because our explanations are not challenged, and there is little interest in improving on their vagueness and imprecision. . . .

Second, there is the problem in testing [L]. In order to employ [L] in the explanation of an action, we need to use [L] to establish that the action's causes—the initial conditions—obtain. But this means that as long as what is to be explained is an action, nothing could even conceivably lead us to surrender [L] itself, and this casts doubt on its claims to be a causal law, as opposed to a definition. Recall that in order to use Smith's answers to questions as a guide to what he believes and desires, instead of an irrelevant sneeze, we had to assume that he wanted to answer our question sincerely and correctly and believed that the way to do so was to use the noise "yes." We had to make these assumptions because we employ [L] as a guide to when behavior constitutes *action*—speech instead of noise, as opposed to "mere" movement of the body.

. . .

In fact, the situation is rather more complicated. For in order to employ behavior as a guide to belief, we have to hold the agent's desires constant. And in order to use behavior as a guide to his desires, we have to hold beliefs constant. Any action can be the result of almost any belief, provided the agent has the appropriate desire, and vice versa. . . . By itself an action never identifies a single belief or desire. It only does so against the background of a large number of other beliefs and desires.

It's worth emphasizing this point: If we know what someone's beliefs and desires are, then [L] will tell us what actions he will undertake. If we know what actions a person performs and we know his beliefs, then [L] will tell us what his wants are. And if we know his wants and what actions he performs, then [L] will tell us what he believes. But without at least two of the three—belief, desire, and action—the third is not determinable. This is the nature of the conspiracy among them. It is the basis of the view that in explaining action, our aim is to render it intelligible by identifying its meaning or significance, in a "hermeneutical circle" where coherence among the three variables is the criterion of explanatory adequacy.

Of course it is clear why commonsense explanations of human action are so disputable and fallible and why folk psychology's predictive powers are so weak. The number of specific beliefs and desires that lead to actions is so large, and the difficulty of identifying them exactly is so great, that our explanations of action cannot help but be seriously incomplete. . . .

Of course [L] has some predictive content. . . . The reason for this sort of predictive success is clear: We can with confidence attribute a certain number of widely held beliefs and desires to everyone, including strangers, and even some more specialized ones to family and friends. Now, the number of such predictions is indefinitely large.

. . .

But predictive power isn't just a matter of numbers of successful predictions. It's a matter of at least two things: proportion of confirmed to disconfirmed predictions and success in providing highly precise and surprising ones. On both these counts [L] fares poorly. Beyond the "safe" predictions, the application of [L] falls down very badly. . . .

It's clear that in order to improve our predictions of human action we need to do either or both of two things: We need to be able to "measure" people's beliefs and desires with greater precision. And we need to improve [L] itself, fill in its ceteris paribus—other things being equal—clause, for example. That is how all causal explanations and causal laws are improved. . . .

This means, however, that we start out with a "law," [L], with only relatively little predictive power, given the difficulty of establishing precisely its initial conditions of application. And then there's little chance to improve it. For to improve it, we need first to find cases where it has gone wrong in its prediction, then "measure" the values of the initial conditions and the actual behavior that it failed correctly to predict, and finally revise [L] in order to accommodate the observed action. But in order to "measure" beliefs and desires, we must use [L] itself, plus the observed action we failed to predict, and then work back to a more accurate determination of the beliefs and desires. Once we've done this and plugged the more accurate initial conditions into the predictive argument, [L] gives us the observed action after all. So there's never any opportunity to add to or subtract from [L] in order to improve it.

One popular way of describing this problem for [L] is to say that it is unfalsifiable: There is no conceivable evidence about human action that could lead us to surrender it. And if it is unfalsifiable, then it cannot provide empirical, scientific knowledge. Therefore, if it does provide knowledge essential to social science, then the explanations of human action that social science uses [L] for are not ultimately empirical ones. Rather, they are interpretative and provide meaning. Moreover, social science's failure to provide predictions beyond those of folk psychology reflect no discredit upon social science, merely its differences in aim from that of the natural sciences. This of course is the interpretative or antinaturalist's view of [L]. . . . All three of the variables of folk psychology, desire, belief, action, are "intentional." This term has a special meaning in philosophy, though one that is related to its ordinary meaning of purposefulness. To say that a state of mind, like belief, for example, is intentional in the philosopher's sense (and this is the only sense in which the term will be used throughout this work) is to say that it has "propositional content"—that beliefs "contain"—in some sense—statements. Thus, there cannot be a belief without a statement believed.

. . .

Wants and desires are also identified by the statements they "contain": My desire to go to the movies is the desire *that* I go to the movies. . . . What shows that a belief or a desire is intentional is not the grammar of the sentence describing it but what happens when you make certain apparently *innocent* changes in the sentences that describe it.

This is easier to explain by illustration: Take the sentence "My eleven-year-old son believes that the *Titanic* sank." Now, he knows little more about the *Titanic* than this. Among the things he doesn't know is that the *Titanic* was the largest ship in the White Star Line. But it was. Now suppose we substitute "the largest ship in the White Star Line" for "the *Titanic*" in our statement of his belief. This will turn our statement about my son's belief from a *truth* to a *falsity,* for he doesn't know that the *Titanic* was identical to the largest ship in the White Star Line, and he does not believe that the largest ship in the White Star Line sank. By contrast, make the substitution in our statement about the cause of the *Titanic*'s sinking and the result will still be a true statement, not a false one. My son, of course, has a belief about the largest ship in the White Star Line, but not "under that description." This is the sense in which the terms used to express a belief are crucial in a way that they are not crucial to express non-intentional facts.

This sensitivity of intentional states to the descriptions and terms we use to identify them is even clearer in the case of desires. Thus, "Lady Astor wanted to sail on the *Titanic*" is a true statement about that wealthy socialite's desires. But the *Titanic* is identical to the only trans-Atlantic liner to sink on its maiden voyage. And under that description of the *Titanic,* Lady Astor certainly had no desire to sail on the *Titanic*. If we substitute "equals for equals" in the true statement that she wanted to sail on the *Titanic,* we get the false one that "Lady Astor wanted to sail on the only trans-Atlantic liner to sink on its maiden voyage." Lady Astor wanted to sail on the *Titanic* "under one description," but under another description she didn't want to.

Therefore, intentional states are ones in which we cannot freely substitute synonymous descriptions without risking the chance of changing a truth to a falsity. If we think about it, this should not really be surprising. Beliefs and desires are "subjective": They are mental or psychological states. They reflect the ways we look at the world: our points of view, which differ from each other and change as we acquire different information about the world. They represent some facts about things in the world or some state of affairs we desire. But never all the facts, the complete picture. A representation of how things are or could be must always be drawn from a perspective, one that is partial and incomplete. Now, there are many objective facts about the world that we don't represent to ourselves because we don't know them or are wrong about them. The subjectivity or incompleteness in our beliefs about the world reflects itself in this curious feature that substitutions that make no difference to truths about objective states of the world make a great deal of difference in descriptions of subjective states.

Philosophers have a special name for this feature of intentional statements. They call them "inten*s*ional"—with an *s* instead of a *t*. This is regrettable, because it breeds confusion between intentionality—a property of psychological states, and intension-ality—a logical property of statements that report them. . . . But we need the notion in order to show that actions are intensional, just like their intentional causes, beliefs, and desires.

The intensionality of desires and beliefs makes the explanation of actions inten-sional as well and thus makes actions derivatively intentional. . . .

What makes "mere" behavior into action is intentionality. Action is intentional, at least derivatively, for behavior is only action if there are intentional states—desire and belief that lead to it. Because desires and beliefs "contain propositions," action reflects them as well; and thus all of the apparatus that common sense and social sci-ence employ to describe what people do (as opposed to what merely happens to them) has an intimate connection with *language.* For it is sentences of a language that give the content of desires, beliefs, and actions, that express the propositions about the world that belief and desire relate us to. It's not just that these states "contain" state-ments; the statements they contain are of their *essence.* . . .

Many social scientists and philosophers have long held that the aim of social sci-ence is to reveal the meaning of behavior or its significance. And they have usually contrasted meaning and significance with causation as incompatible alternative aims. The analysis of the description and explanation of action as intentional doesn't just give new force to this idea. It gives it a hardheaded argument. For to give the mean-ing of an action is now taken out of the realm of the metaphorical and made an es-sential step in explaining it. We cannot explain an action till we know what action it is. We cannot know this unless we know how the agent views it, that is, under which linguistic description the agent brings it. Once we know this, we can explain it by showing its significance, its role in meeting the agent's desires, given his beliefs. Because both desires and beliefs are meaningful states of an agent, the explanation they provide action gives its meaning in a very literal sense. . . . But the main upshot of the intensionality of action and its determinants is that it seems to make the causal approach to human action ultimately impossible. For it shows that there is no way even in principle to provide a description of the beliefs and desires that cause action independent of one another and independent of the actions they are said to cause.

Recall the admission that [L] is employed in everyday life and in social science in order to establish the initial conditions, which are then harnessed together with [L] again, in order to explain an action. Indeed, [L] is also employed in order to deter-mine whether a bit of behavior is action or not and therefore within the purview of social science instead of, say, the physiology of reflexes. For [L] not only links de-sires and beliefs to the action they explain, it is our tool for identifying what beliefs and desires the agent has.

In and of itself this multiple use of [L] in order to carve out its own domain of ex-planation, as well as to establish its own initial conditions, is not *logically* illegiti-mate. It is methodologically suspect, for it makes it impossible to surrender [L] in the light of any empirical evidence. Among social scientists who demand that their the-ories have substantial testable content, [L] will not fare well. [L] certainly does not seem to be falsifiable by any conceivable observable evidence: Whenever a person does something that looks utterly irrational, given the beliefs and desires we have attributed to him, the reasonable thing to do is to change our estimate of his beliefs and desires; in the light of really crazy beliefs and/or desires, any action will look rational. We could, of course, decide that the behavior really is irrational, but then we wouldn't explain it as action, but rather as a form of pathological behavior. What we cannot do is give up [L] to preserve the original estimates of agents' beliefs and desires. For [L] is what we use in order to estimate the beliefs and desires we would be giving up [L] to preserve. If our explanatory generalizations must be falsifiable, then [L] must be surrendered as a causal law.

But the demand that our explanatory hypotheses must be falsifiable is generally viewed as too strong a demand on scientific theorizing. It neglects the fact that theoretical hypotheses often make no claims about observation directly and thus cannot be tested except when brought together with other hypotheses. . . .

. . .The real problem for [L] isn't testability, it's that in applying and improving [L], we need to formulate the right sort of auxiliary hypotheses about desires, beliefs, and actions that will enable us to test and improve it. Even in their absence, [L] might still be said to convey some minimum causal force, as, for example, illustrated in its powers to guide our most basic everyday expectations about how others will and will not behave. If we could but provide an alternative means to establish [L]'s domain and its initial conditions, then we could in fact proceed to test [L] and begin to improve it.

Now, what the intensionality of our descriptions of beliefs, desires, and actions shows is that no such alternative means will ever be found. There are only two sources for a determination of what someone believes or desires: his behavior or his brain. What we need is something that will "measure" what a person believes by some distinct effect of the belief, in the way that a thermometer measures heat by its quite distinct effect, the *height* of a column of mercury or alcohol. We need an equation with a belief (or a desire) on one side of the equal sign and a brain state or description of behavior on the other. But this is impossible because something will always be missing from the brain or behavior side of the equation: intensionality. The description of behavior or brain states is never intensional. It is, in the philosopher's lingo, *extensional.* In fact, it is widely held that all of the rest of science, biological, chemical, physical, and mathematical, can be expressed in extensional terms. That is, any true description of a bit of mere behavior or of a brain state, whether in the language of anatomical displacement, physiology, cytology, molecular biology, chemistry, or electromagnetic theory, will remain true whenever we substitute equivalent descriptions into it, no matter how farfetched. . . .

Philosophers of psychology have expressed this point by saying that mental states are not *reducible* to behavior or brain states. The problem they face is the ancient one of the mind and the body: How is the former related to the latter, and what kind of a thing is the mind anyway? Philosophers of the other social sciences may think they can ignore such arcane questions. But in the end they cannot. For the modern version of the mind-body problem is that of how physical matter can represent, or have content, in light of the fact that a complete description of it will be extensional and never intensional. This becomes a problem for philosophers of social science when they realize that the only way to justify its explanatory strategy as scientific, or to improve on its unity and precision, is by showing the "measurability" of naturalistic social sciences' causes by means that the rest of science recognizes. Only if such linkage is possible will there be, even in principle, alternative means for identifying [L]'s domain of application, and determining the occurrence of its initial conditions, that are independent of [L]. . . . Such linkage is impossible, . . . for there is no description, known or unknown, of the intentional causes of action, which is itself *extensional,* and thus none that is independent of a description of their effects. [L] thus turns out not even to be of limited employment as a causal regularity, for the elements it connects cannot even in principle be shown to bear contingent relations to one another.

This is a pessimistic conclusion for the naturalist who hopes to meet scientific standards in the explanation of human *action.* Whether it is too pessimistic hinges on the resolution of fundamental metaphysical problems about the nature of mind and its relation to the body. . . .

H. L. A. Hart and the Doctrines of Mens Rea and Criminal Responsibility

RICHARD A. WASSERSTROM

In both the English and the American legal systems, a person's liability to punishment is generally made dependent upon certain mental conditions (in addition, of course, to the commission of certain proscribed acts, etc.). In order for a person to be held criminally responsible for his acts, so the generally acknowledged doctrine goes, mens rea must have been present. In his writings on the criminal law, Professor H. L. A. Hart has been concerned in large measure with providing a reinterpretation of the doctrine of mens rea and a new rationale for and defense of the doctrine of criminal responsibility that depends upon it. For Hart the challenge is to defend these doctrines against two positions which threaten them from opposite directions. The first is the claim that the requirement of mens rea only makes sense within the confines of a retributive theory of punishment—within the context of a view that makes the requirement of mens rea dependent upon the appropriateness of punishing people for the immorality of their conduct. The second is the claim that the doctrine of criminal responsibility (and hence mens rea) could profitably be "eliminated" from the criminal law, and the focus of the criminal law shifted thereby from a punitive to a preventive intention. . . .

Any retributive theory of punishment depends in some quite fundamental sense upon the presence of a morally wrong act. Thus, it is not surprising that in one of his most important and influential articles, "Legal Responsibility and Excuses,"

From *University of Chicago Law Review,* Vol. 35 (1967), pp. 92–96, 98–100, 102–104, 114–115, 121–123.

Professor Hart seeks to criticize the thesis, which he attributes to Jerome Hall, that criminal responsibility depends on moral culpability. This, says Hart, is a mistake. Mens rea is not required in order to assure the existence of *moral* culpability. Instead the doctrine's desirability can be seen to depend both upon maximization of the choices that it allows to individual members of society and upon the prevention of the punishment of those who did not voluntarily violate the law.

Hart begins his exploration of these topics by proposing an interpretation of the requirement of mens rea. Those mental conditions that must be present before liability to punishment is allowed can, says Hart, be viewed most profitably in their negative form. As such, they are the conditions that exempt one from punishment on some ground or other. Thus, one way to view these mental conditions is as excusing conditions:

> [T]he individual is not liable to punishment if at the time of his doing what would otherwise be a punishable act he is, say, unconscious, mistaken about the physical consequences of his bodily movements or the nature or qualities of the thing or persons affected by them, or, in some cases, if he is subjected to threats or other gross forms of coercion or is the victim of certain types of mental disease. This is a list, not meant to be complete, giving broad descriptions of the principal excusing conditions; the exact definition of these and their precise character and scope must be sought in the detailed exposition of our criminal law. If an individual breaks the law when none of the excusing conditions are present, he is ordinarily said to have acted of "his own free will," "of his own accord," "voluntarily"; or it might be said, "He could have helped doing what he did."

Given this interpretation of the mens rea requirement, the next question is, of course, why we either do or ought to recognize these excuses as properly exempting persons from criminal liability. The view that Hart wants to reject is that which regards the importance of excuses to any determination of criminal responsibility as being itself dependent upon "the more fundamental requirement that for criminal responsibility there must be 'moral culpability', which would not exist where the excusing conditions are present."

This is the view that Hart ascribes to Jerome Hall in whose book, *General Principles of the Criminal Law,* he finds this position most clearly expressed. In that book, according to Hart:

> Professor Hall asserts that, though the goodness or badness of the *motive* with which a crime is committed may not be relevant, the general principle of liability, except of course where liability is unfortunately "strict" and so any mental element must be disregarded, is the "intentional or reckless doing of a *morally* wrong act." This is declared to be the essential meaning of mens rea: "though mens rea differs in different crimes there is one common essential element, namely the *voluntary* doing of a *morally* wrong act forbidden by the law." On this view the law inquires into the mind in criminal cases in order to secure that no one shall be punished in the absence of the basic condition of *moral* culpability. For it is just only to "punish those who have intentionally committed *moral* wrongs proscribed by law." [citations deleted]

Hart has several reasons for regarding this view as a mistaken one. The first is that the view is false if it is intended to describe the working of actual, rather than ideal, systems of criminal law. In Hart's words, the "doctrine does not fit any actual system of criminal law," and this is so not merely because of the existence of strict liability offenses. Rather, it is so because in every system of criminal law there are of necessity:

> many actions . . . that if voluntarily done are criminally punishable, although our moral code may be either silent as to their moral quality, or divided. Very many offenses are created by legislation designed to give effect to a particular economic scheme (e.g. a state monopoly of road or rail transport), the utility or moral character of which may be genuinely in dispute. An offender against such legislation can hardly be said to be morally guilty or to have intentionally committed a moral wrong. . . .

. . .

If, then, we refuse to be convinced of the falseness of Hall's view by the fact that his doctrine of mens rea does not "fit" completely any actual system of criminal law, and if we ask instead whether Hall's analysis of mens rea as requiring moral culpability does succeed in revealing something of importance to us about the criminal law, what might we say on behalf of such a claim?

The most plausible argument would be that the "core" cases of criminality in almost any legal system are cases of seriously immoral conduct that are proscribed by law. It is surely more than accidental, so this argument might go, that when we search for *clear* cases of criminal behavior we think first of murder, rape, robbery and similar immoral acts. The point is that the immorality or blameworthiness of the action does seem to be conceptually *connected* (but not, perhaps, necessarily) with most typical crimes.

It would be important, however, to emphasize that the claim here is not that the immorality of the action is a sufficient condition for making it criminal (that view is, I think, exposed quite adequately by Hart in *Law, Liberty and Morality,* nor that immorality is a necessary condition (*vide,* strict liability), but simply that it is typically constitutive of acts that are proscribed by the criminal law. . . .

. . . Hart is concerned to establish that Hall's view is mistaken in still another sense—it rests, says Hart, on a related confusion. It supposes that criminal liability must either be based on moral culpability or it must be "strict," i.e., based "on nothing more than the outward conduct of the accused." Given this dichotomy, it does seem to follow, says Hart, that the only plausible explanation as to why we inquire into the mental state of a defendant is that we are concerned to establish the presence or absence of moral culpability.

The difficulty here, Hart tells us, is that the dilemma is an unreal one. There is, in short, a third alternative; namely, that the actor's mental state is relevant just in order to establish that the actor acted *voluntarily.* There is, Hart insists—and this seems to me to be the central point—a rationale for the system of excuses that is different from the one proposed by Hall. It is simply that there is a principle worthy of respect that holds that "it is unfair and unjust to punish those who have not 'voluntarily' broken the law." This, Hart quite rightly insists, is a very different principle from that which holds that "it is wrong to punish those who have not 'voluntarily committed a moral wrong proscribed by law.'" Thus, if Hall had not mistakenly supposed that all liability must be either strict or based on moral culpability, he would have seen the possibility of a rationale for the excuses based upon the fundamental principle that it is unjust to punish a person who did not voluntarily violate the law.

Hart's thesis raises at least three further questions. First, what is there that is unfair or unjust about punishing someone who did not voluntarily break the law? Second, even if it is unjust to punish someone unless he voluntarily broke the law, might it not only be just to punish those who have voluntarily broken the law? And third, is it just to punish those who have voluntarily broken the law? That is to say, even if Hart is right concerning the injustice of punishing in the presence of one of the excuses, this does not imply the justness of punishing in the absence of the excuse—and in particular in the absence of "moral fault." . . .

. . . Hart proposes the following as an answer to the question of why it is unjust to punish in the absence of a voluntary action. Imagine, he says, what it would be like to live in a society in which accidents, insanity, duress, and all of the other excuses were not regarded as entitling an offender to exemption from criminal liability. Imagine what it would be like to live under a system of criminal law that operated on the basis of total "strict liability." At least three things would happen. First, "our power of predicting what will happen to us will be immeasurably diminished." This is so because we cannot predict very accurately when we will, for example, do something by mistake or by accident. Secondly, what happens to us will be dependent very largely on things other than our own choices. And thirdly, "we should suffer sanctions without having obtained any satisfactions." . . . I want to consider the additional but related claim advanced by Hart that there are *affirmative* virtues to a system which recognizes the excusing conditions. Hart identifies at least three advantages in such recognition:

> First, we maximize the individual's power at any time to predict the likelihood that the sanctions of the criminal law will be applied to him. Secondly, we introduce the individual's choice as one of the operative factors determining whether or not these sanctions shall be applied to him. He can weigh the cost to him of obeying the law— and of sacrificing some satisfaction in order to obey—against obtaining that satisfaction at the cost of paying "the penalty." Thirdly, by adopting this system of attaching excusing conditions we provide that, if the sanctions of the criminal law are applied, the pains of punishment will for each individual represent the price of some satisfaction obtained from breach of law.

Here, too, Hart's analysis does provide us with a new and useful way of looking at the role of excusing conditions in the law. By emphasizing the significance that the presence of choice alone can make, Hart permits us to view the criminal law in a substantially more "positive" fashion than is typically the case. It permits us to see the sense in which the criminal law can be seen not so much as a system of prohibitions, the punishment for which is justified either as a means of securing compliance or as a fitting response to wrongdoing, but as a system of "prices" for alternative courses of conduct.

One real danger in this analysis is, of course, that it may lead us significantly to underestimate and understate the non-optional character of criminal laws, that it may lead to an interpretation of criminal laws as mere hypothetical imperatives. . . .

A second objection to Hart's view concerning the affirmative value of the excuses is that it leaves uncertain what we are to think about the punishment of persons for negligent misconduct. . . . What he has done, though, is to insist that the imposition of criminal liability for negligence is *not* like the imposition of criminal responsibility in cases of strict liability, and consequently, that the arguments which obtain against strict liability do not obtain against the punishment of criminal negligence. And he appears further to imply that punishment for negligence is no less permissible (in some circumstances) than the punishment of intentional acts. Very briefly, Hart's position on negligence is that we must (but all too seldom do) distinguish between two distinct questions: (i) "Did the accused fail to take those precautions which any reasonable man with normal capacities would in the circumstances have taken? (ii) Could the accused, given his mental and physical capacities, have taken those precautions?" To punish someone for negligence is only like holding him liable in a system of strict liability if it is the case that the accused lacked the *capacity* to take the precautions that a reasonable man would have taken. What is crucial, Hart tells us in the most complete account that he gives:

> is that those whom we punish should have, when they acted, the normal capacities, physical and mental, for doing what the law requires and abstaining from what it forbids, and a fair opportunity to exercise these capacities. Where these are absent as they are in different ways in the varied cases of accident, mistake, paralysis, reflex action, coercion, insanity, etc., the moral protest is that it is morally wrong to punish because "he could not have helped it" or "he could not have done otherwise" or "he had no real choice." But, as we have seen, there is no reason (unless we are to reject the whole business of responsibility and punishment) *always* to make this protest when someone who "just didn't think" is punished for carelessness. For in some cases at least we may say "he could have thought about what he was doing" with just as much rational confidence as one can say of any intentional wrongdoing "he could have done otherwise."

Hart does surely seem to be saying that the punishment of people for negligence (where they had the capacity to take suitable precautions) is no less justifiable than the punishment of persons for intentional acts. And I think this is false. Hart has shown that there is a sense in which some persons who are negligent could have done otherwise. And he has, therefore, shown that the argument against punishing those who could not have done otherwise does not apply to this class of persons. But, as we have seen, Hart does not rest the case for the excusing conditions solely on their defensive usefulness. Rather, it will be recalled, what Hart did was to identify three virtues of restricting punishment to cases in which mens rea was present: the maximization of the individual's power to predict the future, the introduction of the individual's own choices as a determining element, and the representation of each application of punishment as the price of some satisfaction obtained from a breach of the law.

What must be seen is that at best each of these three elements is most clearly present in the case of *intentional* conduct. The force behind Hart's mercantile analogy and his emphasis upon choice depends at least in part on the presence of intentional, deliberative action. In the case of negligent conduct—even where the actor had the capacity to attend more carefully than he did to the situation—an emphasis upon *choice* and predictability seems misplaced and less convincing. The case that Hart is here making for what he sometimes calls the "moral license" to punish is most persuasive if it is true that the actor chose to break the law. And it is this kind of choice that is hard to find in the case of negligence.

The issue that is involved is in one sense a more basic and fundamental one. Hart is on occasion guilty of confusing two different principles and arguments. Usually, Hart is concerned to establish the desirability of the excuses by invoking the defensive principle that it is unjust to blame or punish someone who could not help doing what he did—someone whose action was not voluntary. This line of argument makes the case for recognizing the excuses, but it hardly ipso facto makes the case for the permissibility of punishing someone who could help doing what he did—someone whose action was not involuntary. Hart appears to recognize this fact, since he also gives an affirmative argument for the permissibility of punishing those who intentionally break the law. And the argument that Hart gives for the permissibility of punishment in the absence of the excuses is that it is possible to say of the offender that he *chose* to do the action in question, and not merely that he could have avoided doing the action in question. In short, "He could have avoided doing X" does not imply "He chose to do X." Yet much of Hart's case for the permissibility of punishment for negligence appears to depend on the permissibility of this inference.

Hart can, of course, meet this objection by insisting that it is morally permissible to punish as long as the action was voluntary, i.e., not involuntary. But then it is not clear that he can continue to insist upon the virtues associated with the mercantile analogy. For they are most plausibly associated with intentional, fully deliberative choices. . . .

. . . Hart is disturbed by Lady Wootton's approbation of the rise of strict liability offenses and of the view that "proof of the outward act alone is enough to make the accused liable to compulsory measures of treatment or *punishment.*" And against this view Hart insists, for the same reasons advanced on other occasions in the defense of legal excuses, that we need not preserve the doctrine of mens rea only if we are prepared to accept a retributive theory of punishment. We need not do so, just because one can hold the non-retributive view that:

> [O]ut of considerations of fairness or justice to individuals we should restrict even punishment designed as a "preventive" to those who had a normal capacity and a fair opportunity to obey. This is still an intelligible ideal of justice to the individuals whom we punish even if we punish them to protect society from the harm that crime does and not to pay back the harm that they have done. And it remains intelligible even if in securing this form of fairness to those whom we punish we secure a lesser measure of conformity to law than a system of total strict liability which repudiated the doctrine of mens rea.

Thus, Hart is once again insisting on the moral importance of the claim that the excuses function as the devices that help to assure that we will not punish those persons who did not, in some meaningful fashion, intend or choose to do the action proscribed by law. . . .

If mens rea is no longer a necessary condition for conviction, then individual freedom will be interfered with in a way in which it is not under our present system. This is so because if mens rea is eliminated then every blow—even accidental ones—will be a matter requiring investigation and consideration of the possibility that cure might be appropriate. . . . Hart does take account of the point made above and he does attempt to distinguish cases of punishment from other pursuits of the social welfare in a fashion relevant to the issue at hand. What he says is this:

> The moral importance attached to these [excusing conditions] in punishment distinguishes it from other measures which pursue similar aims (e.g., the protection of life,

wealth or property) by methods which like punishment are also often unpleasant to the individuals to whom they are applied, e.g., the detention of persons of hostile origin or association in war time, or of the insane, or the compulsory quarantine of persons suffering from infectious disease. To these we resort to avoid damage of a catastrophic character.

The difficulty with this, however, is that while sometimes it is true that we do resort to these measures when "damage of a catastrophic character" threatens, far more often we invoke them in order to prevent social misfortune that is no more catastrophic than the occurrence of serious crime. Indeed, to make the point more forcefully: it seems clear to me that if Hart is to succeed in differentiating the use of persons in punishment to achieve certain ends from the use of persons in other contexts to achieve similar ends, this differentiation cannot depend either upon the seriousness of the damage to be prevented or upon the voluntariness of the actor's behavior.

But despite this, Hart is, I am convinced, getting at something important. Treating or reforming people, in the circumstances described, is something that, like punishment, also has to be justified. Unlike punishment, it does not have to be justified because it necessarily requires the imposition of an unpleasantness. But unlike punishment, too, it does have to be justified because it requires the involuntary submission to the control of another—no matter how benevolent the motive and no matter how beneficial the result anticipated. Preoccupation with the concern of the reformer for the good of the person to be reformed can blind us far too much to the involuntary character of the imposition of so many reforms.

Related to this is the awareness of what will be given up if we cease to care whether a person's action was intentional or not. As Hart so forcefully points out:

> Human society is a society of persons; and persons do not view themselves or each other merely as so many bodies moving in ways which are sometimes harmful and have to be prevented or altered. Instead persons interpret each other's movements as manifestations of intention and choices, and these subjective factors are often more important to their social relations than the movements by which they are manifested or their effects. If one person hits another, the person struck does not think of the other as *just* a cause of pain to him; for it is of crucial importance to him whether the blow was deliberate or involuntary. If the blow was light but deliberate, it has a significance for the person struck quite different from an accidental much heavier blow. No doubt the moral judgments to be passed are among the things affected by this crucial distinction; but this is perhaps the least important thing so affected. If you strike me, the judgment that the blow was deliberate will elicit fear, indignation, anger, resentment: these are not voluntary responses; but the same judgment will enter into deliberations about my future voluntary conduct towards you and will colour all my social relations with you. Shall I be your friend or enemy? Offer soothing words? Or return the blow? All this will be different if the blow is not voluntary. This is how human nature in human society actually is and as yet we have no power to alter it. The bearing of this fundamental fact on the law is this. If as our legal moralists maintain it is important for the law to reflect common judgments of morality, it is surely even more important that it should in general reflect in its judgments on human conduct distinctions which not only underlie morality, but pervade the whole of our social life. This it would fail to do if it treated men merely as alterable, predictable, curable or manipulatable things.

NOTES AND QUESTIONS

1. Did the materials in chapter 2 on the justification of punishment and those in this section on mental states convince you that mental states are crucial to culpability? If the standard, folk psychological, view of human behavior criticized by Rosenberg is so causally vacuous, how do we explain the success of human intercourse and institutions and with what account of human behavior would we replace folk psychology? Suppose that you believed that your mental life was without any causal influence over what you did. What would be the right response? If practical reason is only epiphenomenal, can the law properly premise culpability on it? What would a criminal law that paid no attention to mental states be like?

In *Crime and the Criminal Law* (1963), Lady Barbara Wootton argued that mens rea should be taken into account only for dispositional purposes. Thus, mental states served a purely utilitarian function in her scheme but were not abandoned altogether. Her proposal represents the most serious modern attempt by a policymaker to jettison the need for mens rea in the definitions of crimes and, as Wasserstrom notes, it received intense criticism from H. L. A. Hart.

2. Much of the writing about specific mental states in cases and commentary argues about the precise meaning of intention (purpose), knowledge, recklessness, and negligence. Is there sufficient understanding of these states and clarity of definition to support conviction and imprisonment in part on the basis of their being present at the time of an offense?

3. The usual culpability level ranking of the mental states considers purpose the most culpable, followed by knowledge (although this state is often equated with purpose), and then recklessness. Negligence is always considered the least culpable and, indeed, many influential writers, such as Jerome Hall, would not criminalize negligent conduct. Is this ranking obviously correct? How is it justified? Cannot negligent people be more dangerous than some purposeful miscreants? Can we not imagine reckless conduct that is as heinous as intentional conduct that causes the same result?

4. Support for the criminal law is solidified by its adoption of the standard view of human conduct, but there is a practical, implementation difficulty that arises, which the selections address only briefly. Even if mental states are causal and are a crucial basis for evaluating conduct morally and legally, how can we know what goes on in other minds? No one can read other minds and there is no technological means for doing so. Now, the conduct and circumstance elements of crimes can in principle be verified objectively. But how is it possible practically and thus morally to convict and punish offenders in part on the basis of the alleged presence of objectively unverifiable mental states? We make inferences about mental states based on conduct, including speech, and on our general understanding of practical reasoning and the world around us. For example, if we hear someone say, "I'm going to kill you," and then the agent shoots a bullet through the heart of the person to whom the statement was addressed, we think we are certain that the killer killed the victim intentionally. This

is an easy case, however, and can we be so certain in the vast majority of cases, many of which do not feature such a blatantly incriminating statement?

Mens rea can be identified because humans are necessarily quite good about inferring the mental states of others. If we lacked this ability, coherent human interaction, which depends on gauging accurately what others are up to, would be well nigh impossible. Mental states aren't observable, to be sure, but a high degree of interpersonal agreement—a quite respectable form of objectivity—about the mental states of others is possible. Moreover, the prosecution must meet the "beyond a reasonable doubt" standard of proof concerning the mental state. The ordinary inferences that reasonable people would draw may be wrong, but if so, it will usually be because the defendant has a quite unusual story about what was going on. For example, suppose we see a person hand a known drug dealer money, in return for which the dealer hands the person a glassine envelope containing a powder that turns out to be cocaine. Suppose the person is arrested and charged with the "knowing" possession of a controlled substance, which requires that the defendant *believe* that the possessed substance is a prohibited drug. It is possible that the defendant did not have this belief. After all, it is possible that he mistakenly believed that he was buying sugar to bake brownies or that he delusionally believed it was a sacred substance and the dealer was a priest. In such cases, to avoid conviction the defendant will have to cast a reasonable doubt on the ordinary inferences by conducting a convincing cross-examination of the prosecution's witnesses or by putting on proof of his own. In sum, the identification of the mental states of others is not an insurmountable obstacle to the fair implementation of criminal laws whose moral validity depends upon the inclusion of mental states in the definitions of crimes.

The General Part: Accomplice, Attempt, and Conspiracy Liability

4.1 ACCOMPLICE LIABILITY

Aid and Comfort
LEO KATZ

> Who built Thebes with its seven gates
> The books only name kings
> Did the kings carry the boulders?

So asks the German poet and playwright Bertold Brecht, questioning the way historians like to tell history. He continues,

> Young Alexander conquered India
> All by himself?
> Caesar vanquished the Gallians
> He did not even take a cook along?
> Philip of Spain cried when his fleet
> Was sunk. No one else cried?

From *Bad Acts and Guilty Minds: Conundrums of the Criminal Law* (Chicago: University of Chicago Press, 1987), pp. 252–54.

What goes for history also goes for crime: much of it is teamwork. The laws of complicity and conspiracy are designed to cope with that fact. The law of complicity punishes all who aid and abet in the execution of a crime. The law of conspiracy punishes all who merely agree to commit a crime. Together these two laws see to it that courts, unlike historians, really give credit where credit is due—not merely to the ringleader, but to the ring.

But do we really need the laws of complicity and conspiracy to accomplish that? Let's worry about complicity first. . . . It really isn't obvious why the law couldn't manage nicely without it. Suppose A persuades B to kill C. Under the law of complicity, A would be held liable as B's accomplice for helping, in fact instigating, him to kill C. In modern American jurisdictions that means A could be punished just as severely as the actual perpetrator, B. But it seems that even without the law of complicity, we wouldn't have to let A off the hook. We could simply hold A liable for causing C's death—in short, murder. Why then do we need the law of complicity?

Perhaps, you might say, we need it because not every crime is like murder, not every crime consists of causing some harm. Take burglary, which consists of breaking and entering into a dwelling. Suppose A persuades B to burglarize C's house. Without a law of complicity, wouldn't A go unpunished? We couldn't very well say that A committed the crime of burglary, because A didn't actually break and enter. But perhaps we could: We might say that A broke and entered "using" someone else, just as we might say he broke and entered if he had used a pole to break a window, and, without actually entering, removed a painting from the interior. Admittedly, though, analogizing the use of a human being to the use of a pole may be straining things a bit. Still, it seems the law could do without the law of complicity if it just redefined crimes like burglary to include not just the act of breaking and entering but the act of causing someone else to break and enter. Why hasn't the law taken this simpler tack?

To get at the reason for the law of complicity, it pays to think about the criminal law's civil counterpart, the law of tort. Most crimes are also civil wrongs, torts. The offender faces not just a jail term at the hands of the state, but a damage suit at the hands of his victims. The tort law is quite similar to the criminal law. It also has a law of complicity, called "the law of joint tortfeasors," but its function here is more easily discerned. Suppose A, B, C, and D jointly issue some stock. As the law requires, they prepare a prospectus describing the stock, to be given to every potential purchaser. A number of people buy. Then it turns out that the prospectus contained four egregious misrepresentations, falsehoods deliberately inserted to boost the value of the stock. When the truth comes out, the stock price falls. Some injured shareholders sue A, B, C, and D. The trial reveals that each of the four defendants contributed one of the misrepresentations. A study is performed to assess the damages and it determines them to be $1,111. (The number is small to keep things simple.) The study also determines that had there only been one misrepresentation, damages would have been $1,000, had there been two they would have been $1,100, and had there been three they would have been $1,110. In other words, one misrepresentation did $1,000 worth of damage, a second added only $100 to that total, a third only $10, and a fourth only $1.

Without a law of complicity, each defendant is liable only for the damages that wouldn't have occurred without his participation. But if any of the defendants in this case had not participated, damages would only have been $1 smaller than they were. Thus each defendant would only be liable for $1, the shareholders would only collect

$4, and a $1,107 injury would remain uncompensated. Under the law of complicity, this could not happen. The defendants jointly would be liable for $1,111, which would be divided among them.

The law of complicity works the same magic in criminal law. For suppose we charged the four defendants with some form of fraud. Without a law of complicity, each could claim that because his misrepresentation contributed only marginally to the total harm ($1 out of a $1,111 total) he should either not be punished at all or only very lightly. Under the law of complicity, however, all participants are liable as accomplices in the crime of fraud and the total damage done would be looked to in assessing the punishment they merited.

This explanation also helps one understand a peculiar quirk in the law of complicity. To be an accomplice, it isn't necessary that one actually bring about the commission of a crime; it's enough that one had a hand in it. Imagine that the above example had been even more extreme: it might have involved five defendants and five misrepresentations, and the fifth misrepresentation might not have added anything to the damage total. Then each defendant might argue he should not be liable for anything, since the deletion of his misrepresentation would not diminish damages by a red cent. The argument does him no good because the law of complicity only requires that he participated, not that he brought about the crime.

What makes the law of complicity necessary in the example I gave is the principle of diminishing marginal returns, familiar from economics: The last misrepresentation adds less than the next-to-next-to-last misrepresentation, which adds less than the first misrepresentation. Most cases of group criminality are like this. Generally, when people get together to do something as a group, they are subject to the principle of diminishing marginal returns. The last person contributes less than the next-to-last person, who contributes less than the next-to next-to-last person. That means if every group member has to answer only for the harm that wouldn't have occurred without him, there will be a lot of harm unanswered for. The law of complicity avoids that. Diminishing marginal returns is the real reason for having it.

Complicity, Cause, and Blame: A Study in the Interpretation of Doctrine

SANFORD H. KADISH

A consequence of a person's action may be of two general kinds. It may consist of subsequent events. If I light a match in an area containing explosive vapors that ignite, starting a fire that burns down a building, I may be blamed for the burning of the building because I can be said to have caused it. I started a chain of events that led to the burning of the building through cause and effect relationships governed by laws

From *California Law Review,* Vol. 73 (1985), pp. 323–410.

of nature. But a consequence of a person's action may also consist of the actions of other people. I may have persuaded another responsible person to light the match or helped him by giving him a match for the purpose. The other person then caused the burning of the building. But whether I am to be blamed for the other person's action would not be assessed by asking whether I caused his action in the same sense that his lighting the match caused the fire. Rather, my responsibility would be determined by asking whether my persuasion or help made me accountable for the other person's actions and what they caused.

Responding to these common perceptions of the relationship between actions and consequences, the criminal law has developed two separate doctrines for fixing blame. The doctrine of causation deals with fixing blame for natural events. The doctrine of complicity deals with fixing blame for the criminal action of another person. While the doctrine of complicity is the subject of this article, the doctrine of causation cannot be put aside. For though there are significant contrasts between causation and complicity, there are also important similarities deriving from the common function of both doctrines to fix blame for consequences. In comparing and contrasting these doctrines, I shall draw heavily on the classic treatment of causation by Professors Hart and Honoré.

At the outset, it is important to develop more fully why both in common usage and in law we use different concepts to determine when a person may be blamed for things that happen and when he may be blamed for what other people do. The explanation lies in that singular view of human action that underlies blame. That same view of human action that entails freedom to choose obviously applies to the actions of one who is responding to the actions of another. In the same sense and for the same reasons that a person's genes, upbringing, and social surroundings are not seen as the cause of his actions, neither are the actions of another seen as the cause of his actions. We regard a person's acts as the products of his choice, not as an inevitable, natural result of a chain of events. Therefore, antecedent events do not cause a person to act in the same way that they cause things to happen, and neither do the antecedent acts of others. To treat the acts of others as causing a person's actions (in the physical sense of cause) would be inconsistent with the premise on which we hold a person responsible.

There are exceptions to this general perception of human action that need to be noted here because they figure in the play between the doctrines of complicity and causation. Certain kinds of actions are in fact treated as caused by a prior action of another because we deem them lacking that quality of unconstrained free choice that generally characterizes human actions. Following Hart and Honoré, we may refer to these as nonvoluntary (or nonvolitional), or not wholly voluntary (or not wholly volitional) actions. Of course, an involuntary action, which in law is not regarded as an action at all, is of this character. But the class of nonvolitional actions, in the sense developed by Hart and Honoré, includes actions that are not literally involuntary. It includes all actions that are not wholly unconstrained or that are done without knowledge of those relevant circumstances that give the action its significance. There are two principal circumstances in which we treat human actions as nonvolitional: where they are excusable and where they are justifiable. Actions of persons who are legally irresponsible, actions where the actor acts without a required means rea or where other factors betoken absence of free choice (for example, duress), constitute excusable actions. Actions required by duty (i.e., a police officer's attempt to enforce the law) and actions constrained by the predicament of self-defense are examples of justifiable actions. As Hart and Honoré have shown, there are a variety of other circumstances as well where actions are not regarded as sufficiently volitional to warrant treating them the way human actions are normally treated. But since they are rarely relevant to the kinds of problems discussed in this article, they may be put aside.

I do not mean to say that the language of causation is inappropriate when dealing with one person's influence on the actions of another even when the latter's actions are entirely volitional. We commonly speak of one person occasioning the actions of another or of one person's action being the result of what another person says or does. This is appropriate because causation, broadly conceived, concerns the relationship between successive phenomena, whether they have the character of events or happenings, or of another person's volitional actions. The point I mean to stress is that in dealing with the influence of òne person upon the actions of another, we refer to a different kind of causal concept than that involved in physical causation. However philosophers may dispute the point, as far as the law is concerned, the way in which a person's acts produce results in the physical world is significantly different from the way in which a person's acts produce results that take the form of the volitional actions of others. The difference derives from the special view we take of the nature of a human action. In the course of this article, therefore, I will use causation restrictively to refer to relationships in which succeeding events take the form of happenings, exclusive of individuals' volitional actions.

This view of volitional human action has two relevant implications for understanding the doctrine of complicity. First, when we examine a sequence of events that follows a person's action, the presence in the sequence of a subsequent human action precludes assigning causal responsibility to the first actor. What results from the second actor's action is something the second actor causes, and no one else can be said to have caused it through him. This is expressed in the familiar doctrine of *novus actus interveniens*. Second, when we seek to determine the responsibility of one person for the volitional actions of another, the concept of cause is not available to determine the answer. For whatever the relation of one person's acts to those of another, it cannot be described in terms of that sense of cause and effect appropriate to the occurrence of natural events without doing violence to our conception of a human action as freely chosen.

These two implications of how we conceive of human actions give rise to the doctrine of complicity in the following way. Criminal prohibitions take two principal forms. Most prohibitions threaten punishment for particular kinds of actions (of course, with defined mens rea), sometimes only when some harm eventuates from the action, but sometimes whether it does or not. Examples of this form of prohibition include appropriating another's property, receiving stolen goods, breaking and entering defined structures, obtaining property by false pretenses, having sexual relations with another against her will, and killing a person in the course of operating a motor vehicle. On the other hand, we may punish a person for causing some defined harm, with no further description of the action prohibited: causing the death of a human being (killing) is the most common example. To be guilty of the second kind (result crimes), he must be found to have caused the result, by any actions that suffice to do so.

How then can the law reach those whose conduct makes it appropriate to punish them for the criminal actions of others—a person, for example, who persuades or helps another to commit a crime? Such persons do not commit action crimes, since they do not engage in the prohibited action. Some general doctrine is required through which such persons may be found liable. But what form should the doctrine take? If it were not for the very special way in which we perceive human actions, causation doctrine might serve this purpose, on the view that one who causes another to commit certain actions falls under the prohibition against committing those actions. But our conception of human actions as freely chosen precludes this analysis. Some alternative doctrine is needed, therefore, that imposes liability on the first actor who is to blame for the conduct of another, but that does so upon principles that comport with our conception of human actions. This is the office of the doctrine of complicity.

What then of result crimes? It again follows from our view of human actions that causation doctrine cannot make the first actor liable for a prohibited result caused by a volitional act of the second actor. As Hart and Honoré put it, the latter's action serves as a barrier through which the causal inquiry cannot penetrate to hold the first actor liable. To hold the first actor for the crime, we need an alternative doctrine that is consistent with our conception of human actions. The doctrine of complicity also fills the doctrinal gap for result crimes.

The Theory of Complicity

For the reasons just presented, the doctrine of complicity (sometimes referred to as the law of aiding and abetting, or accessorial liability) emerges to define the circumstances in which one person (to whom I will refer as the secondary party or actor, accomplice, or accessory) becomes liable for the crime of another (the primary party or actor, or the principal). To develop the theory of complicity further, it is necessary now to consider: (a) the nature of the liability imposed on the secondary party, (b) the kinds of actions that create this liability, (c) the intention with which those actions must be committed, and (d) the relevance of the success of those actions in achieving their objective.

The Derivative Nature of the Liability

The nature of complicity liability follows from the considerations that called it forth. The secondary party's liability is derivative, which is to say, it is incurred by virtue of a violation of law by the primary party to which the secondary party contributed. It is not direct, as it would be if causation analysis were applicable. That is ruled out by our concept of human action, which informs much of complicity doctrine. Volitional actions are the choices of the primary party. Therefore they are his acts and his alone. One who "aids and abets" him to do those acts, in the traditional language of the common law, can be liable for doing so, but not because he has thereby caused the actions of the principal or because the actions of the principal are his acts. His liability must rest on the violation of law by the principal, the legal consequences of which he incurs because of his own actions. . . .

The derivative nature of the secondary party's liability explains a variety of outcomes in the law of complicity. It is well settled that a secondary party is liable as an accomplice for influencing or aiding another to commit a crime that the secondary party is not himself capable of committing. An unmarried man, for example, cannot himself commit bigamy, because that crime extends only to those who, already married, marry again. But he can be convicted of bigamy as an accomplice for aiding or influencing a married person to commit the crime. Where a husband is incapable of raping his own wife, he may nonetheless be liable for her rape by another if he helps or encourages the other to do the act. Liability in these cases follows logically from the premise that the liability of the secondary party rests on the liability of the primary party. Since the secondary party could not be held for violating the law himself, his liability must be derivative.

The conventional derivative liability principle is also evident in cases in which one person helps another commit a crime, not realizing that the other is only feigning for the purpose of ensnaring him. For example, suppose a person boosts an ostensible principal into a window and the latter, having previously arranged for the police to arrive, and acting without the intent to steal required for burglary, passes out property to his helper. The helper is not liable as an accomplice so long as the feigning principal has incurred no liability by his actions, since the secondary party's liability derives from that of the primary party.

The relation between the degree of liability of the secondary party and that of the primary party likewise evidences the principle that an accomplice's liability derives from that of the primary party. It is widely accepted that the secondary party's liability need not be as great as that of the principal, who may have acted with a mens rea that makes him more culpable than the secondary party. The latter, for example, may, in the heart of provocation, induce the primary party to kill, while the primary party may act with cool deliberation. But this does not contradict the conception of the secondary party's liability as derivative. The accomplice's liability derives from that of the principal no less because it may derive from some and not all of his liability. These cases do not require attributing to the accomplice the volitional actions of the principal, only his (or some of his) liability. They are therefore consistent with the basic premise of complicity liability. . . .

The Intention

The Basic Requirement. Whether the mode of involvement in another's criminal act is influence or assistance, the law of complicity generally requires that the secondary actor act intentionally; that is, he must act with the intention of influencing or assisting the primary actor to engage in the conduct constituting the crime.

It is important to observe that the intention requirement is independent of the mens rea requirement for the underlying crime. The latter requirement means that to be liable as an accomplice in the crime committed by the principal, the secondary party must act with the mens rea required by the definition of the principal's crime. Thus, if the principal commits larceny by taking another's property with the required intention of permanently depriving its owner of it without consent or claim of right, the secondary party cannot be held as an accomplice unless he influenced or helped the principal intending (or knowing) that the principal would so deprive another of his property. If he believed the principal had a rightful claim to the property, for example, he could not be held for larceny.

It might seem, therefore, that the requirement that the secondary party act intentionally to influence or assist the principal is a consequence of the mens rea requirement of the substantive crime. This view appears plausible, however, only when we focus on cases where the mens rea of the underlying crime is knowledge or purpose. But consider the case described in the paragraph before last where recklessness satisfies the requirement for the underlying crime. In lending his car keys to the inebriated person, the lender acted recklessly, and that is all that is required for the crime of manslaughter committed by the driver. Yet the lender's recklessness about the likelihood that the driver would drive the car in the wrong direction is not enough to make him an accomplice. The lender must have *intended* the very acts that gave rise to the liability. It may be seen, therefore, that the intentionality requirement is not the same as the mens rea requirement. In addition to having the mens rea for the underlying crime, the accomplice must intend that the principal commit the acts that give rise to the principal's liability. . . .

Theory of the Intention Requirement. The theory of the intentionality requirement is not obvious. One possible explanation is social policy; namely, that it would be undesirable to draw the circle of criminal liability any wider. A pall would be cast on ordinary activity if we had to fear criminal liability for what others might do simply because our actions made their acts more probable. This has been the dominant consideration in recent debates over proposals to extend liability to those who know their actions will assist another to commit a crime but who act for reasons other than to further those criminal actions—the supplier of materials, for example, who knows that a buyer plans to use them to commit a crime. The argument that people otherwise lawfully conducting their affairs should not be constrained by fear of liability for what their customers will do has tended to prevail over the argument that it is proper for the criminal law to prohibit conduct that knowingly facilitates the commission of crime. The prevailing argument would seem to have even greater force in the case of a person who was only reckless as to the risk that his actions would lead another to commit a crime.

These policy considerations, however, may not be the whole story. If they were decisive, they should preclude extending criminal liability to knowing, reckless, and negligent actions that *cause* another to commit a criminal harm, as well as to actions that influence or assist another to commit a crime. But in those special situations where causation doctrine applies to interpersonal relationships (because the actions of the primary actor are not regarded as fully volitional), courts have shown no disposition to restrict the reach of causation doctrine, which ordinarily extends to unintended as well as intended consequences.

The explanation for the intention requirement must be found elsewhere. It may reside in the notion of agreement as the paradigm mode by which a principal in agency law (the secondary party in the terminology of the criminal law) becomes liable for the acts of another person. The liability of the principal in civil law rests essentially on his consent to be bound by the actions of his agent, whom he vests with authority for this purpose. Under the prevailing objective approach of contract law, it is the principal's manifestation of consent, rather than his subjective state of mind, that determines the authority of the agent and the rights of third parties. But this is attributable to the policy of facilitating business transactions by protecting people who reasonably rely on appearances the principal creates.

Insofar as manifesting consent to be bound by the acts of another is a general requirement for holding one person liable for the actions of another, the requirement of intention for complicity liability becomes more readily explicable. Obviously, in the context of the criminal law, literal consent to be criminally liable is irrelevant. But by intentionally acting to further the criminal actions of another, the secondary party voluntarily identifies himself with the principal party. The intention to further the acts of another, which creates liability under the criminal law, may be understood as equivalent to manifesting consent to liability under the civil law.

This theory would also explain why intention is not required where the ground of accountability for a result is causation. In causation cases, the actor's liability does not derive from the criminal acts of another. Either there is no other person intervening between the actor's action and the result or, in cases of interpersonal relations, the acts of the later actor are not regarded as volitional because they are excused, and hence are treated the same as any other event that the first actor causes. His liability does not depend on the unlawfulness of the actions of another, but on his own actions, as principal. Intention is therefore not necessary to establish criminal liability.

Assuming this account is correct, there remains a deeper question: why should consent be a general requirement for liability for another's actions? The reason may again involve the characteristic way we view the actions of persons as opposed to events. Persons are autonomous agents, governed by self-determined choices. We are responsible for ourselves and for what our actions cause in the physical world, and we may cause things to happen unintentionally as well as intentionally. However, what other people choose to do as a consequence of what we have done is their action and not ours. Our actions do not cause what they do in the sense that our actions cause events. We become accountable for the liability created by the actions of others, therefore, only when we join in and identify with those actions by intentionally helping or inducing them to do those actions; in other words, by extending our wills to their action.

I am not suggesting that this is a good and sufficient reason for not holding people responsible for the voluntary acts of others that they may recklessly or negligently occasion (though whether this is more suitably accomplished through a causation analysis remains to be considered). I am only proposing that the strong attraction to consent as the necessary condition of accomplice liability may be explained by the law's adherence to the premise of the autonomy of human action.

The Result

By its nature, the doctrine of complicity, like causation, requires a result. It is not a doctrine of inchoate liability. If the primary party does not act in violation of the law, there is no unlawfulness for which to hold the secondary actor accountable. We saw this earlier in considering the derivative (or dependent) character of complicity. But there is another feature of the result requirement: not only must there have been an unlawful action by the principal; in addition, the action of the secondary party must have succeeded in contributing to it.

In this way complicity functions like causation; it fixes blame upon a person for a result. Causation determines when a person is responsible for a subsequent event; complicity determines when he is responsible for the subsequent unlawful action of another. The doctrine of causation and complicity are to this extent cognate.

This is not to suggest that it would be incongruous to apply the concept of attempt to complicity, thereby converting it into a doctrine of inchoate liability. Indeed, a number of American jurisdictions, following the lead of the Model Penal Code, have made it punishable as an attempt to try (even unsuccessfully) to help or influence another to commit a crime (though only where the other does commit a crime). This modification is equivalent to expanding the liability for a result crime to reach those who attempt to cause the result. The fact that a person may be liable for attempting to cause a result does not mean that he may be found liable for causing the result on a finding that he tried. The same is true of complicity and attempted complicity. Complicity cannot be established if the acts of the secondary actor were unsuccessful in influencing or assisting the principal to commit the crime. To this extent, the secondary party's liability depends on his own success.

Successful Contributions and Sine Qua Non Conditions. If these claims are to hold, however, it is necessary to account for some well-established propositions of complicity doctrine that at first blush seem to undercut the requirement of a successful contribution.

The common notion of success is captured in the ordinary locution of something having mattered, of it having made a difference. In causation, the requirement of a condition sine qua non assures this sense of success, since the requirement means that without the act the result would not have happened as it did. In complicity, however, a sine qua non relationship in this sense need not be established. It is not required that the prosecution prove, as it must in causation cases, that the result would not have occurred without the actions of the secondary party. The commonly accepted formulation is that to establish complicity, any influence or help suffices for liability.

Two familiar cases illustrate these propositions. In *State v. Tally,* Tally's responsibility for a killing committed by two others turned on his attempted aid. Tally had sent a telegram that instructed a telegraph operator not to deliver a telegram previously sent by one of the victim's relatives warning the victim of the killers. The operator did not deliver the warning telegram, and the killers were unaware of Tally's attempt to help them. The court found these facts sufficient to establish Tally's liability as an accomplice, stating:

> The assistance given . . . need not contribute to the criminal result in the sense that but for it the result would not have ensued. It is quite sufficient if it facilitated a result that would have transpired without it. It is quite enough if the aid merely rendered it easier for the principal actor to accomplish the end intended by him and the aider and abettor, though in all human probability the end would have been attained without it. If the aid in the homicide can be shown to have put the deceased at a disadvantage, to have deprived him of a single chance of life, which but for it he would have had, he who

furnishes such aid is guilty, though it cannot be known or shown that the dead man, in the absence thereof, would have availed himself of that chance; as where one counsels murder, he is guilty as an accessory before the fact, though it appears to be probable that murder would have been done without his counsel. . . .

In *Wilcox v. Jeffery,* the publisher of a jazz magazine was found guilty of aiding and abetting an illegal public performance by buying a ticket and attending the concert in order to report on it in his magazine. The court upheld the conviction, stating: "The appellant clearly knew that it was an unlawful act for [the saxophonist] to play. He had gone there to hear him, and his presence and his payment to go there was an encouragement."

The doctrine illustrated in these cases raises a question of what it means for the secondary actor's contribution to have made a difference. For in what sense can the contribution be said to have mattered if it was not a necessary condition of the primary party's decision to commit the crime or of his committing it as he did? Should we conclude, after all, that complicity does not require a successful contribution? I think not, for the following reasons.

In at least one class of cases, the same requirement of a sine qua non that prevails in causation also prevails in complicity. There is no accomplice liability where the attempted contribution demonstrably failed to achieve its purpose because it never reached its target. So, for example, if an individual shouts encouragement to another to attack a third person and the attacker is deaf or otherwise unaware of the encouragement, the putative accomplice could hardly be held liable for the assault as a secondary party. He might be held for the independent crime of incitement or solicitation, which by definition does not require success of the inciter's efforts. But he is not liable for the assault because his contribution could not possibly have been effective. The same conclusion applies to demonstrably futile attempts to aid another. The secondary party may be liable if the principal is aware of the proffered aid, since knowledge of the efforts of another to give help may constitute sufficient encouragement to hold the secondary actor liable. But it is well accepted that the secondary actor may not be held liable where his demonstrably ineffective effort to aid is unknown to the primary actor. For example, suppose a person unlocks the door of a building in order to facilitate a burglar's entrance. Unaware of this, the burglar breaks and enters through a window. The secondary actor could not be held as an accomplice to the burglary; he tried but failed to be of assistance. This conclusion would seem necessarily to follow from cases absolving defendants of accomplice liability when their aid arrived after the principal had been apprehended. In these cases, then, the absence of a sine qua non relation between the acts of the primary and secondary actors precludes liability, just as the absence of that relation between the act and a subsequent event precludes liability in causation.

In order to make sense of the apparently conflicting indications the cases give of the requirement of a successful contribution, we need an interpretation of success that accommodates both sets of cases. An interpretation that would do this is one that takes a successful contribution to be one that *could have* contributed to the criminal action of the principal. By "could have contributed," I mean that without the influence or aid, it is *possible* that the principal would not have acted as he did. In complicity cases, unlike causation cases, the prosecution need not prove a but-for relationship. But that does not mean accomplice liability can be imposed if the secondary party fails to influence or aid the principal. When he could not have been successful in any case, there is no liability. But it is enough if the facts establish a possibility of success.

Nevertheless, we are still left with a puzzle. In causation, proof of a but-for relationship is required; in complicity, the possibility of a but-for relationship suffices. How should we account for this difference?

Perhaps the answer follows from the fact that the concept of a sine qua non condition belongs to the natural world of cause and effect, and has no place in accounting for human actions. Physical causation deals with natural events in the physical world. Experience teaches us that natural events occur in consequence of some antecedent events, whether those antecedent events are the conduct of persons or other natural events. Barring miracles, so long as we know the causal laws we can speak with certainty. This permits of the concept of sufficient conditions, enabling us to conclude that if those conditions are present, a certain result has to occur. It also permits of the concept of necessary conditions, enabling us to conclude that if some conditions are absent, the result cannot occur. In cases of causation, therefore, once the facts are established, we can determine with certainty whether a condition was a sine qua non of a subsequent event. We can say in every instance either that the event would not have happened if that condition were not present, or that it would have occurred even if the condition were absent. Of course, the facts may be in dispute or be unascertainable, and we may have to find them on the level of probability. But the future is latent in the past; if we knew all the facts (and all the relevant laws) we could determine what would happen with certainty. The laws of cause and effect permit no other conclusion.

Cases of influencing another to commit an act are different. We do not view a chain of events that includes volitional human actions as governed solely by the laws of nature. In complicity, the result at issue is another volitional human action, which we perceive as controlled ultimately by that actor's choice, not by natural forces. No matter how well or fully we learn the antecedent facts, we can never say of a voluntary action that it had to be the case that the person would choose to act in a certain way.

In a word, every volitional actor is a wild card; he need never act in a certain way. He responds as he chooses to influences and appeals. It may be in a given case that the principal would not have chosen to act without the influence of the accomplice. But this is never necessarily so, in the sense, for example, that my tilting my chair was a necessary condition of its tipping over. Since an individual could always have chosen to act without the influence, it is always possible that he might have. No laws of nature can settle the issue. Sine qua non in the physical causation sense, therefore, does not exist in any account of human actions. On the view of human action I have been postulating, there are no sufficient conditions for an act of will; nor are there any necessary conditions, save those like knowledge and nonconstraint, without which there can be no free act of will at all.

In dealing with the meaning of a successful contribution, I have thus far dwelled mainly on contributions that take the form of influence. Only a few further points need be made where the contribution takes the form of aid. If the principal is aware of the aid, as he is in most cases of complicity, the possibility of influence (through reliance and encouragement) is always present. Apart from this, in most cases where aid has been successfully given, it can be said that without that aid, the crime would not have been committed as it was; in this sense the secondary party's aid is a but-for condition of the crime. That is the very meaning of successful aid in contrast to attempted aid. So, for example, if I provided the crowbar that the principal uses to gain illegal entry, my assistance was a but-for condition of the entry. To be sure, he might have entered anyway—with his own crowbar or by other means. But he did not. My aid was necessary for what actually happened.

This is not the case, however, if the aid is unknown to the principal and takes the form of influence upon a third person to do (or not to do) an action designed to aid the principal. The *Tally* case is an example. It cannot be demonstrated that the deceased's life would have been spared if Tally had not instructed the telegraph operator to withhold the warning telegram. This is because human actions intervened. Hence, all one could demonstrate is that the aid might have made a difference. These cases of aid, therefore, are subject to the same analysis as all cases of influence.

I have argued that the concept of the sine qua non condition is one that involves results occurring as a matter of necessity, and that it therefore has no application to acts of will. Nonetheless, whether the principal would have committed the crime if the secondary party had not acted as he did is determinable as a historical surmise on the basis of a probabilistic inference from the proven facts. Why should the mere possibility that this was the case be enough, rather than some higher showing? This involves the issue of the required extent of the influence or aid, to which I now turn.

NOTES AND QUESTIONS

1. Both Leo Katz in "Aid and Comfort" and Sanford Kadish in "Complicity, Cause, and Blame" offer explanations of why we have a doctrine of complicity. Notice, however, how their explanations differ. Katz thinks that causation would suffice to impose liability on accomplices, except for the inconvenient problem of redundancy (or "diminishing marginal returns"), which is a common feature of group action. Kadish thinks the fundamental reason for having complicity is that the notion of causation would have to be stretched all out of shape to reach accomplices: it would conflict with our basic ideas about free will and responsibility to think of one person as causing another to act as he did.

2. The *actus reus* requirement for complicity has been an abiding puzzle: how much of a contribution does it take to qualify as an accomplice? It would seem at first that to be an accomplice one must somehow make a difference to the outcome. But as Kadish emphatically states and illustrates with several examples, the law does *not* expect the accomplice to make a sine qua non contribution to the outcome. Indeed, according to Katz's analysis, insisting on a crucial contribution would defeat the very purpose of the complicity doctrine, which he says is to deal with cases in which none

of the participants made a crucial difference to the outcome, yet all seem eminently blameworthy. All the law requires, Kadish points out, is that the participant *could* have made a difference. But what does that mean? Why doesn't it include the person who shouts encouragement at a deaf perpetrator? After all, the shout *could* have made a difference—if the perpetrator hadn't been deaf. For that matter, why doesn't it include the person who shouts encouragement at his TV set as he sees Jack Ruby take aim at Lee Harvey Oswald? If his voice carried far enough, and if Ruby weren't sufficiently resolved to consummate the assassination, this encouragement too *could* have made a difference.

To see what the test is really getting at, consider a firing squad taking aim at their victims. Imagine that an approving spectator is present, who evinces no encouragement. We are inclined to classify the soldiers as accomplices, but not the spectator. Yet all of them were superfluous to the outcome (the death would have occurred even if any one of the soldiers weren't firing), and all approved of the outcome. What then is the difference between them? Presumably, that if we started subtracting soldiers from the squad, a point would come where any given soldier *would* make a crucial difference to the outcome. But the point will never come where the (silent, but approving) spectator will make a crucial difference to the outcome. The question being implicitly posed by the law is really whether the reason the defendant did not make a difference to the outcome was redundancy—the raison d'être for complicity—or complete inefficacy. If the former, the *actus reus* requirement for complicity is satisfied; if the latter, it is not.

3. The liability of an accomplice derives from that of the principal. The accomplice is liable because he *assists* the principal in the commission of a crime. If the principal weren't committing a crime, it would seem the accomplice could not be liable in assisting him with it. Or could he? Puzzling questions have arisen in connection with cases like this one: A encourages P to have intercourse with V. P believes V is consenting; A knows that V is not consenting. P is not guilty off raping V, because he does not realize he lacks V's consent. Yet A very much looks like an accomplice to a rape: after all he assisted in what he knew to be unconsented-to intercourse. The puzzle posed by such cases is taken up in the following excerpt from George Fletcher's book *Rethinking Criminal Law*.

The Theory of Derivative Liability

GEORGE FLETCHER

Let "F" stand for the actor-up-front, executing the deed, and "R" for the actor-in-the-rear, who remains behind the scenes. The range of cases we will consider are those in which F is not liable for a criminal act, and the question is whether there is some basis for holding R liable, either as an accessory in F's wrongful act or as a perpetrator acting through an innocent agent. There are three important variations of the problem. F's conduct might be wrongful but excused, it might be justified, or it might be legal in the sense that it does not violate the definition of any offense.

A. F's Conduct is Wrongful but Excused. If F commits the crime while he is insane, under duress or acting under an excusable mistake, his conduct is still wrongful and the "broad" theory of accessorial liability would support treating R, who aided in the deed, as an accessory. There are a few cases of this type in Anglo-American law, but little evidence of a theory of accessorial liability; the consistent approach is to treat R as a perpetrator-by-means acting through his agent F. A good example is the recent decision in *Regina v. Cogan and Leak,* in which Leak allegedly intimidated his wife to have intercourse with Cogan. Leak remained in the room and observed Cogan lie with his wife, who sobbed during the intercourse but did not otherwise resist. Cogan was convicted of rape, and Leak was an aider-and-abettor. On appeal, Cogan's conviction was squashed on the ground that under the newly announced *Morgan* rule (which we take up later), his belief that the woman had consented was a complete defense. The problem was whether Leak's conviction as an aider-and-abettor would have to fall with Cogan's conviction as a principal.

If the appeal had been heard under German law, the critical issue would have been whether Cogan's act was wrongful despite his mistake. The English Court of Appeal gives the impression that it regarded the act as wrongful, for it stresses that Mrs. Leak had been raped even though Cogan was not accountable for it. The argument on the other side would be that the mistake as to consent negates the required intent and that intent is included as an element of wrongful intercourse. . . .

Rather than rely on a theory of accessorial liability in a wrongful act, the English court reasoned that in fact Leak was the perpetrator, and Cogan merely his "means to procure a criminal purpose." The premise of the court's opinion is that whenever accessorial liability is inapplicable, the theory of perpetration-by-means is available to fill the gap. Even if Leak's contribution was barely sufficient to meet the threshold of accessorial contribution, the acquittal of Cogan would be sufficient to treat Leak as a perpetrator.

A German court might also have concluded that Leak was the perpetrator-by-means, but a necessary condition for this finding would be that Leak was the domi-

From *Rethinking Criminal Law* (Boston: Little, Brown, 1978), pp. 664–71.

nant party in carrying out the sexual penetration of his wife. His standing by and watching the act would presumably not be sufficient. In the German idiom, he would have had to have "hegemony" over the act. Cogan would have to function as the actual instrument of his will. Though the English court says that this was the case, the opinion fails to cite facts to show that Leak dominated Cogan in the carrying out of the rape.

There is some Anglo-American authority for the proposition that the party not actually acting must dominate his "instrument" in order to qualify as a perpetrator-by-means. We reasoned earlier that domination and control are implicit in the concept of a principal, particularly as used in the law of agency. In one leading criminal case, the court commented in dictum that a husband can "rape" his own wife through an intermediary, but only if he forces the "unwilling" instrument "by threats and violence, against his will and consent, to have sexual intercourse with the wife." The Model Penal Code requires that the perpetrator-by-means "cause an innocent or irresponsible person to engage in [the prohibited] conduct." If we take this requirement of "causing" to mean something more than "aiding" (which in the language of the code is what accomplices do), then we have a standard much like the German criterion of "hegemony:"

A demanding requirement of causation as a condition for perpetration-by-means fits our original thesis of derivative accessorial liability. What makes the liability of accessories different from that of perpetrators is precisely the weaker causal link. Accessories contribute to the result, but they are not in the control of the process leading to consummation of the crime. They "aid" in the "commission of the offense" but they neither "commit" the offense nor determine its commission.

In the case against Cogan and Leak, the appellate court might have felt that justice required affirmance of Leak's conviction and therefore his reclassification as a perpetrator-by-means. This seemed to be the only option because the theory of accessorial liability remains undeveloped. More precisely, it is the notion of "committing an offense" that has yet to receive the required clarification. If Mrs. Leak was "raped" by Cogan's penetration, as the court maintains, then, in this sense, Cogan committed the offense. His act was wrongful, but excused. If the "broad" theory of accessorial liability would take hold in Anglo-American theory, one could properly hold a subsidiary party as an accessory. This would have the advantage of reserving the notion of perpetration-by-means to cases in which the party behind the scenes in fact dominates and controls an "innocent or irresponsible agent."

B. F's Conduct Is Justified and Therefore Not Wrongful. The theory of complicity becomes more complicated if F acts in self-defense or under another valid justification. The problem is whether R, who aids F's act, can be held either as an accessory or a perpetrator-by-means. Suppose that X attacks F and F responds in knowing self-defense. R comes upon the scene, and thinking that F has started the fight, R hands F a club, the better to finish off his opponent. R acts with the intent to injure and believes that the act is wrongful. The question is whether R's intent is sufficient to hold him accountable for the consequences of F's justified act of self-defense.

This hypothetical problem is important in understanding the foundation of accessorial liability and indeed criminal accountability in general. One of the few premises that guide our thinking about liability is that criminality presupposes a wrongful act. Accessorial liability is a special case, for it is not the actor's wrongful act that is controlling, but the wrongdoing of the perpetrator. In the case of self-defense posed above, the perpetrator does not act wrongfully and therefore there is no wrong objectively to attribute to the accessory R.

It is tempting to conclude that R cannot be liable under any theory of perpetration or complicity. This is the view urged by the Pennsylvania Supreme Court in *Redline,* a case of alleged third-party felony-murder. In response to an armed robbery, a police officer shot at the two fleeing robbers and killed one of them; the survivor was charged with murdering his confederate. Assuming that the issue was accessorial liability, the court reasoned that

> the homicide was justifiable and, obviously, could not be availed of, on any rational legal theory, to support a charge of murder. How can anyone, no matter how much of an outlaw he may be, have a criminal charge lodged against him for the consequences of the lawful conduct of another person? The mere statement of the question carries with it its own answer.

For the Pennsylvania Supreme Court, it was self-evident that there should be no accessorial liability for a justified act of self-defense. The justified act of killing was like the running of a reasonable and justified risk. As the actor's intention cannot make him accountable for the harm resulting from a reasonable risk, his intention cannot make him accountable for the harm resulting from a justified act of self-defense.

All of this seems reasonable, but the argument failed to impress either the commentators or the courts in other jurisdictions, particularly in California. Consider this counter-example devised by Kadish and Paulsen to show that it is intuitively plausible to hold one person accountable for the justified acts of another:

> Suppose two felons are holed up in a house and engaged in a gun battle with surrounding police. One felon tells the other to run for it out the back door where the coast is clear. He does this because he wants the other felon dead and he knows the police have the back door well-covered. As the other felon dashes out, gun in hand, he is shot by police.

Kadish and Paulsen suggest, quite properly, that under these facts the surviving felon should be held accountable for the justified killing by the police. We might agree, but it is important to probe the persuasiveness of this hypothetical case. The critical factor is that the deceiving felon not only dominates but orchestrates the events leading to the death of his confederate. This is a paradigmatic case of hegemony over the act of an unsuspecting instrument. The surviving felon is held not on a theory of derivative liability, but of perpetration-by-means.

It would be difficult to reason from this hypothetical case to the conclusion of liability under the facts of *Redline,* for there the police officer came upon the scene of the robbery and began shooting. It would be difficult to maintain that the surviving felon had caused and dominated the acts of the police officer in the sense required for liability as a perpetrator-by-means. In a trivial sense, the surviving felon "caused" the death, for if the two of them had not committed the robbery, the officer presumably would not have shot the confederate. But something more than "but for" causation is necessary to establish the required dominance over the acts of a third party.

Rejecting the implicit emphasis in *Redline* on accessorial liability, the California Supreme Court approached the problem of third-party killings of co-felons exclusively on a theory of perpetration-by-means. Thus Justice Traynor stressed in *Washington* that the surviving felon must "commit" the homicide himself. This means that he must do something to induce the third party to shoot. The succeeding cases have struggled with the question whether the suspect must "initiate a gun battle" or merely make threatening gestures with a gun. The detailed analysis in the cases implicitly accepts the assumption that the surviving felon must exercise a requisite degree of control over the third-party shooting to be liable as a perpetrator-by-means.

C. F's Act Is Formally Legal. The doctrine of perpetration-by-means extends not only to justified acts, but to acts that are formally legal in the sense that they do not violate the "definition" of any offense. An illuminating case came to the German courts in the early 1950s on the basis of events that transpired under the National Socialists. The defendant had falsely accused her son-in-law of sabotage in order to have him arrested by the secret police. The son was arrested, confined for more than a week and then acquitted of the charge. The defendant was thereafter prosecuted and convicted of intentional false imprisonment. The Supreme Court affirmed her conviction on the theory that she exploited the secret police and thus committed the offense as a perpetrator-by-means. Even if it is assumed that the police had adequate grounds to detain the suspect, the legality of the detention would not shield the suspect from liability.

As a general matter, the fraudulent use of the legal process to impose harm on another entails liability for intentionally bringing about the particular result. This doctrine found early expression in the English common law under the heading *in fraudem legis*. Taking the goods of another under a fraudulently acquired writ of ejectment generated liability for larceny.

We might be able to accept the doctrine of perpetration-by-means in these cases of fraudulently exploiting the apparatus of the law. But a recent case in the United States requires us to think about imposing limits on the principle that R can be liable for the legal acts of F. Suppose that the act of F consists in the assertion of a constitutional right such as the privilege against self-incrimination. *Cole v. United States* holds that if R induces F to claim the privilege to protect both himself and R, the latter can be guilty of "corruptly influencing a witness" and obstructing "the due administration of justice." Part of the problem with this conviction is the vague definition of the offense. That problem aside, we should have some doubts about liability for inducing the assertion of a constitutional right. In the other cases of exploiting F's legal or justified behavior, R manages to bring about an undeniable harm to a specific victim (death, confinement, loss of property). It is far more tenuous to argue that the consequences of asserting a constitutional right constitute a social harm for which the actor-behind-the-scenes should be held accountable. It would be unthinkable (one would hope) to fit the definition of an offense to a case of inducing a homeowner to refuse to allow the police to search his home without a warrant. It is equally dubious to regard convincing another to assert rights under the Fifth Amendment as a basis for criminal liability.

NOTES AND QUESTIONS

1. Consider again the case of A who persuades B to have intercourse with the unwilling C. Again, suppose A knows that C is unwilling but B does not know. Even if we cannot convict A as an accomplice, because B did not commit a crime, it seems we might well succeed in prosecuting him under the perpetration-by-means approach discussed by Fletcher. But would that approach still work if we changed the facts slightly? Imagine that B, convinced that C wanted to sleep with him, was going to have intercourse with C whether A said anything to him or not. Now A still looks blameworthy, looks very much like an accomplice, but cannot be convicted under a perpetration-by-means approach because he is not a but-for cause of the intercourse and, it seems, cannot be convicted as an accomplice either, because B did not commit a crime.

4.2   ATTEMPT LIABILITY

Just because the assassin misses his target, he must not go scot-free. He is guilty of attempted murder. Anyone who seriously attempts to put into practice a criminal plan is guilty of a criminal attempt. But having decided to punish attempted crimes, one is quickly led to the intriguing question of how one should deal with attempts that are doomed from the very outset, crimes that could never succeed, in other words, crimes that are *impossible* to execute. Suppose a thief reaches into a man's pocket but does not know that the pocket is empty. Suppose a man attempts to poison his wife but mistakenly assumes that a milligram of strychnine will do the trick. Or suppose two men furtively engage in homosexual intercourse but erroneously think they are violating a state law. Finally, suppose a traveler tries to smuggle into the country some French lace that he believes is subject to a high tariff; alas, he never learned that the tariff has been lifted. All of these persons are attempting to commit a crime. All of them are doomed to fail, because what they attempt to do is impossible. Which of them should be acquitted, which of them should be convicted of the crime of attempt? Most peoples' instincts, I suspect, give a fairly clear answer to these cases: convict the pickpocket and the poisoner, acquit the homosexuals and the smuggler.

Can we articulate a principle that makes explicit what our instincts tell us? Judges faced with this question focused intently on examples just like the ones given,

Introduction is an excerpt from Leo Katz, *Bad Acts and Guilty Minds: Conundrums of the Criminal Law* (Chicago: University of Chicago Press, 1987), pp. 15–16.

seeking to divine what attribute cases like the first two shared that cases like the second two lacked. Finally, they thought they had spotted the crucial difference between the two kinds of cases. The first two cases involved situations in which the *facts* simply weren't right for what the defendants intended—the picked pocket happened to be empty and the poisoned human immunological system stronger than expected. The second two cases involved situations in which the *law* wasn't right for what the defendants intended—homosexual intercourse happened to be legal and French lace duty-free. The first two attempts thus were dubbed "factually impossible," the second two "legally impossible." The rule courts adopted ran: legal impossibility exonerates, factual impossibility does not.

The principle seemed satisfactory at first, indeed compelling: you can sensibly charge a frustrated pickpocket with attempted theft, but what do you charge the French-lace smuggler with—attempted import of a duty-free product without paying duty? But then two legal scholars, Sanford Kadish and Monrad Paulsen, proposed this ingenious hypothetical scenario.

> Two friends, Mr. Law and Mr. Fact, go hunting in the morning of October 15 in the fields of the state of Dakota, whose law makes it a misdemeanor to hunt any time other than from October 1 to November 30. Both kill deer on their first day out, October 15. Mr. Fact, however, was under the erroneous belief that the date was September 15; and Mr. Law was under the erroneous belief that the hunting season was confined to the month of November, as it was the previous year.

Mr. Fact has attempted to do the "factually impossible." His attempt to hunt deer out of season failed only because of the purely adventitious fact that the date was October 15 and not September 15. Hence he will be convicted. Mr. Law, however, has attempted the "legally impossible." His attempt failed because of a purely adventitious feature in the game law extending the hunting season that year by an extra month. He will be acquitted. But is there any meaningful distinction between Mr. Law and Mr. Fact? Is a criminal law defensible that punishes one and not the other? The example suggests that the proposed principle is seriously deficient, that whatever it is that separates the first two cases from the next two cases has not been captured by it.

Constructing a Theory of Impossible Attempts
GEORGE FLETCHER

There are fewer than twenty recurrent situations that [have shaped the discussion about liability for so-called impossible attempts.] I have grouped them in the accompanying table by the type of interest that the suspect intends to violate. It is worth stressing that in all of these cases the criminal intent is beyond dispute. . . .

The most readily defended position on these eighteen cases is the imposition of liability across the board. The actor's intent, coupled with his act and execution, suffices to justify his conviction and punishment. Of the eighteen cases, only two might pose difficulties for this radically subjective view. In the black magic (A6) and legal sex (C2) cases, intent might not be sufficient to convince the subjectivist to convict. The reasons for balking in these cases, however, seem to be different. In the black magic case, the problem is that the act is not dangerous. From this seemingly scientific fact, subjectivists infer the dubious conclusion that the actor himself is not dangerous: he is not likely to try other, more conventional means of ridding the world of his enemy. In the legal sex case, the argument does not rest on the requirement of dangerousness, but rather on the illusory nature of the offense that the actor believes he is committing. Yet it is not clear why we should give the defendant the benefit of his intended offense's having been recently legalized. One could say that he is not dangerous either—at least as to the legal interest he thinks he is violating. Or one could say as a procedural matter, that the prosecution is barred: there is no code section to cite in the indictment. The latter point seems tenuous. There is no reason why criminal codes should not include a catchall provision covering any intent to violate the law. Though the principles require further clarification, we may note that the aversion to conviction in these two cases counts as common ground between subjectivists and objectivists.

The challenge for my position is to explain why we should acquit in the remaining nine cases in which many if not all subjectivists would be willing to convict. Perhaps some subjectivists would regard the cases of false perjury (E1) and of the bad Samaritan (E2) as sufficiently close to the case of legal sex to acquit in these cases as well. Yet these are not illusory or imaginary offenses in the narrow sense; there is a code provision to support the prosecution. Acquittal in these cases treads on new territory. The simple intuition that no one can attempt a crime that does not exist will not suffice. The problem is to fathom what this additional impulse to acquit might be.

The first step in developing a principle to cover these additional nine cases of acquittal would seem to be the isolation of criteria that would bring these cases into patterns. Are they all the same type of case or are there diverse criteria that might move one to conclude, for different reasons, against liability? It does not seem that one can look for patterns in the cases unless one has some idea what should be relevant for

From *Criminal Justice Ethics,* Vol. 5 (1986), pp. 57–64.

Table 4. Impossible Attempt Situations

Case	Liability for attempt?
A. Intent to kill	
1. *Missed shot case.* D shoots at an intended victim on the scene but misses.	Yes
2. *Pillow case.* D shoots at the bed where V ordinarily sleeps, believing that V is there, but V is absent.	Yes
3. *Shield case.* D shoots at a present, intended victim, but it turns out that the bullet, though on course, is blocked by an invisible shield.	Yes
4. *Real-poison case.* D puts poison in V's coffee cup in the expectation that V will drink the coffee, but V spills the coffee.	Yes
5. *Sugar-arsenic case.* D puts sugar in V's coffee cup in the mistaken belief that the sugar is arsenic and expects V to drink the coffee. V in fact drinks the coffee.	No
6. *Black magic case.* D sticks pins in a doll and recites an incantation in the false belief that this method will banish V to the nether world. V remains unharmed.	No
B. Intent to steal, defraud or acquire stolen property	
1. *Stolen-goods case.* D buys a video recorder from V at a bargain price and believes, incorrectly, that the recorder is stolen. Attempted receipt of stolen goods?	No
2. *Empty-pocket case.* D sticks his hand into V's pocket with the intent to steal whatever is there. It turns out that the pocket is empty. Attempted theft?	Yes
3. *Umbrella case.* D takes an umbrella in the belief that it belongs to B. It turns out to be his own. Attempted theft?	No
4. *Real Picasso case.* D sells V a painting under the representation that it is a real Picasso but believing all along that the painting is a fake. It turns out that it is a real Picasso and the buyer gets fair value for his money. Attempted fraud?	No
C. Intent to have sexual intercourse	
1. *False Lolita case.* D has sex with a nineteen-year-old girl in the belief that she is sixteen, under the age of consent. Attempted statutory rape?	No
2. *Legal sex case.* D engages in private sexual behavior (prostitution, homosexuality, incest) in a jurisdiction that has recently legalized the behavior. D believes the sex act is still illegal and feels guilty. Attempted??	No
3. *Mistaken consent case.* D has intercourse with V in the belief that V has not consented and that she is resisting the act; in fact, V has consented and is merely playing. Attempted rape?	Maybe
4. *Necrophilia case.* D has sex with V in the belief that V is merely unconscious; in fact, V is dead. Attempted rape?	Yes
D. Intent to deal	
1. *Sale case.* D sells harmless powder to V in the belief, shared by V, that it is heroin. Attempted sale of heroin?	No
2. *Buy case.* D buys powder form V in the belief that it is heroin. Attempted purchase of heroin?	No
E. Miscellaneous criminal intents	
1. False perjury case. D lies to a police officer in the mistaken belief that lying to the police constitutes a crime. Attempted perjury?	No
2. Bad Samaritan case. D refuses to render aid to a stranger V who lies injured on the street. D believes that her is thereby violating a newly enacted duty to render aid. Attempted abandonment of someone in distress?	No

the purposes of legal analysis. One might look at these results and conclude that the key factor is the gravity of the threatened interest. Four of the six intended homicide cases come out in favor of liability, but only one of the four property offenses points in that direction. Since we are looking for a general theory of attempt liability, however, the gravity of the intended offense should not matter. Even if we said that it did, we would still confront the problem of explaining why within each category some cases fall one way; and others; the other way.

The issue at the forefront of legal analysis is whether these actors should be held liable for *attempted* offenses. In thinking about patterns in these cases, therefore, we should have some notion of what an attempt is. The legal materials on the nature of attempts do not get us much past the incontrovertible proposition that an attempt is an attempt. The Model Penal Code tells us that, among other things, an attempt is a "substantial step" in execution of the offense. The 1981 English Act winks at us with the equally "firm" rule that an attempt requires something more than "mere preparation." Believe it or not that is all these statutes have to say on this matter. One can only wonder whether these pronouncements are meant as a satire on the principles of legality and fair-warning.

All we know about attempting, therefore, is that the actor must attempt—must try—to commit homicide, theft, fraud, rape, perjury or some other offense. If he is not trying to commit a punishable offense, he is not guilty. This inference from the blurred statutory language furnishes a lens for focusing more sharply on the patterns implicit in the cases.

In his essay defending the subjectivist theory, H. L. A. Hart concurs in taking the concept of attempt seriously. He advances our understanding of the problem by assaying the question whether the verbs "attempting" and "trying" require extensional objects—namely objects that actually exist as opposed to objects that one merely believes to exist (intensional objects). He mentions "finding" as paradigmatic of extensional verbs. "Looking for," in contrast, does not presuppose the existence of the object that one is looking for. A detective might well look for clues to the crime, even though no one knows whether the clues exist. Of course, he could not find them unless they were there to find. "Attempting," Hart claims, is like "looking for." This is a plausible position. As "looking for" stands to "killing." Success in attempting as well as in looking for something presupposes an object of the successful act.

I have two reservations about Hart's argument. The first is simply a reflection on ordinary usage. I don't think that he is right about "attempting" and "trying." I can look or wait for Godot even though I am not sure whether Godot exists. It would be very odd, however, to say that by using a certain incantation, I am trying to kill Godot even though I am not sure whether he exists. Even if I am convinced that Godot is alive and well in Los Angeles, it would be odd to describe my acting on the belief that I am able to kill him as actually trying to kill him. In the cases of "looking for" and "waiting for" a nonexistent person who I believe exists, my first-person description of what I am doing seems to control descriptions of my act by third persons. This does not seem to be the case with attempting and trying. If we know Godot does not exist, we have a sound basis for saying "No, you are not trying to kill even though you think you are."

Further it is not clear that Hart's argument, even if correct, bears on the problem at hand. In all the cases posed, the victim actually exists. The actor's mistake bears merely on the likelihood that his act will endanger the interest protected by law. That the actor believes that the danger to the interest follows from or is attendant upon his act does not establish that he is actually trying to violate that interest. The specific problem we have in clarifying the concept of attempting is understanding the relationship of the actor's beliefs to the proper description of what he is trying to do.

In all of our cases, the actor proceeds on a false belief. If that belief bears on what he is trying to do, then it is proper, at least in English if not necessarily in law, to say that he is trying to kill, steal, rape, etc. It seems obvious, however, that not all of an actor's beliefs can bear on the description of every act that he undertakes. I am trying to finish this article and I am engaged in this effort with a certain set of beliefs about history, politics and perhaps about the ultimate nature of the universe. These beliefs are obviously irrelevant in this description of what I am doing. Let us consider beliefs that are more likely to be on point, such as those about the time and place of my writing. That I believe it is Tuesday does not warrant including this belief in the description of what I am trying to do. If it is irrelevant to me whether I am writing on Tuesday or some other day, it would be inappropriate to say that I am trying to finish the article on Tuesday. Yet if it mattered to me whether I was writing on Monday or Tuesday—as, for example, if my editor expected a manuscript by Wednesday—it would be appropriate to say that I'm trying to finish the draft on Tuesday. From the point of view of including my beliefs in the description of what I am trying to do, it does not matter whether these beliefs are true or false.

A belief is relevant to what I am trying to do if that which I believe "matters" to me in undertaking the particular course of action. More precisely, the question is whether I would change my course of conduct were my beliefs to change. If I am trying to finish the article by Wednesday and suddenly I learn (or come to believe, falsely) that it is Monday, I would presumably relax my efforts and perhaps take off for a movie. This counterfactual test probes the causal connection between my beliefs and a particular action. If "but for" a particular belief, I would not act in a particular way, then one can say that the belief bears causally on my action.

There is nothing extraordinary about testing the relevance of beliefs by probing their causal relevance. Consider the reciprocal case in which my beliefs have an exculpatory effect. The girl is in fact sixteen, but in undertaking sexual relations with her I believe that she is nineteen. Should this belief excuse my conduct? The relevance of this belief depends on whether I would change my course of conduct if I happened to learn that the girl is under age. If I would not, it is hard to see why my incidental belief should generate an excuse. In conventional legal analysis, the causal relevance of exculpatory mistakes is generally assumed. But if there is a good reason to believe that the mistake is irrelevant to me, the case would probably be classified as reckless or intentional conduct. If, for example, I shoot at a target without perceiving that it is in fact a human being, I would get the exculpatory benefit of this mistake only if it is assumed that had I known of it, I would have acted differently. If I am indifferent to whether the target is a human being or not, my killing would be treated as at least reckless. Continental legal systems would typically classify this case of moral indifference as an instance of *dolus eventualis,* i.e., as intentional killing.

My proposal is simply that the same counterfactual, causal test should guide our thinking about inculpatory as well as exculpatory mistakes. The argument does not trade on the symmetry but on what I take to be the correct analysis of attempting. The object of one's attempting depends on the beliefs that matter to one in acting. Beliefs that have no causal relevance do not matter and therefore should not enter into the description of the attempt.

This analysis of attempting is not to be found either in the case law or indeed in the conventional literature. Yet the conceptual analysis of attempting has implicitly shaped the law of attempts, both here and abroad. Consider the problem of determining the intent required for an attempted offense. Suppose, for example, a prisoner blows up the wall in an effort to escape; he knows that a guard is standing nearby. It is not part of his plan to kill the guard, but if the guard dies in the explosion, it is likely that the prisoner's "indirect intent" to kill would be sufficient to convict him of criminal homicide. If the guard does not die, one might be tempted to treat the case as attempted homicide. But so far as I know, no legal system in the Western world would convict of an attempt simply on the basis of a failed, indirect intent. As the requirement is usually stated, the actor must have the "purpose" or "specific intent" to kill in order to be guilty of an attempt. A requirement of an intent focused on death excludes cases where the actor merely knows that the side effect is highly likely. Significantly, Western criminal codes are typically silent on this point. Courts and theorists infer the special requirement from the concept of attempting. As a matter of ordinary usage, it is simply not right to say that the prisoner is "trying" to kill the guard even if he believes that the guard is likely to die in the explosion.

The test of causal relevance explains why it is incorrect to treat the failed side effect as part of the attempt. The prisoner would change his course of conduct if he thought that the exploding wall would not bring him closer to freedom; that is why it is appropriate to say that he is trying to get out of prison. But he surely would not change his course of conduct if he believed that the guard was likely to survive. That he believes that the guard is likely to die, therefore, is not sufficient to say that he is trying to kill the guard.

· · ·

We are still a long way from reflective equilibrium in matching principles to the data and data to the principles. Nearly half of the "no" cases [in Table 4] remain unaccounted for. I could simply change my mind on these cases, but that move would hardly be faithful to Rawls's methodology, which, I take it, envisions some adjustment in one's intuitions but not a radical change in order to let a general principle prevail. Further, my intuitions remain strong that there should be no liability in the sugar and black magic cases even if these actors are trying to kill their intended victims. The challenge is to figure out what it is about these situations that prompts one to balk at imposing liability.

The obvious fact about the sugar-arsenic and black magic cases is that regardless of the actor's beliefs, there is nothing the slightest bit dangerous about what he is doing. There is no chance that the sugar or the sticking of pins will have their intended effect. If we take a glance at the four cases of liability for intended homicide, we find that all of the acts bespeak danger: firing at the victim (A1, A3), firing at the victim's usual bed (A2), putting poison in the victim's coffee cup (A4). Witnessing these events would make one fearful. Even if one knew that the victim was likely to spill the coffee or that a shield stood in the way, it would be difficult not to be apprehensive about the victim's welfare. . . .

There is no doubt that the standard of danger-on-the-face-of-the-act is vague, but it is not more vague than the effort in contemporary legislation to define attempts as "substantial steps" or as something more than "preparation." The issue is not vagueness but whether the standard of danger tells us something relevant about the analysis of liability for attempts.

NOTES AND QUESTIONS

1. Much of Fletcher's analysis critically depends on a point he makes in the hypothetical about an escaping prisoner blowing up the prison wall knowing that a guard is standing nearby. Assuming that the guard survives, Fletcher points out, the prisoner could not be prosecuted for attempting to kill him: "No legal system in the Western world would convict of an attempt simply on the basis of a failed, indirect intent." Why not?

2. Consider again the case of the person who lies to a police officer but mistakenly thinks that that is a crime. Fletcher would not convict because it isn't important to the liar that what he is doing is illegal. But suppose it were important to him. Would you then be willing to convict him? If someone engages in homosexual intercourse as an act of protest, in the mistaken belief that it is illegal, should he then be found guilty of some kind of criminal attempt?

3. Is the following a fair simplification of Fletcher's point about dangerousness: To be guilty of an attempt, one must have gone beyond preparation, one must have achieved a certain level of proximity to success. In the black magic case or even in the sugar-arsenic case, no such proximity was achieved. Therefore the defendant never got beyond the preparation stage; therefore no liability.

5

Justification and Excuse

5.1 DISTINGUISHING JUSTIFICATION AND EXCUSE

This chapter addresses the affirmative defenses, which are claims by the defendant for exculpation, even if the prosecution is able to prove beyond a reasonable doubt that the defendant's conduct satisfied the definitional elements of the crime charged. An affirmative defense provides a reason why conviction is not justified, a reason that is based on the defendant's motivation for the otherwise criminal conduct. For example, suppose the defendant intentionally and coolly kills another human being. Such behavior satisfies the definition of murder in every jurisdiction. But suppose the reason the defendant killed was to save her own life in the face of a wrongful, deadly attack from the person she killed. If she killed properly to save her own life, she should be acquitted, because self-defense can justify homicide under these circumstances. Or, suppose the defendant killed intentionally and coolly because she suffers from a severe mental disorder and as a result delusionally believed that the victim was plotting to kill the defendant. If this is true, the defendant is not a responsible agent because she is incapable of rationality about the events in question, and she ought to be excused. Notice again that affirmative defenses involve mental states. Rather than being concerned with the specific, inculpatory mental states identified by the mens rea requirement in the definitions of crimes, we are here concerned with the defendant's exculpatory reason for action.

The affirmative defenses may be placed in two categories: justifications and excuses. The justified defendant is a responsible agent who has done the *right* thing under the specific circumstances. Although the behavior is usually criminal, in these cases we think doing what is otherwise wrongful is desirable or, at least, permissible. Self-defense is the classic example. The excused defendant does something wrong under the circumstances, but for some reason is not considered a responsible agent. Legal insanity is the classic example.

The proper nature and scope of the affirmative defenses depends on the theoretical justification for punishment that supports the integrity of the criminal law. Consider justifications first. Can it ever be justified to blame and punish a person who has done the right or permissible thing under the circumstances? Can even a purely consequential theory suggest that justifications should not exist? Suppose research could demonstrate that the availability of justifications paradoxically increased undeniably criminal behavior because potential wrongdoers were emboldened by the possibility of beating the rap by establishing a justification when it was not appropriate? Even if one believes that justice demands the availability of justifications, might not their scope, their doctrinal requirements, vary according to one's theory of punishment? Now consider an excuse—the insanity defense. On purely consequential grounds it might be undesirable because limiting defenses increases the overall deterrent efficacy of the criminal law, even if a specific disordered defendant is undeterrable, and incarcerating violent, disordered people would enhance public safety. In contrast, on retributive grounds, justice might require the creation of an insanity defense because some disordered defendants are not responsible agents and it is unjust to blame and punish nonresponsible people. As you consider the selections that follow, keep in mind the influence of theories of punishment.

The literature on the affirmative defenses is huge and hotly contested. As always, theoretical and political preferences play a strong role in discussions about what defenses ought to exist and how wide their scope ought to be. The selections that follow begin by noting that the distinction between justification and excuse is not as clear as the discussion in this introduction seemed to make it. The rest of the chapter investigates the theoretical justifications for the affirmative defenses in general and for some specific doctrines.

The Perplexing Borders of Justification and Excuse

KENT GREENAWALT

Introduction

Most reasons why otherwise criminal acts, such as A's intentional shooting of B, may be noncriminal fall roughly into the categories of justification and excuse. If A's claim is that what he did was fully warranted—he shot B to stop B from killing other people—A offers a justification; if A acknowledges he acted wrongfully but claims he was not to blame—he was too disturbed mentally to be responsible for his behavior—he offers an excuse.

Anglo-American law and scholarly writings about the law recognize a distinction between these two sorts of claims but generally do not do so in any systematic way. For example, a moderately close examination reveals that particular defenses such as self-defense and duress reach instances of both justification and excuse. . . . Anglo-American criminal law should not attempt to distinguish between justification and excuse in a fully systematic way. I explore three possible bases for drawing the distinction: (1) a distinction between warranted and wrongful conduct; (2) a division between general and individual claims; and (3) a distinction based on the rights of others. I show why none of these bases yields a clear and simple criterion for categorization. The difficulty rests largely on the conceptual fuzziness of the terms "justification" and "excuse" in ordinary usage and on the uneasy quality of many of the moral judgments that underlie decisions that behavior should not be treated as criminal. Beyond these conceptual difficulties, there are features of the criminal process, notably the general verdict rendered by lay jurors in criminal trials, that would impede implementation in individual cases of any system that distinguishes fully between justification and excuse. . . .

Although I emphasize borderline problems, I firmly believe that the basic distinctions between justification and excuse are important in the law. My thesis does not deny any of the following propositions: that the distinction between justification and excuse is a fundamental one for moral judgment; that there is value in the law reflecting fundamental moral categories, including, when it is clear, the distinction between justification and excuse; that scholarly attention to the distinction in analysis and criticism of the criminal law can be fruitful, that in most circumstances when justification and excuse are plainly distinguishable, questions of justification have a kind of natural priority over questions of excuse. . . .

When one focuses on paradigm cases, the difference between justification and excuse is pretty straightforward. . . .

Some of the typical features of justification and excuse may be generalized in the

From *Columbia Law Review,* Vol. 84 (1984), pp. 1897–1911, 1913–1919, 1927.

following way. Justified action is warranted action; similar actions could properly be performed by others; such actions should not be interfered with by those capable of stopping them; and such actions may be assisted by those in a position to render aid. If action is excused, the actor is relieved of blame but others may not properly perform similar actions; interference with such actions is appropriate; and assistance of such actions is wrongful.

Though these respective features of justification and excuse often coalesce, they do not always do so. Their imperfect correlation raises the question of what is—or should be—regarded as the central distinction between justification and excuse in ordinary legal discourse. . . .

Systematic distinctions between justifications and excuses might be recommended to further two objectives: (1) producing authoritative determinations of whether persons escaping liability have presented justifications or only excuses and (2) achieving theoretical clarity in the criminal law. The first, more ambitious, goal cannot be fully realized in any system that relies upon a general verdict by lay jurors for tried cases. . . .

The general verdict is hardly a complete answer to the call for greater rigor in the classification of criminal law defenses, however, for precision can serve other objectives. The educative force of a criminal code may be furthered by a labeling of justifications and excuses that promotes in citizens proper views about how to make difficult choices and how to regard the behavior of others. Clarity in distinctions can enhance understanding of the criminal law and its purposes among those who think about that subject and can help lay the groundwork for intelligent reform. Although the boundaries of grounds of defenses should be determined in light of all relevant considerations, not dictated by abstract legal definitions of justification and excuse, exploration of the nature of justification and excuse still may affect perceptions about what the overall scope of defenses should be. Finally, conceptual clarity and comprehensiveness may be worth striving after for their own sake. . . .

If the law's central distinction between justification and excuse is to follow ordinary usage, it will be drawn in terms of warranted and unwarranted behavior. That, indeed, is the central distinction in existing American law insofar as one can be discerned; and exploration of the desirability of greater precision sensibly begins with it. . . .

The major barriers to precise classification along this line lie in two uncertain borderlines between justified and excused action and in divergences of moral evaluations of why actors should escape criminal conviction. The price of much greater rigor in the law would be to press concepts beyond their natural capacity, to generate avoidable disagreements or submerge controversies with misleading labels, and, likely, to complicate the tasks of jurors.

1. Permissible Acts that Are Less than Ideal. If A performs the morally best possible act in the circumstances, he is morally justified. If he performs an act that is wrongful, he is not justified, though he may have an excuse. Regrettably, these two categories do not necessarily exhaust acts that are subject to moral evaluation.

An act may be thought to be morally permissible even though it is not the best possible among the available alternatives. A person may act in a manner that reflects what most people would do or that in some sense is "within his rights," although a different response would be morally preferable. For example, after Bruce betrays Al's confidence, Al refuses to speak to Bruce. One may acknowledge that Al's anger and hostile response are "natural" and that Al has not wronged Bruce, while at the same time believing that Al would have acted in a morally preferable way if he had forgiven Bruce. How are we to summarize such an evaluation? Blaming Al may not be appropriate; his claim that his response was normal and consonant with Bruce's wrong is not really an excuse. yet we may feel uncomfortable about calling Al's behavior *justified.* What we have, in fact, is a claim in defense of action that may not fit smoothly into either of the two categories.

The perplexity here not only concerns the common problem of classifying situations at the edges of competing categories; it goes much deeper, raising fundamental questions about the exercise of moral evaluation. People who accept some version of perfectionist ethics—for example, that a person should always act to promote the greatest happiness or should always act with loving concerns—will tend to view Al's claim as an excuse. All of us fall short of what we should do and Al's yielding to his natural emotional feeling, though an instance of ordinary human shortcoming, is not a justification for what he has done. On the other hand, people who believe that ethical "oughts" mainly concern duties involving minimal requisites for behavior toward others, will tend to regard Al's claim as justificatory, bringing his actions within the wide range of morally permitted behavior. Innumerable other examples raise similar questions about evaluation, but the most pervasive instances involve the pursuit of one's own interests at the expense of the greater interests of others. . . .

The criminal law does not demand ideal behavior from people. Basic definitions of criminal behavior leave untouched many actions that fall below even modestly rigorous standards of moral acceptability, and privileges to engage in otherwise criminal acts also make concessions to the realities of human nature.

Permissions to use physical force in self-defense are an example. Even when a person knows he can retreat safely and fears no damage to his property, he may use deadly force rather than retreat from his home in the face of an assailant who threatens his life, and in many jurisdictions he can use deadly force rather than retreat from a public place as well. Many people would say that safe retreat is morally more commendable than attempting to take an enraged assailant's life. A legal privilege not to retreat might be supported on the ground that those defending their rights have a basic moral right not to retreat, or that nonretreat deters future aggressions, or that factfinders are incapable of judging when retreat would clearly be safe, or that the law should accommodate the outraged feelings of victims of aggression.

Imagine that a jurisdiction in which the rule of retreat for dwellings is being considered believes that precise classification of justifications and excuses is an important objective of the criminal code. One member of the legislative drafting committee thinks refusal to retreat is positively desirable, deterring aggression and symbolizing the sacredness of dwellings. The second thinks that refusal to retreat is morally less desirable than retreat, when retreat can be carried out safely, but that refusal to retreat is within the range of morally permissible responses. A third member thinks refusal to retreat is decidedly wrong and doubts whether a person aware that retreat would be safe has even a moral excuse for using deadly force instead; yet this member is hesitant to impose his moral conviction and demand behavior many people find unnatural, and he is also skeptical of the capacity of jurors to determine when someone knows he can retreat safely. Each legislator agrees that criminal liability should not be imposed on people who decline to retreat from their homes; the first plainly thinks failure to retreat is justified, the second regards it as justified only in the broad sense of morally permitted, the third thinks that the actor who declines to retreat when he knows he can do so safely has only an excuse, an excuse based on common human weakness and administrative difficulties. If the legislators believed that the law had to label precisely what constituted an excuse and what constituted a justification, they would somehow have to iron out that troublesome issue in respect to retreat. On the other hand, if the law's approach to that distinction does not purport to be rigorous, they would not need to worry too much about whether the privilege received one label or another, or indeed received either label. In this instance, since the general privilege to use deadly force in self-defense is a justification, any provision for retreat could be handled most conveniently within the category. . . .

2. "Mistakes" in Judgment. People often engage in conduct that would be justified if the actual facts were precisely as they believed them to be, but would not be justified if the actual facts had been fully comprehended. How should such acts be characterized?[1] Does that depend on whether the factual mistake involves some fault of the actor? If, as I contend, the act based on a faultless mistake of fact should be regarded as justified by the law, should the law try to distinguish the faultless misperception from one that is faulty but will still relieve the actor from liability?

I begin with a situation in which from the standpoint of all existing human knowledge an action appears to be desirable, but unforeseeable consequences make it turn out to be undesirable.

> Employing the most advanced techniques for predicting wind patterns, Roger decides that a fire in a national forest that threatens human lives can be halted only by carefully burning out a section of the forest that is in the path of the fire. That section is burned on Roger's orders; shortly thereafter the wind shifts in a wholly unexpected way that halts the forest fire before it reaches the burned section.

We may hesitate to classify a situation like this simply as an instance of justification or excuse, and our natural language is rich enough to convey the reasons for our hesitation. We may say, "the risk Roger took was justified," or, somewhat more precisely, "the actor, but not the act, was justified," or more precisely yet, "Roger's choice and action were justified, but what they actually produced turned out fortuitously not to be justified." Such language conveys succinctly our evaluation of what has transpired.

Despite the difference between this situation and paradigm examples of justification, that the law should treat Roger's defense as one of justification seems plain, at least if the law's crucial distinction is to be between warranted and wrongful action. In respect to Roger's behavior, society would expect and hope that a similar actor with

---

[1] . . . Conceptually we can distinguish five major positions on mistakes about justifying circumstances: (1) that the actual circumstances control; (2) that the circumstances believed by the actor control; (3) that circumstances reasonably believed by the actor control; (4) that the act must be justified under *both* the actual and the believed circumstances; (5) that the act may be justified under either the actual or the believed circumstances.

a similar set of available facts would make the same choice. And society's view of the morality of the manner in which he acted, its moral judgment about him, should not be affected by the unfortunate outcome. Roger is not asking to be relieved of responsibility for his choice because of some personal inadequacy like mental disturbance; rather, he has acted as the most competent practitioner in hiss field would have acted. . . .

Some intermediate cases are less simple to classify. Suppose that Roger is dealing with a situation that requires a quick on-the-spot choice. He makes a choice that is the best possible under the circumstances, but one that could correctly have been seen as wrong in advance by experts using sophisticated weather-predicting equipment. Whatever else the law may allow, certainly any choice that is the best that could be expected in the circumstances must be regarded as justified.

A more troublesome question is how much the inherent talents and training of the particular person making the choice should count. Suppose Roger is careful and conscientious, but he makes what turns out to be the wrong choice because he is less skilled or experienced than most other forest rangers with such responsibilities. His actions are the best that could be expected of him but are not the best that could be expected of the average ranger. Given the law's inability to make infinite gradations in skill and experience, it should not label the behavior in a manner that will encourage emulation. This consideration points in favor of calling Roger's factual misperception an excuse. How society should regard him is less clear. In a sense his choice has rested on a personal inadequacy, but one that does not involve the carelessness or diminished responsibility associated with typical excuses. I shall not try to resolve this particular borderline problem, which relates to the more general issue of how far legal elements of justification and excuse should be cast in objective or subjective terms. . . .

However these cases are treated, the crucial point for our purposes is that were the law to attempt precise categorization, some actions grounded in factual mistake should be viewed as justified, others as only excused. The critical question is whether for cases in which the criminal law is to relieve actors of liability in either event, it should try to distinguish justifications from excuses. . . .

. . . If the law really should be precise and label as excuses all negligent beliefs about justifying circumstances, then it should also label as excuses negligent perceptions about likely harm to legally protected interests. The logic of a program for systematic clarification of justification and excuse thus reaches how primary bases of liability are treated as well. Conversely, if it is acceptable not to resolve the reasonableness of a mistaken perception that negates a required intention or recklessness concerning the basic elements of an offense, then the absence of resolution for mistaken perceptions about justifying circumstances is also acceptable. That the present approach to primary bases of liability is so widely perceived as unobjectionable supports the view that the law need not always differentiate between reasonable and unreasonable beliefs about justification. . . .

Overarching Principles of Justification and Excuse in a Criminal Code

Instead of introducing sharp distinctions between justification and excuse in the definition of specific defenses, a jurisdiction might adopt general and abstract definitions of justification and excuse that would cut across specific defenses that themselves did not sharply distinguish the two general grounds of defense. Such abstract definitions might be developed by judges, but it is hard to imagine isolated cases in which judges would need to develop a full-blown theory of justification and excuse. Moreover, incremental development that would also be consistent and systematic does not seem likely, especially in the present climate of relative undevelopment of theories of justification and excuse. Thus, I shall address the possibility of abstract definitions in the context of a criminal code.

Definitions designed to capture common understandings about justification and excuse would be too vague to resolve troublesome borderline cases. On the other hand, definitions precise enough to work clean distinctions between justified and excused actions would have to employ a sense of the terms that was partly creative. Since such definitions would provide no important guidance to juries resolving cases, the aim of such definitions would be to serve clarifying and educative functions.

Their possible value would depend on what exactly was "clarified" and what the basis of the clarification was. We have difficulty articulating our moral evaluation when action is based on a perfectly reasonable factual misperception, but sifting out the actual elements of the evaluation is rather simple. A legal categorization of such actions as justified or excused would not alter the evaluation or increase our understanding of it. The character of other behavior, such as a failure to retreat safely, is subject to genuine dispute. For such behavior, a sharp classification by the law might achieve a resolution affecting to some degree how people would regard the behavior in the future, but the resolving definitions could not remain faithful to the complexity and diversity of a society's moral views.

There is a further problem with any legal "clarification." By selecting more crucial factors for examination, the law is bound to exclude others that will appear of moral relevance in some circumstances. Any definition of legal justification that is more specific than an open-ended reference to morally relevant factors is virtually certain to treat as justified some instances in which special factors would make the act only excused, at best, from a moral point of view (e.g., refusing to retreat when the aggressor is an angered spouse). The law's current lack of clarity itself may help foster the healthy notion that legal categorization does not determine moral appraisal.

If one conceives the criminal law as a proper and important medium for transmitting correct moral views to a confused public, despite certain inevitable variations between the optimal moral and optimal legal judgments, then departing from conventional understanding and existing moral consensus in defining justification and excuse will not be worrisome. One's opinions on how far the law should depart from conventional morality are likely to reflect a bundle of complex views about the role of law and the nature of moral understanding. . . .

What does it mean to say that excuses are individual and justifications general? Roughly, the idea is that an excuse does not reach others who perform similar acts, but a valid justification would apply to anyone else in similar conditions. Exactly what this contrast amounts to is somewhat cloudy. In the broad sense of "universalizability" common to discussions of moral philosophy, excuses as well as justifications are general: all persons with similar mental disturbances committing similar acts would have a similar excuse based on mental illness. The point must be that excuses, but not justifications, are based on personal characteristics or subjective attributes. But, however, the distinction is understood, its fit with the distinction between justification and excuse is less than perfect.

Some justifications depend upon the social role of the actor or his relation to a person affected by the act. Police and parents, for example, have special authorizations to use physical force when others may not. Traditionally, relatives of potential victims had greater rights than strangers to intervene against aggressors, though the movement now is to eliminate this distinction. If "the situation" is defined broadly enough, it may include roles and relational characteristics; so perhaps their relevance to justification is not at odds with the idea that justifications are general and objective.

One subjective characteristic of the actor is crucial, however, for justification in both ordinary usage and in the law: his belief in the presence of justifying circumstances. . . .

Some excuses include features that are not individual and subjective. A person may be blamed morally for giving way to threats if the vast majority of people would have had the strength to resist. In most jurisdictions the duress defense has an objective component, formulated in the Model Penal Code as whether a "person of reasonable firmness" would have yielded. Since one kind of situation in which this objective component matters is when a person is so overwhelmed that he makes a choice that would be indefensible for a cool and rational actor, the objective element obviously applies to duress as an excuse as well as to duress as a justification.

Although some excuses may now have an objective component, perhaps they are misconceived, because excuses *should* be exclusively individual and subjective. Such an argument might be mounted, but if it rested on wooden application of abstract bases of categorization, it would lack persuasiveness; and closer scrutiny reveals that whether duress should have an objective component is not intuitively obvious.

Whether a wholly subjective test for blame is practically comprehensible when a person has yielded to fear and committed an undesirable act is subject to some doubt. . . .

Even if one opts to resolve these troubling questions by sticking to a wholly subjective standard for moral blame, the law's use of objective elements in excuses cannot be declared wrong in principle. The law must concern itself with judgments that strangers (members of a jury) are capable of making. Absent strong evidence that a particular actor is highly idiosyncratic, a jury must be largely guided by intuitive judgments about the resistability of threats, inferring a great deal about the actor's reactions from the normal reactions of most people. . . .

The discussion in this section has shown that although the distinction between justification and excuse may correlate substantially with the distinction between bases for relief from liability that are general and objective and bases that are individual and subjective, the latter distinction is not, and cannot reasonably be made, the central method for dividing justifications from excuses. . . .

A final possibility is that the crucial line between justification and excuse concerns the rights of others. The idea is that a justified act may be supported but not stopped, whereas an excused act may be stopped, by its victim or an intervenor, but not supported.

What may be said on behalf of this line? First, as I have suggested earlier, if one began with some very rough categorization between justifications and excuses, the claimed consequences in terms of the rights of others would correlate pretty well with the respective designations. Second, this distinction is sharper and practically more significant than the distinction between warranted and unwarranted action. It is practically more significant because actual legal consequences would turn on the characterization of the defense as a justification or excuse; these legal consequences would not directly concern the law's treatment of the actor who offers the defense, but they would make a difference for the actual or possible actions of others. The distinction is sharp-edged because it admits of no gray area of uncertainty of the sort that would exist between warranted and wrongful action; either others have a right to prevent an act or they do not. Third, the distinction appears to fit well with the idea that real justifications depend on accurate assessment of the facts; persons who know that their rights are being impaired because of the mistaken perceptions of others are generally allowed to defend those rights.

Despite these reasons in favor of a distinction drawn in terms of the rights of others, an effort to reform the law in this direction would be misguided, both because the distinction deviates from what is most fundamental about judgments of justification and excuse, and because it unravels. Rights of defense, intervention and support do not always correlate with each other or with the actual facts in the manner supposed. How the law should handle the intervention of others is too complicated a matter to be determined by initial characterization of a defense as a justification or excuse, and were that labeling to await careful judgment about intervention, legislatures or courts would be pushed to resolve immensely troublesome hypothetical issues that might never arise.

I have suggested that the central distinction between justification and excuse involves the difference between warranted actions and unwarranted actions for which the actor is not to blame, and concerns the moral appraisals these sorts of actions call forth. The rights of others is an inadequate substitute for this distinction. . . .

Neither the rights of others nor any difference between general and individual claims provides an adequate basis for distinguishing between justifications and excuses. Rather, the central distinction between justification and excuse is between warranted action and unwarranted action for which the actor is not to blame. Although the law's failure to be as precise as it might in reflecting this distinction is partially due to correctible inattention or indifference, much of the imprecision is a consequence of the troubling borderlines of the two concepts, of legal rules that compromise disagreements about substantive morality, and of canons of convenience that support placing similar factual situations under the same rubric in order to focus the jury's efforts on the questions crucial to liability and nonliability.

Achieving greater clarity between justification and excuse is a laudatory goal, deserving the serious attention of scholars. I want to reemphasize this point, because my lengthy discussion of borderline problems may tend to obscure both my conviction that the basic distinction between justification and excuse is very important for moral and legal thought, and my hope that this essay will contribute to understanding some of the complexities of that distinction. A fully comprehensive system *could* divide up all instances of justification and excuse, but it could do so only by distorting of ordinary concepts or by employing some complicated subcategories reeelecting significant policy judgments. A program to achieve that objective is not an appropriate one for Anglo-American penal law.

NOTES AND QUESTIONS

1. Greenawalt's article neatly shows that the boundaries between justification and excuse are indeed perplexing. The distinction has given rise to an enormous, important literature in the last few decades. The distinction is central to understanding the limits of criminalization and responsibility. Can a unitary theory of punishment rationalize all the difficulties and provide a coherent, satisfying answer?

Consider the following standard hypothetical case. An agent commits an act that the agent honestly and reasonably believes is entirely unjustified, but in fact, unbeknownst to the agent, the act is "objectively" right, creates positive social value. Should the agent be justified, excused, or neither? If the objective rightness of the result is the touchstone, the agent is justified, but does this seem right? Subjectively the agent fully believed the act was wrong and clearly was willing to do it knowing this. It is just a matter of luck that it turned out to produce positive value. Indeed, a particularly malevolent agent may be disappointed that this occurred. Is it simply the principle of legality that suggests that the agent is justified, or is a deeper principle at work? Doesn't the agent deserve conviction and punishment? Should the agent at least be convicted of attempting to commit the crime? Don't deterrent and incapacitation rationales both suggest that the agent should be convicted and punished?

Now consider the agent who honestly and reasonably believes that the conduct is justified, but who has made a mistake. Subjectively, the agent is blameless, but objectively negative social value resulted because in fact the victim need not have been harmed to produce positive value. Once again, what legal response is appropriate? Is this the sort of conduct we want to proclaim was right under the circumstances? After all, the agent behaved in an ethically appropriate way in making a reasonable judgment. In future cases, don't we want people faced with the balance of evils to make reasonable judgments? Do we want to deter people from harmdoing when the honest and reasonable judgment is that the balance of evils will thereby be positive? Is this a person who needs further restraint? Did the agent do something "wrong" that demands an excuse? Which meaning of "wrong"—objective or subjective—is appropriate here? How does one decide?

Note that much turns on a preference for subjective or objective modes of analyzing these cases, but what theory suggests that either mode is self-evidently true?

2. For many years, little was made of the justification/excuse distinction and some still argue that it makes little difference because the outcome—acquittal and

freedom—is the same, whichever theory of affirmative defense is employed (with the exception of a successful insanity defense, which leads to involuntary hospitalization in all jurisdictions). But is the distinction so simply disposed of on pragmatic grounds? After all, the law is a teacher and source of social standards. Doesn't it matter whether the law deems behavior right or wrong? Won't it matter to defendants? Don't we care whether we have done the right thing? Moreover, there can be other consequences, such as whether one can *rightly* defend oneself against justified and excused agents. Surely it is not right to harm a justified agent to protect oneself, but the hapless harmdoer may have an excuse. On the other hand, isn't there a right to harm a wrongdoer who may be excusable, say a disordered person threatening death, in order to save oneself? Can you think of any other theoretical or practical differences that the distinction may produce?

5.2 JUSTIFICATION: DEFENSIVE FORCE

Putative Self-Defense and Rules of Imputation in Defense of the Battered Woman

B. SHARON BYRD

Mistakes as to Justifying Circumstances and their Effect on Imputation

In an article entitled "A Theory of Justification: Societal Harm as a Prerequisite for Criminal Liability,"[1] Paul Robinson made a considerable breakthrough in my opinion in the analysis of mistakes as to justifying circumstances. The main purpose of the article was to locate justification defenses in the failure of an actor to cause objective societal harm. One of the main cases Robinson discusses is the burning of a field to create a fire wall and prevent a city from being destroyed by a raging forest fire. Generally, this type of conduct would be justified under a lesser evils defense since the harm caused to the field is significantly less than the harm avoided to the city. Accordingly, Robinson argues, the real basis of the justification is the prevention or minimization of societal harm.

But what if the person burning the field was not aware that the city was in danger from a forest fire. Instead, he only wanted to harm his neighbor by destroying the field. Should this make any difference? If the basis of the justification defense is indeed the prevention or minimization of objective societal harm, then even the unknowingly justified actor has fulfilled this prerequisite. His motive, Robinson claims, should make no difference because we in society in fact want to encourage people to

From *Jahrbuch für Recht und Ethik,* Vol. 2 (1994), pp. 291–304.
    [1] 23 UCLA Law Review 266 (1975).

burn the field in such situations. In parting, Robinson suggests "It is conceded here, however, that a beneficial act done with knowledge of the justifying circumstances or for bad motive arguably gives rise to an intangible harm similar to that associated with impossible attempts.[2]

The suggestion that lack of knowledge of justifying circumstances should be treated like an attempt[3] seems to me to make a lot of sense, particularly from the point of view of structural analysis within the criminal law.[4] His article faced a fair amount of criticism, however, from George Fletcher,[5] who chose for good reason to focus more on the self-defense cases. Fletcher posits the following hypothetical: "A physician P is about to inject air into the suspect X's veins with the intent to kill him. Ignorant of P's intentions, X decides to use this opportunity to assault him. As the needle is poised, X grabs the physician and begins to choke him." Since X does not have a justificatory intent, Fletcher does not want to give him the benefit of the justification defense. To do so, Fletcher claims, would be collapsing elements of the offense definition with claims of justification for violating the prohibitory norm. Killing an attacker in self-defense would be just like doing something that is not criminally prohibited at all.

Fletcher's criticism, however, overlooks the real elegance of Robinson's analysis. Although Fletcher is correct in saying that treating mistakes as to justificatory circumstances like mistakes as to the definition of the offense essentially means collapsing the criminal law norm with the exceptions to that norm, that does not mean that the unknowingly justified actor will be treated like someone who has done nothing wrong. The real insight in Robinson's analysis is the imposition of attempt liability in these cases. As a result, the unknowingly justified actor will be treated just like the actor who thinks an unloaded gun is loaded and shoots it at his victim. In both cases, the actor has in fact caused no objective societal harm but instead has done something which, if the circumstances were as he supposed them to be, would have resulted in criminally prohibited harm.

Fletcher, of course, focuses on self-defense cases rather than on lesser evils cases. Providing a person who does not even know he is being attacked with any benefit from the self-defense justification is clearly problematic. Both physician P and suspect X in Fletcher's example, seem to be equally offensive persons. That makes it more difficult to say that no societal harm has occurred when X assaults P. It makes killing P like killing a fly, Fletcher claims. Accordingly, Fletcher would convict X of the fully consummated offense. But I think the basic problem here is that Fletcher is

---

[2] Id. at 291.

[3] Presumably Robinson uses the phrase "impossible" attempts to distinguish them from what in the common law sometimes is referred to as "unfinished steps" attempts, the former involving a situation where the actor has done everything he thinks necessary to consummate some criminally prohibited harm but the harm does not occur, the latter involving a situation where the actor is interrupted, by the police for example, before he has finished doing everything he intended to do to bring about the harm. I will use simply "attempt" here to mean the former type of situation.

[4] For a detailed discussion of Robinson's theory and the implications it has for mistakes regarding justifying circumstances, see *B. Sharon Byrd*, "Wrongdoing and Attribution: Implications beyond the Justification-Excuse Distinction", 33 Wayne Law Review 1289, 1314–1332 (1987).

[5] See *George P. Fletcher*, Rethinking (op. cit. fn. 9) p. 555 et seq. See also *George P. Fletcher*, "The Right Deed for the Wrong Reason: A Reply to Mr. Robinson", 23 UCLA Law Review 293 (1975).

not really regarding self-defense as a pure justification within his own definition of justifactory defenses. Fletcher rejects any balancing of evils approach toward self-defense. It is not the case that we simply discount the life of the aggressor to come out in favor of the self-defender.[6] Instead, self-defense is an absolute right to protect oneself against wrongful aggression. If that is so, then X would indeed have a right to protect himself and kill P if necessary. And in Fletcher's example, if X had done nothing to prevent P's attack, X would have died and P would have been subject to prosecution for murder. If, on the other hand, X had known of the attack, then, according to Fletcher, he would not have been acting wrongfully in killing P. Where, from the point of view of the omniscient third party observer, X does have a right to kill P, P does not have that same right to kill X.

Fletcher's real problem, it seems to me, is that he is collapsing justifications with excuses. Let us [consider the] case of Franny threatening to kill George if George does not kill Herbert. This case [includes] a possible duress excuse. Because we understand George's fear of death, we might excuse him in this situation if he does kill Herbert. But suppose that George does not know he is being threatened by Franny and he simply kills Herbert to get rid of him. I do not think there is any question here that lack of knowledge of the excusing circumstances bars the excuse entirely. That is because the whole basis of the excuse is the psychological pressure on George. If there is no psychological pressure, there is no reason to excuse. Yet it is Fletcher himself who claims that justifications do not depend on the presence of psychological pressure. Instead, the reason for the justification is that the conduct is *not wrongful*. If it is not wrongful, then it is permissible to engage in it, just like it is permissible, at least with respect to the prohibition against murder, to shoot empty guns at people and not kill them.

The correct comparison is not between the unknowingly justified actor and the unknowingly excused actor, but instead between the unknowingly justified actor and the actor who thinks the gun is loaded when it is not. In both cases, the objective circumstances indicate that the conduct is not wrongful. It is not wrongful to shoot empty guns and it is not wrongful to ward off attackers. The only thing that makes the actor seem worthy of criminal sanction is the thoughts he has at the moment of the act. The former thinks he is shooting a loaded gun at his victim and the latter that he is attacking someone for no good reason. Admittedly, Fletcher is correct when he states: "The consensus of Western legal systems is that actors may avail themselves of justifications only if they act with a justificatory intent."[7] But he is wrong if he means that not having the justificatory intent requires treating the unknowingly justified actor the same as the unknowingly excused actor. In Germany, the leading opinion in the scholarly literature is that the unknowingly justified actor is to be punished for attempt.[8]

---

[6] See *George P. Fletcher,* "Proportionality and the Psychotic Aggressor: A Vignette in Comparative Criminal Theory," 8 Israel Law Review 367 (1973); *George P. Fletcher,* "The Psychotic Aggressor—A Generation Later", 27 Israel Law Review 227 (1993).

[7] *George P. Fletcher,* Rethinking (op. cit. fn. 9) p. 557.

[8] *Karl Lackner,* Strafgesetzbuch mit Erläuterungen (20th ed. 1993) Munich: C. H. Beck, § 22, note 16; *Adolf Schönke/Horst Schröder,* Strafgesetzbuch Kommentar (24th ed. 1991) München: C. H. Beck, § 32 ff., preliminary note 15 (*Theodor Lenckner*) and the authorities cited therein.

It is all the more surprising that Robinson fails to see the relevance of his analysis to the case of putative self-defense. In the case in which an individual believes incorrectly that he is being attacked, Robinson opts for an excuse.[9] Both Fletcher and Robinson lament the Model Penal Code and other typical common law definitions of justifactory defenses that justify an individual who believes, or reasonably believes, in the need to use justified force. The problem here, both of them assert, is that the mistaken actor will be justified as long as his mistake was reasonable. Since the putative attacker, however, is not acting wrongfully, he too would be justified in warding off the putative defender. As a result, two people would be justified in doing contradictory things. And since the putative self-defender is wrong, he is objectively causing societal harm in carrying out his defense.

I would agree with Fletcher and Robinson that the objective circumstances are of primary relevance in determining whether an actor is justified. Therefore, I would also agree that belief language is inappropriate in a self-defense provision. Still I do not agree that the appropriate defense is an excuse. Instead, I think one again must analyze the problem on the level of the offense definition, just like Robinson analyzes the problem with the unknowingly justified actor.

Consider the following two cases. Jeremy thinks he is shooting at a tree stump. Instead it is Katie, who is hit by the bullet and dies. Laura thinks she is being attacked by Maurice. Instead Maurice has a water pistol and is merely trying to be cute. Laura shoots in putative self-defense and kills Maurice. These two cases share a number of things in common. Of primary relevance is that if the situation were as assumed, then no wrong would in fact occur. Jeremy would have hit a tree stump and Laura would have saved her own life from unlawful aggression. Furthermore, the natural question to ask in both of these cases is whether Jeremy and Laura were negligent in making the mistake. Could they have avoided it had they exercised more care? If not, then one cannot impute the commission of a wrongful killing to them. . . .

Quite different is the parallel case on the excuse level. Returning to George and Franny, suppose George only thinks Franny is threatening to kill him if he does not kill Herbert. Here it is *not* the case that no wrong would occur if George were not mistaken. Herbert will be the innocent victim regardless of whether Franny is in fact threatening George or George only thinks he is being threatened by Franny. Although here too the question of George's fault for making the mistake would be relevant, it would be relevant on a different level. We would not only ask whether he was at fault in making the mistake but also whether the mistakenly assumed threat was sufficient enough to excuse his wrongful killing of Herbert. Furthermore if George is at fault for getting into the situation of duress, we tend to lose all sympathy for him.

In Germany, an actor loses the excuse of duress entirely if he was at fault in getting into the situation.[10] The Model Penal Code, on the other hand, denies the duress defense entirely when the actor was at least reckless in bringing about the situation. If, however, the actor was negligent, then he is to be punished for the negligent offense.[11] Again, this treatment shows the inability of the common law to adequately

---

[9] *Paul H. Robinson,* (op. cit. fn. 9) vol. 2, § 184 (a), p. 398.

[10] German Criminal Code § 35 (1).

[11] Model Penal Code (op. cit. fn. 8). § 2.09 (2).

distinguish between the imputation of conduct to an actor as his deed and the imputation of blame to an actor for his wrongful conduct. If George were negligent in getting into a situation where Franny could threaten to kill him if he did not kill Herbert, he would still be killing Herbert intentionally and not negligently. And if he were negligent, he could have avoided the situation by exercising more care. Why should we want to diminish his culpability for intentionally killing Herbert?

If one is serious about distinguishing conduct rules from decision rules, then one has to accept that justifications, as exceptions to norms, are part of the body of conduct rules. If so, then mistakes as to justifying circumstances have to be dealt with like mistakes as to circumstances relevant under prohibitory norms and not like mistakes as to excusing conditions. Accordingly, the unknowingly justified actor who has objectively caused no prohibited harm should be punished as Robinson suggests for an attempt. The real basis for his liability is his evil design. Furthermore, the person who assumes that justifying circumstances exist (Laura with respect to Maurice) should be treated like the actor who assumes that he is doing something that in fact is not wrongful (Jeremy with respect to Katie). If the mistake was unreasonable then it makes sense to impute negligent commission to him.

The Appropriate Standard of Reasonableness

One of the most common standards used in the common law for judging almost every form of conduct is that of "reasonableness."[12] The use of this standard essentially turns the issue of liability over to the jury, presumably a group of twelve reasonable people, who are to decide whether they would have acted differently in the particular situation in which the defendant found himself. If so, they impose liability on the defendant, if not, they do not.

A major problem with this approach is deciding how to define the defendant's situation. Defining the defendant's situation is essentially deciding (1) what evidence may be presented to the jury and (2) how the jury will be instructed on the relevance of this evidence to the issue of "reasonable" behavior. The different treatment in the United States given the battered woman who kills her sleeping husband illustrates quite well how these two decisions directly bear on the issue of her guilt via the reasonableness standard.

Generally, the right to exercise deadly-force self-defense in the United States depends on a reasonable belief that the force is immediately necessary to ward off a danger of death or serious bodily harm.[13] A problem is raised in the battered women cases

---

[12] For a discussion of the reasonableness standard in the battered women self-defense cases see *Holly Maguigan* (op. cit. fn. 7); *Elizabeth Schneider,* "Particularity and Generality: Challenges of Feminist Theory and Practice in Work on Woman-Abuse" 67 New York University Law Review 520 (1992).

[13] The Model Penal code (op. cit. fn. 8), § 3.04 defines self-defense in relevant part as follows: "(1) . . . the use of force upon or toward another person is justifiable when the actor believes that such force is immediately necessary for the purpose of protecting himself against the use of unlawful force by such other person on the present occasion . . . (2) (b) The use of deadly force is not justifiable under this Section unless the actor believes that such force is necessary to protect himself against death, serious bodily harm, kidnapping or sexual intercourse compelled by force or threat; nor is it justifiable if: . . . (ii) the actor knows

when the batterer is sleeping at the time he is killed in alleged self-defense. Although I think there are cases where one can indeed argue as an *objective* matter that exercising deadly-force self-defense was immediately necessary, or at least necessary before the batterer re-awakens, I would like here to focus merely on the battered woman's *subjective* assumption that the force was immediately necessary. I am thinking of a case in which a woman has suffered serious physical harm accompanied by threats of death over an extended period of time. She may have tried to escape in the past with the result that her husband has found her and beaten her even more brutally. There may be a number of reasons why she is afraid of leaving again—fear that her children will be in danger if left alone with the batterer, fear of being found again and killed, lack of financial means of effective escape, etc. She has just gone through an extended period of brutality and her husband has gone to sleep. Fearing what will confront her when he awakens, and seeing no way out of the situation, she kills him in his sleep.

The question for the jury in this case is whether she reasonably believed that the deadly force was immediately necessary. In defining her situation for the jury, some states will (1) exclude evidence of the effects of the battering relationship:[14] (2) include evidence of the effects of the battering relationship but instruct the jury to apply an "objective" standard of reasonableness:[15] (3) include evidence of the effects of the battering relationship and instruct the jury to apply a "subjective" standard of reasonableness.[16]

---

that he can avoid the necessity of using such force with complete safety by retreating . . . except that: (1) the actor is not obliged to retreat from his dwelling or place of work, unless he was the initial aggressor . . ." The Model Penal Code does not directly impose the "reasonableness" standard on the defendant's belief in the need for force. In § 3.09, however, it is provided that "(2) When the actor believes that the use of force upon or toward the person of another is necessary for any of the purposes for which such belief would establish a justification . . . but the actor is reckless or negligent in having such belief . . . the justification afforded . . . is unavailable in a prosecution for an offense for which recklessness or negligence . . . suffices to establish culpability." This solution, at least with regard to the false assumption of justifying circumstances, seems to me to be correct. The problem with the Model Penal Code is that the belief language is included at all in the definition of self-defense, with the result that the unknowingly justified actor will be liable for the intentionally consummated offense. This solution, as I have indicated above in section III, seems to be incorrect. Many jurisdictions in the United States do not follow the Model Penal Code and instead insert the reasonableness standard in the definition of self-defense. Here the result is not only that the unknowingly justified actor will be liable for the intentionally consummated offense, but also that the actor who "unreasonably" assumes that deadly force is immediately necessary will also be liable for the intentionally consummated offense.

[14] See *State v. Thomas,* 423 North Eastern Reporter 2d 137 (Ohio 1981) excluding expert testimony on the battered woman syndrome (overruled in *State v. Koss,* 551 North Eastern Reporter 2d 970 (Ohio 1990).

[15] *State v. Norman,* 378 South Eastern Reporter 2d 8, 15 (N. C. 1989).

[16] *State v. Koss,* 551 North Eastern Reporter 2d 970, 973 (Ohio 1990); *State v. Leidholm,* 334 North Western Reporter 2d 811 (N. D. 1983); *State v. Stewart,* 763 Pacific Reporter 2d 572, 579 (Kan. 1988) claiming to use a two-pronged subjective and objective standard of reasonableness but confusing the honest belief requirement with the subjective standard and applying the "reasonably prudent battered wife" standard as an objective test (rejecting *State v. Hodges,* 716 Pacific Reporter 2d 563 (Kan. 1986) to the extent that a purely subjective standard was sanctioned); *State v. Gallegos,* 719 Pacific Reporter 2d 1268 (N. M. App. 1986) claiming to apply a hybrid standard of subjective and objective reasonableness but also confusing the honest belief requirement with a subjective standard and applying a so-called "objective" test under consideration of circumstances peculiar to the battered woman.

My position is that solution (3) applying the subjective standard is appropriate for criminal law determinations. Furthermore, I think confusion as to the exact role of the reasonableness standard leads to the use in the United States of a more or less objective standard of reasonableness.[17] This confusion arises, firstly, from equating the reasonableness requirement with an objective *standard of behavior,*[18] as would be appropriate in the tort rather than the criminal law context. The confusion, I think, rests secondly on the assumption that a subjective standard of reasonableness collapses the requirement that the defendant believe in the justifying circumstances with the standard for judging those beliefs.[19] Finally, the U.S. Supreme Court's decision in *Foucha v. Louisiana,*[20] and other similar state court decisions pose a newer problem with regard to applying the subjective standard of reasonableness. In *Foucha,* the Court held that a criminal law defendant acquitted on an insanity defense could not be civilly committed after regaining his sanity even though he remained generally dangerous for society. The argument then is that applying a subjective standard of reasonableness will lead to the acquittal and thus release of dangerous offenders. I shall discuss each of these problems individually.

Equating Reasonableness Requirement with Objective Standard of Behavior

The first problem of equating the reasonableness standard with a standard of behavior results from failing to distinguish making mistakes from taking risks. I think this distinction is generally understood but tends to get lost in discussions of reasonable or unreasonable mistakes in the criminal law context. In tort law, the reasonableness standard is used indeed to define a minimum of acceptable conduct regarding an individual's adversity or inadversity to risk taking. When economists discuss the issue, they speak in terms of the cost of taking precautions in comparison to the probability of causing a certain amount of harm. This approach indicates that the defendant is considered capable of taking more or less precaution to avoid this harm. In turn, this means that although the defendant may not have intended to cause the harm in the particular case, still he was aware of the alternatives for avoiding potential harm and could have taken them.

The precaution cost analysis, however, is inapplicable to the battered woman problem for two reasons. Firstly, within the framework of her own beliefs, the bat-

---

[17] See Holly Maguigan, "Battered Women and Self-Defense: Myths and Misconceptions in Current Reform Proposals," 140 University of Pennsylvania Law Review 379 (1991), pp. 409–413, 442–448 arguing that in fact most jurisdictions use a mixed standard but label it "objective." See also table at 464–478 with complete rundown on the use of the objective or subjective standard of reasonableness and on the admissibility of expert testimony on the battered woman syndrome.

[18] See, for example, George P. Fletcher. *A Crime of Self-Defense: Bernard Goetz and the Law on Trial* (New York: Free Press, 1985), p. 41, discussing whether the objective or subjective standard of reasonableness is appropriate: "One would think that there would be little dispute about jurors' applying an objective *standard of acceptable behavior.*" (emphasis added)

[19] Id., p. 41: ". . . it is hard to make a case for a subjective standard that enthrones the private judgments of every person. A sensible legislature or judge would not choose a rule that allowed people to escape liability for homicide or attempted homicide simply because *they believed in good faith* that they were about to be robbed." (emphasis added)

[20] 112 S. Ct. 1780 (1992).

tered woman acts "intentionally" to kill her husband. At the time she pulls the trigger, she is not engaged in a debate as to what precautions she should take to avoid the criminally prohibited harm. Secondly, the precaution cost analysis assumes that one can calculate probabilities of causing harm with some degree of exactitude. Whereas a dam owner may know the highest water level attained over the past one hundred years and will know how high a dam has to be built to avoid flooding with a particular degree of certainty,[21] no one will ever know whether the batterer would have caused death or serious bodily harm upon awakening. The fact that a relatively high percentage of women homicide victims are indeed killed by their husbands,[22] would not provide an adequate basis for a woman to assume that her particular husband posed this risk. The only information she has is that he has *not* killed her in the past. But this information is completely unsuitable for predicting the possible outcome of the next battering incident.[23]

Accordingly, I would suggest that the risk-taking analysis of negligence is inappropriate in the mistake context. This conclusion is not surprising since tort law is aimed at defining minimum levels of acceptable conduct. Harm-causing conduct below this level is the primary basis for tort liability, partly because the legal system is more concerned with compensating the victim, than with casting blame on the tortfeasor. The criminal law, on the other hand, is primarily concerned with the issue of individual guilt. If the particular defendant could not help making the mistake, it may make sense to impose tort liability to maintain a certain minimum standard of behavior and to ensure that the victim is compensated.[24] But if that individual did everything within his own abilities to avoid the mistake, it makes no sense to cast blame on him in the criminal law context.

Collapsing Honest Belief Requirement with Standard of Reasonableness

A second major argument against the subjective standard of reasonableness is that it supposedly collapses the belief requirement with the reasonableness requirement and thus essentially abolishes the reasonableness requirement altogether. The rationale behind this argument seems to be that whatever an individual in good faith believes is the only thing he could be said to reasonably believe in a subjective sense. I think that is clearly wrong. Consider the case of Natalie and Otto. Natalie has an I.Q. of 180

---

[21] For an economic analysis of this type of case see Mark F. Grady. Proximate Cause and the Law of Negligence," 69 *Iowa Law Review* 363 (1984).

[22] A recent *Time* magazine article (January 25, 1993) reported: "Anywhere from one-third to as many as half of all female murder victims in America are killed by their spouses or lovers, compared with 4% of all male victims . . . [T]he average sentence for a woman who kills her mate is 15 to 20 years: for a man. 2 to 6."

[23] Indeed Lenore E. Walker, *The Battered Woman Syndrome* (New York: Springer 1984), p.29 indicates that without professional assistance, abuse will tend to "escalate to homicidal and suicidal proportions." Consequently, the evidence shows that surviving past violence but staying in the relationship becomes increasingly dangerous as time passes: "As we begin to see more battered women, we also realize the high probability that as the violence escalates. they will eventually be killed by or kill their men (p. 53). See also discussion of separation assault in Martha R. Mahony, "Legal Images of Battered Women: Redefining the Issue of Separation," 90 *Michigan Law Review* 1 (1991).

[24] That would certainly seem to be the rationale behind strict tort liability.

and Otto an I.Q. of 80. They both attend mathematics classes together. Both Natalie and Otto believe in good faith that $2 + 2 = 5$. If we were to evaluate their performance on a mathematics examination in the form of a grade, it is reasonable to fail both of them. But if we were considering the issue of blameworthiness for the good faith but incorrect belief, I think we could easily come to the conclusion that Natalie is lazy and thus at fault for her mistake, but that Otto is doing the best he can. Thus the good faith but false belief may be reasonable considering Otto's abilities but unreasonable considering Natalie's. In imposing tort liability we may treat them equally (as in giving both a failing grade) because this judgment indicates that their conduct fell below the accepted minimum. In casting blame for the mistake, however, it makes no sense to judge them according to the same standard.

Subjective Standard and Acquittal of Dangerous Offenders

A third argument against using the subjective standard of reasonableness is that it would permit a not-guilty verdict of potentially dangerous individuals, dangerous because they perceive the world differently from the normal individual. Jeffrie Murphy gives the example of a delusional psychotic who "says he kills in order to protect himself from the death rays emanating from the tongue of Mr. Brown (a dangerous assassin from Mars)." If we apply a subjective standard of reasonableness then we have to apply "the standard of the *reasonable psychotic*—a standard that invites each member of the jury to ask himself 'If I were crazy as hell, might I believe that I was under immediate threat of death and that my use of deadly force was necessary to repel the attack against me?'"[25] Since, as Murphy points out, the answer would obviously be yes, we would have to acquit dangerous offenders. The acquittal becomes even more problematic under the U.S. Supreme Court's *Foucha v. Louisiana*[26] decision, since the acquitted but dangerous criminal defendant could not be civilly committed.

My suggestion essentially involves not imputing wrongful conduct to the putative self-defender if the mistake as to the justifying circumstances was subjectively reasonable. A subjectively reasonable mistake as to the justifying circumstances would essentially negate the mens rea required for conviction. If it were the standard generally applied, it would arguably require the acquittal and, under *Foucha,* release of dangerous individuals, such as the delusional psychotic in Murphy's example.[27]

A number of U.S. jurisdictions have already responded to the limitations imposed on the civil commitment of dangerous individuals. Some of them have abolished their diminished capacity defense as a means of negating a required offense culpability element.[28] Others have adopted a "guilty but mentally ill" provision to substitute for

[25] Jeffrie G. Murphy. "Some Ruminations on Women, Violence, and the Criminal Law," forthcoming in Jules Coleman, ed.. *In Harm's Way: Essays in Honor of Joel Feinberg,* Cambridge: Cambridge University Press (1994).

[26] 112 S. Ct. 1780 (1992).

[27] I thank Jeffrie Murphy for his discussion of this issue at the Erlangen symposium "Imputation of Conduct in Law and Ethics," October 3–9, 1993, where I originally presented the first draft of this paper.

[28] Paul H. Robinson, "The Criminal-Civil Distinction and Dangerous Blameless Offenders," 83 *Journal of Criminal Law and Criminology* 693, 704 (1993). See id., 698–706 for a discussion of the historical development of the insanity defense before and after court-mandated limitations on the use of civil commitment.

the mental illness excuse defense and to permit criminal commitment of dangerous offenders. If a defendant is found "guilty but mentally ill," he will generally be awarded the same sentence he would have received on a simple "guilty" verdict. He will then be examined by psychiatrists to determine whether he is in need of treatment, and if so will be criminally committed to a mental health facility. If not, he will serve his full sentence in prison or the part of his sentence remaining after he has regained his mental health. In this way, society can avoid the risk of the "not guilty by reason of insanity" verdict where the defendant must be released from civil commitment as soon as he is sane, even though he still may be dangerous.[29]

The first approach of abolishing the diminished capacity defense altogether and barring the introduction of mental disease or defect to negate the mens rea requirement relates more directly to the problem posed for my suggested analysis of battered women cases. Although this approach represents the helplessness occasioned by judicially imposed limitations on civil commitment and not any well-reasoned doctrine of criminal responsibility,[30] it would appear to permit the acquittal of battered women and the conviction of Murphy's delusional psychotic.

Battered women who kill their sleeping husbands are not usually suffering from any form of mental disease or defect. Accordingly, there would be no need for the introduction of this type of evidence at trial as there would be for the delusional psychotic. Admittedly, expert testimony on the battered woman syndrome and the effects it has on the woman's belief in her ability to leave the relationship would be needed. But this testimony relates directly to the objective facts of the case and the effects of the actual, and not imagined, battering relationship on the defendant. In the case of the delusional psychotic, there are no objective data whatsoever for the belief in the death rays emanating from the tongue of Mr. Brown, the dangerous assassin from Mars. Consequently here a psychiatrist is needed to explain that this belief is the product of the defendant's delusions. Here evidence of mental disease or defect to negate mens rea could still be barred without sacrificing the subjective standard for battered women.

A counter-argument of course could be made by simply changing Murphy's example to make the delusional psychotic's beliefs based on some odd experiences he has had throughout his lifetime that led him to think that Mr. Brown was a dangerous assassin from Mars. These experiences and the effect they produced on the delusional psychotic, however, would be particular to that specific individual. Battering relationships on the other hand, tend to generally affect women's perceptions of their ability to flee because of what Lenore Walker describes as the feeling of "learned helplessness".[31] According to Walker, experiments on animals and human beings show that this is a *normal* response on the part of the subject of the experiment to being conditioned that all attempts at avoiding certain unpleasant circumstances are to no avail. Presumably the delusional psychotic's response is not the normal response to the type of experiences he has had in the past, otherwise we would not classify him as psychotic. The battered woman, on the other hand, is not mentally ill as a result of the battering relationship.

---

[29] Id. at 702.

[30] See id. passim and Note, "Fourteenth Amendment—The Continued Confinement of Insanity Acquittees," 85 *Journal of Criminal Law and Criminology* 944 (1993).

[31] Lenore E. Walker, *The Battered Woman* (op. cit. fn. 23) pp. 42–54.

Applying a subjective standard of reasonableness does not invite a jury to put itself in the position of someone who has psychotic responses to objectively neutral circumstances based on some former factual scenario. Instead it requires the jury to consider what would be a reasonable response for someone subjected to the type of violence battered women are actually exposed to with regard to judging the amount of danger in fact posed on the particular occasion and the likelihood of being able to safely flee. Furthermore, as argued, the subjective standard of reasonableness does not reduce the reasonable belief standard to the actual belief standard. That reduction would be necessary, however, before the delusional psychotic's beliefs could be classified as "reasonable," since these beliefs are indeed only "reasonable" for the particular individual. Accordingly, applying a subjective standard will not permit the acquittal of dangerous psychotics, but will permit the acquittal of the battered woman, who is not insane.

When a court refuses to permit the jury to evaluate evidence of the past battering relationship, it essentially asks the jury whether an average woman could reasonably believe that deadly force is necessary to ward off an attack from her sleeping husband. That question borders on absurdity since it excludes any consideration of the reasons for the battered woman's fear of serious bodily harm or death. A court that permits the jury to hear evidence of the battering relationship, but instructs the jury to apply an objective standard, essentially tells the jury to ignore the evidence. It is only by applying a subjective standard that one can arrive at a determination of fault in the criminal law context for making the (perhaps false) assumption that circumstances exist warranting the use of deadly-force self-defense.

One Solution to the Battered Woman Dilemma

I have argued two positions that now need to be synthesized and applied to the battered woman case where the woman mistakenly assumes that deadly force is immediately necessary to ward off a threat of death or serious physical harm. The first argument was that mistakes as to justifying circumstances should be treated like mistakes as to the definition of the offense and not like excuses. The second argument was that the reasonableness standard for judging the mistake should be subjective rather than objective.

The effect of the first argument on the battered woman would be that if she in good faith believed that she was in danger of being seriously injured or killed on her husband's awakening and that killing him was the only alternative for warding off the danger then no wrongful conduct should be inputed to her as intentional wrongdoing. The argument essentially is that (1) the imputation of wrongful conduct depends on goal-directed or willful behavior; (2) an individual who is mistaken about circumstances constituting the notion of criminal wrong is not acting willfully with respect to causing that harm (Jeremy); (3) circumstances justifying the infliction of otherwise criminally prohibited harm are, as exceptions to criminal law rules of conduct, circumstances constituting the notion of criminal wrong; (4) an individual who mistakenly assumes that justifying circumstances exist is not acting willfully with respect to the criminally prohibited wrong; (5) therefore, wrongful conduct cannot be imputed to that individual.

It is extremely important to realize that this argument does *not* mean that the battered woman in my example is justified (nor is she excused). Instead, she will be treated like Jeremy who honestly believes that he is shooting at a tree stump rather than at Katie, a human being. Just as we cannot impute the intentional wrongful killing of Katie to Jeremy, so too we cannot impute the intentional wrongful killing of the batterer to the battered woman.

The next question raised in Jeremy's case is whether Jeremy could have discovered that the tree stump was really a human being. This question moves us to Jeremy's negligence (recklessness) in making the mistake. If Jeremy could have detected with a reasonable amount of effort that the tree stump was really a human being, then the negligent killing of Katie could be imputed to him. Similarly, if a judge or jury determines that as an objective matter, the battered woman did not need to use deadly force self-defense before her husband awakened, then the question should be raised as to whether she was negligent in making the mistake. If so, then the negligent killing of her husband (not in self-defense) could be imputed to her. If not, then no wrongful conduct could be imputed to her at all as her deed. Consequently, she (although not justified) would not need to be excused.

The second argument was that when judging the reasonableness of a mistake as to circumstances constituting the offense definition or as to circumstances constituting a justification for committing a criminally prohibited wrong, a subjective standard of reasonableness should be applied. The argument essentially was that judgments of negligence in the criminal law are different from judgments of negligence in tort law, the former relating to the actor's personal failure to correspond to criminal law norms, the latter relating to a certain minimum standard of behavior and victim compensation. Still, the subjective standard of reasonableness is a standard that differs from the determination of a good faith belief. Consequently, a jury should be permitted to hear all of the evidence regarding the battering relationship and should be instructed to put themselves in the position of the woman when determining whether she could have avoided the mistake as to the need for deadly-force self-defense.

NOTES AND QUESTIONS

1. Abigail has wrecked the family car. She knows she will be able to keep that fact secret from her husband for about a week. But then he will know for sure, and given his choleric temper she quite reasonably believes that he will beat her to within an inch of her life once he finds out. She knows that the law of self-defense does not permit killing someone unless an imminent danger looms. Nevertheless she kills him. How should she fare?

2. Suppose you are a committed retributivist. You believe that punishment should be proportional to blameworthiness. Does that mean that you would not allow someone to defend himself against an attacker if in the process of defending himself

he inflicts disproportionate punishment on the attacker? Presumably not. But that makes for an interesting problem, explored in the following article by Larry Alexander.

The Enterprise of Prevention and the Principle of Proportional Response

LARRY ALEXANDER

The Enterprise of Prevention and the Principle of Proportional Response

The enterprise of retribution has, as we have seen, an array of philosophical difficulties. What is the proper basis of retributive desert—act or character—and what is the role of luck in that basis? Does ill-desert permit, justify, or compel retribution? Is retributive desert comparative or noncomparative, and is it distinct from positive, distributive desert? And there are other difficulties, to only some of which I have alluded. But despite those difficulties, the intuitive support for the enterprise of retribution remains strong, especially for two related principles of the enterprise on which all retributivists agree: no punishment of the innocent, and no punishment greater than culpability. The two are related if culpability is a matter of degree; once one is punished to the extent of his culpability, further punishment is "undeserved" and thus tantamount to punishment of the innocent.

The principle forbidding punishment greater than culpability, which I label the *principle of proportionality,* will be the focus of this section of the article. It is a principle that is important not only for its role in the retributivists' attack on excessive punishment, but also for its role in the American legal system's limit on the amount of force that can be used to defend rights. I intend to demonstrate, not that the principle of proportionality is mistaken, but rather that it is often invoked where it does not in fact apply. In short, although some instances of "punishment" are in fact applications of the *enterprise of retribution* and thus limited by the principle of proportionality, other instances are applications of the *enterprise of prevention.* In the latter enterprise, the principle of proportionality in its ordinary form plays no role.

I begin my discussion of the principle of proportionality by asking the reader to consider an example commonly used by retributivists to demonstrate the concept of excessive punishment violative of the principle of proportionality—the example of hanging pickpockets in Victorian England. (I really don't know or care if they did hang pickpockets, or cut off their hands, or what, but the example is a good one, fic-

From "The Doomsday Machine: Proportionality, Punishment and Prevention," *The Monist,* Vol. 63 (1980), pp. 208–14.

titious or not.) Was such punishment for the minor crime of pickpocketing excessive, if one assumes that the punishment did have some deterrent effect? (If it had had a perfect deterrent effect, of course, it would not have been a problem, as it would never have been used.)

If the reader feels that hanging pickpockets was excessive—and most people I have polled feel that way—I now ask the reader to consider a product solely of the imagination. Assume there is a super-sophisticated satellite that can detect all criminal acts and determine the mental state of the actors. (The society that has invented this device has made criminal only those acts that are clearly violations of the moral rights of others.) If the satellite finds that the actor knew his act was a crime, that he had no recognized excuse or justification for committing it, that he was not acting in the heat of passion or under duress, and that he was not too young, enfeebled, mentally unbalanced, and so forth to be deemed without capacity to commit a crime, the satellite immediately—and without regard to the seriousness of the crime—zaps him with a disintegration ray. Once the satellite detects the crime, it is impossible to prevent punishment of the criminal, no matter how merciful the authorities might feel. The definitions of crimes and the punishments attached thereto can be charged only prospectively. The entire population is informed of the existence of the satellite and what it does.

Now, if, as hypothesized, the punishment of pickpockets is regarded as excessive, is the punishment meted out by my imaginary device (the Doomsday Machine, I call it)—obliteration for all crimes committed with certain mental states, right down to intentional overparking—excessive?

At first the reader might feel that the Doomsday Machine is indistinguishable from the practices of Victorian England, and so, for consistency's sake, answer that its punishment *is* excessive. But something about the Doomsday Machine example as it relates to the notion of excessive "punishment" is no doubt unsettling (aside from the idea of being obliterated by a ray for a parking ticket). So consider some further hypotheticals.

Suppose a man receives a phone call from a burglar who says, "I've been spying on you and know you're going out tonight. I plan to burglarize your house in order to steal your valuables. But I want you to know that I have a very bad heart, and if you hide your valuables, I might very well suffer a heart attack by expending a lot of energy and suffering anxiety in looking for them. So please leave them in plain slight; for I am definitely going to enter your house and look for them until I find them or drop dead." The listener hangs up the phone, takes his valuables, hides them on the very top shelf of his closet, and leaves. He returns home and finds the burglar, dead from a heart attack, on the floor. Excessive punishment for a nonviolent burglary?

Consider some other examples that I feel are parallel. What if a man keeps a moat to protect his castle (or an electric fence to protect his house), and he receives a letter from someone who says that the first time the castle (house) is deserted he will attempt to enter it; and because he cannot swim (is not shockproof), his death will be on the owner's hands if the moat is not drained (the current not turned off). Is there a duty to drain the moat (shut off the current) in order to avoid excessive punishment? And what if one hides his jewels on top of an unscalable cliff after having been told by a thief that the latter would attempt to climb it if the jewels were placed there?

I might go on in my hypotheticals to drag out vicious dogs, crocodiles, and spring guns to protect persons from petty crimes, and pit these devices against petty criminals, whose common denominator is that they all know of the certain consequences of their acts, know that their acts are illegal, are determined to proceed with them anyway, and are acting premeditatedly without any recognized legal excuse, justification, or incapacity. (In all of my hypotheticals the protective devices are somehow programmed, like the Doomsday Machine, to be absolutely no threat to anyone acting in ignorance of their existence, or on a mistake of law or fact, or with a legal excuse, justification, or incapacity.)

At this point I expect a certain response to materialize among most of the readers. Most will not feel the above examples involve excessive punishment. Indeed, many are probably unsure whether the examples involve "punishment" at all. Perhaps only a few readers will maintain that in the examples one has a duty to render a violation of his rights reasonably safe in the face of a violator's threat of, in effect, suicide.

But if these examples do not involve excessive punishment, then the Doomsday Machine does not mete out excessive punishment either. The structure of the Doomsday Machine hypothetical and the other hypotheticals is the same. A person bent on violating another's moral rights is fully aware of a condition that renders such an attempt life-threatening to him but not to others who might have an excuse or justification or who might be unaware of the dangerous condition. There is a trap, but it is only one for the wary. And once the violation occurs or reaches a certain stage, no human intervention will be effective will be effective to prevent the threat from being carried out.

But if the Doomsday Machine does not mete out excessive punishment, then perhaps neither did those oft-maligned judges in Victorian England. Does the Doomsday Machine differ in any relevant respect from an ordinary system of criminal law that imposes harsh sentences, if the harsh sentences are imposed only under the same conditions as restrict the Doomsday Machine?

Well, one difference surely is that getting caught and severely punished are never certainties for criminals facing an ordinary system of criminal law. Indeed, my Doomsday Machine and other hypotheticals all made the choice to commit a criminal act indistinguishable from the choice to commit suicide. In the real world, the chances of escaping detection or conviction are substantial.

Most people I have polled, however, when asked whether it would make any difference to the question of excessive punishment if the Doomsday Machine were imperfect and could detect only, say, one out of three crimes (or the moat were swimmable, the shock survivable, the cliff scalable, and so forth, one in three times), replied that it would not. I concur. The difference, if any, between Doomsday Machine "punishments" and ordinary harsh punishments must lie in something other than the chance of escaping them.

One difference between the Doomsday Machine and ordinary harsh punishments lies in the Machine's infallibility in detecting all the factors relevant to guilt, in contrast to the fallibility of even the most enlightened criminal justice system. But fallibility, logically, has more to do with whether we should punish at all, or how harsh our harshest punishment should be, than with whether our punishments should be scaled according to the gravity of the crime and should not exceed the supposed "desert" of the criminal (assuming we have not been fallible in assessing it). We are equally as fallible in determining who is guilty of petty larceny as we are in determining who is guilty of murder. If the former crime but not the latter were punishable by death, fallibility would be as great but no greater a concern.

Another difference between the Doomsday Machine and ordinary harsh punishments lies in the fact that the punishment the former metes out occurs substantially contemporaneously with commission of the crime. However, when I reprogrammed the Doomsday Machine to mete out the punishment a day, or six months, or a year after the crime, none of the participants in my informal polls felt that the change was morally significant, especially after I replaced, in my other hypotheticals, my moats, fences, dogs, crocodiles, and so forth, with snakes whose venom took a year to kill.

Another possible distinction between some of my hypotheticals, although not my Doomsday Machine, and ordinary harsh punishments is that the former involve a danger that materializes *before* the criminal achieves his aim. The heart attack, the drowning in the moat, the shock from the electric fence—all occur before the criminal makes off with the booty and thus look like true instances of prevention. The Doomsday Machine and the Victorian punishments occurred *after* the crime and thus look like excessive punishment. This distinction is only apparent, however. First, in all of the hypotheticals a violation of a right had already occurred when the violator triggered the death-dealing mechanism. True, in some of the hypotheticals, the triggering violation—for example, trespass or breaking and entering—was but a means to a further, and usually more serious, violation—for example, theft. But in all cases there was *some* prior violation. Moreover, if attempted violations suffice to trigger just punishment, then whether the "excessive" punishment meted out in the hypotheticals occurs before or after a consummated violation appears to be irrelevant so long as there is an attempted violation.

If violations have occurred in all the hypotheticals, perhaps the hypotheticals can be distinguished on a different though related basis. In some of the hypotheticals, the criminal's death, though it occurs after he violates the victim's rights, nonetheless prevents a further or more serious violation. In the examples of the Doomsday Machine and the hanging of pickpockets, there may be no further or more serious violation contemplated by the criminal to be prevented by his death. (An extreme example where the death of the criminal cannot prevent the harm of a violation is that of the diamond that carries the notice, "Anyone who reads and understands this notice and who, without excuse or justification, attempts to steal this diamond, will be blown up by a bomb inside it." Because the explosion will destroy the diamond along with the thief, it will not prevent the harm.) Thus, although in all the examples the *threat* is designed *to prevent the harms of violations,* in only some, not including the Doomsday Machine, is the *consummation of the threat* designed *to prevent the harms of violations.*

I confess that although I perceive the distinction just described, I fail to perceive its relevance to the question of whether the threatened injury is excessive, that is, morally impermissible. If the potential victim is willing to create a particular risk to *his* rights in order to increase the threat to violators and thus to decrease the overall risk to his rights, I see no valid moral objection on behalf of the violators.

The only remaining difference between the Doomsday Machine and ordinary harsh punishments that might be deemed significant is that the Doomsday Machine, unlike ordinary punishment, requires no human intervention between the criminal act and the punishment. (Indeed, in my hypothetical, human intervention to prevent the punishment is ineffectual.) Is our moral compunction against imposing harsh punishment, despite such punishment's deterrent value, related to our inability to make the punishment automatic and not subject to our control after the criminal act? Is the relevant analogy to a judge in a regime of harsh punishment that of a person returning to his castle to find a forewarned trespasser in the middle of the moat being attacked by crocodiles that the owner can call off by means of a whistle? Would the owner be morally compelled to call them off? If so, then perhaps we have a great incentive for building a Doomsday Machine. If not, then the Doomsday Machine example draws into question the whole concept of excessive punishment and our adverse moral reaction to it.

Once it is clear that it makes no difference whether the disproportionate harm befalls the criminal before or after he succeeds in violating another's rights, so long as he is threatened with the harm before he acts, we can see that the electric fence, the moat, the cliff, and so forth, on the one hand, and harsh criminal punishment administered by human beings on the other, as well as the Doomsday Machine programmed for either instantaneous or delayed zapping, are all related phenomena. They are all instances of the *enterprise of prevention,* an enterprise that I maintain appears to be morally justifiable when conducted according to certain principles, among which is *not* the principle of proportionality. The principles which are germane to proper conduct of the enterprise of prevention are the principle that requires that the person threatened with the harm have no right to engage in the act which triggers the harm (the *wrongful act principle*) and the principle that requires adequate notice of the threat before it may be carried out (the *notice principle*).

Once these two principles are compiled with, a harm disproportionate to ill-desert may be imposed on an actor, even if it is more harm than is necessary to effect a similar degree of prevention of the act in question.

NOTES AND QUESTIONS

1. Would it be all right for the state to adopt a law imposing the death penalty, or life imprisonment, for drunk driving, even if no one has been injured in the course of it? If it is all right to protect even trivial valuables by threatening death to the thief—by surrounding them with a moat or electric fence or guarding them with a vicious dog or crocodile—then why isn't it all right to protect the lives of the citizenry by threatening death to drunk drivers? How would Larry Alexander respond to this proposal?

5.3 EXCUSE GENERALLY

Brain and Blame

STEPHEN J. MORSE

Introduction

The discovery of biological pathology that may be associated with criminal behavior
lures many people to treat the offender as purely a mechanism and the offensive conduct as simply the movements of a biological organism. Because mechanisms and
their movements are not appropriate objects of moral and legal blame, the inevitable
conclusion seems to be that the offender should not be held legally responsible. I suggest in contrast that abnormal biological causes of behavior are not grounds per se to
excuse. Causation is not an excuse and, even within a more sophisticated theory of
excuse, pathology will usually lay a limited role in supporting an individual excuse. . . .

The Law's Concept of the Person

Intentional human conduct, that is, *action,* unlike other phenomena, can be explained
by physical causes *and* by reasons for action. Although physical causes explain the
movements of galaxies and planets, molecules, infrahuman species, and all the other
moving parts of the physical universe, including the neurophysiological events accompanying human action, only human action can also be explained by reasons. It
makes no sense to ask a bull that gores a matador, "Why did you do that?" but this
question makes sense and is vitally important when it is addressed to a person who
sticks a knife into the chest of another human being. It makes a great difference to us
if the knife-wielder is a surgeon who is cutting with the patient's consent or a person
who is enraged at the victim and intends to kill him.

When one asks about human action, "Why did she do that?" two distinct types of
answers may be given. The reason-giving explanation accounts for human behavior
as a product of intentions that arise from the desires and beliefs of the agent. The second type of explanation treats human behavior as simply one bit of the phenomena of
the universe, subject to the same natural, physical laws that explain all phenomena.
Suppose, for example, we wish to explain why Molly became a lawyer. The reason-
giving explanation might be that she wishes to emulate her admired mother, a prominent lawyer, and Molly believes that the best way to do so is also to become a lawyer.
If we want to account for why Molly chose one law school rather than another, a perfectly satisfactory explanation under the circumstances would be that Molly chose the
best school that admitted her.

The mechanistic type of explanation would approach these questions quite differently. For example, those who believe that mind can ultimately be reduced to

From *Georgetown Law Journal,* Vol. 84 (1996), pp. 527–37.

the biophysical workings of the brain and nervous system—the eliminative materialists—also believe that Molly's "decision" is *solely* the law-governed product of biophysical causes. Her desires, beliefs, intentions, and choices are therefore simply epiphenomenal, rather than genuine causes of her behavior. According to this mode of explanation, Molly's "choices" to go to law school and to become a lawyer (and all other human behavior) are causally indistinguishable from any other phenomena in the universe, including the movements of molecules and bacteria.

As clinical and experimental sciences of behavior, psychiatry and psychology are uncomfortably wedged between the reason-giving and mechanistic accounts of human conduct. Sometimes they treat actions as purely physical phenomena, sometimes as texts to be interpreted, and sometimes as a combination of the two. Even neuropsychiatry and neuropsychology, the more physical branches of their parent disciplines, are similarly wedged because they begin their investigations with *action* and not simply with abnormal movements. One can attempt to assimilate reason-giving to mechanistic explanation by claiming that desires, beliefs, and intentions are genuine causes, and not simply rationalizations of behavior. Indeed, folk psychology, the dominant explanatory mode in the social sciences, proceeds on the assumption that reasons for action are genuinely causal. But the assimilationist position is philosophically controversial, a controversy that will not be solved until the mind-body problem is "solved"—an event unlikely to occur in the foreseeable future.

Law, unlike mechanistic explanation or the conflicted stance of psychiatry and psychology, views human action as almost entirely reason-governed. The law's concept of a person is as a practical reasoning, rule-following being, most of whose legally relevant movements must be understood in terms of beliefs, desires, and intentions. As a system of rules to guide and govern *human* interaction—legislatures and courts do not decide what rules infrahuman species must follow—the law presupposes that people use legal rules as premises in the practical syllogisms that guide much human action. No "instinct" governs how fast a person drives on the open highway. But among the various explanatory variables, the posted speed limit and the belief in the probability of paying the consequences for exceeding it surely play a large role in the driver's choice of speed. For the law, then, a person is a practical reasoner, a being whose action may be guided by reasons. The legal view of the person is not that all people always reason and behave consistently rationally according to some preordained, normative notion of rationality. It is simply that people are creatures who act for and consistently with their reasons for action and are generally capable of minimal rationality according to mostly conventional, socially constructed standards.

On occasion, the law appears concerned with a mechanistic causal account of conduct. For example, claims of legal insanity are usually supported and explained by using mental disorder as a variable that at least in part caused the defendant's offense. Even in such cases, however, the search for a causal account is triggered by the untoward, crazy *reasons* that motivated the defendant. Furthermore, the criteria for legal insanity primarily address the defendant's reasoning, rather than mechanistic causes. For example, in addition to a finding of mental disorder, acquittal by reason of insanity requires that the defendant did not know right from wrong or was unable to appreciate the wrongfulness of her act. Conduct motivated by crazy reasons is intentional human action. The law excuses a legally insane defendant, however, because her practical reasoning was nonculpably irrational, not because her behavior was caused by abnormal psychological or biological variables. Indeed, it is a simple matter to devise irrationality criteria for legal insanity that would excuse all people now found legally insane, but which make no mention whatsoever of mental disorder or other alleged mechanistic causes.

Reasons, Responsibility, and Excuses

The law's conception of responsibility follows logically from its conception of the person and the nature of law itself. Once again, law is a system of rules that guides and governs human interaction. It tells citizens what they may and may not do, what they must or must not do, and what they are entitled to. If human beings were not creatures who could understand and follow the rules of their society, who could not be guided by reasons, the law and all other systems, such as morality, that regulate conduct by reasons and rules would be powerless to affect human action. Rule-followers must be creatures who are capable of properly using the rules as premises in practical reasoning. It follows that a legally responsible agent is a person who is so capable according to some contingent, normative notion of both rationality itself and how much capability is required. For example, legal responsibility might require the capacity to understand the reason for an applicable rule, as well as the rule's narrow behavior command. These are matters of moral, political, and, ultimately, legal judgment, about which reasonable people can and do differ. There is no uncontroversial definition of rationality or of what kind and how much is required for responsibility. But the debate is about human action—intentional behavior guided by reasons.

Specific legal responsibility criteria exemplify the foregoing analysis. Consider the criminal law and criminal responsibility. Most substantive criminal laws prohibit harmful conduct. Fair and effective criminal law requires that citizens must understand what conduct is prohibited, the nature of their own conduct, and the consequences for doing what the law prohibits. Homicide laws, for example, require that citizens understand that unjustifiably killing other human beings is prohibited, what counts as killing conduct, and that the state will inflict pain if the rule is violated and the perpetrator is caught and convicted. A person incapable of understanding the rule or the nature of her own conduct, including the context in which it is embedded, could not properly use the rule to guide her conduct. For example, a person who delusionally believed that she was about to be killed by another person and kills the other in the mistaken belief that she must do so to save her own life, does not rationally understand what she is doing. She of course knows that she is killing a human being and does so intentionally, but the rule against *unjustifiable* homicide will be ineffective because she delusionally believes that her action is justifiable.

The inability to follow a rule properly, to be rationally guided by it, is what distinguishes the delusional agent from people who are simply mistaken, but who could have followed the rule by exerting more effort, attention, or the like. We believe that the delusional person's failure to understand is not her fault because she lacked the ability to understand in this context. In contrast, the person capable of rational conduct is at fault if she fails to exercise her rationality. In sum, rationality is required for responsibility, and nonculpable irrationality is an excusing condition. Blaming and punishing an irrational agent for violating a rule she was incapable of following is unfair and an ineffective mechanism of social control.

Responsibility also requires that the agent act without compulsion or coercion, even if the agent is fully rational, because it is also unfair to hold people accountable for behavior that is wrongly compelled. For example, suppose a gunslinger threatens to kill you unless you kill another innocent person. The balance of evils is not positive: it is one innocent life or another, so the killing would not be justified. But it might be excused because it is compelled. Compulsion involves a wrongful hard choice that a rational, otherwise responsible agent faces. If she yields to the threat, it will not be because she doesn't understand the legal rule or what she is doing. She knows it is wrong and acts intentionally precisely to avoid the threatened harm. Still, society, acting through its legal rules governing such cases, might decide that some choices are too hard fairly to expect the agent to behave properly and that people will be excused for making the wrong choice. If the hard choice renders the person irrational and incapable of rationality, then there is no need to resort to notions of compulsion to excuse.

In sum, an agent is responsible for a particular action if she was capable of rationality and acted without compulsion in this context. If she was incapable of rationality or compelled to perform the particular action, she will be excused.

Causation Is *Not* an Excusing Condition

The "fundamental psycholegal error" is the mistaken belief that if science or common sense identifies a cause for human action, including mental or physical disorders, then the conduct is necessarily excused. But causation is neither an excuse per se nor the equivalent of compulsion, which is an excusing condition. For example, suppose that I politely ask the brown-haired members of an audience of lawyers to whom I am speaking to raise their hands to assist me with a demonstration. As I know from experience, virtually all the brunet(te)s will raise their hands, and I will thank them politely. These hand-raisings are clearly caused by a variety of variables over which the brunet(te) attorneys have no control, including genetic endowment (being brunet(te) is a genetically determined, but-for cause of the behavior) and, most proximately, my words. Equally clearly, this conduct is human action—*intentional* bodily movement—and not simply the movements of bodily parts in space, as if, for example, a neurological disorder produced a similar arm-rising. Moreover, the conduct is entirely rational and uncompelled. The cooperating audience members reasonably desire that the particular lecture they are attending should be useful to them. They reasonably believe that cooperating with the invited lecturer at a professional meeting will help satisfy that desire. Thus, they form the intention to raise their hands, and they do so. It is hard to imagine more completely rational conduct, according to any normative notion of rationality. The hand-raisings were not compelled, because the audience was not threatened with any untoward consequences whatsoever for failure to cooperate. In fact, the lecturer's request to participate was more like an *offer,* an opportunity to make oneself better off by improving the presentation's effectiveness, and offers provide easy choices and more freedom, rather than hard choices and less freedom.

The cooperative audience members are clearly responsible for their hand-raisings and fully *deserve* my "thank you," even though their conduct was perfectly predictable and every bit as caused as a neuropathologically induced arm-rising. My "thank you" was not intended simply as a positive reinforcer for the hand-raising behavior the audience members performed. Gratitude is the appropriate moral sentiment in response to the willingness of the audience to satisfy the normatively justifiable expectation that they should cooperate and the reasonable assumption that a group of lawyers is composed of rational and therefore responsible moral agents. "Thank you" is the appropriate and deserved expression of that moral sentiment.[1] Although the hand-raising conduct is caused, there is no reason why it should be excused.

All phenomena of the universe are presumably caused by the necessary and sufficient conditions that produce them. If causation were an excuse, no one would be responsible for any conduct, and society would not be concerned with moral and legal responsibility and excuse. Indeed, eliminative materialists, among others, often make such assertions, but such a moral and legal world is not the one we have, nor I daresay, one that most of us would prefer to inhabit. Although neuropathologically induced arm-risings and cooperative, intentional hand-raisings are equally caused, they are distinguishable phenomena, and the difference is vital to our conception of ourselves as human beings. This is not the appropriate place to offer a defense of the importance of responsibility and excuse and praise and blame, but I will simply assume that such human ideas and practices enrich our lives and encourage human flourishing. In a moral and legal world that encompasses both responsible and excused action, all of which is caused, the discrete excusing conditions that should and do negate responsibility are surely caused by something. Nevertheless, it is the nature of the excusing condition that is doing the work, not that the excusing condition is caused.

The determinist reductio—everyone or no one is responsible if the truth of determinism or universal causation underwrites responsibility—is often attacked in two ways. The first is "selective determinism" or "selective causation"—the claims that only some behavior is caused or determined and that only this subset of behavior should be excused. The metaphysics of selective causation are wildly implausible and "panicky," however. If this is a causal universe, as it most assuredly is, then it strains the imagination also to believe that some human behavior somehow exits the "causal stream." To explain in detail why selective causation/selective excuse is an unconvincing and ultimately patronizing argument would require a lengthy digression from this essay's primary purpose. I have made this argument in detail elsewhere and shall simply assert here that good arguments do not support this position.

The second attack on the determinist reductio claims that only abnormal causes,

---

[1] I am borrowing here from Jay Wallace's excellent, compatibilist account of what it means to hold someone responsible. According to Wallace, holding people morally responsible cannot be reduced to a behavioral disposition positively and negatively to reinforce good and bad conduct, respectively. It is a susceptibility to experience the appropriate moral sentiments if another agent meets or breaches a justifiable moral obligation that one accepts and then to express these emotions through the appropriate positive or negative practices, such as praise and blame. *See* R. Jay Wallace, *Responsibility and the Moral Sentiments* (Cambridge: Howard University Press, 1994), 51–83.

One can imagine a world in which praise and blame were used solely for their operant conditioning success, but I suspect that they would then be quite unsuccessful, and the world would be a quite cheerless place in general.

including psychopathological and physiopathological variables, excuse. Although this argument appears closer to the truth, it is a variant of selective determinism and suffers from the defects of that approach. Pathology can produce an excusing condition, but when it does, it is the excusing condition that does the work, not the existence of a pathological cause per se. Consider again the delusional self-defender, who kills in response to the delusionally mistaken belief that she is about to be killed. Human action to save one's life is not a mechanistic, literally irresistible cause of behavior, and crazy beliefs are no more compelling than noncrazy beliefs. The killing is perfectly intentional—the delusional belief provides the precise reason to form the intention to kill. Moreover, the killing is also not compelled simply because the belief is pathologically produced. A nondelusional but unreasonably mistaken self-defender, who feels the same desire to save her own life, would have no excuse for killing. A desire to save one's own life furnishes a justification or excuse only under limited circumstances. There is also nothing wrong with our defender's "will," properly understood as an intentional executory state that translates desires and beliefs into action. The defender's will operated quite effectively to effectuate her desire to live when she believed that she needed to kill to survive. Nor does our delusional self-defender lack "free will" simply because she is abnormal. I don't know what free will is in any case, and it is often just a placeholder for the conclusion that the agent supposedly lacking this desirable attribute ought to be excused. The real reason our delusional self-defender ought to be excused, of course, is that she is not capable of rationality on this occasion. This is the genuine excusing condition that distinguishes her from the nondelusional but unreasonably mistaken self-defender.

When agents behave inexplicably irrationally, we frequently believe that underlying pathology produces the irrationality, but it is the irrationality, not the pathology, that excuses. After all, pathology does not always produce an excusing condition, and when it does not, there is no reason to excuse the resultant conduct. To see why, imagine a case in which pathology is a but-for cause of rational behavior. Consider a person with paranoid fears for her personal safety, who is therefore hypervigilant to cues of impending danger. Suppose on a given occasion she accurately perceives such a cue and kills properly to save her life. If she had not been pathologically hypervigilant, she would have missed the cue and been killed. She is perfectly responsible for this rational, justifiable homicide. Or take the case of a hypomanic businessperson, whose manic energy and heightened powers are a but-for cause of making an extremely shrewd deal. Assume that business conditions later change unforeseeably and the deal is now a loser. The deal was surely rational and uncompelled when it was made, and no sensible legal system would later void it because the businessperson was incompetent to contract. Even when pathology is uncontroversially a but-for cause of behavior, that conduct will be excused only if an independent excusing condition, such as irrationality or compulsion, is present. Even a highly abnormal cause will not excuse unless it produces an excusing condition.

Brain and Blame

The foregoing analysis of excusing conditions applies straightforwardly to cases in which brain or nervous system pathology is part of the causal chain of intentional behavior. To begin, biological causation will only be part of the causal determinants of any intentional conduct, which is always mediated by one's culture, language, and the like. The best accounts of the relation between brain and behavior suggest that no discrete bit of physiology always and everywhere produces exactly the same intentional conduct in all human beings experiencing that physiological state, that no stimulus produces exactly the same brain states in all people responding to it, and that no bit of exactly the same behavior emitted by different people is attended by exactly the same brain state in all the similarly behaving agents. For example, the same pathophysiological (or psychopathological) processes may produce delusional beliefs in all people with the processes, but the delusional content and resultant behavior of delusional, thirteenth-century subcontinental Indians will surely differ from that of delusional, late-twentieth-century Americans. For a second intuitive example, consider the demonstration about hand-raising discussed previously. Large numbers of people behave (approximately) exactly the same for the same reasons in response to the same stimulus. It is implausible to assume that their brains and nervous systems are in identical biophysical states. In sum, biological variables will rarely be the sole determinants of intentional human action.

More fundamentally, biological causation will not excuse per se, because people are biological creatures and biology is always part of the causal chain for everything we do. If biological causation excused, no one would be responsible. Intentional human action and neuropathologically produced human movements are both biologically driven, yet they are conceptually, morally, and legally distinguishable. Moreover, if biology were "all" the explanation and everything else, including causal reasons for action, were simply epiphenomenal—as the eliminative materialists claim—then our entire notions of ourselves and responsibility would surely alter radically. But eliminative materialism is philosophically controversial, and science furnishes no reason to believe that it is true. Indeed, it is not clear conceptually that science could demonstrate that it is true. Thus, until the doctor comes and convinces us that our normative belief in human agency and responsibility is itself pathological, biological causation per se does not excuse.

Abnormal biological causation also does not excuse per se. Human action can be rational or irrational, uncompelled or compelled, whether its causes are "normal" or "abnormal." Whatever the causes of human action may be, they will ultimately be expressed through reasons for action, which are the true objects of responsibility analysis. Suppose, for example, that a confirmed brain lesion, such as a tumor, is a but-for cause of behavior. That is, let us suppose that a particular piece of undesirable behavior would not have occurred if the agent never had the tumor. Make the further, strong assumption that once the tumor is removed, the probability that this agent will reoffend drops to zero. Although one's strong intuition may be that this agent is not responsible for the undesirable behavior, the given assumptions do not entail the conclusion that the agent should be excused. The undesirable behavior is human action, not a literally irresistible mechanism, and the causal role of the brain tumor does not necessarily mean that the behavior was irrational or compelled.

Moreover, it is a mistake to assume that specific brain pathology inevitably produces highly specific, complex intentional action. Certain areas of the brain do control general functions. For example, Broca's area in the left frontal lobe controls the ability to comprehend and produce appropriate language. A sufficient lesion in this site produces and enables us to predict aphasia. But there is no region or site in the frontal lobes or anywhere else in the brain that controls specific, complex intentional actions. No lesion enables us to explain causally or to predict an agent's reasons and consequent intentional action in the same direct, precise way that a lesion in Broca's area permits the explanation or prediction of aphasia. Neurological lesions can dissociate bodily movements from apparent intentions, producing automatisms and similar "unconscious" states. But such states rarely produce criminal conduct, and when they do, the agent is exculpated. In these cases we need not even reach the issue of whether the agent's intentional action is rational, because action itself is lacking. The story relating brain or nervous system pathology to intentional conduct will be far more complicated and far less direct than the already complicated correspondence between brain and nervous system lesions and the reduction or loss of general functions.

Brain or other nervous system pathology affects agents more generally. Suppose, for example, that the tumor in the previous example makes the agent irritable or emotionally labile. Such emotional states surely make it harder for any agent to fly straight in the face of other criminogenic variables, such as provocation or stress, but per se they do not render an agent irrational. Other agents may be equally irritable or labile as the result of environmental variables, such as the loss of sleep and stress associated with, say, taking law exams or trying an important, difficult, lengthy case. But these people would not be excused if they offended while in an uncharacteristic emotional state, unless that state sufficiently deprived them of rationality. People with criminogenically predisposing congenital abnormalities or lifelong character traits would have even less excuse for undesirable behavior, because they had the time and experience to learn to deal with those aspects of themselves that made flying straight harder.

Consider the case of Charles Whitman, who killed many victims by shooting passersby from the top of the tower on the University of Texas campus. He suffered from a brain tumor, and let us assume that we could demonstrate incontrovertibly that he would not have shot if he had not suffered from the tumor. But whether he is nonetheless responsible depends not on the but-for causation of his homicides, but on his reasons for action. If Whitman believed, for example, that mass murder of innocents would produce eternal peace on earth, then he should be excused, whether the delusional belief was a product of brain pathology, childhood trauma, or whatever. But if Whitman was simply an angry person who believed that life had dealt him a raw deal and that he was going to go out in a blaze of glory that would give his miserable life meaning, then he is unfortunate but responsible, whether his anger and beliefs were a product of the tumor, childhood trauma, an unfortunate character, or whatever.

All human action is, in part, the product of but-for causes over which agents have no control and which they are powerless to change, including their genetic endowments and the nature and context of their childrearing. If people had different genes, different parents, and different cultures, they would be different. Moreover, situational determinants over which agents have no control are but-for causes of much behavior. A victim in the wrong place at the wrong time is as much a but-for cause of the mugging as the mugger's genetics and experiences. If no victim were available, no mugging occurs, whatever the would-be mugger's intentions. Such considerations are treated by philosophers under the rubric "moral luck." Our characters and our opportunities are in large measure the product of luck, and if luck excused, no one would be responsible. A brain tumor or other neuropathology that enhances the probability of the sufferer engaging in antisocial behavior is surely an example of dreadful bad luck. But unless the agent is irrational or the behavior is compelled, there is no reason to excuse the agent simply because bad luck in the form of biological pathology played a causal role. A cause is just a cause. It is not per se an excuse.

Convicting the Morally Blameless: Reassessing the Relationship between Legal and Moral Accountability

PETER ARENELLA

Does "knowledge" of what morality proscribes combined with the capacity and a "fair opportunity" to make a "rational choice" about whether to comply with community norms provide adequate grounds for assessing whether an offender deserves moral blame for what he has done? . . .

Our inquiry must begin by examining the meaning of our moral culpability judgments. An individual is not considered morally culpable for his behavior unless he *deserves moral blame* for what he has done. Thus, an account of moral culpability must identify the circumstances under which an individual (including criminal defendants charged with *mala in se* crimes) deserves moral blame for engaging in conduct that breaches community moral norms. . . .

There are many different accounts of when individuals deserve moral blame for causing some undesirable state of affairs. Some view moral blame as deserved even when the actor's breach of morality can be attributed to factors beyond his meaningful control. In contrast to such visions, the liberal paradigm requires actors to have some form of knowledge, reason, and control of their actions before they can be fairly blamed for what they have done.

Criminal law theory and doctrine has, for the most part, embraced this liberal paradigm for moral responsibility and articulated a *conduct-attribution* version of it. According to this account, individuals deserve moral blame for conduct that breaches community norms when that conduct can be fairly attributed to them. The law's *conduct-attribution* model of moral responsibility generally requires a demonstration that the actor made a knowing, rational, and voluntary choice to act in a manner that breached community norms. . . .

From *UCLA Law Review,* Vol. 39 (1992) pp. 1511, 1516–24, 1543–44, 1609–10, 1614, 1616.

Moral theorists have identified four principal conditions that must be satisfied under the liberal paradigm before someone deserves moral blame for their conduct. A (1) *moral agent* must be implicated in (2) *the breach of a moral norm* that (3) *fairly obligates the agent's compliance* under circumstances where that (4) *breach can be fairly attributed to the agent's conduct.*

To qualify as a blameworthy *moral agent,* the individual must have the capacity to make moral judgments about what to do and how to be and the ability to act in accordance with such judgments. We view moral evil as a corruption of this human potential for moral concern, judgment, and action. Thus, individuals do not *deserve* moral blame if they lack these moral capacities.

What are these moral capacities? Since Aristotle, moral theorists have generally agreed that the necessary attributes of moral agency fall under three categories: knowledge, reason, and control. But, describing the types of knowledge, reason, and control that are necessary for moral agency is no small task. To articulate a coherent and defensible normative conception of moral agency, one must grapple with metaphysical issues in moral theory and empirical issues in moral psychology.

To identify the capacities an individual must possess to qualify as a moral agent, one must provide answers to the following questions. What does it mean to be a moral actor? What are the grounds for making moral decisions and evaluations? Do the grounds for making moral judgments themselves motivate moral choices? What types of reasoning ability, emotions, feelings, desires, and social understandings, if any, does a person need before she can exercise moral judgment and make moral choices? What special skills, if any, does she need to control those aspects of her character that may impair her ability either to see the morally salient aspects of a situation or to make the appropriate moral choice once she recognizes it? Finally, how does a person develop these moral capacities and what degree of development is sufficient to render the person an appropriate addressee of moral norms and a suitable object for moral evaluation by other members of the community?

To complicate matters, there can be no single account of moral agency. The capacities one needs for moral judgment and action will depend in part on what morality demands of the agent. Thus, any account of moral agency must concern itself with the type and rigor of the moral norms that we are expecting the agent to understand and apply in her practical judgments. For example, moral norms that require the actor to achieve a state of virtue will implicate a far more robust account of a moral agent's necessary attributes than the minimalist moral norms implicated by our criminal laws. . . . The criminal law's *mala in se* crimes implicate, for the most part, moral norms that impose minimal demands on the agent. [T]his essay attempts to identify a minimal threshold account of what it takes to be a moral agent.

Qualifying as a moral agent is only the first prerequisite for being the object of a deserved attribution of moral blame. Even if the actor is a moral agent, the remaining three conditions must be satisfied before he deserves moral blame for being implicated in some undesirable state of affairs. . . .

The fourth requirement is that the breach of the moral norm must be fairly attributed to the moral agent's conduct. This *fair attribution* condition ensures that the agent will only be blamed for conduct breaching a moral norm when that conduct can be fairly imputed to his agency and he is at fault for engaging in that conduct. Thus, a moral agent will not deserve moral blame when his breach of a moral norm occurs under circumstances that deprived him of a fair opportunity to avoid the breach. . . .

The criminal law does provide an account of the first and last prerequisites for moral blame: the moral agency and fair attribution conditions. To be morally culpable for his criminal conduct, the individual must also qualify as a blameworthy moral agent. Who satisfies the threshold condition of moral agency in the law's eyes? Everyone except for the very young, the very crazy, and the severely mentally retarded. . . . What is the law's account of the capacities and abilities an individual must possess before we consider him a blameworthy actor who can be fairly subjected to the law's moral culpability judgments? And does the law's description of a moral agent's necessary attributes offer a persuasive account of our capacity to engage in moral judgment and moral action?

Legal theorists have not seriously considered these questions. Some ignore the question of moral agency altogether. Others assume that the concept of moral agency can be derived from what they view as the more fundamental prerequisite for moral blame: the fair attribution condition. In their eyes, moral agents are simply individuals whose conduct can be fairly attributed to them.

I shall label these scholars *conduct-responsibility* theorists because they articulate a *conduct-attribution model of moral responsibility*. Their work focuses on the type of reason, knowledge, and control any actor must have before any specific culpable conduct can be fairly attributed to him. From their perspective, a moral agent is simply a human being who is capable of having such reason, knowledge, and control over his conduct. Since criminal law doctrine roughly reflects this conduct-attribution model of moral responsibility, the law derives its account of the moral agency condition from its version of the fair attribution condition.

The criminal law's account of the fair attribution condition contains two basic components: the state must prove that the actor engaged in *culpable conduct* and that he was *morally responsible for that culpable conduct*. The culpable conduct requirement includes within it act- and fault-imputation elements. To show that the criminal engaged in culpable conduct, there must be proof that the act and/or harm can be fairly imputed to the actor. . . .

Satisfaction of the culpable conduct requirement creates a defeasible presumption that the defendant was morally culpable for his crime. But, the defendant can defeat this presumption of moral fault by denying that he was morally responsible for engaging in the culpable conduct, thereby invoking the second component of the law's fair attribution condition. In the criminal law, the dominant account of conduct-responsibility requires proof that the actor made a rational and voluntary choice to engage in behavior that he knew (or more controversially, that he should have known) would (or might) breach community norms under circumstances that gave him a fair opportunity to avoid the breach. Thus, a defendant can negate his moral culpability by showing that he "could not have acted otherwise" in the following sense: the circumstances preceding the crime deprived him of a *fair opportunity* to make a rational choice to comply with the law's commands.

Criminal defendants are generally treated as morally culpable for their crimes when they satisfy the law's fair attribution condition. However, the law does recognize two defenses, immaturity and insanity, that permit a defendant to argue that she is not the sort of individual who can be fairly subjected to the law's moral culpability judgments. Who isn't a fully accountable moral agent in the law's eyes? Someone who lacks the general capacity for rational and voluntary choice presupposed by the law's conduct-attribution model of moral responsibility.

In sum, the law's conduct-attribution model of moral responsibility generates a very thin account of a moral agent's necessary attributes.

What unifies situations in which either of the law's fair attribution conditions is negated is that they involve circumstances in which we find it difficult to view the actor's specific conduct as evidence of his ill will or indifference to the moral norms regulating our interpersonal interactions. We still consider the actor a worthy participant in our moral discourse. He is a suitable object of deserved attributions of moral blame because he is a moral agent, but his behavior or attitudes toward the norm breached on this specific occasion do not warrant moral condemnation.

In contrast, excuses that deny the offender's status as a moral agent identify individuals who are outside our moral discourse. Their specific criminal conduct may provide evidence of indifference towards some or all community moral norms, but we can not sustain our resentment towards this indifference once we realize that the offender lacks the capacity to understand their significance or respond appropriately to their demands.

In sum, the moral agency component identifies those individuals who are capable of participating with us in moral discourse and moral judgment because they share our attitudes and are capable of integrating their understanding of morality's meaning and value into their practical judgments about what to do and how to be. Satisfaction of the law's fair attribution conditions will identify the circumstances in which a moral agent's conduct appears to show his culpable lack of respect for the norm he has breached on this particular occasion. . . . How descriptively accurate is the analogy between legal and moral blame?

To answer this question, one must identify conceptions of moral agency and fair attribution conditions that best "fit" how we conceive of these themes in our most considered private blaming practices.[1] To construct an account of how the formal criminal law[2] conceives of moral culpability, one must look at how criminal law doc-

---

[1] Since we live in a morally pluralistic culture, one might doubt whether such an interpretivist enterprise could generate any single coherent account of moral blame. After all, one facet of our pluralistic culture is the difficulty of reaching any intersubjective agreement about the appropriate moral evaluation of actors and their acts. How can there be any consensus when we rely on conflicting moral principles and differing characterizations of the facts, acts, and consequences that are relevant in applying moral principles?

One must acknowledge that there is no cultural moral consensus concerning a broad range of actions and how those actions shape our moral evaluation of the actor in our private blaming practices. In short, there is no single coherent account of the "breach of moral norm" blaming condition. This obvious truth does not, however, prevent us from examining whether our moral educational practices as well as moral psychology reflect some common presuppositions about the moral nature of human action that might generate coherent accounts of two other blaming conditions under the liberal paradigm for moral responsibility: moral agency and fair attribution. Whether these common presuppositions are justifiable depends in part upon whether they rest on a defensible vision of human nature.

[2] The criminal law's formal conception of moral culpability can itself be revised by how criminal law decision-makers apply it in their practices of charging crimes, negotiating pleas, and adjudicating guilt. As noted earlier, these legal decision-makers may apply non-liberal notions of moral desert in making their judgments about who "deserves" blame. . . . For purposes of this essay, I am interested only in comparing the law's formal conception of moral culpability against the most defensible account of moral blame we can draw from moral theory, psychology, and educational practices.

trine and theory reflect and reshape such accounts about the moral significance of human endeavors.

Our accounts of *moral* evil presuppose that the wrongdoer has the capacity for moral concern, judgment, and action. We view moral evil as a corruption of this moral potential. Our p-r [participant-reactive] attitudes of resentment and blame rest on such presuppositions. We find it difficult to sustain our initial reaction of blame towards an actor who has breached some moral norm when we come to believe that the actor, through no fault of her own, lacked these moral capacities. We blame people not just for morally bad acts, but for the morally objectionable attitudes that (we believe) the actor conveyed through such behavior. But the liberal model of moral responsibility insists that we should not blame someone for failing to show moral concern for the interests of others if the actor is incapable of feeling such concern or acting on its basis.

What enables us to be moral actors who can understand the moral norms implicated by the criminal law? What *threshold* capacities do we need before we are able to use these norms in our practical judgments? . . . A moral agent must possess the following character-based abilities and attributes: the capacity to care for the interests of other human beings, the internalization of others' normative expectations (including self-identification as a participant in a culture's moral blaming practices), the possession of p-r attitudes concerning one's own and others' characters and acts, the ability to subject one's non-moral ends and values to moral evaluation, the capacity to respond to moral norms as a motivation for one's choices, and the power to manage those firmly entrenched aspects of character that impair one's ability to make an appropriate moral evaluation of the situation one is in and the choices open to one.

None of these attributes are properties, skills, or capacities whose development is totally a matter of our own responsible choices. Some of them can only develop through time and appropriate interpersonal relations and experiences with adults who nurture us. A child cannot develop the character-management skills listed above until she develops her character, becomes aware of its nature, and learns how to manage those aspects of it that can motivate the wrong types of choices.

The character-based model of moral agency reminds us that "desert" does not "go all the way down." We neither choose nor control the process that determines whether we become moral agents. For the most part, our status as moral agents is a matter of constitutive and social luck. Moreover, we do not voluntarily take on the burdens and obligations of being a moral agent: they are thrust upon us. . . .

A coherent conception of moral blame under the liberal model requires some defensible version of the moral capacities described above. The criminal law's conception of moral agency does not offer such an account. Instead, it identifies the two capacities, rationality and control over one's actions, that the individual needs to make a rational and knowing choice about whether to comply with community norms. The law's conception of moral agency explains why criminal conduct can be fairly attributed to us. But, this conduct-attribution model of moral responsibility is incomplete because it never addresses the threshold question concerning the attributes one needs to make moral choices about whether to engage in criminal conduct. . . .

The concept of moral agency outlined in this essay has attempted to identify at a conceptual level the *threshold* capacities someone needs to qualify as a morally accountable actor. Implicit in this conceptual analysis is the assumption that some, albeit few, human beings lack *any* capacity to feel concern for the interests of others, to subject their ends to moral evaluation, to respond to moral norms as a motivation for their choices, or to control those aspects of their character that may motivate immoral choices. Conversely, this analysis argues for the proposition that once the actor possesses these threshold capacities, he qualifies as a moral agent for purposes of the criminal law even if others possess far greater ability to exercise these capacities than he does. Is this fair?

Perhaps not if the moral norms we expected the actor to understand and comply with were very demanding. But, the moral norms implicated by crimes barring physical and sexual violence against other human beings place minimal restraints on the agent's ability to pursue his own interests. . . .

While the character-based model of moral agency might broaden moral-agency-defeating excuses, it could narrow the scope of some controversial conduct-responsibility-defeating excuses that suggest the moral agent was denied a fair opportunity to avoid engaging in culpable conduct. Remember that to qualify as a moral agent under the character-based model, the individual must have the capacity to manage her character traits which motivate wrong choices. Accordingly, moral agents who are raising conduct-responsibility excuses would not be permitted to argue that some aspect of their character made it too difficult for them to either appreciate what they were doing or conform their behavior to applicable moral norms. One consequence of this narrowing of excuses negating moral responsibility for specific culpable conduct might be increased pressure to recast these controversial defenses as moral agency excuses.

Choice, Character, and Excuse

MICHAEL S. MOORE

I wish to isolate two theories of excuse, each of which instantiates its own distinctive theory of responsibility. One is what I shall call *the choice theory of excuse,* according to which one is excused for the doing of a wrongful action because and only because at the moment of such action's performance, one did not have sufficient capacity or opportunity to make the choice to do otherwise. Such a choice theory of excuse instantiates a more general theory of responsibility, according to which we are responsible for wrongs we freely choose to do, and not responsible for wrongs we lacked the freedom (capacity and opportunity) to avoid doing. The second I shall call *the character theory of excuse,* according to which one is excused for the doing of a wrongful action because and only because such action is not determined by (or in some other way expressive of) those enduring attributes of ourselves we call our characters. Such a character theory of excuse instantiates a more

From *Social Philosophy and Policy,* Vol. 7 (1990), 29, 31, 33, 35, 37–41, 43–51, 53–58.

general theory of responsibility, according to which the primary object of our responsibility is our own character, and responsibility for wrongful action is derivative of this primary responsibility, our actions being proxies for the characters such actions express. . . .

What I call the choice theory of excuse is also called the "capacity conception of responsibility," the "responsibility principle," the "voluntarism principle," the "Kantian theory of responsibility," the "value of choice" theory of excuses, the "voluntariness principle," the "personhood principle," and my own earlier label, the "disturbed practical reason" theory of excuse. . . .

Despite its long history and its many current adherents, the choice theory's classical modern expression is to be found in the writings of Herbert Hart. In examining legal excusing conditions, Hart thought:

> What is crucial is that those whom we punish should have had, when they acted, the normal capacities, physical and mental, for abstaining from what it forbids, and a fair opportunity to exercise these capacities. Where these capacities and opportunities are absent, as they are in different ways in the varied cases of accident, mistake, paralysis, reflex action, coercion, insanity, etc., the moral protest is that it is morally wrong to punish because "he could not have helped it" or "he could not have done otherwise" or "he had no real choice."

Such a theory of excuse is itself but an instance of a more general principle of moral responsibility: "what the law has done here is to reflect, albeit imperfectly, a fundamental principle of morality that a person is not to be blamed for what he has done if he could not help doing it." . . .

Hart's second and later justification for the choice theory of excuse—and the way he is usually read today—grounds it in considerations of fairness and justice that are not themselves products of utilitarian calculation. That is, the excuses and the "could have done otherwise" principle they instantiate are seen as deontological, or non-consequentialist, side constraints that constrain the maximization of any utilitarian goals, crime-prevention and choice-maximization included. As Hart himself later recognized, there are constraints "which civilized moral thought places on the pursuit of the utilitarian goal by the demand that punishment should not be applied to the innocent." One of those constraints is "that out of considerations of fairness or justice to individuals we should restrict even punishment designed as a 'preventive' [i.e., utilitarian punishment] to those who had a normal capacity and a fair opportunity to obey." . . .

What is required is a third, compatibilist, reading of the principle, which is this: "he could have done otherwise" is elliptical for "he could have done otherwise if he had chosen to." His choice, in other words, was not made *impossible* by factors over which he had no control; his choice was a cause of his behavior (even if it itself was caused). . . .

. . . What makes choices impossible or very difficult is either an incapacity in the agent or the lack of fair opportunity to use a non-defective capacity. Hart thus subdivides the ability presupposed by his sense of "could" into two components. One relates to the equipment of the actor: does he have sufficient choosing capacity to be responsible? The other relates to the situation in which the actor finds himself: does that situation present him with a fair chance to use his capacities for choice so as to give effect to his decision? . . . Does the responsible self who chooses include any emotions, or is the responsible self who chooses only to be identified with the conscious will, against which all emotions are alien and potentially disturbing (incapacitating) factors? . . .

[T]he choice that is the touchstone of responsibility for the choice theorist includes much more than this. It includes the deliberative processes that lead up to the initiation of bodily movements. It is here that intentions and plans are formed in light of the actor's desires and beliefs. It is here that the actor chooses his actions under more complex descriptions than simply "moving my body": descriptions such as "taking my revenge on X" or "eliminating that hateful X." Choice, to be morally interesting, must include not only the initiation of basic actions but also the formation of the intentions and beliefs that guide and motivate the doing of basic actions. We choose our plans (complex actions), and not simply the (basic) actions that execute them.

If this is what is meant by "choice," then some emotions will necessarily have a place in this process. As Sabini and Silver observe: "the emotions are connected to cognition, connected to desires and plans." On this view, the emotions are not invaders of our processes of reasoned deliberation, nor are they preemptors of such processes. Rather, our emotions are both products and causes of the judgements we make as we decide what to do. When we get angry, for example, our anger can itself be caused by judgment: e.g., that an innocent person has just suffered undeserved punishment. Such anger reflects our judgment that something immoral has just taken place. Further, such anger at unjust treatment need not make reasoned choice more difficult. It may instead make choice easier by highlighting what we otherwise might have missed. Anger at injustice is at least as effective as reciting Kant when keeping the priority of justice before one's mind as one decides how to respond. . . .

The choice theory just examined has come to be regarded as the traditional or orthodox view of excuse. There has recently arisen something of a chorus that is critical of the choice theory and instead puts forward a character theory of excuse. This excuse theory is grounded in a general view of moral responsibility. On this general view, the ultimate object of our responsibility is our own character. Our responsibility for actions is derivative of our more fundamental responsibility for character.

On this view, the excuses, in both law and morality, serve a kind of filtering function. We are prima facie morally responsible and legally liable for wrongful and illegal acts, but we are only prima facie responsible and liable because we do not yet know whether such wrongful acts were truly expressive of our characters. If they are, we are actually responsible and liable; if they are not, we are neither. The excuses, in such a case, serve to filter out wrongful actions for which we are not responsible because they are not expressive of our character. In such a way the excuses reconcile the ultimate nature of moral responsibility—it is for character, not action—with the surface features of our moral and legal ascriptions: namely, that they are for actions and not character.

This theory of excuse, and the conception of responsibility that stands behind it, are both in considerable need of clarification. Let us begin with the more general conception of responsibility and work towards the filtering function of the excuses. First of all, what is it we are responsible for when we are said to be responsible for our *characters?* . . .

The choice faced by the character theorist is this: how broadly does he wish to identify character? Does the character of a person include only that which he reflectively identifies as "me"? This would be a narrow and subjective view of character, for it excludes those actions, thoughts, and feelings that the person himself subjectively experiences as ego-alien. Or does the character of a person include not only those items *he* identifies as part of his sense of self, but also those he experiences as an *id?* This we shall call the broad and objective view of character, since it includes more items and does so on a nonsubjective basis. . . .

. . .[A] commonly perceived difference between the character and the choice theories does not exist. It is commonly thought that the choice theorist cannot hold a person responsible for those of his actions that stem from strong emotions because such emotions impede choice (and should thus excuse on the choice theory of excuse), whereas the character theorist can easily hold such persons responsible for such actions because (on the character theory) responsibility for actions is only a proxy for responsibility for the emotional makeup such actions express. Yet, as we have seen, this difference can only exist if we make asymmetrical assumptions about the two theories: namely, we stick the choice theorist with a narrow view of choosing agency while we allow the character theorist the broad view of character. Whereas if we allow each theorist the most plausible assumptions about what choosing and character include, this difference disappears.

One last nuance in our usage of "character" needs attention here in order to keep clear the real differences that do exist between the two theories. Sometimes our talk of character is not about character *traits* or *attributes;* indeed, such talk does not use "character" to name universals of any kind. Rather, we talk of characters doing things, and what we mean to designate is some particular agency. . . .

. . . If "character" simply names our choosing agency, then responsibility for character is simply responsibility for choice, and there is no debate to have about which is the correct theory of responsibility. For the two theories to be as different as they seem to be, there must be a metaphysical difference between that aspect of our selves we call our character and that part we call our agency of choice. One can heighten the difference between the two theories by claiming that either character or will *constitutes* the self exclusive of the other; to maintain any difference at all between the two theories, however, one must see a metaphysical difference between character and will.

If we are clear about what character is, we next need to inquire whether and in what sense we can be *responsible* for our characters. One debate a choice theorist could have with a character theorist about the excuses is whether there is a responsibility for character at all.[1] If there is not, if there is only responsibility for actions, then the excuses cannot have as their function the isolation of actions expressing bad character; if one is not responsible for one's character, then responsibility for action cannot be derivative of that responsibility.

This route to denying the character theory of excuse (by denying the character

---

[1] This appears to be the point at which Nicola Lacey believes the two theories of excuse diverge. See Lacey, *State Punishment,* (London: Routledge, 1988), p. 68.

conception of responsibility that lies behind it) is not one I adopt. For I think it is obvious that, in some sense, we are responsible for being the kind of people that we are—i.e., for our characters.

There is room for disagreement as to exactly how, and in what sense, we are each responsible for our characters. With regard to the "how" question, there are two possibilities: (1) we are responsible for our characters because we *choose* to become persons with such character, or (2) we are responsible for our characters because we *are* (at least in part) our characters. The first possibility, of course, collapses the character conception of responsibility back into a choice conception of responsibility. . . .

Despite the distinguished lineage of this first view in Aristotle, there are two reasons to doubt its correctness. One is an empirical worry: do we really have much capacity to mold our characters? We do have some such capacity. We do form "second-order desires" or "ego-ideals" about what kind of person we would like to become, and we have some causal power to effect changes in ourselves in conformity with such desires or ideals. Yet the social science on this issue gives little encouragement to thinking we have much of this power.

Secondly, there is a conceptual worry: who is the "he" who is choosing character? Does he himself have any character, and, if so, was it chosen too? To the character theorist who grounds responsibility for choice and action in responsibility for character, a characterless chooser is an odd legitimator of responsibility for the character he chooses; yet a chooser of character who already possesses character before he chooses invites an infinite regress.

One might attempt to alleviate both these worries by what might be called the weak Aristotelian view. This view concedes that our characters are formed initially by processes over which we have little choice or control; however, our responsibility for character comes from our later choices to *maintain* these already formed character traits. . . .

The weak Aristotelian view at least sounds empirically more plausible. Even so, the weak view cannot accommodate all the attributes of self that intuitively are the proper subject of moral judgement. Take the emotions, for example. There seems very little that we can do about willing our emotions into or out of being. . . . Yet we do hold people responsible for their emotional makeup, including the presence or absence of particular emotions on particular occasions. This inclines me to think that it is the second possibility that captures our responsibility for our character: we are responsible for our character because we are, in part, constituted by our characters. . . .

. . . Although I have just rejected the claim that moral judgments about character are merely a disguised form of moral judgments about choice, that rejection says nothing in favor of the claim that moral judgments about choice are merely a disguised form of moral judgments about character. And it is this latter claim that the character theorist about excuse must establish.

Before we assess this crucial claim of the character theorist on its moral merits, we have one last clarifactory question to explore about the claim itself. This is the question of the sort of relationship that the character theorist asserts to exist between character and action that makes an actor responsible for action. The character theory of excuse variously asserts that we are excused from responsibility for our actions when those actions do not *manifest, express, reveal,* or *indicate* bad character; when such actions are not the *result* of, not *determined by, explained by,* or are not *attributed to* bad characters; when such actions are not an *exercise* of a character defect; or when such actions are not *evidentiary of* bad character. We need to be clearer about what is meant by these expressions.

Three different sorts of relations might be meant by them. The first would be a logical relation between character and actions that are "in character." On this view, the relation between someone's greedy action on a particular occasion and his greedy character is the logical relation between a particular and the universal that it instantiates. Such a view of the relation commits one to a behavioral view of what character is, and that is sufficient reason for the character theorist to avoid it.

Preferable on this ground is a second view of the relation, which is that it is a causal relation. A greedy action, on this view, is in character for a person only if that action was caused by that person's greedy character. This view of the relation presupposes a nonbehavioral view of what character is, but that is a virtue—not a defect—of this relational view. There is a problem with this second view, however; it stems from the non-discriminating nature of the causal relation. Greedy character in a person can cause any number of behaviors besides greedy actions. My greed can cause my heart rate to go up (e.g., I get excited when I see large amounts of money). It can cause overtly generous behavior (e.g., Bulstrode in *Middlemarch,* who compensates for his greediness by overtly generous behavior). Indeed, any given character trait can probably cause virtually any kind of behavior on a given occasion. For example, suppose Van Gogh was greedy; his greed could have caused him to cut off his ear (e.g., by way of punishment of himself for not being paid enough for a picture).

. . . [T]he character theorist has need of a more discriminating relation. The evidentiary relation is his best bet. Some act A will evidence some trait C if and only if not only C causes A, but also states of type C typically cause events of type A. Effects are evidence of their causes only when there is some general connection between the *class* of events that includes the effect and the *class* of events that includes the cause. Evidentiary inference is the more discriminating relation sought by the character theorist. Then acts of refusing to give to charities, forcing poor debtors to pay, paying employees as little as possible, etc., are acts "in character" for the greedy person; lopping off one's ear, or giving away all of one's money, are not acts "in character" for some greedy person even if they happen on some occasion to be caused by his greed.

This last clarification allows us to pinpoint what are and are not the differences between the two theories of excuse. . . .

The difference between the two theories has to be in the kinds of causes of action they each find to be the touchstone of responsibility: character or choice. Whether there is any difference between the two theories boils down to the question of whether there is any difference between a person's character and his choices. On the assumption that choices are possible only if a person has and exercises a choosing agency (will), the question is whether there is a difference between a person having a character and a person having a will. The evidentiary relation just discussed seems to isolate just such a difference: any action evidences the possession of a will, because a will can typically will anything and still be a will. But as we have seen, while a character *can* cause any action, to be possessed of a character precludes the possibility that one's character can *typically* cause any class of actions equally well. Characters, to be characters, can only typically cause some classes of actions, but not others. Character in this sense is inherently general, requiring typical causal connections to classes of actions; will and the choices that issue from it are in this sense particular, being equally capable of causing any particular act and not being tied to any general class of actions.

Perhaps the place to start in assessing the moral merits of the two theories of excuse is with the main arguments put forward by the character theorists in favor of their theory. Unfortunately, of the five main arguments, four are irrelevant to the moral issue I wish to raise. . . .

One is the argument that proceeds from utilitarian (or, more broadly, consequentialist) theories of punishment. . . . Briefly, the argument is that the preventive goals of punishment do not require its infliction on those whose actions have not manifested bad character, because such persons are not dangerous nor can their punishment have any significant deterrent effect. It is not clear to me that the character theory of excuse would better serve crime-prevention goals than would the choice theory. But in any case, the argument for me is a non-starter since it proceeds from an unacceptable theory of punishment.

A second argument, one that also does not address the moral issue about excuses focused for us by the mixed and retributivist theories of punishment, is the argument of Michael Bayles and others which is designed to show how well the character theory fits the legal excuses that presently exist in American law. This is an exercise in doctrinal exegesis that is relevant to deciding what theory of excuse our present law comes closest to instantiating. It is not an exercise capable of answering the normative question of which theory of excuse our law ought to recognize.

A third argument in favor of the character theory is by far the major consideration which in fact motivates character theorists to adopt their theory. This is the argument that proceeds from hard determinist premises. The assumption is that the choice conception of responsibility is in trouble because it is hostage to the questionable truth of libertarian (Strawson: "panicky") metaphysics; if determinism turns out to be true, the choice conception is assumed to have the unhappy implication that no one is responsible for anything. Whereas, the character theorist thinks, responsibility can be preserved by his theory even in the face of determination. So long as he rejects Aristotle's notion that we are responsible for our characters because we choose them, and sticks to the idea that we are responsible for our characters because we are our characters, he escapes any threat from determinism. For his idea of responsibility does not depend on an actor's choices being free. Rather, he can happily admit that responsible choices are caused by character, and that character in turn is caused by factors not themselves chosen by the actor. By *his* idea of responsibility, the actor is responsible for any actions in character just because he is his character. This is known in the trade as the "character-stop" answer to determinism.

There is nothing wrong with the character-stop strategy. This is why that part of morality known as the theory of the virtues is not hostage to the falsity of determinism. However, the character theorist overlooks the fact that the choice conception of responsibility has an answer just as good to the hard determinist: we are at least in part the agency that chooses whether to act or not; that agency's choices can themselves exist even if caused by factors external to the will; it would make choice a very peculiar event if it has to be uncaused in order to exist; there is no persuasive argument showing that choices have this peculiar feature; and the fact that some people find such argument persuasive can be explained in ways having nothing to do with the truth of the arguments in question. . . .

A fourth argument for the character theory proceeds from a very general intellectual fashion prevalent today. This I have elsewhere called "interpretivism." Briefly, the idea is that moral questions (if not the explanatory questions of social and even natural science) are interpretive questions, questions that seek the best interpretation of various social practices. To ask what responsibility is, or when a person is responsible, is to ask what the best interpretation of the "blaming stories" prevalent in our society might be. The character theory of excuse appears to be favored by interpretivists because such a theory requires "more story" than does the choice theory. That is, to see whether an action expresses the agent's character requires a longer, more complete narration of what sort of person, in general, he is; whereas to see whether an action was freely chosen by an agent seemingly requires a more limited enquiry into his capacities and opportunities at the moment of acting.

It is hard to get a handle on just what this argument comes to. Even if one's metaethics commits one to viewing moral reasoning as storytelling and [story]/retelling, why should one prefer "more story"? Are not "short stories" an appropriate genre? The interpretivists here sounds like the psychiatrists of the 1950s who criticized the M'Naughten definition of insanity on the ground that it did not allow them to tell their psychiatric stories. In both cases, we should like to know why the stories someone wants to tell are better because they are closer to some relevant truth.

It is a fifth kind of argument in favor of the character theory of excuse that raises the relevant issues. Consider George Fletcher's nonutilitarian appreciation of the need for this kind of argument:

> An inference from the wrongful act to the actor's character is essential to a retributive theory of punishment. A fuller statement of the argument would go like this: (1) punishing wrongful conduct is just only if punishment is measured by the desert of the offender, (2) the desert of the offender is gauged by his character—i.e., the kind of person he is, (3) and therefore, a judgment about character is essential to the just distribution of punishment.

It is the second premise, of course, that the character theorist must defend.

. . . Nicola Lacey presents some defense of this essential premise. She defends the moral view that "it is unfair to hold people responsible for actions which are out of character . . .[;] fair to hold them so for actions in which their settled dispositions are centrally expressed." In order to test the moral correctness of these conclusions, we should construct examples of two kinds: (1) an actor freely chooses to do wrong (i.e., he had the capacity and a fair opportunity not to so choose), and yet the action is "out of character" for that actor; (2) an actor's behavior is good evidence for a settled disposition (character) of a bad kind, and yet he has not (yet) chosen to act on that disposition. If Lacey is right, we ought to find it fair to punish the second but not the first, because the first but not the second has a moral excuse. However, I shall contend that we rightly find it fair to punish the first but not the second, because we rightly think the second but not the first to have a moral excuse.

Character theorists have two responses to such examples. They might deny that someone . . . is culpable. Or they could deny that . . . action was really out of character. I shall first deal with the second kind of response. . . .

. . . [T]he character theorist has to be careful here, lest "hidden character defect" become her label for "free choice." "Character," as we have seen, has to mean something considerably more general than merely a disposition to do the particular act done—on pain of this kind of collapse of the character theory into the choice theory.

. . . Lacey elaborates that the criminal law should "treat seriously the individuality and sense of identity of each citizen by responding punitively only to actions which are genuinely expressive of the actor's relevant disposition: with which the agent truly identifies, and can call her own." If this means what it seems to mean—what I have called the metaphysical intuition that actions we do are not *our* actions unless they are in character for us—then it is hostage to a very problematic theory of personal identity. This is the theory that holds character to swamp both spatiotemporal contiguity and unified consciousness as the touchstone of personal identity. On this theory, we are only our character, a conclusion that has two startling implications. First, when "we" radically change our character over time, we literally become someone else—not just another kind of person, but a different person. Second, multiple-personalitied persons are not single persons with multiple characters; they are rather many persons with one character each. This allowance of the possibility that many persons can inhabit one body—either over time or even at one time—raises havoc with some basic metaphysical, moral, and legal ideas that are difficult to imagine giving up. One of the those ideas is just the sort of thing Lacey is apparently willing to abandon: namely, how we individuate and attribute basic actions to persons. Normally we do this by the body involved in the action: one movement by one body, one basic action. . . . [W]e should not think of character as exclusively constituting the identity of persons—and if we do not think this, then we cannot think that an action out of character is no action of ours.

. . . I now turn to the second kind of example, where there is behavior revealing bad character, but no free choice to do wrong.

. . . May someone . . . fairly be punished even though he has done nothing wrong?

The question is a hard one for the character theorist. After all, he thinks that we are ultimately responsible for our characters and that action-responsibility is only a derivative of this more basic character-responsibility. If this is true, then why not punish people directly for bad character, since that is the locus of their just deserts? Why punish bad character indirectly, only through punishing actions expressive of it? George Fletcher seeks to answer this question in terms of a value distinct from the justice of the guilty getting their just deserts: namely, privacy.

. . . But our moral question has only to do with the *fairness* of dispensing with the *actus reus* requirement. That punishment would be *deserved* because of bad character alone is something the character theorist seems committed to, however much other values prevent punishment of this class of deserving persons.

. . . [N]o one deserves to be punished for being a poor specimen of humanity. The aesthetic kind of responsibility that we admittedly do have for so much of our characters as are unchosen cannot fairly lead to punishment, because we could not have avoided possessing these aspects of ourselves. . . .

Responsibility for negligence *is* difficult to square with the choice conception of responsibility for the obvious reason that a negligent actor does not choose to do the complex act (such as killing) that is forbidden. True, such an actor does choose to do some basic action, such as moving his finger on the trigger of his gun; and it also may be true that he chooses to do more complex acts (such as hitting a target) through his doing of the basic act of moving his finger. But in the sense of choice earlier described, he does not choose to do the complex action forbidden by morality and law (such as killing the man standing behind the target) because his mind was not adverting to that aspect of his action.

. . . What makes the intentional or reckless wrongdoer so culpable is not unexercised capacity—although that is necessary—but the way such capacity to avoid evil goes unexercised; such wrongdoers are not even trying to get it right. Their capacity goes unexercised because that is what they choose. Choice is essential to their culpability, not one way among others that they could have been seriously culpable.

Does this mean that when we blame for negligence we blame for character (the second of the character theorist's two claims here)? Interestingly enough, although the choice theorist cannot easily accommodate responsibility for negligence, neither can the character theorist. For the character theorist must bridge two gaps in order to link her theory with responsibility for negligence. The first is the gap between the failure of a negligent actor to advert to the risk that made his action negligent *at the time of that action,* on the one hand, and the *general tendency* of such an actor to be inadvertent about such risks, on the other. . . . Put simply, judgments of negligence don't depend on any general traits of carelessness; an isolated act of negligence suffices for responsibility for the harm that act causes.

The second gap is between the actor who does "systematically, characteristically make unreasonable mistakes" and the bad character of such an actor. . . . But one can be careless—even characteristically so—without having a bad character in this sense. Such carelessness can be due to awkwardness and stupidity as easily as indifference. And, again, we blame for carelessness irrespective of *why* one is careless.

Thus responsibility for negligence fits poorly with either conception of responsibility. . . .

Negligence does not exhaust the kinds of moral thought-experiments the character theorist might use to support her theory. . . .

In thinking through such thought-experiments, two things should be borne in mind. One is that it is not enough to show that *usually* an inference of bad character can (or cannot) be drawn when moral excuse fails (or succeeds). A theory of excuse has to do better than this, and tell us what it is that always makes us responsible and, in its absence, always excuses us. Secondly, it is not enough to show the presence or absence of bad character whenever an excuse fails or succeeds; one must also show that the presence or absence of bad choice does not stand in that same relation to the excuse in question. After all, bad choices are usually made by bad people, and bad people usually make a lot of bad choices, so it shouldn't be surprising if the two theories overlap greatly when they excuse. Still, they do not always excuse in the same situations. Moreover, even when both theories yield the same conclusions about responsibility, it is important that we understand the reasons on which these conclusions are based. If I am right [,] . . . we excuse because culpable choice is lacking, not because the action fails to manifest bad character.

NOTES AND QUESTIONS

1. One of the most perplexing questions is why the law provides any excuses. The puzzle can be explored from two directions. This first is based on consequential objections. For example, why should the law exculpate any unjustified agent who behaves antisocially? Shouldn't such offenders be locked away to insure the public safety and to deter anyone who might offend from thinking that the possibility of a successful excusing claim reduces the risk of conviction and punishment? The obvious answer is that some offenders are not responsible and don't deserve punishment, even if they commit crimes. This leads to the second objection, the argument from a determinist account of the universe that suggests that determinism and genuine responsibility are incompatible. So, even if the law's view is that we are choosing creatures and that choice is the basis of responsibility, isn't this account mistaken? How can the law fairly hold anyone accountable as a moral agent? Morse suggests the most common principled defense, which argues that determinism or universal causation and responsibility are compatible, but compatibilist accounts are themselves controversial. As a recent commentator puts it, "Understanding how free will is possible is perhaps the most vexing of the traditional problems of philosophy."[1]

On the entirely plausible assumption that this problem will not be "solved" anytime soon, if indeed it is soluble at all, how should the law respond? The standard pragmatic response is to claim that responsibility is a necessary fiction that the law must adopt. But can it be just to blame and punish people on grounds that are admittedly fictive? If one is willing to adopt such a consequentialist approach, why not adopt a pure consequentialism that jettisons responsibility altogether? Defenders of the standard view respond that compatibilism is not subject to an uncontroversially destructive counterargument and they believe it is right. Consequently, they are morally entitled to premise ascriptions of responsibility on that basis. What does seem clear, however, is that if determinism or universal causation is a relevant consideration, it should excuse everyone or no one.

2. The importance of the causation issues has arisen frequently in recent years as more and more alleged causes of criminal conduct are propounded, many of which are arguably syndromes of mental abnormality. Examples are battered spouse syn-

[2] Timothy O'Connor, "Introduction," in T. O'Connor, ed., *Agents, Causes, and Events* (Oxford: Oxford University Press, 1995) p.3.

drome, abused child syndrome, urban survival syndrome, and the like. Although these alleged conditions have different scientific validities, the claims they foster are similar. In each case, the defendant claims that the criminal behavior was the product of the syndrome and the defendant should therefore be excused. But what is the basis of this claim? If it is that a cause excuses, we know this is mistaken, both theoretically and descriptively. The theoretical objection was described in note 1 above. The descriptive objection comes from traditional, insanity defense claims. Many mentally disordered defendants can demonstrate that disorder was part of the causal chain that produced their crimes, but not all of them succeed with the defense, because causation is not the basis of the excuse. What is needed are a convincing account of what conditions should excuse and evidence that the new syndromes are relevant.

3. The excusing conditions accepted by the law and ordinary morality alike are based on the standard view of human behavior addressed in Chapter 3—that is, that human beings are capable of rational, practical reasoning. But this observation does not take one very far. As the selections demonstrate, the excusing conditions can be based on "thin" or "thick" accounts of what it means to be a rational, practical reasoner. Arenella objects to versions of rationality that ask simply whether the defendant was narrowly in touch with reality, reasoned instrumentally logically, and exercised a "choice." In addition, he suggests that the capacity for genuine moral evaluation of one's conduct is a necessary part of the definition of rationality and responsibility. Is he right? Should psychopaths be excused: Has he gone far enough? Should even more capabilities be included within rationality and responsibility? How does one decide which capabilities should be included?

4. A currently active, related debate is whether responsibility analysis should focus on the offender's specific criminal offense or on the offender's character. Thinner views of responsibility tend to focus on the act, thicker ones on the character. Those who adopt the former view believe that the characteristics of the offense are a sufficient warrant for punishment. They claim that the character theory requires too much for responsibility, often collapses into the act theory, or results in unwarranted inferences or mitigation. Moore provides an excellent analysis of the issues. Once again, however, it is apparent that one's underlying normative theory crucially determines the outcome. This is why "foundations" are so important: deriving a comprehensive, coherent view requires an adequate defense of one's underlying commitments. Starting with intuitions about act and character is fine, but the next step of justifying those intuitions is harder and more important.

Do the different theories of justification for punishment suggest different outcomes of the act versus character debate? Can either be justified by all the theories of punishment?

5. Should the law conform to the ordinary person's perception of appropriate excusing conditions, even if this perception appears misguided? For example, suppose that people tend to believe that a particular cause is an excuse and thus tend to excuse any time that variable can be identified as a cause of the offender's conduct.

Remember that this is almost certainly a conceptual mistake. The criminal law may gain legitimacy by appearing congruent with peoples' expectations and practices, but is that legitimacy bought at too high a price? Should the lawmaker throw up his or her hands and simply go along with popular sentiment for fear of losing that legitimacy? What is the alternative? This issue arises in every substantive criminal law context. For an attempt to discover empirically what common expectations are and how congruent they are with the criminal law's doctrines, see Paul Robinson and John Darley *Justice, Liability & Blame* (Boulder, CO: Westview, 1995). They argue that if the law is too incongruent with the common person's expectations, the law should yield. If careful reflection leads the lawmaker to believe that the common expectations are misguided, however, how can a rational legislator support laws that will blame and punish or fail to excuse people based on a misguided conception of justice?

6. What excusing conditions do you think the law should adopt? Should they be defined to permit acquittal readily or under limited circumstances? What answers do the different theories of punishment suggest?

5.4 EXCUSE: DURESS

Duress as Justification

JOSHUA DRESSLER

Why does coercion exculpate? More precisely, does society acquit persons who act under duress because their actions were *justifiable,* or is it that we *excuse* them—render them personally blameless—for their unjustifiable conduct?

Lesser-Harm Justification Theory

Professors LaFave and Scott consider duress a justification. Their statement seems intended merely as a description of the common law. In the paradigmatic case, D commits a crime short of homicide because of an imminent deadly threat by C. Under these circumstances, commission of the crime is a lesser evil or social harm than that threatened. D's conduct is, therefore justifiable.

By this view, duress lacks any independent force as a defense. It is simply a special version of the justification defense of necessity, special only because the circumstances were produced by a human rather than a natural force. The moral rea-

From "Duress as Justification," *Southern California Law Review,* Vol. 62, 1989, pp. 1331–1386.

soning (whether utilitarian or nonconsequentialist) that justifies performing a lesser evil in the latter case would similarly justify the coerced actor to accede to the threat.

This explanation of duress is unsatisfactory. . . .

Not all common law duress cases involve the commission of the lesser evil. Duress exculpates not only when the actor is threatened with death, but also when the actor accedes to a threat of serious bodily injury. The actor can be acquitted although the actor has caused equal or slightly greater harm than was threatened. For example, suppose that C threatens to cut off D's arm unless D rapes V. Presumably, D will be acquitted for of rape; yet it is unlikely that the exculpatory force of the case depends on the analysis of whether the loss of an arm or rape is the greater evil.

Or, suppose the harm threatened is precisely the same as the harm commanded: D must cut off V's right arm or else lose his own right appendage. The harm is equal, and the defense applies. Yet, the usual view is that conduct is not justified (although excusable) unless it prevents a greater, not simply an equal, harm. . . .

If the lesser-harm theory does not adequately explain our reaction to cases of duress (or, at least, not to all cases), is there another, more satisfying, explanation to justify committing an otherwise criminal act as the result of coercion, *even when the harm caused by the coerced actor is equal to, or greater than, that threatened by the coercer?* The answer depends in part on one's understanding of the concept of justification. If one believes that a justified act "typically reflects well on the actor's courage or devotion to the public interest," duress hardly qualifies as a justification defense. But, this view of justification is surely too narrow; it could not even justify most cases of self-defense.

It is also difficult to justify compelled conduct if, as many scholars assert, justifications are truly universal principles (i.e., if A is objectively the right thing to do, anyone should be justified in doing A, or assisting another to do A), and, further, incompatible justifications are necessarily impossible (i.e., no one can be justified in resisting the commission of justified act A). Therefore, notice the implications of the universalization-incompatibility view of justification. If coerced actor D is justified in raping V to protect his child from serious harm or death, it necessarily would be justifiable for X, a stranger, to rape V, in order to protect D's child, or for X to assist D in raping V by holding a knife at V's throat. Consequently, it would also be unjustifiable for V forcibly to resist the attack. It is unlikely that such conclusions satisfy ordinary moral intuitions. If so, then the initial premise justifying coerced conduct should be questioned.

The conclusion that duress is not based on justification analysis may be correct, but the universalizability-incompatibility premise, which is thought to support the conclusion, is incorrect. Justifications can be agent-relative. In another context, it is not morally incoherent for society to permit an on-duty police officer to use deadly force in self-defense without retreating to a place of known safety because he acts in our behest, while society often denies the same justification to a nonretreating private person who acts solely in self-defense. Indeed, many criminal codes take precisely this position.

Similarly, a limited, intellectually coherent argument for a nonuniversizable version of duress as a justification is possible, and has been suggested. The duress-as-justification argument is based on the general principle that, at least within certain limits, self-interested conduct, even when it results in equal or greater social harm, is morally permissible.

On this theory, it would be morally justifiable for a person to value his own interests, or perhaps that of a family member, over the equivalent interests of a stranger, although a noninterested person and society would value the interests equally. For example, under this theory D could justifiably kill V to avoid his own death because D may value his own life over V's, although society would treat the losses as equal. Or, D could justifiably kidnap V, rather than allow C to kidnap D's child, although the harms again are equal. Yet, in each of these cases, X, a third person unrelated to D, would not be justified in committing or assisting in the intended crime.

It cannot be gainsaid that such a moral position is plausible. Even if it is accepted, it would have rather limited applicability. First, and most obviously, it does not apply to the case where a coerced person causes harm to an innocent person in order to protect a stranger from less harm. Such conduct ordinarily exculpates, so one must look elsewhere to explain such a rule.

Second, it is likely that few who would justify self-interested conduct are willing to take the theory to its logical conclusion. Some people might only permit an actor to cause rather minor harm to another to protect himself from similar or lesser harm. For example, D is arguably justified in pushing V in order to avoid a similar battery threatened by C, wrongdoing that results from coercive nonhuman threats or from poor socioeconomic conditions. These three situations—kill-or-be-killed threats, coercive natural conditions, and environmentally induced crime—raise a more general question: In light of the underlying rationale of the excuse, what are the proper outer limits of the defense?

At the outset, certain overarching considerations that ought to go into the line drawing process deserve brief attention. First, and most simply, it must be remembered that since duress is a normative excuse reasonable minds can and will differ regarding its proper boundaries. Hence, this author cannot suggest that the lines drawn below are beyond fair controversy. Second, line drawing in duress cases is a highly sensitive matter. The rules of duress say something very important about the actor (i.e., that the actor is, or is not, a person of reasonable moral strength) as well as the characteristics of the hypothetical objective person to whom the actor is compared (i.e., the degree of moral strength that human beings may fairly be expected to manifest). In setting standards, therefore, we need to be honest about our weaknesses and optimistic about our strengths. We must avoid unfairly stigmatizing persons who find themselves in compelling circumstances by setting standards too high, yet we must not demean ourselves by setting standards that are too low. We need to avoid the conflicting evils of hypocrisy and overzealousness, on the one hand, and moral abstention, on the other.

First, we must refrain from acting hypocritically. In the realm of duress, hypocrisy is the result of holding others to a standard of moral strength to which we would not hold ourselves if we were similarly situated. The MPC Commentary makes this point, albeit inartfully, when it warns that:

> [T]he law is ineffective in the deepest sense, indeed . . . it is hypocritical, if it imposes
> on the actor who has the misfortune to confront a dilemmatic choice, a standard that

his judges are not prepared to affirm that they should and could comply with if their turn to face the problem should arise. Condemnation in such a case . . . is unjust.

But, as wrong as hypocrisy is, the MPC drafters have overstated the problem with regard to duress cases. It is not inevitably hypocritical for a juror to concede that most people in the same situation, including the juror, would have acted as the defendant did, yet still believe that the coerced actor deserves to be punished. As long as the juror believes that the juror also would be deserving of punishment (and, presumably, would accept it) in the same situation, there is no hypocrisy. We avoid duplicity by only blaming others when we are prepared to blame ourselves.

But, *should* we blame others whenever we would blame ourselves? If we do, we run a second risk: overzealous or even self-righteous use of the criminal law. The criminal law is not intended to correlate perfectly with our personal moral values. More specifically, the introspective form of guilt persons are apt to feel when they do something wrong should not be treated as a perfect measure of the criminal law's denunciatory version of guilt. Most of us are harder on ourselves than we are on those around us. We attempt to live virtuous lives. We are apt to reproach ourselves when we fail to live up to our highest moral standards. Although we cannot be perfect, we try to be, and feel guilty when we fail. We do not excuse our shortcomings.

However, the criminal law is not perfectionistic. It sets only minimum standards of conduct. It does not, nor should it, function as the moral police, requiring us, upon threat of death or loss of liberty and resulting stigma, to act virtuously. Thus, although in the general run of cases we should expect excuse law to conform roughly with our feelings about blame and guilt, a perfect relationship should not be expected. In some cases, it is proper for the law to excuse me, although I do not excuse myself. We should set criminal law standards of conduct somewhat *below* the level to which we tend to hold ourselves in our private lives.

Nevertheless, we also should avoid the conflicting danger of setting standards too low or, even worse, abstaining entirely from expressing moral judgments of others. Our compassion for the coerced actor should not cause us to treat human beings as if they cannot be expected to demonstrate a reasonable degree of moral courage. Nor should we fall prey to the idea that because we share a moral fault with the actor (namely, our mutual lack of absolute moral strength), and because the difference between us and the wrongdoer may simply be a matter of moral luck, that it is not "our business" to blame the actor, or that we should be "cleaning our own house first."

Notice the significance of the latter argument. It is *not* a claim that the coerced wrongdoer is not blameworthy. It is not an argument to excuse. Rather, it is an argument against imperfect people throwing stones at other imperfect wrongdoers. It suggests that those who would judge the wrongdoer lack the moral standing to do so or, at least, should voluntarily abstain from invoking their standing. If accepted in the context of the criminal law, its effect is not to have us draw liberal lines of excuse, but to draw no lines at all.

Society will not do that, nor should it. As long as we remain mindful of our connection to the wrongdoer, including our shared fallibilities, it is not unseemly for us to set reasonable, minimal standards of personal responsibility (standards to which, lest we forget, we are willing to be held ourselves), codify them in our criminal codes, and punish those who fail to live up to them.

NOTES AND QUESTIONS

1. Consider the following case. Master Sergeant William Olsen was captured during the Korean war by the Communist forces in late 1950 and taken to the Kangye prisoner of war camp. There the Chinese who ran the camp set out to educate him and his fellow prisoners as to the "true" nature of the war, namely, "that they [the prisoners] were the victims of the warmongers and were the aggressors in Korea." The education was in no way haphazard. It was systematic and relentless, involving countless hours of lecturing, group discussion, and interrogation. The Chinese called this treatment of the POWs "lenient policy," because it was short on threats and long on "persuasion." Over the course of the war, it proved remarkably successful. It got American POWs to do things the Germans had never gotten them to do. They informed on each other, frustrated each others' escape attempts, and in one way or another almost all collaborated with the enemy.

The capstone of the Chinese strategy was "start small and build," which the psychologist Robert Cialdini describes thus:

> Prisoners were frequently asked to make statements so mildly anti-American or pro-Communist as to seem inconsequential. ("The United States is not perfect." "In a Communist country, unemployment is not a problem.") But once these minor requests were complied with, the men found themselves pushed to submit to related yet more substantive requests. A man who had just agreed with this Chinese interrogator that the United States is not perfect might then be asked to make a list of these "problems with America" and to sign his name to it. Later he might be asked to read his list in a discussion group with other prisoners. "After all, it's what you believe, isn't it?" Still later, he might be asked to write an essay expanding on his list and discussing these problems in greater detail.
>
> The Chinese might then use his name and his essay in an anti-American radio broadcast beamed not only to the entire camp but to other POW camps in North Korea as well as to American forces in South Korea. Suddenly he would find himself a "collaborator," having given aid and comfort to the enemy. Aware that he had written the essay without any strong threats or coercion, many times a man would change his image of himself to be consistent with the deed and with the new "collaborator" label, often resulting in even more extensive acts of collaboration.[1]

On Christmas Day of 1950 Olsen and his fellow prisoners were assembled for a Christmas party and bullied into making some speeches. Olsen was one of those who spoke. He noted that the Communists were treating their prisoners better than the Germans did theirs during World War II. He also said that the Korean War was a "millionaire's war and that the prisoners had innocent blood on their hands." Later Olsen and some other prisoners were moved to a camp for newly arrived POWs. Olsen would greet the new arrivals by telling them "how to get along with" the Communists, "that escape was impossible, that the Chinese were not guards but were there to pro-

---

1. Robert Cialdini, *Influence: The New Psychology of Persuasion* (New York: William Morrow, 1984), 76.

tect the prisoners from the Koreans, and [that] they, the prisoners, had been cannon fodder for the imperialists and warmongers." He contributed articles to some POW publications, lauding the Communists' treatment of POWs and saying that America "was engaged in an imperialistic war to fatten certain capitalists and that the blood of innocent victims was on the hands of Americans." After the war Olsen was charged with aiding the enemy. His main defense: "They made me do it. I wasn't myself." Should he be convicted?[2]

2. *United States v. Olsen,* 20 C.M.R. 461 (1955).

5.5 EXCUSE: MENTAL ABNORMALITY

The Abolition of the Special Defense of Insanity

NORVAL MORRIS

Abolition of the defense of insanity has received exhaustive attention in the literature; the informed reader is entitled, therefore, to be notified of where the argument leads so that he may avoid the sharper irritations of redundancy. In accordance with the thesis of separation of the mental health law and the criminal-law powers to incarcerate, I propose the abolition of the special defense of insanity. . . .

The problem is to cut through the accumulated cases, commentaries, and confusions to the issues of principle underlying the responsibility of the mentally ill for conduct otherwise criminal. The issues are basically legal, moral, and political, not medical or psychological, though, of course, the developing insights of psychiatry and psychology are of close relevance to those legal, moral, and political issues.

A glance at the history of the common-law relationship between guilt and mental illness may help to structure the discussion. Until the nineteenth century, criminal-law doctrines of mens rea (criminal intent) handled the entire problem. Evidence of mental illness was admitted on the question of intent, and as the infant discipline of psychiatry claimed an increased understanding of mental processes, such evidence on the question of intent grew in importance. Psychiatrists, then generally known as "alienists" (separating, alienating, the citizen from the community because of mental illness), claimed increasing competence to classify, explain the origins, and predict the course of mental illnesses, with and without diverse treatment interventions. The dramatic events of major criminal trials became important battlegrounds for psychiatry and psychiatrists, public dramatic ceremonials in which professional standing

From *Madness and the Criminal Law* (Chicago: University of Chicago Press, 1982), pp. 53–64.

was proclaimed and tested. Inexorably, conflict developed between the disciplines of law and psychiatry with their distinct supporting epistemologies, the language and concepts of the law—free will, moral choice, guilt, and innocence—confronting those of psychiatry—determinism, degrees of cognitive and volitional control, classification of diseases, and definition of treatments. Complicating these inherent confrontations were the different consequences of the application of the two competing systems: the binary system of the law, guilt or innocence, and, if the former, punishment to close the equation; the continuum of psychiatry, degrees of illness and opportunities for "cure," to be determined in the last resort only by the fact of nondestructive life in the community.

In a multipurposive society these epistemological and purposive differences between law and psychiatry are to be welcomed, but they carried, and still carry, the seeds of confusion. The pre-*McNaughtan* position was correct and clear: the psychiatrist could contribute useful evidentiary insights to the issues correctly defined by the common law of crime—did the accused intend the prohibited harm? But by the time of *McNaughtan* (1843) this clear position was frustrated by the increasing tendency of lawyers, psychiatrists, public opinion, and legislators to turn questions of evidence into matters of substance, to transmute medical evidence about legal issues into substantive legal rules. *McNaughtan* was just such a substantive rule, confusing the evidence for a proposition with the proposition itself.

How would the pre-nineteenth-century position now stand, taking into account advances in the discipline of psychiatry? The sick mind of the accused would be relevant to his guilt since he may, because of sickness, have lacked the state of mind required for conviction of the offense with which he has been charged or of any other offense of which he may be convicted on such a charge (in the language of the trade, "lesser included offenses"). If guilty of such a crime, his sick mind is relevant to fair sentencing. If innocent, that is all the criminal law has to do with the matter—though, of course, like any other citizen he may be civilly committed if he is mentally ill and is a danger to himself or others or is incapable of caring for himself. On many of these issues the psychiatrist has useful insights; on none should psychiatry frame the operative rule, define the dividing line between guilt and innocence, between detention and freedom. Whenever this happens, the law is perverted in practice, and psychiatry is brought into disrepute. The English and American judges went wrong in the nineteenth century; it is time we returned to older and truer principles.

I must stress that in advocating the abolition of the special defense of insanity, the nuances of difference among the *McNaughtan* Rules, the *Durham* Rule, the rules offered by the American Law Institute and accepted in *Brawner* and in many state criminal codes, the irresistible impulse test, the recommendations of the Group for the Advancement of Psychiatry, and other suggested special defenses, though important in practice and meriting close analysis, are not essential to the present discussion. All vary around the following structure: a definition of mental illness, as a threshold to the invocation of the defense, and a statement of a required causal relationship between that "mental illness" and the otherwise criminal behavior of the accused. My thesis stands, whatever definition of illness and whatever language to capture a causal relationship are offered. And, of course, variations on where the burdens of proof are placed on those two issues, and on how heavy are those burdens, are also irrelevant.

It would be a mistake to read these dogmatisms as an attack on psychiatry. The lawyers have been quite content to strap a mattress to the back of any psychiatrist willing to appear in court to answer questions like: at the time of the killing did the accused "know the nature and quality of the act"? did he "know that it was wrong"? did he have "substantial capacity to appreciate the criminality of his conduct"? did he have "substantial capacity to control his conduct"? Wiser psychiatrists and those not tempted by the bright focus of public interest have avoided these philosophically impossible questions. Nor does it assist materially to direct the psychiatrist to give information to the jury to help them answer these elusive questions but to avoid offering answers himself, since it is the questions themselves that are philosophically in error that pretend to a precision beyond present knowledge.

Why, then, go beyond the simple rule, to give mental illness the same exculpatory effect as, say, blindness or deafness? Evidence of the latter afflictions may be admitted as indicative of lack of both the *actus reus* (prohibited act) and the mens rea of a crime. Why go further? The answer lies in the pervasive moral sense that when choice to do ill is lacking, it is improper to impute guilt. And hence there is pressure for a special defense of insanity, just as there is pressure for a special defense of infancy or duress. Let us consider what has been offered by way of larger statements of the ends to be served by a special defense of insanity.

The major commissions of inquiry in the United States and in England have been less than compelling on the underlying justifications of this defense. Here is the American Law Institute's rationale for the special defense of insanity which now dominates the field:

> What is involved specifically is the drawing of a line between the use of public agencies and public force to *condemn* the offender by conviction, with resultant sanctions in which there is inescapably a punitive ingredient (however constructive we may attempt to make the process of correction) and modes of disposition in which that ingredient is absent, even though restraint may be involved. To put the matter differently, the problem is to discriminate between the cases where a punitive-correctional disposition is appropriate and those in which a medical-custodial disposition is the only kind that the law should allow.

This seems to me descriptive of what is to be done and not at all a justification of the doing. . . .

In *Durham*, Judge Bazelon put the matter curtly and clearly: "Our collective conscience does not allow punishment where it cannot impose blame." Such a rationale claims too much, assumes our possession of finely calibrated moral scales, and flies in the face of observation of the dross daily work of our criminal courts. It is hortatory rather than descriptive but it does state a justification that a generous mind may accept as an aim though doubt as a reality.

Historically, of course, the special defense made good sense in relation to one punishment. Capital punishment infused it with meaning. But even perfervid advocates of capital punishment do not favor the execution of the mentally ill, and this justification for the special defense is now sufficiently covered by the rules and practices of sentencing.

One is left, therefore, with the feeling that the special defense is a genuflection to a deep-seated moral sense that the mentally ill lack freedom of choice to guide and govern their conduct and that therefore blame should not be imputed to them for their otherwise criminal acts nor should punishment be imposed. To the validity of this argument we will several times return, but it is important not to assume that those who advocate the abolition of the special defense of insanity are recommending the wholesale punishment of the sick. They are urging rather that mental illness be given the same exculpatory effect as other adversities that bear upon criminal guilt. And they add the not unfair criticism of the conventional position that they observe the widespread conviction and punishment of the mentally ill, the special defense being an ornate rarity, a tribute to our capacity to pretend to a moral position while pursuing profoundly different practices.

The number held as not guilty by reason of insanity in the United States as a whole and in some states will illustrate the relative rarity of the special defense. Nationally, in the 1978 census of state and federal facilities, 3,140 persons were being held as not guilty by reason of insanity. . . . No one acquainted with the work of the criminal courts can think that these numbers remotely approximate the relationship between serious mental illness and criminal conduct. The defense is pleaded only where it may be advantageous to the accused and that balance of advantage fluctuates with sentencing practice and rules and practices relating to the release of those found not guilty by reason of insanity. Hence statistics will not lead us to principle in this matter; a more fundamental inquiry is necessary.

A useful entering wedge to principle is to inquire, What is the irreducible minimum relationship between mental illness and criminal guilt? What is the least the criminal law could do in this matter?

It is unthinkable that mental illness should be given a lesser reach than drunkenness. If a given mental condition (intent, recklessness), is required for the conviction of a criminal offense, then, as a proposition requiring no discussion, in the absence of that mental condition there can be no conviction. This holds true whether the absence of that condition is attributable to blindness, deafness, drunkenness, mental illness or retardation, linguistic difficulties, or, if it could be established, hypnotic control. But this states basic principles of criminal law, not a special defense. The main reasons for defining a "special defense" beyond the traditional common-law relationship between mental illness and the *actus reus* and mens rea of crime are, I think, twofold: expediency in crime control and fairness.

The expediency rationale can be quickly advanced and disposed of; the fairness rationale is more difficult.

In an important article in 1963, "Abolish 'The Insanity Defense'—Why Not?" J. Goldstein and J. Katz accurately perceived that "the insanity defense is not a defense, it is a device for triggering indeterminate restraint" of those who were mentally ill at the time of the crime but are not civilly committable now. In considerable part, that has been its role since 1800 when the emergence of the special defense in England led to the Criminal Lunatics Act of 1800, which provided indeterminate custody for those found not guilty by reason of insanity, with similar legislation spreading in the states and federal systems in this country.

Few are prepared any longer to justify the special defense on this crime control basis, as a means of confining the dangerous though not civilly committable. It would be a strange "defense," an unusual benevolence, whose purpose is confinement of those who could not otherwise be confined.

Hence we are brought to the central issue—the question of fairness, the sense that it is unjust and unfair to stigmatize the mentally ill as criminals and to punish them for their crimes. The criminal law exists to deter and to punish those who would or who do choose to do wrong. If they cannot exercise choice, they cannot be deterred and it is a moral outrage to punish them. The argument sounds powerful but its premise is weak.

Choice is neither present nor absent in the typical case where the insanity defense is currently pleaded; what is at issue is the degree of freedom of choice on a continuum from the hypothetically entirely rational to the hypothetically pathologically determined—in states of consciousness neither polar condition exists.

The moral issue sinks into the sands of reality. Certainly it is true that in a situation of total absence of choice it is outrageous to inflict punishment; but the frequency of such situations to the problems of criminal responsibility becomes an issue of fact in which tradition and clinical knowledge and practice are in conflict. The traditions of being possessed of evil spirits, of being bewitched, confront the practices of a mental health system which increasingly fashions therapeutic practices to hold patients responsible for their conduct. And suppose we took the moral argument seriously and eliminated responsibility in those situations where we thought there had been a substantial impairment of the capacity to choose between crime and no crime (I set aside problems of strict liability and of negligence for the time being). Would we not have to, as a matter of moral fairness, fashion a special defense of gross social adversity? The matter might be tested by asking which is the more criminogenic, psychosis or serious social deprivation? In an article in 1968 on this topic I raised the question of whether there should be a special defense of dwelling in a black ghetto. Some literal-minded commentators castigated me severely for such a recommendation, mistaking a form of argument, the reductio ad absurdum, for a recommendation. But let me again press the point. If one were asked how to test the criminogenic effect of any factor in man or in the environment, the answer would surely follow empirical lines. One would measure and try to isolate the impact of that factor on behavior, with particular reference to criminal behavior. To isolate genetic pressure toward crime one might pursue twin studies or cohort studies, one might look at patterns of adoption and the criminal behavior of natural fathers and adoptive fathers and see whether they were related to the criminal behavior of their children. Somewhat similar measuring techniques would be followed if one were trying to search out the relationship between unemployment and criminality, or a Bowlby-like study of the effects of maternal separation or maternal deprivation on later criminal behavior. Our answers to the question of the determining effects of such conditions would be found empirically and not in a priori arguing about their relationships to crime, though there may be ample room for argument involved in the empirical studies.

Hence, at first blush, it seems a perfectly legitimate correlational and, I submit, causal inquiry, whether psychosis, or any particular type of psychosis, is more closely related to criminal behavior than, say, being born to a one-parent family living on welfare in a black inner-city area. And there is no doubt of the empirical answer. Social adversity is grossly more potent in its pressure toward criminality, certainly toward all forms of violence and street crime as distinct from white-collar crime, than is any psychotic condition. As a factual matter, the exogenous pressures are very much stronger than the endogenous.

But the argument feels wrong. Surely there is more to it than the simple calculation of criminogenic impact. Is this unease rationally based? I think not, though the question certainly merits further consideration. As a rational matter is hard to see why one should be more responsible for what is done to one than for what one is. Yet major contributors to jurisprudence and criminal-law theory insist that it is necessary to maintain the denial of responsibility on grounds of mental illness to preserve the moral infrastructure of the criminal law. For many years I have struggled with this opinion by those whose work I deeply respect, yet I remain unpersuaded. Indeed, they really don't try to persuade, but rather affirm and reaffirm with vehemence and almost mystical sincerity the necessity of retaining the special defense of insanity as a moral prop to the entire criminal law. . . .

. . . The special defense of insanity may properly be indicted as producing a morally unsatisfactory classification on the continuum between guilt and innocence. It applies in practice to only a few mentally ill criminals, thus omitting many others with guilt-reducing relationships between their mental illness and their crime; it excludes other powerful pressures on human behavior, thus giving excessive weight to the psychological over the social. It is a false classification in the sense that if a team of the world's most sensitive and trained psychiatrists and moralists were to select from all those found guilty of felonies and those found not guilty by reason of insanity any given number who should not be stigmatized as criminals, very few of those found not guilty by reason of insanity would be selected. How to offer proof of this? The only proof, I regret, is to be found by personal contact with a flow of felony cases through the courts and into the prisons. No one of serious perception will fail to recognize both the extent of mental illness and retardation among the prison population and the overwhelming weight of adverse social circumstances on criminal behavior. . . . The special defense is thus a morally false classification. And it is a false classification also in the sense that it does not select from the prison population those most in need of psychiatric treatment.

Excusing the Crazy: The Insanity Defense Reconsidered

STEPHEN J. MORSE

The Moral Basis of the Insanity Defense

The basic moral issue regarding the insanity defense is whether it is just to hold responsible and punish a person who was extremely crazy at the time of the offense.[1] Those who believe that the insanity defense should be abolished must claim either that no defendant is extremely crazy at the time of the offense or that it is morally proper to convict and punish such people. Neither claim is easy to justify.

In all societies some people at some times behave crazily—that is, the behavior at those times is recognizably, aberrantly irrational. A small number of these people behave extremely crazily on occasion, including those times when an offense is committed. A hypothetical defendant with a delusional belief that he is the object of a murderous plot, who kills one of the alleged plotters after hallucinating that he hears the plotter's foul threats, is crazy. Such cases are rare, but clearly exist; the influence of extreme craziness on some criminal behavior cannot be denied. . . .

The insanity defense is rooted in moral principles of excuse that are accepted in both ordinary human interaction and criminal law. Our intuition is that minimal rationality (a cognitive capacity) . . . or lack of compulsion (no hard choice) are the essential preconditions for responsibility. Young children are not considered responsible for the harms they cause precisely because they lack these capacities. Similarly, adults who cause harm while terrifically distraught because of a personal tragedy, for instance, will typically be thought less responsible and culpable for the harm than if they had been normally rational and in control. Aristotle recognized these fundamental requirements for responsibility by noting that persons may be less blameworthy for actions committed under the influence of mistake (a cognitive problem) or compulsion. . . .

From *Southern California Law Review,* Vol. 58 (1985), pp. 777–780, 782–785, 787–791.

1. I use the word "crazy" advisedly and with no lack of respect for either disordered persons or the professionals who try to help them. It refers to behavior that is weird, loony, or nuts; less colloquially, it is behavior that seems inexplicably irrational. I chose the word "crazy" because I believe that it is the best generic term to describe the type of behavior that leads to a diagnosis or label of mental disorder. At the same time, it avoids begging questions about whether the crazy person was capable of behaving less crazily. When one engages in the discourse of illness, disease, or disorder, it is often assumed that the phenomena being discussed are uncontrollable manifestations of abnormal biological processes. But the truth is that our understanding of behavior, including very crazy behavior, is limited, and neither mental health scientists nor laypersons really know to what degree behavior of any sort can actually be controlled. Thus, I prefer to use a nonjargon word to describe the type of behavior—crazy behavior—with which the law is concerned in insanity defense cases.

Criminal law defenses that focus on the moral attributes of the defendant are based on these same intuitions and principles. Even if the defendant's conduct fulfills the usual requirements for prima facie guilt—that is, act, mental state, causation, result—the defendant will be found not guilty, not culpable, if the acts committed were the products of cognitive (e.g., infancy) or [hard choice] circumstances (e.g., duress) that were not under the defendant's control. . . . To convict a person with a meritorious defense would offend our conception of the relationship between legal guilt and blameworthiness. . . .

In sum, the moral basis of the insanity defense is that there is no just punishment without desert and no desert without responsibility. Responsibility is, in turn, based on minimal cognitive and volitional competence. Thus, an actor who lacks such competence is not responsible, does not deserve punishment, and cannot justly be punished.

The discussion so far has been premeditatedly vague about two issues that must now be clarified: the meanings of rationality and compulsion and the extent to which these factors affect moral accountability. Rationality is notoriously hard to define, but a reasonable working definition would include reference to both the sensibleness of the actor's goals and the logic of the means chosen to achieve them. It is, of course, difficult to say that the preferences or goals of another are irrational or not sensible, but there is no alternative to making these judgments within the social context in which those preferences are held. In a rough-and-ready fashion, we may ask whether, given the social context, any sense can be made of the actor's goals, whether any reasonable person could hold them, whether they are logically or empirically intelligible. Thus, in our society, it is generally considered rational to be a member of a so-called "fringe" religion because our society approves of diverse religious beliefs. In contrast, it does not make sense to want (truly) to be a Martian. These judgments about the intelligibility or rationality of goals can be made so long as we recognize that few goals are rational or irrational in an ultimate sense and we make a general presumption in favor of rationality.

It is easier to assess the rationality of the means an actor chooses to achieve goals because this assessment involves factual beliefs about the world or logical relationships. The inquiry becomes whether instrumental behavior is rationally connected to achieving identified goals. In Aristotelian terms, is the actor a good "practical reasoner"? . . .

. . . If one tests this framework with cognitive craziness, say a delusional belief system, it works very well indeed. For instance, the person who gouges his eye out because he believes he is the Lord's prophet and that mutilating himself will produce peace on earth, surely has an intelligible, rational goal, but the means chosen violates instrumental rationality in a number of ways. If the actor has beliefs that are simply not justifiable on any reasonable view of the world and seems incapable of correcting the errors by logic or evidence, then it is fair to conclude that the actor is irrational with respect to the behavior in question.

Now let us turn to a discussion of the criteria for compulsion. Although it is a vague concept at best, we may define compulsion generally as hard choices that society cannot ask defendants to make at their peril. But what are the criteria of choices so hard that a defendant's "wrong" choice should be excused? First, it must be the case that the defendant will experience substantially greater physical or psychological pain if he or she behaves lawfully/rightly than if he or she behaves unlawfully/wrongly. In other words, the pain produced by performing the lawful/right act must outweigh the pain produced by performing the unlawful/wrong act, the latter of which is usually a strong counterweight to wrongdoing. Let us consider a range of examples. First, the typical case of duress fits this criterion: the defendant will suffer greater pain if he or she does not perform the commanded, wrongful deed than if he or she does. Now consider the drug-dependent person (DDP) who is physically addicted to the drug. A DDP who does not take the drug will undergo the psychological and physical pain of withdrawal. This pain may very well be greater than the pain produced by fear of violating the law or by other psychological factors such as the loss of self-respect. Finally, take the hypothetical of a driver who rounds a turn on a mountain road and sees two children lying in the road. If the driver runs over the children, surely killing both of them, the driver lives; if the driver swerves to avoid them, the driver will go over the edge of the cliff, plunging to a certain death. Although theoretically all lives are equal, the immediate pain of losing one's own life is greater than the pain produced by the possibility that the law may punish the driver in the future. In all these cases, the actor is reasonably rational: the practical syllogism leading to action is logically intact, but he actor faces a very hard choice. . . .

The criteria I have offered for compulsion comport with our moral intuitions and practices. If a choice is too hard, it is *unfair* to blame and punish the actor who has no reasonable alternative. This is not to say that the actor has no choice. Saintly persons might be willing to undergo any pain rather than harm another, but the criminal law cannot expect such saintly behavior from ordinary persons. In addition, possible future criminal punishment will have little deterrent effect on a person faced with the immediate and severe pain of making the "right" choice in a hard-choice situation.

How much irrationality and compulsion are necessary for moral and legal excuse? The degree of rationality or self-control that may be involved in a specific act is rarely an all-or-none matter, and these factors may vary in degree over time during one's life. Similarly, the degree of rationality or self-control that society and the law require for responsibility may vary over time within a society and among societies. One need not be totally irrational or compelled to be excused, but at various times and in various places more or less may generally be expected from people.

The most important point to recognize, however, is that mental health science cannot set the legal standard for irrationality or compulsion in the context of legal accountability because setting the standard is not a scientific issue. The standard is a moral and social standard, to be set by those legal institutions empowered by a society to make individual moral and social decisions. In our society, for example, the substantive standards for legal insanity should be set largely by the legislature and interpreted by the courts, and individual cases should be decided by juries and judges.

The criteria for lack of responsibility also include the requirement that the irrationality or compulsion must be nonculpable. In other words, the actor should not be excused if the irrationality or compulsion was the result of the person's rational, voluntary act. If the irrationality is produced by the voluntary and knowing ingestion of a hallucinogen, for example, the actor is entirely responsible for the subsequent irrationality and will therefore not be excused. Similarly, a mentally disordered person who is able to control the disorder or its effects will be held responsible if such a person could have taken medicine, exercised willpower, or whatever.[2]

The insanity defense issue, then, is whether in some cases extreme craziness (involved in the defendant's offensive conduct) so compromises the defendant's rationality or creates such compulsion that it would be unjust to hold the defendant responsible. Whatever skepticism exists about the scientific status of psychiatry and psychology, it is clear that a small number of persons commit offenses under the influence of extremely crazy states of mind.[3] Even resolute opponents of the insanity defense, such as Norval Morris, admit that there "is indeed some quite florid psychopathology [i.e., crazy behavior] . . . among those for whom these pleas are made." The law should mitigate the punishment of such people because, presumably, they are less responsible. These admissions concede that craziness can affect the foundational capacities for responsibility. In light of such a concession, opponents of the insanity defense should have the burden to demonstrate that no mentally disordered defendant should be excused entirely.

Norval Morris has presented the most recent, important, nonconsequentialist argument for abolishing the insanity defense in his book *Madness and the Criminal Law*. Professor Morris suggests numerous consequentialist arguments for rejecting the insanity defense, but, believing in desert as a limiting principle in criminal law, he confronts directly "the question of fairness, the sense that it is unjust and unfair to stigmatize the mentally ill as criminals and to punish them for their crimes." Professor Morris denies that the mentally disordered lack the capacity to choose their behavior.[4] In brief, he argues that other causes, such as social disadvantage, are far more criminogenic than mental disorder (including severe disorder), yet we do not excuse those who are poor or the products of broken homes. Professor Morris concludes, "[a]s a rational matter it is hard to see why one should be more responsible for what

2. Note, however, that in these latter cases the actor's culpability may be affected although an excuse based on irrationality or lack of self-control does not obtain. For instance, a hypothetical actor who is delusional because of a controllable mental disorder or the voluntary ingestion of a hallucinogen, and consequently does not realize the victim killed is a person, cannot be guilty of intentional homicide because the actor lacks the requisite mens rea of intending to kill a person. The actor may be guilty of negligent or even reckless homicide, however, because a reasonable person should have been aware, or the actor may in fact have been aware, that the homicidal behavior was foreseeable. Again, the lack of culpability in this case is based on the absence of a requisite mens rea, not on the presence of the excusing condition of irrationality.

3. Consider again the case of our hypothetical, wildly deluded and hallucinating person who kills in response to the delusional belief, buttressed by nonexistent voices, that there is a murderous plot against him.

4. Professor Morris uses the locutions "freedom of choice" and "absence of choice" to characterize the criteria for responsibility and nonresponsibility. *Id.* I believe that these locutions and related terms such as free will and determinism are entirely confusing in the legal and psychiatric literature. Rather that being the criteria for responsibility, they are typically used as conclusory synonyms for responsibility. For instance, what does it mean to say that a person lacks free will? If it means that the person's behavior is uncaused, then it is conceptually confused and morally irrelevant. In a causal universe, all phenomena, including behaviors, are caused. If free will means that the person is not compelled, then it is a reasonable synonym for one criterion of responsibility—as long as compulsion is not simply the equivalent of "caused." In any case, terms such as free will are notoriously obscure. Writers should try to describe the behavioral criteria for responsibility rather than using conclusory metaphysical terms.

is done to one than for what one is." This conclusion is surely correct. It does not follow from the argument presented for it, however, which makes a morally irrelevant comparison between the poor and the mentally disordered.

Professor Morris confuses causation with excuse, a confusion that has consistently bedeviled criminal law theorists. Causation is not an excuse, however, for all behavior is caused. If causation were an excuse, no one would be held responsible for *any* behavior, criminal or not. Moreover, causation is not the equivalent of the subspecies of excuse that we term compulsion. Compulsion exists when the person faces a regrettable hard choice that leaves one with no reasonable alternative to wrongdoing. Again, if causation were the equivalent of compulsion, no one would be responsible because all would be compelled. Causation is not the issue; nonculpable lack of rationality and compulsion is. Understood in these terms, Professor Morris's conclusion that a person should not be more responsible for what is done to one than for what one is does indeed follow. These are not the terms in which he makes his argument, however.

Consider the case of a person whose extreme irrationality stems from the involuntary ingestion of a powerful hallucinogen. Such a defendant, who is not responsible for the ingestion of the drug, is not held responsible for a consequent crime. How can we distinguish this case from that of a person who commits a crime in response to motivations produced by severe mental disorder, say, a sudden command hallucination buttressed by a consistent delusional belief that the action is necessary? Crazy defendants who are not responsible for what they are should also be excused. In both cases the defendant is excused not because the behavior was caused—all behavior is caused—but because the defendant was sufficiently irrational and was not responsible for the irrationality.

The reason we do not excuse most disadvantaged criminals (or those whose criminal behavior can be explained by powerful causes) is not because we lack sympathy for their unfortunate background or because we fail to recognize that social disadvantage is a powerful cause of crime, as it surely is. Rather, most disadvantaged defendants are held responsible because they possess minimal rationality and are not compelled to offend. A disadvantaged defendant driven sufficiently crazy by circumstances will be excused because that defendant is crazy, not because the crazy behavior is caused and the defendant is disadvantaged. Similarly, most mentally disordered persons are held responsible for acts influenced by their disorders because they are sufficiently rational to meet the low threshold standards for responsibility. In sum, the criteria for moral autonomy and responsibility are rationality and lack of compulsion, whereas the criterion for excuse is that the actor is nonculpably lacking either reasonable rationality or is compelled.

The other major recent attack on the insanity defense, the American Medical Association's (AMA) report recommending abolition of the "special" defense of insanity, provides another instructive but confused counterargument to the defense's moral basis. The AMA's most important argument is that the insanity defense undermines the moral integrity of the criminal law because it impermissibly confuses psychiatric and legal concepts. The AMA writes:

> A defense premised on psychiatric models represents a singularly unsatisfactory, and inherently contradictory approach to the issue of accountability. . . .

The essential goal of an exculpatory test for insanity is to identify the point at which a defendant's mental condition has become so impaired that society may confidently conclude that he has lost his free will. . . . Because free will is an article of faith, rather than a concept that can be explained in medical terms, it is impossible for psychiatrists to determine whether a mental impairment has affected the defendant's capacity for voluntary choice, or cause him to commit the particular act in question. Accordingly, since models of mental illness are indeterminant in this respect, they can provide no reliable measure of responsibility.

Rather than being a persuasive argument against the moral basis of the defense, this quote exhibits a confusion about moral responsibility akin to Professor Morris' equation of causation with excuse. The AMA believes that the insanity defense confuses moral and legal concepts with medical concepts, but it is the AMA analysis that is guilty of this confusion.

The legal defense of insanity is not based on the psychiatric premise of determinism, and the essential goal of the defense is not to identify those actors who lack free will. The legal defense of insanity is based on the premise that rationality and lack of compulsion are the touchstones of moral responsibility, and the various tests seek to identify those actors who lack these attributes. The AMA correctly notes that free will cannot be explained in medical terms or identified medically, but this is entirely beside the point. Medical models cannot provide a "reliable measure of responsibility" because they are not meant to do so. The AMA errs by claiming that free will is the basis for responsibility and that mental disorder is somehow necessarily the antithesis of free will. Free will is not the basis for responsibility, and mental disorder per se does not negate responsibility: irrationality or compulsion negate responsibility.

The Idiom of "Involuntariness" and the Law

HERBERT FINGARETTE AND ANNE FINGARETTE HASSE

[T]he aim of this section is to illustrate how the use of idioms of loss of self-control do not systematically imply nonvoluntariness or involuntariness in the context of assessing criminal responsibility. This is important to realize because there is no doubt that idioms of loss of self-control are doubtless often used, *and used aptly,* in connection with insane conduct. This idiomatic usage unquestionably encourages the tendency to think that the conduct is in a relevant legal sense not voluntary. This, in turn, seems to provide an easy and direct answer to the question, "Why are the insane not responsible?"

From *Mental Disabilities and Criminal Responsibility* (Berkeley: University of California Press, 1979), pp. 49–63.

Fortunately, we need only explore a few clear-cut illustrative users of such idioms in order to make explicit what have, tacitly, been the relevant elements of meaning when we use these idioms.

"I couldn't help myself" is used aptly, for example, in situations ranging from the most obviously voluntary to the most obviously involuntary. At one extreme: "I couldn't help myself from doing it; it gave me such pleasure because the child seemed so eager to have the toy, and was so delighted when I gave it to her." No court would consider this to amount to involuntariness in defense against a larceny charge. At the other extreme: "I couldn't help myself; his sheer strength forced my arm back." Assuming the facts as stated, this is a clear case of involuntariness. The idiom "I couldn't help myself" thus provides no basis, per se, for distinguishing in the context of criminal responsibility the voluntary from the involuntary. It takes only a reasonable fluency in the language to imagine a number of illustrative and apt uses of this idiom, ranging along the spectrum from the most obvious through the intermediate and borderline cases of involuntariness and voluntariness in criminal law.

"I lost control—I couldn't prevent myself." Was it because I had found his ideas so unpalatably snobbish and racist that at last I had become annoyed enough to respond with a personal insult that provoked a fight? It is, then, perfectly proper English, and quite apt, to say that I lost my self-control. But what I did was plainly voluntary in law in the context of assessing criminal responsibility. Or did I "lose control" in the sense that I was dizzy and faint, physically unable to keep from falling and injuring a bystander in my fall? In that case my behavior was, in that same legal context, involuntary. . . . The essence is that these idioms are in fact entirely ambiguous on the issue of voluntariness in law; in themselves, even assuming they are aptly used, they have no weight with respect to the assessment in law of voluntariness.

It may seem that the preceding discussion of the idioms of informal, lay discourse is misdirected. The law, one might argue, should rely on the presumably unambiguous terms of medicine or science generally, not on the common idiom. Do not "mental disease," "irresistible impulse," and "compulsion" necessarily imply "involuntary"? As to this it should be recalled that the reliance on medical terms to settle legal issues in the areas of mental malfunction has been criticized again and again by the courts. And related to this is the fact that the common law concept of the voluntary derives from the common store of morally oriented notions about human conduct, not from technical and esoteric notions of science.

. . . In every criminal law use of "involuntariness" as a defense—excepting, of course, the uses we here question—the evidentiary structure of fact is simple and its significance immediate. The coma, the epileptic seizure, the faint, the use of superior physical force to compel, the clear and believable threat of imminent grave injury— these are very different forms of externally or internally caused, physically or psychically grounded, authentic involuntariness in law. But they all share in this: once the few simple and (in principle) observable elements essential to the defense are established, their significance—the exculpatory involuntariness they manifest—typically lies on their face. Of course, the court may on occasion lack direct eyewitness proof of the facts; or the significance of the facts may on occasion be challenged by reference to exceptional circumstances. But the model, and in real life very often the actuality, is one in which a few simple observations have an import that is self-evident.

The situation is just the contrary where the person is conscious but irrational, as in insanity. Here the structure of fact that establishes the condition is in principle complex. . . . The judgment of insanity requires thoughtful deliberateness, since it is an overall assessment of complex characteristics and workings of a man's mind. The judgment of involuntariness is typically in profound contrast: Was the defendant in a coma? Was there an order backed by a gun at his head? Was he physically constrained by some person or thing?

Such general considerations as the preceding suggest that when we have to do with what we may call insane defects in self-control, we are dealing with something substantively very different from any of the things we deal with in connection with the usual defense of involuntariness. . . .

. . . Viewed from the standpoint of involuntariness as strictly conceived in criminal law, the conduct one sees in insanity seems to be a model of *voluntary* conduct. It is (typically) purposeful, intentional, and effectively executed; it is often premeditated, planned, and prepared; and it is not infrequently tenaciously and ingeniously pursued in spite of external obstacles.

The facts in some instances of insane criminal conduct, particularly in some types of paranoid states or agitated, destructive depressions, suggest a wilfulness reaching passionate and stubborn intensity. But passionate intensity has not in itself served in criminal law as proof of involuntariness. On the contrary, passionate wilfulness may evidence a morally culpable failure of "self-restraint," and it generally establishes in law the *voluntariness* of the act, not its involuntariness.

It has been stressed in the immediately preceding discussion that the insane "loss of self-control," by contrast with the strictly involuntary act, is very often aware and purposeful—but then, so also are certain acts that are "*non*voluntary," i.e., acts done under coercion, necessity, and provocation. Can we not infer, then, that awareness and purposiveness may be compatible with action that is not voluntary, and is so in some either fully or partly exculpatory sense?

Here we must bring to bear in a more specific way the earlier general remarks made in reference to simplicity and complexity. In coercion, necessity, and provocation, the integrity of mind of the defendant is not challenged; his mind is not internally analyzed and characterized in its complex inner relationships. He is viewed, in impersonal terms, as the "standard" reasonable man, the citizen responsible to law. However, in this group of defenses an immediate, urgent, readily identified, and highly defined motive to unlawful conduct, peculiar to an objectively defined situation, becomes legally relevant. It becomes legally relevant because its immediacy, extreme intensity, and universal efficacy is such that *any* person, i.e., any *reasonable* and *law-abiding* person, may be expected to succumb at lest momentarily. . . . Here, then, as in the cases of coma or physical restraint, we have simple, immediate, impersonally defined circumstances whose significance leaps to the mind's eye. There is no essential analysis of the internal complexities and individuality of the mind and personality of the defendant.

What becomes of the concept of nonvoluntary conduct when the presumption of the rational, responsible person no longer holds, when the mind is internally in fundamental disarray, when it can no longer respond rationally to circumstance (and, in particular, to law)? We can now see that to speak of a lack of voluntary conduct here is to wrench the concept from its very roots, to apply a concept that in *every other* criminal law use presumes an integral, "standard" mind faced with impersonally defined constraints. To shift to the context in which the supposition of the rational mind itself is questioned is in effect to shift to a context in which "voluntary" and "nonvoluntary" no longer have their usual application, for now a basic *precondition* of their usual use in lacking. Of course, the *words* could be *given* some new and partially analogous meaning in this new context. No one has ever clearly done this in the law, because the issue has remained obscure. Moreover, such a verbal move would be likely to continue to obscure the fundamental differences between nonvoluntariness and irrationality. It would seem far more helpful to mark the radical differences by using different terms rather than to purchase a specious terminological economy by use of radically ambiguous language.

The tendency to become preoccupied with certain analogues between irrational behavior and nonvoluntary behavior has been vastly reinforced by certain pseudo-analogies that easily take root. The chief of these is probably the pseudo-analogy based on viewing the concept of "mental disease" as a reference to a reified "external" cause acting "on" the mind. The power of this apparently scientific model, and of related pseudo-analogies, has been so pervasive that it is essential to explore the issues in order to dissolve the illusions. . . .

It often seems to be tacitly assumed that once one introduces the concept of "disease," and links certain conduct to disease, this at one stroke establishes involuntariness in the disease-related behavior. Commonly, those who rely on this presupposition seem to have either of two forms of the presupposition in mind.

One, the more general, amounts usually to the supposition that if an act is the "product" or "effect" or "symptom" of a "mental disease," then that is not a voluntary act—the "victim" of the disease "can't help behaving as he does." The variant form of the presupposition makes a narrower claim. It is acknowledged that mental disease per se need not render behavior involuntary, but it is asserted that *some* forms of mental disease do in fact produce certain specific symptoms: "compulsive" behavior, or "irresistible impulse," or some form of "incapacity to conform" behavior to the law. Each version will be considered in turn.

What is it about "disease" that suggests that, in general, its manifestations are involuntary? . . . There is, in truth, no escape from the substantive question—what is there about a "diseased" mind that, in spite of the purposiveness of the conduct and often the skill of its execution, renders that conduct involuntary?

There is no answer to this question. Or perhaps one should answer that there is indeed a feature of a disordered mind that can justify exculpation—i.e., irrationality—but there is no common law principle justifying the characterization of this feature as "involuntariness"—for, in any usual criminal law sense of the word, it is not appropriate.

One might, as a last resort, speak in terms of familiar but vague notions like the "will," and say that if at lest it is the *will* that is "diseased," and not merely the mind generally, then the mere fact that the will is "diseased" renders the behavior not voluntary. But the question remains—why should behavior that *is* willed, even though the will be "diseased," be called *in*voluntary? This seems to be a corruption of language in order to achieve a desired conclusion, since it is natural and usual to hold that behavior, if *willed,* is voluntary. Indeed, it is not to be denied that it may be relevant to exculpation that the "will" is "diseased." But we shall quickly lose from sight whatever it is about such a will that negates responsibility for the conduct if at the outset we describe the conduct as *un*willed! This way lies total confusion. If, on the other hand, we acknowledge that the conduct is willed, but willed by a diseased will, we have to ask why *this* (rather than involuntariness) should make the conduct in that respect nonculpable.

There is, as mentioned earlier, another, narrower form of the argument designed to establish that disease of the mind produces nonvoluntary conduct. In this second and qualified form of the argument, it is not the existence of "mental disease" per se, not even "diseased will" per se, that renders the conduct involuntary. It is the purported fact that, in some cases, mental disease can produce as a particular symptom an "irresistible impulse" or a "compulsion" to act in a certain way regardless of whether the act is criminally prohibited. Here the claim is not that the impulse is nonvoluntary merely by virtue of being diseased; it is that this particular symptom is a distinct effect or manifestation of the disease, and can be judged by *independent* criteria to amount to a compelling, irresistible inclination to act in a certain way.

Here again, in spite of the temptation to speak of involuntariness, if we do so we face a profound paradox. For the person who acts "compulsively," or under the sway of some "irresistible" impulse or mood or passion, is one who is *absolutely intent upon* acting in a certain way. He will not allow himself or anyone else—if he can help it—to divert him from *his* purpose. It is the peculiar intensity and single-mindedness with which he *wills* to act in a certain way that strikes us. No *other* motive or wish that he brings to bear leads him to temper or put aside his purpose. If, as we are supposed to do here, we leave aside any claim that this is involuntary *merely* because it arises out of mental disorder, by what other, independent criterion could such conduct be classed as involuntary? On the face of it, one would see "compulsive" conduct as an expression of (stubborn) "will" par excellence.

Of course, there is in some of these cases something odd, something that can at times be responsibility-negating, in the mental condition underlying such single-mindedness and obstinacy, such persistence, such absolute undissuadability. That this is so is both true and important. For such a will may be irrational. But on what grounds should we characterize this irrational will as an *absence* of will?

If, however, one argues that the "will" has been "overthrown," this quickly generates familiar controversies of a "metaphysical" rather than an empirical kind. What is the "true" will? Is an irrational commitment a "false" will? And by what independent computation or other criteria do we determine that this "true will" was not "strong" enough to resist the irrational impulse or resolution rather than having been lax in not using its available "power" to resist? One expert says one thing; another says otherwise. Some, understandably, wash their hands of all such debate.

Commonly the experts do not differ about some objective measurement or specific observation of this particular defendant. Dispute arises because they adhere to competing psychological doctrines, or because they have different attitudes toward the justice or future therapeutic efficacy of criminal conviction of the defendant. Differences in expert opinion often amount to a covert expression of such differences. A jury, asked to assess the strength of a mysterious "inner" and "true" will, can only look to the experts. The question is not factual in the way it would be if one were dealing with such a paradigmatic form of irresistibility as compulsion by a superior external physical force, or coercion with a shotgun at the head. In such cases, objective measurement assures us that the one force is greater than any counterforce the defendant's muscles could exert, and common experience assures us that a reasonable man of good will could not fairly be expected to ignore the threat and disobey. There is no question in these latter cases of covert rivalry among speculative doctrines, or of covert and conflicting philosophies as to the justice of punishing the defendant, all masquerading as quantitative medical assessment of "resistibility."

No doubt, one of the chief influences in perpetuating the assimilation of some of these forms of "compulsive" conduct to "involuntariness" is the explicit or tacit background metaphor of the person as victim: we view him *as if* he were being subjected to a superior external force.

There can be benefits from such an approach—but not to the law. There can be dangers from such a way of speaking—and particularly so for the law.

From the private standpoint of the person himself, characterizations in terms of being "compelled" or "irresistibly driven" may genuinely and helpfully reflect the subjective sensation of inclinations to incompatible lines of conduct. The idiom reflects one's frustration that one is not acting on one's own reasonable and nobler inclinations, but instead acting on an inclination that, even as one indulges it, one judges to be less admirable, less in keeping with one's ideas of prudence, or decency, or morality. This language expresses one's desire to resist being identified, by oneself or by others, with the inclination that one in fact follows. It is also a way of expressing both self-exculpation and self-condemnation: What I do is contrary to what I approve. Yet by condemning what I do, I reveal that there is another, better side of me, a side of me that aspires to the higher, even while I follow the lower.

Such talk may truly be part of a moral battle, genuine or self-deceptive, in one's attitude to oneself and one's conduct. Yet such subtle and inner "battles," conceived in various idiomatic and metaphorical terms, significant though they may be in one's personal life, are obviously not the proper subject matter of judgments of culpability with respect to criminal law. However important, however authentic or self-deluding they may be from the standpoint of morality or religion, however fascinating and useful such modes of analysis may be to the novelist or the psychologist, such "internal tensions" and "battles" constitute a different order of subject matter for analysis than anything the law can legitimately concern itself with.

Conclusions about Addictions and Criminal Responsibility

HERBERT FINGARETTE AND ANN FINGARETTE HASSE

[I]n spite of a vast literature, professionals in the field of drug and alcohol addiction acknowledge that no satisfactory scientific understanding of addiction has been reached. Thus there is no medical foundation for adopting the general proposition at the crux of the exculpatory legal arguments, the proposition that addictive conduct is involuntary. On the other hand, massive descriptive evidence indicates that individuals often make choices to abandon addictive conduct or abstain from drug or alcohol use permanently or temporarily. Moreover, authorities observe that in the specific case of narcotic addiction there is often little in the way of chemical or biological influences. Yet such addiction may provide an important individual or group identity for many who lack socially approved skills or are socially alienated. Popular beliefs about the chemically induced hell of narcotic withdrawal agony or the insatiable craving for ecstatic pleasures are profoundly at odds with the facts, though they have deeply colored the thinking of the courts. Since narcotic addiction is officially classified as the most "compelling" form of the addictions, this information forces abandonment of the argument that behavior associated with addiction, whether alcoholic or narcotic, should be regarded as legally involuntary.

Once we conclude that addictive conduct is legally voluntary, however, we do not express a basic substantive insight into addiction, but merely free ourselves from a false idea. Courtroom cliche has obscured the fact that the problems at issue concern intricate and poorly understood relationships that link character, personality, and mind to upbringing, social setting, and cultural values, and in turn to biochemical and neuropsychological processes. Indeed, courts have been ill-served by those psychiatrists who have promoted the notion that addiction is involuntary and who have seen this notion as a legal formula that will permit medical models to supersede the use of criminal sanctions.[1] The very complexity of the problem calls for legislative determinations concerning rehabilitation, regulation of alcohol and drug commerce, and the general administration of criminal law in this area.

Undoubtedly there are those who regard possible legal approaches to addiction in polar terms: either we inflict harsh, punitive, and degrading measures on the addict, or we declare the person sick and therefore not responsible for his conduct. What is needed here is the abandonment of such extreme and fixed positions.[2] Nothing we

From *Mental Disabilities and Criminal Responsibility* (Berkley: University of California Press, 1979), p. 191–95.

1. This imputation of motive rests upon inferences that seem repeatedly apparent as one reads the court records and psychiatrists' statements about the irrelevance and inappropriateness of the criminal law in the areas of mental disease and addiction.

2. A recent polar formulation reflects a common doctrinaire approach: "Medicine views the drug misuser as a patient who needs treatment; law enforcement views him as a criminal who must be punished"

have said precludes in any way the many legislative options for establishing rational procedures and institutions, whether within penal or civil systems, for "detoxifying" the acutely intoxicated, for counseling, for treating, and for otherwise helping the addict. Nor is there any support in anything we have said for the irrational, expensive, and inhumane harassment of addicts, especially those who have been impoverished and alienated, an approach still so prevalent today. In the present antipunitive atmosphere in many enlightened circles, however, it is appropriate to recall that the lawful and proper threat of sanctions may be not only a pragmatically effective approach, but also a morally humane one. It regards the addict as an autonomous person, responsible for guiding his own life and subject to law.

Of course, the medical approach can also reflect a humane concern, a concern for the weak and ailing and for those who cannot, in some respects, handle their own lives. But by now it is no news that both of these approaches, the medical and the legal, however inspired, can in practice disregard human dignity when ignorance, social prejudice, well-intentioned dogma, lack of funding, or routinization take over. We need to rethink the implications of both approaches against the background of the limited knowledge that we have. Coordinating the attack on the complex problem of drug and alcohol abuse is preeminently a legislative responsibility. For the courts to assume that addictive drug or alcohol use, or addiction-related conduct, is involuntary, and for the courts then to build such an unwarranted assumption into constitutional and common law doctrine would be a grave error.

The fundamental substantive question that the criminal law properly faces here is whether, in a particular case, the defendant's capacity to act rationally in regard to the criminal significance of the act has been so impaired as to have rendered him nonresponsible at the time of the act. At first blush this may look like a more complex question than such apparently limited and technical questions as: Is defendant diseased? or Was the conduct involuntary? But as we have seen, these latter questions are confusing pseudo-simplifications; insofar as they point toward an authentically relevant issue, it is in substance the responsibility issue that is of concern.

There is, unfortunately, no single, simple sign or label that identifies the condition at issue here. Only a review of the defendant's history, conduct, physical health, and general demeanor can provide an adequate picture. This is not a picture that can be read off with scientific precision, or even with science at all, though scientific data may be of help. It is a picture that can only be assembled and assessed from the perspective of practical lay judgment, the judgment of ordinary people who know how to get along in life taking practical account, as they go, of the bearing of law on their conduct. The test they apply to the defendant is a test they themselves pass every day of their lives: Is the defendant, as portrayed up to the moment of the offending act,

(Group for the Advancement of Psychiatry, New York: Group for the Advancement of Psychiatry, 1971, p. 12). Too often such a formulation merely sidesteps a set of complex personal, social, legal, and spiritual problems: "Oftentime . . . the desire to avoid the implications of criminality while maintaining formal control has resulted in compulsory treatment of an "illness" which has never been adequately defined. The Commission warns against the tendency to assume that when its motives are benevolent, society need not attend to the philosophical and constitutional issues raised by its actions" (National Commission on Marijuana and Drug Abuse, Drug Use in America: Problem in Perspective, Washington, D.C.: U.S. Gov't. Printing Office, 1973, p. 257).

and in the circumstances of that act, on the whole able to take into account in a practical way, in acting as he does, the criminal significance of his act?

The facts about the life and personality of "addicts" or "alcoholics," as we have reviewed the current state of knowledge, suggest that in some cases there is some impairment of this capacity. Specifically, this is likely to be true of the person who has had a longtime involvement with heavy use of alcohol or other drugs, whose life circumstances by now reveal deep rootlessness and alienation from human contacts, and who also suffers serious physical debilitation and disease in consequence of this unhealthy mode of life. Such persons are typically skid-row "down-and-outers" who have already shown persistent imperviousness to moral values, to rewards or sanctions, or to social pressures. They can readily present the picture of seriously impaired capacity for responsible conduct under law. Given this stage of generalized demoralization, the criminal law should be required to take cognizance of the issue as one touching fundamental criminal law principle, and not merely as a problem properly left to be handled through legislative health and welfare policies more generally. On the other hand, as has been emphasized, mere heavy involvement with drug or alcohol abuse, and related unlawful modes of life, do not per se manifest irrationality. The myth of "slaves to addiction" should not go unchallenged. . . .

It seems expectable that where the evidence shows that the defendant regularly took into account the criminal significance of the act in a practical way—for example, took intelligible and planned measures to escape police detection, etc.—the jury will not find irrationality in regard to the act. Where, however, the evidence shows genuine incapacity to take such measures, or to take them in relatively regular and reliable ways, or to make simple and obvious plans to carry through even criminal acts efficiently, or to escape detection for them—this, along with the rest of the evidence if it forms a suitable pattern of incapacity for rational conduct, could lead to a finding that the defendant was at least to a material extent irrational. This lack of rationality calls for some mitigation of punishment. The finding would also mandate posttrial medical examination, as well as whatever health, welfare, and safety measures were then applicable under the relevant policies at the time.

Only where there was a finding of irrationality that was both predominant and nonculpable in origin would criminal punishment be entirely precluded, with medical supervision remaining as the sole consequence. Such gross debilitation of character and mind would entail, in practice, significant constraints on the defendant for the safety of the public and for the defendant's own welfare and safety.

NOTES AND QUESTIONS

1. Mental abnormality is a classic foundation for an excusing condition. Notice that mental abnormality itself, even extreme abnormality, is *not* sufficient to warrant an excuse. The mental abnormality must produce some other defect in the person that

undermines responsibility. For example, tests for legal insanity variously require that the mental disorder produces a substantial reasoning problem or causes the agent to lack the ability to control his or her conduct. Reflection will disclose, however, that these difficulties could be produced by other innocent causes, such as fatigue or stress. The real excusing condition, then, is innocently caused irrationality or the inability to control one's conduct. Nevertheless, at least the insanity defense is tied to a mental abnormality as the cause of the excusing condition. The reason for the limitation is that mental abnormality is "gross and verifiable," but is it any more so than stress or fatigue? Why does the criminal law limit the possibility of excusing for mental abnormality to cases of diagnosable mental disorder?

2. Suppose that the law did adopt generic excusing conditions, such as irrationality and the inability to control conduct, which could be supported by credible evidence of any kind, including mental abnormality. Would such a scheme be more theoretically sensible? Would it work?

3. Would it be just to abolish the insanity defense altogether? Critics of the defense can mount a consequential attack on the defense, but that still leaves the fairness claim. Would you be morally comfortable blaming and punishing a person who is grossly out of touch with reality, that is, vastly delusional about what he or she was doing at the time of the crime? Remember, the outcome of acquittal by reason of insanity is not that the defendant goes free. Rather, in all jurisdictions, the successful insanity defendant is committed to a mental hospital for treatment and to protect society. There is no blame, at least in theory, but there is loss of liberty. Still, the period of confinement is tied to the person's recovery and lack of dangerousness, rather than to the period of years deserved for the offense. Research evidence does show that people acquitted by reason of insanity do spend about as much time in hospital as people convicted of the same crime spend in prison, but the purpose and, one hopes, the conditions of confinement are different.

Four states have abolished the insanity defense, allowing the defendant to use evidence of mental abnormality only to negate the mental state required by the definition of the crime charged. In fact, mental abnormality seldom negates mens rea: it gives agents crazy reasons for doing what they do, but it does not prevent them from forming the intention to do what they do. Consequently, mental disorder will rarely have much mitigating effect in the absence of an insanity defense, unless it is considered at sentencing.

4. Insanity defense scholars are divided about whether mental abnormality is a status excuse or an excuse specific to the individual offense. Infancy is an illuminating analogy. Very young children seem incapable ever of having sufficient understanding to be held fully morally responsible for their deeds. Thus, infancy does seem to be a status excuse: it is simply being a (young) child that excuses. But older children, as the common law recognized, might very well have sufficient understanding to be held fully responsible. Indeed, the United States Supreme Court has held that it is constitutional to execute sixteen- and seventeen-year-olds convicted of capital of-

fenses. Surely, starting in early adolescence, youths might have sufficient understanding in some cases to be responsible for some deeds, even if not for all. Similarly, mentally disordered people typically are not grossly out of touch with reality about all aspects of their lives, nor are they necessarily totally irrational about those behaviors most influenced by mental disorder. Irrationality at a given time is certainly a feature of the person, but does that mean it is the status of being irrational that excuses? Is the real basis for excusing more specific: for example, that the practical reasoning for the offense in question was "infected" with irrationality? Does anything turn on the distinction?

5. Probably the most controversial substantive insanity defense issue in the wake of John Hinckley Jr.'s acquittal by reason of insanity for the attempted murder of President Reagan was the validity of a "control" test for legal insanity. There appears to be general agreement that some agents are irrational and that they can be identified with reasonable reliability, but there is intense dispute about whether people really lack the ability to control themselves because of mental disorder and, if so, whether these people can be reliably identified. Some have argued that we lack the ability to distinguish the inability from the unwillingness to control oneself and that in cases of extreme mental disorder, when we would be tempted to say that the defendant was unable to control the offending conduct, it is highly likely that the defendant was sufficiently irrational to meet the irrationality standard for legal insanity. It is clear that there is no reliable and valid test for the inability to control oneself and, so far, the critics of the control test have won in the legislatures and courts, but control test advocates continue to press their case.

6. The effect of so-called "addiction" on criminal responsibility is also problematic. To begin, the meaning of "addiction" is itself contested. The term brings to mind a condition manifested by uncontrollable behavior dictated by uncontrollable desires that the ingestion of certain substances produces. The modern diagnostic terms are "substance dependence" and "substance abuse," which do not sound as malignant, but the connotation of uncontrollable behavior persists. If criminal behavior, including the use of controlled substances, were genuinely the uncontrollable symptom of a substance-induced disorder, then it might seem unfair and ineffective criminally to prohibit and to punish such behavior. Indeed, this has been the claim of many, both in cases and commentary. In *Powell v. Texas,* involving the constitutionality of punishing a so-called "alcoholic" for the crime of being drunk in public, the Supreme Court narrowly avoided constitutionalizing a prohibition on punishing allegedly irresistible conduct. But whether substance-related behavior *should* be excused is still much debated.

Herbert Fingarette, a philosopher and noted expert on "addiction" presents with Ann Hasse what is surely the minority view, which Fingarette has reaffirmed in his more recent book, *Heavy Drinking.* Fingarette argues that the medical model of addictions raises more questions than it answers and that the empirical evidence strongly disputes the assumption of uncontrollability. These claims anger many, but can the arguments be so readily dismissed? Consider the evidence that there may be a genetic predisposition to having trouble controlling one's heavy drinking, evidence that is often used to support the position that heavy drinking is the uncontrollable symptom of a disease. Suppose there is a genetic component involved in having difficulty handling drink. What follows? Does it mean that the complex repertoire of behavior involved in obtaining alcohol and drinking it is not human action? The movements involved in obtaining a drink, bringing it to one's lips, sipping, and swallowing are hardly the same as the physically involuntary tremor a neurological disorder may produce. Still, some people may metabolize ethanol in ways that, in interaction with their drinking culture, predispose them to develop particularly strong desires for ever greater amounts of consumption. So genetics may in part produce abnormally strong desires. Do abnormally strong desires excuse and, if so, on what theory of excuse? Suppose genetics in part produced abnormally strong sexual desires, which, under conditions of frustration, led to sexual assault. There is no diagnosis for abnormally strong sexual desires, but the notion of disease is really doing no work in the analysis of why we excuse. In both cases we are considering abnormally strong desires, which, under the right conditions, are associated with criminal behavior to satisfy them. What theory of excuse, if any, is at work?

As you think about the vexing problem of substances and criminal responsibility, ask yourself what theory of excuse is at work and what facts about "addiction" would have to be true, at least in a specific case, to justify excusing. Remember, too, that in many cities from one-half to over eighty percent of all felony arrestees test positive for one of the most important classes of controlled substances. Does this have any bearing on the proper substantive doctrines of excuse for substance related criminal conduct?

7. In the criminal justice system, mental abnormality arises most frequently in contexts other than as the basis for an excusing condition; for example, incompetence to stand trial is a far more common claim. Some have used this observation to suggest that the insanity defense is raised too infrequently to be worth the cost of adjudicating it. But is it raised less frequently than duress, for example? And even if it is raised infrequently, is this a persuasive, sufficient reason to convict and punish an offender who may be morally blameless?

6

Sentencing Theory and Practice

Theories of sentencing are largely dependent on justifications for punishment, because sentences are precisely the punishment the criminal law aims to impose on violators. Should sentences reflect the desert of the criminal, satisfy consequential concerns about public safety, or achieve mixed goals? The answers depend on values, data, and, of course, politics. For the pure retributivist, public safety may be of only marginal concern in setting sentences, because justice demands that sentences be proportional to the offender's desert. But how does the retributivist know what punishment is proportionate? It is difficult to quibble with the consequentialist's desire to employ sentences to lower crime rates and to protect the public, but what if public safety goals would lead to sentences that are far too harsh or too lenient according to most peoples' sense of justice? Moreover, how often does the consequentialist possess data sufficiently valid to warrant the sentencing scheme proposed? A mixed justification seems to solve the problems that purity creates, but achieving a coherent mix is difficult because each contributor suffers from its own flaws and no combination is easily justifiable.

The types of punishment that may be meted out have changed as society has changed. At least in the United States, mutilation, torture, transportation, public flogging, drawing and quartering, and burning at the stake are not acceptable, either because they are unconstitutional under the Eighth Amendment's ban on cruel and unusual punishments or because the public finds them unacceptable for some reason. But death by "relatively humane" methods, incarceration, and fines are all constitutional, including imprisonment for virtually any term of years for any crime. The death penalty is of course much and hotly debated, but it is comparatively rarely sought and even more seldom imposed. Although it is a topic of intense moral and factual interest, it is simply too large an issue to address in our selections without risking unacceptable superficiality.

At present, imprisonment is our society's pain of choice to impose on serious and not-so-serious offenders. For most defendants convicted of relatively serious crimes, the important issues are whether imprisonment will follow and, if so, for how long. Fines and other generally less painful punishments are also common, but they usually require fewer resources to impose and because they are less painful, they are correspondingly easier to justify. Consequently, the selection in this chapter focuses on imprisonment.

Sentencing practices vary historically according to public conceptions about how well the criminal justice is working, the changing popularity of different justifications of punishment, and the political response to the former concerns. For about a century, beginning in approximately the last three decades of the nineteenth century, there was an increasing tendency to view imprisonment as a means of reforming the convict. People differed about what would work during imprisonment to achieve this goal, but the prison was supposed to do more than simply incapacitate and deter. Probably the most influential consequence of the reform ideal was the indeterminate sentence, which would allow sentencing judges and the correctional authorities the flexibility needed to individualize the terms of imprisonment. Although convicted of the same offense, a less heinous and more quickly reformed criminal would do less time, and a more evil, recalcitrant offender would do more. By the late 1960s and early 1970s a powerful critique of the reform ideal and its practices arose. Commentators pointed out that criminals often did not receive their just deserts, questioned whether reform was an adequate justification for punishment and whether the technology of reform really worked, and criticized what appeared to be arbitrary sentencing decisions.

As a result, there was a turn toward the "just deserts" model of sentencing, according to which convicted criminals were supposed to be sentenced to a determinate terms of years from a narrow and fixed range for each crime that was based largely on desert. Some jurisdictions created "guidelines," which were attempts to achieve rational, guided discretion for the sentencing judges by providing them with both the proper set of variables to consider and a method for combining them. The most comprehensive guidelines effort was mounted by the federal government, whose sentencing guidelines applicable in federal criminal cases are comprehensive, leave federal judges little room for discretion, and arguably are quite harsh. Although the federal guidelines have been much criticized for their inflexibility and harshness, they have withstood constitutional and political challenges.

The turn toward "just deserts" sentencing occurred simultaneously with rising rates of crime. In the 1980s the use of imprisonment increased, as more prisons were built and legislatures tended to increase the terms imposed for many crimes. The "war

on drugs" also escalated markedly in the 1980s in response to the growing use of cocaine during that period, especially after 1986 when the "crack" or "rock" form was
increasingly used. The perceived need to imprison drug offenders with ever more
onerous sentences also contributed to the escalation of prison building, as larger numbers of drug offenders were sentenced to longer terms of years. Whether increased
rates and terms of incarceration and concomitant increased prison space are sensible
responses to the crime problem are, like most important criminal justice issues, hotly
contested and too often ideologically fraught. You should consider again who belongs
in prison, for how long, and under what conditions. For example, do minor drug offenders—say, users or low-level street dealers—deserve lengthy terms of imprisonment, and is imprisoning them a successful strategy in the war on drugs? Should recidivists receive enhanced sentences? If some rehabilitative methods can be shown
to work for at least some prisoners, should society spend the resources necessary to
implement them? These are the types of questions society at large and the criminal
justice system must confront as we decide what to do with convicted criminals. We
can confidently predict, however, that the current fondness for harsh imprisonment
will not last forever, because styles of sentencing always change as society inevitably
is disappointed by whatever practice is current.

Sentencing Aims, Principles, and Policies
ANDREW ASHWORTH

The Aims of the Criminal Justice System

. . .

It is important to distinguish the aims of the criminal justice system from the aims of
sentencing, which merely relate to one element. The system encompasses a whole series of stages and decisions. . . . It would hardly be possible to formulate a single
meaningful "aim of the criminal justice system" which applied to every stage. It is
true that one might gather together a cluster of aims: for example, the prevention of
crime, the fair treatment of suspects and defendants, due respect for the victims of
crime, the fair labelling of offences according to their relative gravity etc. But to combine these into some overarching aim such as "the maintenance of a peaceful society
through fair and just laws and procedures" is surely to descend into vacuity, since such
a formula says almost nothing when applied to any one of the stages in the system. A

From *Sentencing & Criminal Justice*, 2d ed. (London: Butterworths, 1995), pp. 57–81.

preferable approach is to recognise that different stages may have their distinct aims and purposes, but to attempt to ensure that various decision-makers do not pull in opposite directions.

Unrealistic aims should not be set for individual decisions in the criminal justice system. . . . Only a small proportion of crimes come before the courts for a sentencing decision. . . . Thus the potential of sentencing for altering the frequency and patterns of offending in society is severely handicapped by the fact that relatively few offences result in the passing of a sentence. On the other hand, it may be assumed that sentencing fulfils an indispensable public function. There is at least some evidence that law and order break down in the absence of police, for example. So, without judicial sentencing, and the panoply of police, penal agents, and courts, there would surely be more crime. But it does not follow from this that general crime prevention can be increased or decreased by changes in sentencing levels—even if those changes would be acceptable on other grounds, which they might not be. . . .

Sentencing is no more than one aspect or stage in the criminal justice system. Nonetheless, it has considerable social significance in its own right. Conviction involves the public labelling of people as offenders. The sentencing decision can often be seen as the core of the labelling or denunciatory process by giving a judgment of "how bad" the offence was, and by translating that judgment into the particular penal currency of this country at this time. Sentencing has an expressive function and, as Durkheim argued, "the best punishment is that which puts the blame . . . in the most expressive but least costly form possible."

This expressive or censuring function is carried out by means of imposing coercive measures on convicted offenders. The imposition of punishment requires justification. We should not be satisfied with the proposition that anyone who commits any offence forfeits all rights, and may be dealt with by the State in whatever manner the courts decree. Instead, we should seek justifications for the institution of punishment, for sentencing decisions, and for the forms of sentence available to the courts. The importance of the last element is evident from the widespread use of imprisonment and the increasing restrictiveness of non-custodial sentences in many countries. The "aims of sentencing" are not so much a set of abstract propositions as a group of key assertions about the social justifications for the imposition of imprisonment, fines, community service, curfew, etc., on individuals for offences.

The Rationales of Sentencing

The Argument for Declaring a Primary Rationale

When judges are discussing sentencing, one of the most frequent topics is discretion. . . . There are many who would agree that sentencers ought to have some discretion so as to take account of the peculiar facts of individual cases. But does that remove the argument for bringing the rule of law as far into sentencing decisions as possible? The rule of law, in this context, means that judicial decisions should be taken openly and by reference to standards declared in advance. It is one thing to agree that judges should be left with discretion, so they may adjust the sentence to fit the particular combination of facts in an individual case. It is quite another to suggest that judges should be free to choose what rationale of sentencing they will adopt in particular cases or types of case. Freedom to select from among the various rationales is a freedom to determine policy, not a freedom to respond to unusual combinations of facts. It is more of a license to judges to pursue their own penal philosophies than an encouragement to respond sensitively to the facts of each case.

It is fairly well established that a major source of disparity in sentencing is the difference in penal philosophies among judges and magistrates. . . . One notable decision of the Supreme Court of Victoria states:

> The purposes of punishment are manifold and each element will assume a different significance not only in different crimes but in the individual commission of each crime . . . Ultimately every sentence imposed represents a sentencing judge's instinctive synthesis of all the various aspects involved in the punitive process.[1]

The inscrutable idea of an "instinctive synthesis" comes close to another notion, which is that the various aims of sentencing should be "balanced" in each case. Indeed, the Sentencing Reform Act of 1984 in the United States required the U.S. Sentencing Commission to devise guidelines that reflected proportionality, deterrence, public protection, and offenders' treatment needs—aims that were listed without recognition that they conflict and that priorities must be established. If there is thought to be some value in each of these purposes, what should be done?

It is often assumed that there are only two alternative courses: either (1) to declare a single rationale, or (2) to allow sentencers a fairly free choice among several rationales. Critics of the first approach argue that it is too rigid, especially when there is such a wide range of crimes and criminals. They may then assume that the second approach is the only "realistic" one. They may argue that the second approach is more "balanced" or is "multi-faceted," thereby contrasting its practicality with the academic, even ascetic regime of a single rationale. But there is a third possibility, which may be both practical and consistent with the rule of law: (3) to declare a primary rationale, and to provide that in certain types of case one or another rationale might be given priority. . . .

Deterrence

Deterrence is one of several rationales of punishment which may be described as "consequentialist," in the sense that it looks to the preventive consequences of sentences. In fact, deterrence is merely one possible method of producing crime prevention through sentencing: it relies on threats and fear, whereas rehabilitation and incapacitation adopt different methods of achieving a similar end. . . . It is important to draw the distinction between individual (or special) deterrence and general deterrence. The latter aims at deterring other people from committing this kind of offence, whereas individual deterrence is concerned with deterring this particular person from reoffending. A system which regarded individual deterrence as the main goal would presumably escalate sentences for persistent offenders, on the reasoning that if non-

1.*Williscroft* [1975] VR 292, at pp. 299–300.

custodial penalties fail to deter then custody must be tried, and if one year's custody fails to deter two years must be tried, etc. It would not be the gravity of the crime but the propensity to reoffend which would be the main determinant of the sentence. Although traces of this approach can often be discerned in the sentencing of repeat offenders, it is rarely adopted as the primary rationale of a sentencing system.

More significant is general deterrence. Jeremy Bentham was its chief proponent, and he started from the position that all punishment is pain and should therefore be avoided. However, punishment might be justified if the benefits (in terms of general deterrence) would outweigh the pain inflicted on the offender punished, and if the same benefits could not be achieved by nonpunitive methods. Sentences should therefore be calculated to be sufficient to deter others from committing this kind of offence, no more and no less. The assumption is that citizens are rational beings, who will adjust their conduct according to the disincentives provided by sentencing law. Modern economic theorists such as Richard Posner adopt a similar approach, viewing punishments as a kind of pricing system. . . .

Criticisms of deterrence theory may be divided into the empirical and the principled. The main empirical criticism is that the factual data on which a deterrent system must be founded does not exist. We lack reliable findings about the relative deterrent effects of various types and levels of penalty for various crimes. For example, sophisticated techniques have been applied in attempts to assess the deterrent efficacy of the death penalty, without yielding clear and reliable results. A necessary element in research is a proper definition of deterrence, to establish that fear of the legal penalty was the factor which determined conduct. The few studies which satisfy the criterion are no basis for broad policies. On the other hand, there is research which suggests that certain forms of offence which tend to be committed by people who plan and think ahead may be susceptible to deterrent sentencing strategies: Richard Harding, for example, found that robbers tended to desist from arming themselves with guns if there was a significant extra penalty for carrying a firearm. This may be taken to bear out the proposition that general deterrence is more likely to be effective for planned or "professional" than for impulsive crimes, although Harding argues that deterrent sentences need to be combined with publicity and appropriate "social learning" opportunities if they are to have significant preventive effects.

A counterexample is David Riley's study of drunk drivers, in which he shows that the problems of a general deterrent strategy lie in drivers' optimism about the risk of not being caught, ignorance of the penalty, and ignorance of the amount of consumed alcohol to commit an offence. Further studies have examined the potential deterrent effect of increased enforcement by the police, but it seems that a general crime prevention strategy with publicity and attempts to change people's attitudes is likely to be more effective than either sentencing or enforcement changes alone. Another area in which the potential for legal deterrence appears not to be great is burglary: interviews with burglars suggest that most of them are not rational calculators but rather short-term hedonists or eternal optimists. The 1990 White Paper was concerned to point out that sentencers and others who talk about deterrence often overestimate the likely consequences of increases in penalty levels:

> much crime is committed on impulse, given the opportunity presented by an open window or unlocked door, and it is committed by offenders who live from moment to mo-

ment. . . . It is unrealistic to construct sentencing arrangements on the assumption that most offenders will weigh up the possibilities in advance and base their conduct on rational calculation. Often they do not.[2]

One might wish to argue that armed robbery and, perhaps, drug smuggling are exceptions to this; but the reality is that reliable evidence of what types of offender can be deterred from what types of crime by what types of penalty is rare. The dearth of evidence leaves some authors undaunted, since they argue that "commonsense reasoning about general prevention" can be used instead. But if the available research yields any conclusion, it is the danger of generalising from one's personal experience to the probable reactions of others—as the examples in the next paragraph suggest.

Principled criticisms of deterrence theory might be maintained whether or not there is satisfactory evidence of general deterrent effects. One such criticism is that the theory could justify the punishment of an innocent person if that were certain to deter several others: a simple utilitarian calculus would allow this to happen, without any respect for the rights of the innocent person. Another, more realistic criticism is that the theory can justify the imposition of a disproportionately harsh sentence on one offender in order to deter several others from committing a similar offence. This is the so-called "exemplary sentence." English judges have passed such sentences from time to time, and some would argue that such decisions have been the product of political or "media" pressure to respond to public anxiety about a certain type of crime. One incident which has become part of judicial lore is the passing of exemplary sentences on certain offenders after the Notting Hill race riots in 1958. It is argued that such sentences may be justified by the consequences, which in this case were reductions in racial troubles in Notting Hill (although there were similar troubles in other cities in the following months). But who can assert that it was the exemplary sentences which caused the reduction in the number of offences which otherwise would have taken place? Might it not be the case that the police had arrested and charged the ringleaders, and without them there would be no continuation? Or that increased police patrols dramatically increased the perceived risk of being caught? The Notting Hill case serves only to emphasise the formidable difficulties of gathering evidence on the effectiveness of exemplary sentences as short-term deterrents. One can rarely be confident of interpreting a sequence of social events correctly, and that there are no other plausible explanations for changes in people's behaviour. . . .

The argument has returned to the empirical objection. The real test of the principled objection is this: even if one believes the Notting Hill anecdote, would this justify the extra long sentences on the first people to be sentenced for the crime? Should, for example, an extra two years of one person's liberty be sacrificed in the hope of deterring several others? The objection to this is often expressed in the Kantian maxim, "a person should always be treated as an end in himself [or herself], and never only as a means." Respect for the moral worth and autonomy of the individual means that citizens should not be regarded merely as numbers, to be aggregated in some calculation of overall social benefit. It may be true that the fundamental justification for the whole institution of punishment is in terms of overall social benefit, in the same

2. White Paper, Crime, Justice and Protecting the Public (London: HMSO, 1990), para. 2.8.

way as this is the justification for taxes. There are also plenty of other examples of compulsion "for the greater good," such as quarantine, compulsory purchase of property, etc. These measures do not, however, have the censuring dimension which sentences have. If there is an argument for civil detention of individuals in the hope of deterring others from committing crimes, it has yet to be heard. Exemplary sentences, by heaping an undeserved portion of punishment on one offender in the hope of deterring others, are objectionable in that they condemn an individual in order to achieve a social goal—and do so without any real criterion of how much extra may be imposed. A deterrent theory which incorporates no restrictions to prevent this shows scant respect for individuals' choices and invests great power in the State and the judiciary.

A number of mixed theories of punishment have been advanced in an attempt to preserve elements of deterrence theory while avoiding the principled objections. The most notable is that of H. L. A. Hart, who argued that the general justifying aim of punishment must be found in the prevention and control of crime, but that in deciding whom to punish and how much to punish the governing principle should be desert. That is, only the guilty should be punished, and then only in proportion to the seriousness of their offences. This does away with deterrence as a rationale for particular sentences, but on the other hand it finds no place for desert in the basic justification for punishment. There is a strong argument that punishment both incorporates and requires reference to individual desert as well as to overall social benefit.

Sentences are not the only form of general deterrent. In some cases it is the process which is the punishment—being prosecuted, appearing in court, receiving publicity in the local newspaper—rather than the sentence itself. In some cases the shame and embarrassment in relation to family and friends are said to have a more powerful effect than the sentence itself. On the other hand, the deterrent effects of sentencing and of the process may be diluted considerably by enforcement policy, or at least by beliefs about the risk of detection. Thus it is sometimes argued that it is beliefs about the probability of detection rather than about the quantum of punishment which are more likely to influence human behaviour. Once again, research suggests that a preventive strategy focused on detection probabilities has uncertain prospects, at least for some types of offence. What matters, for deterrence theory, is potential offenders' beliefs about the risk of being caught, and we have little information about that. . . . [T]here are grounds for believing that any deterrent effect which sentence levels have upon the reasoning of potential offenders may be diluted considerably by the fairly low risk of detection. These suggestions surely confirm that it is naive to assume a kind of hydraulic relationship between court sentences and criminal behaviour.

Rehabilitation

Like deterrence, rehabilitation as an aim of sentencing (sometimes termed reformation or resocialisation) is a method of achieving the prevention of crime. It proclaims that the principal rationale of sentencing is to achieve the rehabilitation of the offender. This usually requires a range of sentences and facilities designed to offer various programmes of treatment. Sometimes the focus is upon the modification of attitudes and of behavioural problems. Sometimes the aim is to provide education or skills, in the belief that these might enable offenders to find occupations other than crime. Thus the crucial questions for the sentencer concern the perceived needs of the offender, not the gravity of the offence committed. The rehabilitative approach is closely linked with those forms of positivist criminology which locate the causes of criminality in individual pathology or individual maladjustment, whether psychiatric, psychological, or social. Whereas deterrence theory regards offenders as rational and calculating, rehabilitative theory tends to regard them as in need of help and support. One key element in determining those needs is a report from an expert—for example, a pre-sentence report prepared by a probation officer or, occasionally, a psychiatric report. The sentencer should then decide on the form of treatment which matches the perceived needs of the offender, and make the appropriate order. Those jurisdictions which have operated a "treatment model" of this kind have usually made their sentences indeterminate, on the basis that a person should only be released from obligations when, in the opinion of the experts, a cure has been effected.

This approach to sentencing reached its zenith in the 1960s, particularly in certain American jurisdictions, but the early 1970s are said to have brought the decline of the rehabilitative ideal. There seem to have been two major objections. One was the criticism that few of these treatment programmes seemed to be better at preventing reoffending than ordinary, non-treatment sentences. There had been many studies of the effectiveness of particular programmes, usually judging them on reconviction rates in subsequent years, and the conclusions of a widely-publicised survey of the research by Martinson and others were represented as "nothing works." In fact, Martinson disavowed such a totally negative conclusion, and an English survey by Stephen Brody was more circumspect in pointing out that only a limited number of programmes have been tried and evaluated. Research into intensive probation in England and in the United States has not been particularly encouraging, but there remains the possibility that research findings on rehabilitation conceal "interaction effects." In other words, there may be small groups of offenders for whom a certain kind of treatment has markedly better or markedly worse results, but such effects might not be apparent by looking simply at reconviction rates for all offenders. The early English survey of intensive probation was not encouraging in this respect either. Moreover, even if interaction effects are identified, there would have to be elaborate screening of offenders to discover which group or typology each of them falls into.

The second objection to rehabilitative policies is that they considerably increase the powers of so-called experts and recognise no right in individuals to be regarded as worthy of equal respect and concern. Indeterminate or even semi-determinate sentences place the release of offenders in the hands of prison or probation authorities, usually without firm criteria, clear accountability, or avenues for challenge and reasoned decision-making. There is no question of recognising an individual's right not to be subjected to compulsory state intervention which is disproportionate to the seriousness of the crime committed. Even if the crime is relatively minor, an offender who is assessed as needing help might be subject to state control for a considerable period. The motivation may be benevolent and "in the person's best interests." In effect the individual offender may be regarded more as a manipulable object than as a person with rights.

Despite these two objections, it can be argued that rehabilitative approaches have not been properly tested, and a fuller commitment to its goals of treatment and reso-cialisation would result in a more humane and more effective sentencing system. There has never been adequate provision of the kinds of help and support which might be necessary. But this leaves several questions unanswered. Do we have rehabilita-tive programmes which could work for large numbers of offenders? Do we have pro-grammes which could work for lesser, but still significant groups of offenders, whose suitability could be identified in advance? Should these programmes be available to courts, even in cases where the duration of the programme exceeds the proportionate sentence? Even if all these questions are answered in the negative, there are sound humanitarian reasons for continuing to experiment with rehabilitative programmes for offenders. However, respect for individual rights suggests that participation in programmes should be voluntary and that the duration of programmes should remain within the bounds set by proportionality.

Incapacitation

A third possible rationale for sentencing is to incapacitate offenders, that is, to deal with them in such a way as to make them incapable of offending for substantial peri-ods of time. In its popular form of "public protection," this is sometimes advanced as a general aim. However, it is usually confined to particular groups, such as "danger-ous" offenders, career criminals, or other persistent offenders. Capital punishment and the severing of limbs could be included as incapacitative punishments, but there are formidable humanitarian arguments against such irreversible measures. The de-bate has usually concerned lengthy periods of imprisonment and disqualification for driving. Other measures such as curfews and additional requirements in probation or-ders may now raise similar problems.

What has been claimed for incapacitative sentencing strategies? . . . Two such strategies can be mentioned here. One is the imposition of long, incapacitative cus-todial sentences on offenders deemed to be "dangerous." It is claimed that one can identify certain offenders as "dangerous,"—i.e., as likely to commit serious offences if released into the community in the near future—and the risks to victims are so great that it is justifiable to detain such offenders for longer periods. The chief objection to this is overprediction: studies suggest that incapacitative sentencing draws into its net more "non-dangerous" than "dangerous" offenders, with a "false positive" rate that has often reached two out of every three. Indeed, the main British study found that only 9 out of 48 offenders predicted as dangerous committed "dangerous" offences within five years of release from prison and, what is equally significant from the point of view of public protection, that an equal number of "dangerous" offences was com-mitted by offenders not classified as dangerous. . . .

The empirical basis of the second incapacitative strategy is likewise open to ques-tion. It was claimed by Greenwood in the United States that one can identify certain high-risk robbers and incarcerate them for substantial periods, achieving a reduction in the number of robberies and reducing sentence levels for other robbers. The crime preventive benefits of this are obvious, but the strategy has been shown to have ma-jor flaws. A subsequent report in America for the National Academy of Sciences demonstrates that Greenwood exaggerated the incapacitative effects and based his calculations on imprisoned robbers rather than robbers generally, and that a reworked version of his prediction method had disappointing results.

Apart from the empirical objections, there is also a principled objection to incapacitative sentencing, which parallels the objection to general deterrent sentencing: individuals are being punished, over and above what they deserve, in the hope of protecting future victims from harm. The force of such an objection is particularly strong where the successful prediction rate is low. The more difficult question is whether the objection should be given absolute force if a fairly high prediction rate could be achieved. There are some cases where the prison authorities, doctors, and others feel sure that a certain prisoner presents a serious danger to others, in terms of violent or sexual assault. Should the Kantian objection be upheld even if there was an agreed high risk of serious offences? The Floud Committee thought that a just redistribution of risk should result in the prolonged detention of the high-risk offender rather than an increased danger to victims. Some critics of their approach, who would wish to uphold an individual's right not to be punished more than is proportionate to the offence(s) committed, also seem willing to concede that in cases of "vivid danger" it would be justifiable to lengthen detention for incapacitative purposes. This means overriding the individual's right because of the danger to the rights of victims. The point is an important one, because the emphasis of liberal theories on individual rights does not necessarily lead to absolute rights which ignore the social context and the possibility of conflicting rights. Thus, even the staunchest advocate of individual rights might concede that, where there is a conflict between the rights of two people (albeit that one of them is merely a potential or predicted victim), it is the right of the convicted offender which should yield. All this depends on an acceptably high rate of successful prediction. Even then, it is questionable whether it justifies the prolongation of incarceration in a prison: David Wood puts the case for transfer to a form of civil detention, if disproportionately long isolation of certain offenders is thought proper.

Desert

If the 1960s were the heyday of the rehabilitative approach, then the 1970s and 1980s were characterised by the re-emergence of desert as a primary rationale of sentencing. Desert theory is a modern form of retributive philosophy, and, like retributivism, it has various shades and hues. Its leading proponent is undoubtedly Andrew von Hirsch, the author of the American report *Doing Justice* in 1976 and the writer of several subsequent articles and books. In his view, punishment has a twin justification. One element is that there is an intuitive connection between desert and punishment: thus, desert is "an integral part of everyday judgments of praise and blame," and state punishment institutionalises this censuring function. Thus sentences communicate official censure or blame, the communication being chiefly to the offender but also to the victim and society at large. However, censure alone is not enough: the fallibility of human nature makes it necessary to attach a prudential reason to the normative one. Thus the second justifying element lies in the underlying need for general deterrence: without police, courts and a penal system, "it seems likely that victimising conduct would become so prevalent as to make life nasty and brutish, indeed." This preventive element of the rationale is regarded as subsidiary, operating only within a censuring framework.

The main thrust and chief contribution of desert theory is to the quantum of punishment, where proportionality is the touchstone. There is not one but two senses of proportionality, which must be distinguished with care. Ordinal proportionality concerns the relative seriousness of offences among themselves. Cardinal proportionality relates the ordinal ranking to a scale of punishments, and requires that the penalty should not be out of proportion to the gravity of the crime involved. Different countries have different anchoring points for their penalty scales, often evolved over the years without much conscious reflection and regarded as naturally appropriate. . . . Some have alleged that the rhetoric of desert is likely to lead to greater severity of penalties, but that is by no means the general outcome. . . . So much depends on general political trends and judicial disposition in the jurisdiction concerned: there is no natural connection between desert theory and severity, and in some states desert has been an integral part of policies of stabilising or reducing the use of custody.

Nevertheless, it must be conceded that to draw the theoretical distinction between cardinal and ordinal proportionality is not to provide much concrete guidance on the severity level which enables one to describe particular sentences as deserved. It does suffice to rule out extreme punishments such as ten-years' imprisonment for shoplifting; but the argument as to whether a person committing a particular house burglary deserves 18 months' imprisonment, three months, or a community service order has to be conducted on penological and social grounds. . . .

The parameters of ordinal proportionality are also difficult to establish. Most countries have a fairly traditional ordering of offences, but this has usually not come to terms with modern offences concerned with safety risks, environmental crimes, etc. Changes in the relative positions of certain offences have taken place—for example, in England during the 1980s a more serious view was taken of rape and of causing death by reckless driving—but without any overall theory of what makes offences more or less serious. . . . Criteria . . . need to be refined considerably if there is to be a framework which can cope not only with "new" forms of criminality like breaches of safety regulations and incitement to racial hatred, but also with the longstanding contrast between property crimes and offences against the person. The subject calls for further philosophical and social enquiry. . . .

Critics of desert theory have attacked it at various points. It is said to be unsatisfactory to rest such a coercive institution, even partly, on the mere intuition that punishment is an appropriate or natural response to offending. Furthermore, exactly what is deserving of blame and punishment—culpable acts or dispositions? It is also said to be unfair to rest desert partly on individual culpability when strong social disadvantages may be at the root of much offending. One answer to this is to recognise grounds for mitigation of sentence for any offender who has suffered significant social deprivation, while maintaining that the unequal distribution of wealth and opportunity in society ought to be tackled by means other than sentencing. Where social injustices are widespread, this "does not diminish . . . the harmfulness of common victimising crimes," although it strengthens the case for reducing overall punishment levels. Critics have also argued that the key concepts of ordinal and cardinal proportionality are too vague and open to divergent interpretations, but these criticisms are likely to apply to any approach to sentencing which invokes a notion of proportionality. . . . [D]esert theorists have tried to grapple with the awkward question of the relevance of previous convictions to sentence, rationalising the concessions to first offenders in terms of human frailty and evaluating the relevance of various types of previous record. . . . Desert theorists have also tackled the problems of introducing proportionality into non-custodial sentencing. . . . Many of the proposals require further refinement, but the strengths of desert theory are to be found in its apparent concordance with some widely held moral views, in its respect for the rights of the individual offender, and in its placing of limits on the powers of the state. Thomas Mathieson has attacked desert theory for the implicit claims of precision and objectivity embodied in terms such as "commensurate," "ordinal and cardinal proportionality," "culpability," and "offence seriousness." An alternative evaluation would be that this analysis has enabled considerable advances in framing questions which should be asked about the justifications for punishing people and about the justifications for imposing different punishments on different offenders, with its proponents still seeking to refine the answers.

Social Theories of Sentencing

Several contemporary writers are dissatisfied with the tendency of the four "traditional" theories of punishment, especially desert theory, to deal with sentencing in isolation from its wider social and political setting. Various theories are being developed which attempt to make sentencing principles more responsive to social conditions and community expectations. . . .

Barbara Hudson's work insists that priority should be given to crime prevention and to reducing the use of custody by the penal system. Changes in social policy relating to employment, education, housing, and leisure facilities are far more important to justice than narrow debates about proportionality of sentence. And when it comes to sentencing, there should be greater concern with "the problems of whole human beings" rather than with particular pieces of behaviour: the state should not "privilege events over people" and should place more emphasis on the provision of rehabilitative opportunities. This would be the best way of showing respect for offenders as individuals.

Nicola Lacey likewise argues that the first step must be the state's recognition of its duty to foster a sense of community by providing proper facilities and fair opportunities for all citizens. Once this has been achieved in a community, punishment is justified as reinforcing the values that it has been decided to protect through criminal law. Proportionality would then be important in sentencing, but so would the conflicting value of promoting the welfare of the community. Lacey disagrees both with desert theorists and with preventionists in their insistence on assigning general priority to a single value: for her, while the core of each value must be preserved, compromises have to be negotiated separately and sensitively.

John Braithwaite and Phillip Pettit develop what they term a republican theory of criminal justice. Its central value is dominion, defined in terms of each citizen's ability to make life choices, within a social and political framework which each citizen has participated in shaping, and then to be protected in those choices. In its responses to offending, the criminal justice system should adopt a system of minimum intervention but may pursue policies of prevention through sentencing where appropriate. Proportionality of sentence is not a primary concern. Indeed, republican theory would decouple censure from sentencing. Censure might be achieved more effectively by shaming and other forms of social reaction, and a particular sentence might be lower if the prospects for shaming seem good. Otherwise, while the authors gesture vaguely towards upper limits of proportionality, they seem to accept that substantial sentences based on predictive and preventive rationales might be acceptable. . . . What is characteristic of these social theories is that, to various extents, they assign greater importance to overall levels of penalty than to the relative fairness of individual sentences.

Restoration and Reparation

One of the major developments in criminal justice in the 1980s was the increasing recognition of the rights and needs of the victims of crime. . . . It has also been manifest in the growing number of restorative theories of criminal justice. . . . The argument is that justice to victims should be placed first as the goal of the criminal justice system and of sentencing. Thus the primary aim would be to ensure that an offender compensates the victim and the wider community for the results and effects of the crime. This would not necessarily avoid onerous sentences, because some crimes have deep and long-lasting effects, both for the victim and for the community, and the responsible offenders would then be expected to provide substantial compensation or reparation. Custodial sentences would be fewer, since those in custody would be less able to make reparation. Sentences would be more clearly related to the harm done by the offence, and more constructive in seeking (where possible) to rectify or remedy the harms. Thus, as Lucia Zedner puts it:

> Criminal justice should be less preoccupied with censuring code-breakers and focus instead on the process of restoring individual damage and repairing ruptured social bonds. In place of meeting pain with the infliction of further pain, a truly reparative system would seek the holistic restoration of the community. It would necessarily also challenge the claim of the state to respond to crime and would instead invite (or perhaps demand) the involvement of the community in the process of restoration.

As such, restorative theory is not a rationale for punishment but a justification for rather different responses to lawbreaking. So far as courts are concerned, apart from those few cases in which the offender was thought to require custody in order to protect potential victims from danger, the primary task would be to assess the compensation or reparation required. Harm done would be the chief criterion, whereas the offender's fault is often crucial in the present system. The restorative approach seems less straightforward in cases with no individual victim: where it is a crime without an ascertainable victim (e.g., drugs, pornography), or a crime against a company or against the state, the matter becomes more difficult.

A fully restorative approach to criminal justice remains untried, and many of the questions it raises have no obvious answers. Is it realistic, in times of world economic recession, to construct a theory based on offenders working for years to pay compensation to their victims? If the theory also requires symbolic reparation to the community, how is this to be calculated if not on grounds of proportionality and desert? Can victim-offender mediation really cope with serious crimes? The modest successes of mediation schemes cannot be denied, but most of them have operated at a fairly low level of seriousness and, even then, some victims have been unwilling to participate. Moreover, if the compensation ordered has to be acceptable to the victim, is it right that the feelings of different victims should determine the obligations of those who commit similar offences? Although some restorative theorists do not take the view that victims should play an influential role in deciding what the offender's obligations should be, others insist that the crime "belongs" to the victim to such an extent that victims should have a say in sentencing. That is to give restorative theory a populist turn which is far from inevitable. More promising, even if less strongly heard above the populist tumult of recent years, is the potential of restorative justice to achieve a genuine form of social integration to an extent that theories of punishment cannot, and often do not, aspire.

Deprivation of Profits

Further complications arise when the aim of depriving offenders of the profits of their crimes is examined. Its justice can scarcely be doubted: it is quite wrong that offenders should be allowed to keep any profits from their offending. . . .

While the elementary justice of confiscation orders may be conceded, this should not divert attention from other concerns. Political pressures to "combat" organised crime lead too easily to provisions which are overzealous and which trample on what are ordinarily considered to be defendants' rights. Does the legislation create presumptions against offenders which, in effect, require them to make a case for keeping their property? If so, is there a sufficient justification, or is it simply that normal rights were swept aside by a tide of moral panic? . . .

. . .[T]he deprivations they impose ought to be taken into account when determining whether the overall penalty is proportionate to the seriousness of the offence. . . . Yet it has also been argued that the exercise of depriving an offender of profits is distinct from and additional to the task of sentencing. . . . What should be avoided, in all instances, is a disparity of result which means that an offender who can readily discharge obligations under the confiscation order receives a lower sentence—especially, a lower prison sentence—than one who cannot. There is a long-standing principle that a wealthy offender should not be allowed to "buy a way out of prison." So, even if courts do take account of the onerous effects of a confiscation order, they should bear in mind the principle of equality before the law, and consider whether the order really is an additional penalty or merely an attempt to remove an unfair advantage gained from the crime by restoring the status quo.

Some Principles and Policies

Justifying sentences and the sentencing system is not merely a matter of considering overall or ultimate aims. A number of discrete principles and policies may also impinge on general decisions on sentencing policy and individual decisions. It would be extravagant to claim that there is a settled core of these principles and policies, which can be drawn together and put forward as a coherent group. The reality is that they form a fluctuating body at different stages in penal history and are invoked selectively as the tides of penal politics ebb and flow. Punishment may be regarded as one of the institutions of society (along with the family, religion, the armed forces, etc.), and in this context sentencing is an institution for the expression of social values as well as an instrumental means to a clinical penological end. . . .

The Principle of Equal Respect and Dignity

This is one way of restating the master principle which may be a focus of argument about the types of sentence which ought to be permitted or excluded. . . . The argument of principle must be that individuals have a right not to be stripped of their essential human dignity. It is an argument which is quite independent of the proportion between the offence and the punishment, for it concerns not the relative severity of punishments but whether certain types of sentence should be excluded absolutely. The concepts of equal respect and dignity are relatively vague, and probably acquire their meaning in the light of cultural expectations at different stages in the history of societies.

If one considers the historical changes in the acceptability of punishment, it seems that there has been a movement away from corporal penalties—those which affect the body, in the sense of the direct infliction of pain   towards punishments which affect the mind. . . . Yet why is it that these [corporal] forms of punishment are ruled out? If they might be effective as deterrents (of which we cannot be sure), why should a consequentialist or preventive theorist exclude them? If some of them might appear to be apt or proportionate responses to some types of crime, why should the desert theorist disavow them? The answer must surely lie in a concept of "cultural sensibility:" they are regarded as unacceptable in a humanitarian sense, as things which it is wrong to do deliberately to a human being in the name of the state. There is no objective or timeless benchmark of what is inhuman or degrading: it is culturally specific.

. . .

There are two counter-arguments which must be identified and then dismissed. One is that a person who commits an offence forfeits all rights vis-à-vis the state: this is unacceptable in principle, although it is less clear what limits the state ought to observe when sentencing offenders. To allow the counter-argument would be to admit torture, amputation, etc., without limit. The other counter-argument is that, if a non-custodial measure is used instead of custody, the offender has no grounds for complaint. This is also unacceptable—not merely because it would tend to allow the return of torture and amputation, but more widely because it recognises no restrictions on sentences for crimes which do not warrant immediate custody. The proper approach is to examine the intrusiveness of electronic monitoring and of additional requirements in probation orders, to see whether the degree of intrusion or humiliation is such that it ought not to be countenanced.

The Principle of Restraint in the Use of Custody

In recognition that imprisonment is a severe deprivation for most of those incarcerated, there has been widespread formal acceptance that it should be used with restraint. . . .

The Policy of Controlling Public Expenditure

Recent years have seen the increasing influence of economic considerations on the shape of penal systems. As governments have scrutinised their expenditure programmes, the large sums spent on the penal system in general and prisons in particular have come to be questioned. To ask whether the state gets "value for money" from this expenditure is to enquire whether the offenders could be dealt with equally effectively in some cheaper way. This was undoubtedly one reason behind the development of new or altered noncustodial measures, and economic considerations became an unexpected ally to those who had long argued on criminological grounds that prisons may be counter-productive and that "more severe" does not mean "more effective."

...

The Principle of Equality before the Law

This is the principle that sentencing decisions should treat offenders equally, irrespective of their wealth, race, colour, sex, or employment or family status. . . . The principle of equality hardly needs justification, for it is surely unjust that people should be penalised at the sentencing stage for any of these reasons. Yet in practice there are difficulties. There is evidence of discrimination according to wealth, some evidence of race and sex discrimination in certain respects, and clear evidence of discrimination on grounds of employment status. The last is a peculiarly difficult issue: courts often try to pass a sentence which ensures that a person who has a job is able to keep it, although the implication is that unemployed offenders are discriminated against, since that source of sentence reduction is not open to them. Another major question raised by this principle is how far it should be taken: . . . There is keen argument about whether it is right to speak of "just" or "fair" sentences in a society riven with inequality and injustice.

The Principle of Equal Impact

This principle argues that sentences should be so calculated as to impose an equal impact on the offenders subjected to them. Or, to phrase the principle negatively, the system should strive to avoid grossly unequal impacts on offenders with differing resources and sensitivities, because that would be unjust. The most obvious application of the principle is to fines, which ought to be adjusted to reflect the different means of different offenders. Another application is to imprisonment, where the offender has some special mental or medical condition which may make custody significantly more painful or perhaps where the offender must spend a prison term in solitary confinement for his own protection. On the other hand, the principle leads in a different direction if it is applied to first offenders and persistent offenders, because it could yield the argument that someone who has been in prison often before needs a longer term of custody in order to make an equivalent impact, whereas the first offender may need only a short term. . . .

The Principle of Parsimony

On the basis that all punishment is pain and ought therefore to be avoided or minimised where possible, Bentham argued for a principle of frugality in punishment. In all cases the least sufficient punishment should be chosen. . . . What is not always clear is the level at which proponents are urging the principle. It could be regarded as a principle applicable to policy-makers—a broader version of the principle of restraint in the use of custody, perhaps phrased in terms of minimum intervention. It would recognise the punitive effects of the criminal process and publicity on many offenders, and would argue for the greater prominence of formal cautions and other diversionary measures for less serious forms of crime. It would also support the approach of reserving community penalties for cases that are too serious for a fine or conditional discharge. . . . A more thoroughgoing "decremental strategy" would involve a progressive reduction in penalty levels over time.

Alternatively, or even additionally, the principle of parsimony could be regarded as a principle for the sentencer in individual cases. The question is how far this should be taken, if the court has two cases before it—both offences of stealing, one by a person of lowly status (e.g., from a "criminal" family or neighbourhood), the other by a citizen whose background leads the court to believe it unlikely that he will ever offend again. If the court gives a lesser punishment to the second one, it may be following the principle of parsimony, but would this be fair? It would certainly breach the principle of equality before the law (above). . . . [W]hile the principle of parsimony ought to be pursued at the general or legislative level, the principle of equality before the law should prevail in individual sentencing decisions.

NOTES AND QUESTIONS

1. The authority to sentence, to impose state punishment on a human being, is a power of immense magnitude and responsibility. How should the state create and justify a sentencing scheme, and how does the judge impose and justify individual sentences? The introduction to this chapter suggested that the justification for sentencing was dependent upon the justifications for punishment, which should be clear from Ashworth's selection. What should also be clear is that once one enters the domain of consequential justifications, facts about consequences become terribly important. As sentencing schemes and resultant individual sentences are altered to

achieve particular goals, do they do so? If one believes that sentences of incarceration are too few and too short to effectuate general deterrence and incapacitation, one will imprison more offenders for longer terms. But, holding everything else constant, do crime rates decrease when harsher sentences are imposed? Ashworth's review is an efficient statement of sentencing aims and evidence. Does it indicate that the various forms of sentences imposed meet their goals? Suppose that the evidence for the efficacy of incarceration is as weak as many claim. What follows? If you are a pure retributivist, you won't care. As long as criminals deserve to be imprisoned, lock them up. But if you are a mixed theorist or consequentialist, would you be willing to imprison fewer people and for shorter terms? If not, why not? How strong must social science evidence be to persuade you to abandon intuitively held, commonsense beliefs—say, that incarceration deters?

2. Attempts to achieve consequential goals always threaten to run afoul of justice claims. The fear is that some offenders are punished more than they deserve to serve the goals of public safety. These fears are important because most people believe that just deserts sets necessary constraints on whether and how much offenders may be punished. As a result, analysts for whom crime reduction is the primary goal are nonetheless at pains to demonstrate that various sentencing schemes aimed at reducing crime are *not* inconsistent with just deserts. How difficult is this task? What principled argument consistent with a just deserts rationale would permit a sentencer to sentence two criminals convicted of the same crime committed under similar circumstances to different terms?

3. Proponents of just deserts sentences are always asked, "How much?"—that is, how does the just deserts theorist know what sentence is proportionate to the criminal offense or, depending on one's type of just deserts theory, to the background of the offender as well? Even if one is a "moral realist," who believes that there are objectively correct answers to such questions, the just deserts sentencer must still admit epistemological doubt: can that "right answer" be known? But even if the properly proportionate sentence cannot be known with certainty, must the just deserts theorist abandon the attempt to develop a coherent sentencing scheme and to impose just sentences in individual cases? Many theorists have suggested schemes for a fair ordinal ranking of sentences,[1] and the Department of Justice's *Report to the Nation on Crime and Justice* reports that a careful national survey, The National Survey of Crime Severity, found that "many diverse groups of people generally agree about the relative severity of specific crimes" (2d ed., 1988, p. 16). Compared to nonvictims, crime victims tended to rank the severity of crimes higher, but the relative severity apparently did not change for the victimized group. So, if there is general agreement about relative severity, is a justly proportional scheme impossible?

Critics respond that even if "accurate" ranking is possible, the whole scheme

---

1. E.g., Michael Davis, "How to Make the Punishment Fit the Crime," in *How to Make the Punishment Fit the Crime* (Boulder, Colo: Westview Press, 1992). But see David Dolinko, "Mismeasuring 'Unfair Advantage': A Response to Michael Davis," 13 *Law and Philosophy* 493 (1994).

may be too lenient or, more likely, too harsh. Indeed, one of the fears of retributive sentencing is that it is always unjustly harsh (see D. Dolinko, "Three Mistakes of Retributivism," *UCLA Law Review,* Vol. 39 [1992], pp. 1623–1657). But this outcome isn't analytic. Retributivism can be coherently and consistently lenient. Nonetheless, whether the retributive scheme is harsh or lenient or somewhere in between, how can the retributivist fairly punish without knowing that the scheme *is* proportionate? Is asking for such perfect knowledge unfair to the retributivist? Can any sentencing scheme be as sure of itself as it would like to be? Can a consequential sentencer really assure us that the consequential scheme has produced the promised net gain to society?

4. Determinant sentences and rigid guidelines were created to avoid arbitrary sentencing that treated like cases unalike. Opponents believe that such schemes are inherently unjust because they fail to individualize sentences sufficiently. Tonry reports that surveys disclose that average citizens routinely support individualization, but this is not a principled argument about why and how individualization should be accomplished. The real claim is that the newer, determinate sentencing schemes have established "equality" only by obliterating morally important differences among offenders convicted of the same crimes.

As always, how one responds depends on one's theory of "likeness." Recall the difference between the "act" and "character" theories of criminal responsibility, raised in Chapter 5, Section 5.3. Both can be plausibly and coherently proposed and defended. An act theorist is more inclined to believe that the crime committed is sufficient grounds for individualization to apportion punishment; a character theorist believes that more information about the offender's life and circumstances must be considered. Assuming one believes that the act theory produces an unduly narrow sentencing scheme, the burden then is on the proponent of greater individualization to identify the further variables that the sentencing authority should take into account, to justify why those variables are relevant to a proper sentence according to the theory of punishment that supports the proponent's sentencing scheme, and to justify how much the sentence should be adjusted.

Consider the following example. Assume, as many do, that there is reasonable evidence to believe that a history of being abused as a child predisposes people to violent conduct in adolescence and adulthood. Holding all else constant, should the previously abused criminal be sentenced the same or differently from an offender not previously abused who is convicted of the same crime under similar circumstances? Holding all else constant, we are more likely to be sympathetic to the life of the abused offender, but how is this relevant to the just sentence that may be imposed? If sympathy is a criterion for individualization, when is it warranted and how much? How would sympathy variables be ranked? Let us assume that previous abuse is genuinely a partial cause of later violence. Remember that causation per se is not an excusing circumstance. Indeed, the causal history may suggest that the abused offender, despite our sympathy, presents a greater risk of future violence. But most proponents of individualization do not recommend *harsher* sentences based on developmental variables.

In *Determinism, Blameworthiness, and Deprivation* (New York: Oxford University Press, 1990), Martha Klein has argued that offenders with unfortunate histories that produced antisocial motives have "paid in advance" by the suffering their unfortunate circumstances produced. No child, for example, is responsible for the suffering of being abused, and if the abuse later produces antisocial behavior, the childhood suffering was payment in advance for later, deserved punishment. This proposal is attractive as a justification for individualizing toward leniency, but how would it work in practice? If such people really are more dangerous, should they serve shorter terms? Even if they have paid in advance, does earlier suffering suggest that they are less responsible now? Why?

In the writings of many, most notably the late Judge David Bazelon and more recently Michael Tonry, there is an implicit or explicit social justice claim for individualization. The argument is that our society's unjust institutions have unfairly pushed many citizens into lives of crime that the more fortunate find easy to avoid. It is therefore unfair to punish the less fortunate, who are truly victims of unjust circumstances, as if they were not victims. This is the "rotten social background" or "deprivation" theory for punishing less harshly. Once again, however, how would this work in practice and are deprived offenders less responsible?

What factors should be used to individualize sentences and how would you justify them?

5. There is a danger that any sentencing scheme, no matter how coherent and fair, may provide an unjust sentence in individual cases. A common response is that the judge should have the discretion to exercise mercy. As Jeffrie Murphy points out in his book *Forgiveness and Mercy* (coauthored with Jean Hampton, Cambridge: Cambridge University Press, 1985), however, mercy is a problematic concept for the law. It is not clear that it is independent of justice, and if it is not, shouldn't the sentencing scheme formally incorporate the considerations that would justify a grant of "mercy?" If you believe that mercy is independent, will it be possible to grant it in a nonarbitrary manner? Will there be sufficiently objective criteria to permit different judges to treat like cases alike?

6. Perhaps the most important sentencing issue in the United States today is the validity of the current preference for longer sentences, increased rates of incarceration, and additional prisons. Are we sending too many people to prison, about the right number, or too few? In *Malign Neglect* (excerpted in Chapter 1), Michael Tonry demonstrates that American sentences are far longer than those permitted in other developed nations. He argues that our sentences are far too harsh and that we send far too many people to prison, a policy that has a particularly pernicious effect on already disadvantaged groups, especially young African American males. He cites data that suggest that proponents of incarceration overstate the proportion of people in prison who are terribly dangerous or serious recidivists.

Are we putting too many people in prison or simply not using the cells for the right offenders? At the very least, is the cost of imprisoning minor drug dealers and the like worth it? Should we be imprisoning property offenders? Assuming that you don't want to imprison such offenders for the first offense, how much recidivism would justify the use of incarceration? If you emptied cells by decarcerating or refusing to incarcerate such minor criminals, would you fill those cells with new violent offenders not incarcerated and increase the terms of such offenders? In other words, are there at present substantial numbers of serious violent offenders convicted but not incarcerated or incarcerated but not for sufficient terms? If there are such people, would the prisons be refilled if the former were sent to prison and all were imprisoned longer? What kind of research evidence would be required to conclude that it would be safe to release offenders convicted of violent crimes?

7. Once an offender is incarcerated, the question of what resources should be allocated to rehabilitative services in prison is of great practical importance, but it is not a matter of substantive criminal law. Nonetheless, it needs to be considered, because if successful interventions could reduce the period of incarceration necessary to render an inmate reasonably safe to return to society, it would be both humane and arguably cost effective to do so. Some interventions do seem to work for some prisoners, but for a program to be effective, its subjects need to be carefully chosen, and all programs should be subject to rigorous evaluation. Finally, note that a just deserts theorist might still claim that even if rehabilitation is efficient, no offender should be released until the minimum deserved sentence has been served.